Paul Cop for several years and is the author of twelve titles on a diverse range of subjects, most recently *Pop Charts*, *Movie Charts* and *The Mammoth Book of Drug Barons*. He began to research the criminal underworld while working as an editor in London.

The Mammoth Book of
Undercover Cops

Edited by
Paul Copperwaite

RUNNING PRESS
PHILADELPHIA · LONDON

Constable & Robinson Ltd
55-56 Russell Square
London WC1B 4HP
www.constablerobinson.com

First published in the UK by Robinson, an imprint of Constable & Robinson, 2011

A copy of the British Library Cataloguing in Publication
Data is available from the British Library

UK ISBN 978–1–84901–619–3 (paperback)
UK ISBN 987-1-84901-733-6 (ebook)

1 3 5 7 9 10 8 6 4 2

Digit on the right indicates the number of this printing

US Library of Congress Control number: 2010941555
US ISBN 978–0–7624–4274–4

Running Press Book Publishers
2300 Chestnut Street
Philadelphia, PA 19103–4371

Visit us on the web!
www.runningpress.com

Printed and bound in the UK

For Daisy

Contents

Acknowledgements

The editor would like to thank all those who made this book possible by allowing us to reprint the extracts listed below:

Eryl Humphrey Jones and Duncan Proudfoot at Constable & Robinson for use of various extracts from Part 1, Chapter 2 of YOU'RE NICKED! by Dick Kirby, © Dick Kirby, 2007, (Robinson, 2007); Janne Moller at Black and White Publishing Ltd for use of extracts from Chapter 14 of GLASGOW CRIMEFIGHTER by Les Brown and Robert Jeffrey, © Les Brown and Robert Jeffrey, 2005 (Black and White Publishing, 2005); Mrs Catherine Trippett at Random House UK for permission to quote various extracts from Chapter 19 of THE INFORMER: The Real Life Story of One Man's War Against Terrorism by Sean O'Callaghan, © Sean O'Callaghan, 1998, (Bantam Press, a division of Transworld Publishers Ltd, 1998); Nicholas Hewitt and Sage Journals Online for the use of extract from "MURDER IN THE MÉTRO: Masking and Unmasking Laetitia Toureaux in 1930s France" by Gayle K. Brunelle and Annette Finley-Croswhite, *French Cultural Studies 14* (February 2003), © Gayle K. Brunelle and Annette Finley-Croswhite. (Published in book form in Chapter 2 of MURDER IN THE MÉTRO: Laetitia Toureaux and the Cagoule in 1930s France, Gayle K. Brunelle and Annette Finley-Croswhite, Louisiana State University Press, 2010.) With thanks to Colin Wilson for permission to quote from Chapter 17 of SERIAL KILLER INVESTIGATIONS by Colin Wilson, © Colin Wilson, 2007 (Summersdale Publishers Ltd, 2007);

Susan Howe at Orion for permission to quote from Chapter 7 of BENT COPPERS: The Inside Story of Scotland Yard's Battle Against Police Corruption by Graeme McLagan, © Graeme McLagan, 2003, (Weidenfeld & Nicholson, 2003), and Part 1, Chapter 5 of CRIME BEAT: True Stories of Cops and Killers, by Michael Connelly, © Hieronymous, Inc. 2004 (Bloomsbury Publishing, 2007, originally published as CRIME BEAT: Selected Journalism 1984–1992, by Steven C. Vascik Publications, 2004); Jack Sargeant and Chris Barber for permission to quote from ANOTHER BRICK IN THE LAW: Met. Detective Sergeant Challenor, Building up Evidence, © Chris Barber (published in *Bad Cop, Bad Cop*, ed. Jack Sargeant, Virgin Books 2003); Katie Smith at Bloomsbury publishing for permission to quote from Chapters 10 and 16 of THE FRENCH CONNECTION by Robin Moore, © R. & J. Moore, Inc, 1969; Jack Sargeant and Martin Jones for permission to quote from INVESTIGATING OFFICER X: Operation Countryman vs. the Metropolitan Police, by Martin Jones, © Martin Jones, (published in *Bad Cop, Bad Cop*, ed. Jack Sargeant, Virgin Books 2003); Paul Swallow at Vision Paperbacks for permission to quote from Chapter 6 of ONE CHILD AT A TIME: Inside the Fight to Rescue Children from Online Predators, by Julian Sher, © Julian Sher, 2007 (first published in the UK by Vision Paperbacks, a division of Satin Publications Ltd, 2007); Jack Sargeant and John Harrison for permission to quote from DENIS TANNER AND THE BONNIE DOON BODIES by John Harrison, © John Harrison (published in *Bad Cop, Bad Cop*, ed. Jack Sargeant, Virgin Books 2003); Raphael Sagalyn of the Sagalyn Agency for the use of various extracts from HOMICIDE: A Year on the Killing Streets, by David Simon, © David Simon 1991, 2006 (Canongate Books Ltd, 2008); Kate Choi at Fletcher & Company for permission to quote from Chapter 2 of DONNIE BRASCO: Unfinished Business, by Joe Pistone and Charles Brandt, © Joseph D. Pistone, 2007 (Running Press Book Publishers, 2007); Nat Sobel of Sobel Weber Associates for permission to quote from Chapter 6 of THE ONION FIELD by Joseph

Wambaugh, © Joseph Wambaugh, 1973 (Quercus, 2008); Farley Chase at the Waxman Literary Agency for the use of various extracts from GODFATHER OF NIGHT: My Life in America's Hidden Greek Mafia, by Kevin Pappas, © Kevin Pappas, 2009 (Sphere, 2009); Kimberly Rossetti at John Wiley & Sons Canada, Ltd for permission to quote various extracts from FALLEN ANGEL: The Unlikely Rise of Walter Stadnick in the Canadian Hell's Angels, by Jerry Langton, © Jerry Langton, 2006 (John Wiley & Sons Canada, Ltd, 2006).

Every effort has been made to trace the original copyright holders of the following without success; the editor and publishers would be pleased to hear from any claimants to the legal copyright of:

Chapter 7 of *Famous Stories of the Murder Squad*, Leonard Gribble, © Leonard Gribble, (Arthur Barker, London, 1974).

Introduction

Before the growth of today's sophisticated, hi-tech surveillance techniques, sending a woman or man undercover to infiltrate organised crime at the highest level possible was often the only way to gather credible evidence for a prosecution. This collection features extracts that chart the growth of undercover and plain-clothes policing from the 1930s and 1940s to the present day. It features true stories from the 1970s and 1980s – the "glory days" of major undercover operations against the Mafia and organised crime, and closes with a look at the future of covert police work in today's terror-stricken, Internet-driven age.

From stake-outs to sensitive operations in which officers can spend weeks, months or even years high on the adrenaline required to live a life-threatening lie, many of the chosen extracts exhibit the sustained bravery, presence of mind and care required when even the smallest inaccuracy could be enough to expose an undercover officer to certain death, whether fast or slow.

In many undercover operations, a police officer need only make one mistake. A corporate director who falls out of favour can rue the day from the relative comfort of a golden parachute, or at least the provisions of a pension plan. The undercover cop who puts a foot wrong may face a more grisly fate altogether. And of course your typical gang leader is far more mercurial, menacing and capricious than your average bunch of share-holders (even if that is an image cultivated to a purpose), increasing the relative likelihood of that fall from grace.

* * *

Additionally, the deployment of undercover cops and even surveillance techniques has always been problematic as well as dangerous: for starters, there is the costly infrastructure required to establish fake identities and subsequently support them in the field.

One person's undercover cop can be another's secret policeman. Laws that necessarily exist to protect the civil rights and personal freedoms of those without criminal intent – just as a cop works to preserve the order of these people's lives, allowing them to exercise those freedoms in peace and in line with their reasonable expectations – can mean that a cop operating "in the field" must weigh and balance the legal implications of their actions day by day or even minute by minute.

In undercover and surveillance work, there is a significant chance that evidence gathered undercover at great risk and expense would, at least in broadly democratic countries, be found to be inadmissible. This would undermine a case were it presented in court or, if it provided the sole basis for the prosecution, mean that a case could not be brought at all, however "bang to rights" a suspect may be. The latter has applied to phone-tap evidence in the UK, for example, where several terrorism suspects live under T-PIMs (or Terrorism Prevention and Investigation Measures – which "control orders" were rebranded as in January 2011), because Whitehall argues that there is conclusive evidence against them that would not be admissible in court.

Second only to their personal safety, an undercover cop must consider the case they're building, and this can also be undermined where the cops themselves have participated in crimes or even could be said by an attentive defence lawyer to have precipitated them, acting as an agent provocateur. It does not matter if the accused has a history of drug trafficking; any case is tried on its specifics. If you were carrying drugs at the behest of a police officer, well, my learned friends, the laws on entrapment may be complex but few would put money on your being found guilty, were the case even allowed to proceed to a verdict.

The simple-seeming principle of gathering admissible evidence proves highly complex in practice: there's a thin line between preserving a cover story and participating in crime in order to do so, especially when crime is the business of the people you are hanging out with and you are there to gather evidence of it! (And how do you rise to the inner circle of a ruthless criminal gang without being involved in policy decisions?) An undercover cop must remain aware of when to make this call. If the slightest reluctance to take part in a job would arouse potentially fatal suspicion on the part of crooks hip to the possibility of infiltration, then it requires the most acute and focused judgement to determine what to do. Do you participate in a crime? Can you contrive to excuse yourself while preserving your cover? Do you abort your mission altogether (the de facto consequence of your non-participation)? That's if you still have the time and opportunity to do so and it's not your fate to be haplessly carried along by events.

Joe Pistone, for example, in *Donnie Brasco: Unfinished Business*, describes an incident that occurred while he was undercover with the Bonnano crime family, in which he was due to take part in a hit. In the US, situations have occurred in which undercover cops have been required, in order to maintain their cover, to discharge their guns into a still-twitching corpse. However in Pistone's case, even this course of action would not have been enough to allay the suspicions his associates would have had, had he not been as eager as any of them to deliver the kill shot. What happened is detailed in the extract in Part 3, Chapter 12.

Participation in crime can not only weaken an undercover cop's credibility as a witness, but there's also a real risk that an agent may "go rogue", seduced by the fringe benefits of their assumed identity and their new-found loyalties to associates who, as personal contacts, may be more sympathetic than they were portrayed as being in briefings. Many crooks are able to do what they do because they're possessed of a loyalty-inspiring personal charisma that's matched only by their sociopathic, manipulative tendencies. To the undercover cop's handlers there is, ironically, little to choose in appearance between an undercover operative who is feeling compromised as to their allegiances, and an undercover officer who is simply excellent at what they do.

Pistone, again, details how, to his extreme annoyance, his FBI superior in a major southern US city resented Pistone's secondment to his regional office. Pistone's operation had begun in New York, but the Bonnanos' business took him to Florida. Either his superior resented having the responsibility thrust upon him for a cop engaged on a long-term operation who was not going to expedite any fast arrests and help him meet his targets, or he really believed that Pistone – a seamless operator – was a rogue officer.

To generalize, authority abhors this ambiguity, especially when long-term operations can tie up resources for years and, even if successful, may not produce arrests until the authorizing officers who would deservedly take the credit are drawing their pensions and tending rosebushes instead.

In the UK, any covert activity on the part of a police force must be open to inspection by the Office of Surveillance Commissioners, and carried out in line with the Police Act (1997) and the Regulation of Investigatory Powers Act (2000), and its Scottish Parliamentary equivalent. Police forces differ from intelligence agencies in that for what they do to have a point, it must be credible enough to present to the Crown Prosecution Service, collated in case files.

Having a single office for the supervision of all ongoing police-run intelligence operations at any time is designed to serve the dual purpose of ensuring that surveillance is not used against any individual as a punishing form of harassment in itself, and that resources are not wasted in duplication or with a lack of proper process that would leave a prosecution flawed.

The legislation identifies three types of covert activity open to police forces: intrusive surveillance, which is covert and involves a cop working on someone's private premises or in their vehicle, and also covers surveillance devices; and

directed surveillance, which is covert but does not intrude on
their property. When these ways of obtaining private information about people are insufficient, it authorizes the use of
Covert Human Intelligence Sources (CHIS) – or undercover
cops, with the following guarantees: "The authorizing officer
must be satisfied that the authorization is necessary, that the
conduct authorized is proportionate to what is sought to be
achieved and that arrangements for the overall management
and control of the individual are in force."

Whether or not these conditions were fully met in Mark
Kennedy's case is bound to remain a matter of debate in
the UK for the time being, with ongoing inquiries into the
nature of undercover policing, and questions asked in
parliament. Kennedy was an undercover police officer
who, as Mark Stone, was tasked with infiltrating a group of
environmental activists. Events came to a head in 2009 as
protesters planned to occupy a coal-fired power station at
Ratcliffe-on-Soar in Nottinghamshire, and are open to a
number of interpretations: as Stone, Kennedy was an excellent infiltrator – perhaps too good, with the irony that his very
suitability for the role seems to have contained the seeds of
his downfall, based as it was on his pre-existing sympathies
with the environmental movement.

He excelled in his first undercover job in south London,
buying drugs and guns and passing information back to
Scotland Yard. Resulting from this, he was recruited by the
National Public Order Intelligence Unit, which maintains a
database of political activists, to gather information on race-
hate crimes. Kennedy considered himself a modern copper,
respectful of minorities in a way that Sir Ian Blair would be
proud of, one who saw police work as a means of guarantee-
ing a democratic and fair society.

Whereas the dealers, however, had wanted to know as little
about him as possible, gaining the trust of Nottinghamshire's
environmental activists required a comprehensive back story
(which, conveniently, involved drug dealing), together with
the ability to empathize and, quite simply, a willingness to get
his round of beers in. With his ponytail, tattoos and a childhood

eye injury that was, at least, atypical of a policeman, Kennedy took his job as seriously as a student in Lee Strasberg's method-acting classes, and rationalized that, when not collecting information on potentially violent extremists, he would be using his time to benefit the environmental cause, out of a personal commitment as much as the need for a cover story.

For seven years until 2009, Kennedy involved himself ever more deeply in the group, and describes his long-term girl-friend from this period as the most real relationship of his life, despite his wife and two children. In effect, Mark Kennedy *became* Mark Stone.

Nottinghamshire police had Stone earmarked as a ring-leader within the group, a person of special interest. He was even jumped by five officers in 2006 during a protest at Drax power station – when he had tipped them off about the protest. Kennedy still feels that some of the best, most inspirational experiences of his life happened while he was Stone: "So many people I knew, or Mark Stone knew, became really good friends. It wasn't just about being an activist all the time."

In April 2009, 114 activists were arrested ahead of the planned occupation of the Ratcliffe-on-Soar power plant. Twenty-seven were due to be charged with public-order offences, one of whom was Stone. Kennedy was told, natu-rally, not to worry about being charged. But he did worry, wishing for a number of reasons to preserve his cover. The Nottinghamshire detectives putting together the prosecu-tions had had no idea that an undercover officer had been involved. If charges were dropped against him alone, this would look highly suspicious when it came to continuing as Stone. Kennedy's planned role in the protest had been as a driver, and he argued with his handlers that charges should be dropped against other drivers too. Shortly after this, he was told that the operation was being wound up, and that he should tell his cohorts in the environmental movement that he was off to America to visit family.

Following his extraction, Kennedy returned to the Met in October 2009, and found himself a square peg. According to him, he was seen as having, however unavoidably, failed to keep abreast of the changes in policing and its technology and, he maintains, was told he wasn't really qualified to do anything. Incredibly, he returned to his Nottingham friends, as Mark Stone, in early 2010, having left the employ of the police. But the discovery of a passport in his real name led to his unmasking.

At the outset, Kennedy had rationalized that he would be helping both sides. In the end, perhaps he fantasized vainly about being accepted by his girlfriend and friends for who he was, or at any rate despite who he had been. Psychologists might offer such an explanation, or one involving guilt, as to why a former undercover officer experienced in tradecraft would leave his real passport in the glove compartment of his van. Unmasked but to date unharmed, Kennedy seems relieved to be no longer deceiving the people he came to care about.

Twenty activists were convicted of trespass offences in relation to Ratcliffe-on-Soar, but the case against the remaining six collapsed. One version of why has Kennedy going rogue, threatening to give evidence for the defence. Another says that he had become an agent provocateur, thus undermining a credible prosecution, although in tapes of meetings he passed to his handlers, he demurs from climbing the power station himself, lest he be seen as leading the protest. (This is Kennedy the thoughtful copper, still keen in April 2009 not to prejudice the case his handlers were putting together.) It may simply be that the tapes not only provided insufficient evidence for a prosecution, but would have helped the defence, showing that the campaigners concerned were in fact vacillating about whether or not to take part in the protest, and to what extent. Using them could have undermined the prosecution case, begging the question as to whether the operation mounted involving Kennedy had been proportionate to the threat in the first place, while not to have done so could have led to allegations of non-disclosure from the defence.

According to Kennedy, the police have distanced themselves from him, but it would appear that the role confusion he experienced is not unique. Similar stories have emerged, including that of the undercover cop who married a "fellow" activist from protest-group Reclaim the Streets. But psychological confusion has not altogether elbowed out the good old British cock-up, such as the officer embedded for four years with anti-capitalist group Globalise Resistance, who inadvertently called a campaigner on his mobile phone while discussing photographs of demonstrators with a fellow officer while at a police station. According to the BBC's *Newsnight*, the activist's recording contains such gems as, "She's Hanna's girlfriend, very overt lesbian. Last time I saw her, hair about that long, it was blonde, week before it was black."

The Kennedy case, along with others, would appear to be bringing about a rethink in the way the UK conducts its covert policing. If so, it is to be hoped that resources remain directed where they belong: at apprehending the prime movers of terror and organised crime.

Undercover policing is fraught with legal difficulties. (For one thing, for example, if an officer has sex undercover, it could raise the question as to whether the consent his partner gives is properly informed.) No wonder, therefore, that the number of specialized undercover operatives – those who assume false identities to gain credibility within criminal groups – is relatively small when compared to the number of police officers deployed in other frontline roles.

For the most part, where they exist, undercover activities take their place alongside covert surveillance and the use of informers in any given investigation – activities less likely to induce a tendency to go beyond their boundaries, as undercover work can, it seems. Therefore, the following tales present undercover investigations in the context of police work as a whole, together with the plain-clothes detection and surveillance activities that bring in collars for cops as quickly and efficiently as possible. It shines a broad torch beam across cases that have been made or broken by cops acting covertly. Enjoy.

PART 1

OLD SCHOOL: The UK and Europe

1

You're Nicked!

Dick Kirby

Dick Kirby's series of memoirs capture the flavour of life in the Flying Squad during the 1970s and 1980s. Tasked with busting London's gangs of blaggers, grafters and hooligans, these cops were every bit as tough as the characters they surveilled, infiltrated and arrested. This is the world harked back to in the TV series *The Sweeney* and, more recently, *Life on Mars*.

These "glory days" of British policing, with their certainties, cynicism and villains straight out of central casting, are the subject of nostalgia today, but were the stuff of everyday life to cops like Kirby. In our terror-obsessed culture, the idea of things being what they seem is oddly comforting, however ruthless the villains concerned.

In the following extract, operations aimed at busting one gang of fraudsters and a separate gang of forgers are described in Kirby's characteristic, to-the-point tone. From its inception, the Flying Squad, otherwise known as "the Sweeney" from rhyming-slang "Sweeney Todd" was tasked with apprehending robbers and – importantly back then, in 1919 – pickpockets, and originally consisted of twelve specialized detectives answerable to Scotland Yard. Today, they tackle the toughest of Britain's bank robbers.

Since a conspiracy to rob can pose a huge threat to the public at large, intelligence has always been of paramount importance to the Sweeney in solving the dilemma of gathering enough evidence for a prosecution that is effective in taking villains off the streets, without having to allow a crime to be committed in order to do so. The Mobile Patrol Experiment, as the Flying Squad was originally known, was tasked with gathering intelligence on known robbers, and to do this it made use of horse-drawn carriages with eyeholes cut into their canvas! When a conspiracy is brought to the Sweeney's attention, more often than not, covert surveillance plays a key role in gathering subsequent intelligence, as the following two episodes show . . .

It was around about this time that Charlie Kray was released from prison, having served a ten-year sentence for being an accessory after the fact in the murder of Jack "The Hat" McVitie, for which his brothers Reggie and Ronnie had been convicted and had been sentenced to life imprisonment. Now that the Dixon brothers and the Tibbs family were out of the way, would Charlie try to fill the gap?

We concentrated on Charlie and his known associates and followed him everywhere but very little was happening; Charlie was attempting to muscle in on the strength of his brothers' reputation, although not with any great success or, indeed, enthusiasm. He seemed to be spending more and more time in the country and several individuals were brought to our attention.

But there was one person that Charlie did keep in contact with, more than any other, someone who had been a friend of the family for twenty-five years. His name was Geoffrey Leonard Allen.

The friendship had a fairly inauspicious beginning. During the 1950s, Allen had threatened Reggie and Ronnie Kray with a shotgun when they had tried to collect the winnings from a crooked game of cards. But their acquaintance blossomed to such an extent that Allen later purchased a restaurant in the Essex town of Thaxted and renamed it "The Blind Beggar" in honour of the twins – and you can't get much chummier than that, can you? To the locals in Pulham Market, Norfolk, Allen, then fifty-seven years of age, was a ruddy-faced, wavy-haired, portly and rather flamboyant businessman, the owner of "Whiteoaks", who specialized in buying property. But, as Charlie Kray, through his own inactivity, started to drift further into the background, so we became more and more interested in the activities of Allen. It appeared that many of the properties which he had purchased had been heavily insured, before being burnt to the ground. The insurance companies had started refusing to pay out, and Allen commenced civil litigation proceedings against them; in the meantime, he continued buying up properties but put up "front men" as the purchasers; these properties, too, were going up in flames. And on just about every occasion, Allen had convincing alibis; he was, it appeared, nowhere near the scene of the blaze. Unsurprisingly, he was known as "The Godfather".

A whole team of us was moved up to Suffolk; the chief constable obliged us by stopping recruitment and we took over the training wing accommodation at Halesworth Police Station, situated in the north of the county. From there, now much closer to Allen and his associates, we followed and kept an eye on them. Our presence had caused a great deal of speculation among the locals, but the word had been put about that we were working with Customs and Excise on immigration matters, and given the close proximity of the coastline this was accepted.

The Criminal Investigation Department had been in existence for almost a hundred years when, that autumn, its members were, for the first time, paid for overtime. Until then, detectives had been paid an allowance which, for detective constables, amounted to just £38 per month. Now, given the tremendous number of hours we were working up in East Anglia, our salaries doubled. We carried out an enormous amount of observation and surveillance; at the time, I was driving a Ford Corsair 2000GT, an exceptionally powerful, fast car, and it was much needed.

We had been there for months, quietly gathering evidence, before we were ready to make arrests. On one occasion, we heard that one of Allen's properties was going to be torched and we kept observation on it all night; it wasn't until the following day that we discovered that it was another of his properties which had gone up in flames! I later followed Allen to a hotel, where I saw him meet up with one of his top associates in the lounge. I managed to get close enough to hear Allen say:

"How did that bit of business go, the other night?"

"Like a house on fire!" was the response, and both men roared with laughter.

This revelation drew predictable, scathing cross-examination from Allen's barrister at the trial at Norwich Crown Court the following year:

"So you, disguised, one assumes as an aspidistra plant, got close enough to hear one comment, and one comment only – of a highly incriminating nature – from my client?" he asked, and sorrowfully shook his head. "What a clever, *fortunate* Serious Crime Squad officer you are!"

When Allen and his associates came to be arrested, my goodness, it was a testing time. At 3 o'clock in the morning, on Saturday, 13 September 1975, we were assembled for a briefing, which included every available Serious Crime Squad officer from London, officers from No. 5 Regional Crime Squad, local officers and the Special Patrol Group, after which we went out and made the arrests. Many of the officers found that the early start had thrown their body clocks right out of kilter. I helped search a large industrial complex. Suddenly one of the constabulary officers came hurrying towards me, his face contorted.

"Quick!" he groaned. "Where's the shit-house?"

I pointed. "Down there, second left."

"Thanks!" he grunted and hobbled away.

I saw him again, about twenty minutes later; he looked considerably relieved. "Everything all right, now?" I grinned.

"Ah!" he beamed. "It come out like a flock a'starlings!"

Twenty-three people were arrested – six of them women – and we worked; and when I say we worked, I mean we worked for twenty-four hours straight off. Then we fell into our beds for four hours and then we worked for twenty hours, followed by another sleep of four hours and then working for another twenty hours. We all found different ways to keep going: my own patent way was to sip cups of hot, weak, sugary, milkless tea. We would have regarded any officer who drank alcohol during that time as being potty and, in fairness, I don't believe anybody did. But by the time the gang was charged, the officers from the Serious had the appearances of zombies; bumping into each other was commonplace and I managed to excel by walking straight into a wall.

By the morning of Tuesday, 16 September, Allen and nine others were charged and en route to Great Yarmouth Magistrates' Court. The charge for Allen and seven others was that they had conspired together, and with other persons unknown, to induce the Royal Insurance Company to settle £153,369 for a fire insurance claim for Briggate Mill, Worstead, near North Walsham, Norfolk, with intent to defraud. Despite a number of ardent pleas for bail being made by all of the defendants, it did them no good at all.

A delicious moment occurred when the senior officer who had outlined the circumstances of the case and the objections to bail was cross-examined by the defence. There were two matters which weighed heavily against any of the defendants getting bail. The first was that the officer giving evidence was Detective Superintendent Randall Jones, a tall, knowledgeable and very frightening ex-Flying Squad officer, who had a loathing of violent criminals. And the second was that the defence barrister who was cross-examining him was a dope.

The barrister's client had a conviction for an assault occasioning actual bodily harm, for which he had been fined £75. Therefore, thought the brief, the circumstances of the assault must have been so trivial that, in all probability, it had been no more than his client giving someone (who probably deserved it) a clip round the ear.

"It was, officer," the brief intoned, "no more than a very minor type of assault, was it not?"

Randall raised his eyebrows. "Depends, I suppose, on what you would describe as being 'minor'," he replied.

Now, I should mention that in those days, three things were quite different regarding bail applications as opposed to the present time. Firstly, police officers, rather than the Crown Prosecution Service, voiced their objections to bail, which made sense because they knew all the ins and outs of the case and, what was more, knew the defendants. Secondly, convicted felons' CRO files were made out of paper, rather than microfiche. And lastly, one could refer to any part of that paper file, which not only showed the result at court but also revealed the offence for which the prisoner had originally been arrested.

Sadly, the defence counsel had much to learn because he was obviously unaware of the cardinal rule of all competent briefs: "Never ask a question, unless you know the answer!" So in a sustained bout of silliness, he gave a contrived sigh of exasperation and drawled, "Pray tell the court of the circumstances of this ghastly assault for which my client was fined the staggering sum of £75."

Unfortunately, he was so wrapped up in the sound of his own rhetoric that he failed to notice the wild anxiety in his client's eyes, nor his vigorous and negative head-shaking.

A smile flitted across Randall's face as he looked up from the prisoner's CRO file and nodded. "Certainly."

He waited a couple of seconds to ensure that he had the undivided attention of the Bench before casually replying, "He pulled the victim's toenails out, with a pair of pliers!"

The prisoner buried his face in his hands, the barrister's face turned chalk-white and the beak roared, "*WHAT!*" Rightly or wrongly, he tarred all the defendant's co-accused with the same brush and remanded the lot in custody for seven days. The magistrate then demanded to know how anybody could have been fined such a paltry sum for such a serious assault and an investigation was launched.

This was the explanation. The prisoner had been arrested by a police constable and, given the gravity of the offence, he had quite rightly been charged with inflicting grievous bodily harm with intent, to be tried only at the Old Bailey and punishable with life imprisonment.

However, between arrest and the initial court appearance,

the prisoner had been spoken to – interviewed would have been far too harsh a term – by a venal CID officer whom I shall refer to as Detective Constable Barry Smithson. Both the charge and the evidence were impressively watered down, hence the resultant fine of just £75; I have no doubt that the arrangement and consultancy fees were somewhat steeper.

At the conclusion of the discipline board which followed, Smithson was sacked in double-quick time and although his senior officers probably sighed with relief, they were not the only ones to experience a sense of salvation.

With the gang locked up, there was no need for any further secrecy. For many years, it had been suspected that Allen had been carrying out his fire-raising; now sweeping enquiries could be made.

Between 1955 and 1969, eight of the properties which Allen had purchased in the mid-Anglia region had gone up in flames. In the weeks and months following the arrests, I went all over Essex, Hertfordshire, Suffolk and Norfolk, investigating those fires and the people who witnessed them. Because of the time that had passed, some of the witnesses were dead, but I found others who, though elderly, possessed memories which were amazingly sharp. One old chap, then in his eighties, had been a volunteer fireman in the 1950s when a fire occurred in the middle of the night at the Oast House, Saffron Walden, which was one of Allen's properties.

"I went along because it was in an out-of-the-way place and only I knew where it was," he told me. "We had nearly got there when I saw Mr Allen's car coming towards us; I knew it was his – there wasn't all that many cars round here after the war and you couldn't miss his one – it was a great big flash American job!" He chuckled. "The next day, I read in the paper that Mr Allen said he'd been at a club in Southend at the time of the fire, but he couldn't have been – could he?"

The retired fireman was just one of many witnesses I found. I would work one week from home – meaning that I would carry out all the enquiries closest to home, so that I could return each night; and then the following week, I would cram in as many enquiries, as far afield as I could, moving from hotel to hotel. And remember, in all of these enquiries, it would not be the case of completing one enquiry before going on to the next; quite often, while carrying out one particular investigation, the result would be three or four more different lines of enquiry. It was nothing other than pure detective work, and I loved it.

In some of these cases, straw was brought into the property prior to the blaze occurring; not only because straw was a good accelerant, but because it burnt away to almost nothing and what was left was usually washed away, courtesy of the firemen's hoses.

One such case occurred when Allen purchased Witham Lodge Farm, Witham, Essex, which lies back from the Hatfield Road, in 1965. The premises were run-down, and in fact had been used as a barn. In an effort to be helpful, the previous owner removed bales of straw which had been deposited in the library. To his amazement, Allen was furious, saying that he *wanted* them in the library. Even more astounding was that on the night of the fire, the previous owner witnessed the firemen throwing out bales of burning straw, which had mysteriously found their way back into the library.

A year later, Allen purchased Shortgrove Hall, Essex, for £47,000. It had been intended, so it was said, to turn it into a hotel and a casino and, it was further said, Allen went to the Colony Club in London's West End, seeking advice on this venture from the Hollywood film star (and gangster) George Raft. It was during that night that the premises burnt down. The same fate was in store for Coldham Hall, Stanningfield, Suffolk, where the model Claudia Schiffer now lives.

The latest venture had been the purchase of Briggate Mill, in March 1975, for £10,500. It was the subject of planning permission to convert it into six flats and three maisonettes and had been insured for £175,000. On the evening of 7 August 1975, six fire appliances were called to deal with a fire at the premises. In the fifteen minutes it took them to arrive, the blaze had gutted the building. By an incredible coincidence, the fire was witnessed by the manager of the Royal

Insurance Company, who had insured the building, and who was visiting friends next door; the heat was so intense, it was feared that the blaze would spread to the neighbour's property, which fortunately proved not to be the case.

The trial began on Friday, 10 September 1976 at Norwich Crown Court, before Mr Justice MacKenna. John Marriage QC, a highly competent barrister, appeared for the prosecution and he was assisted by the late James Crespi. Three years previously, Crespi had fortuitously escaped death when an IRA bomb had exploded outside the Old Bailey, and he was one of the 162 persons who sustained injury. A press photograph depicting the blood-splattered torn shirt on his corpulent body was flashed around the world. A great character and a lover of good food, his enormous girth precluded fast movement; during Crespi's stay at Norwich, his journey between the court and the Old Crown Hotel opposite, was covered by taxi.

In the dock were eight defendants; all of them were charged with conspiracy to cheat and defraud in respect of the insurance claim at Briggate Mill and to this charge, all of them pleaded not guilty. In addition, Allen and his former wife were charged with conspiring to defraud the County Fire Office Ltd of £150,000 in respect of Shortgrove Hall, Saffron Walden, and both of them pleaded not guilty to this charge. She would later be acquitted.

Quite simply, the case for the Crown was that all of the defendants had played a part, to a lesser or greater degree, in burning down buildings, preparing false insurance claims or in some way covering-up; all, except for Allen, who was described as the organizer.

Just as simply, the case for the defence was that none of the defendants had done anything of the kind and the police had fitted them up. Allen went further – he made no secret of his friendship with the Kray brothers and that he had considered bringing Charlie into his businesses in East Anglia (although this had not happened). Moreover, he claimed, the police had never recovered the proceeds of the Kray crime empire and they had maliciously decided to bring charges against him, because of his association with them. Sounds as though the stage was set for a no-holds-barred fight, doesn't it? You'd be right.

Everything witnessed, overheard or written down by the police, said the defence, was a lie. Allen, said the prosecution, had suggested to several police officers that he could "put them on to big things", if only they would drop the charges. If they would not, he said, he would have no option but to "turn Queen's Evidence" and tell the truth, this being the only way out for him. This was *definitely* disputed by Allen. Since the police thought that this would certainly be the case, Detective Sergeant Terry Brown GM went to the remand prison where Allen was being held, in the hope that he would repeat himself. Brown had been fitted with a "Nagra" or concealed tape recorder. So had Allen. It's what's known as "A Mexican Stand-off".

And so it went on, "Yes, you did," "No, I didn't," until the defence suddenly dropped a bombshell.

Detective Chief Superintendent Len Gillert was being cross-examined by Allen's barrister, who suddenly, and out of the blue, asked him:

"Have you been tapping my client's telephone?" Consternation in court!

Gillert swallowed and then replied, "I can neither confirm nor deny the question."

The barrister furiously stated that that was not an answer; Gillert replied that it was. Eventually, the judge decided that he would make a ruling on whether the question should be answered or not, but not until Gillert had had the opportunity of legal advice, to discuss all the imputations of the question. Which is what happened: Gillert consulted with the director of public prosecutions and the attorney general, who came to the conclusion that, if the judge decided that Gillert should answer the question, he must do so. And the judge *did* ask the question and the answer which Gillert gave was, of course, "Yes".

Knowledge of what one criminal is saying (or indeed writing) to another is an immensely important weapon against crime and it has been for years. Special Branch officers tapped the telephone lines of insurgents before and during the First World War, and the whole business has always been shrouded in secrecy. Many people think that when the police wish to intercept a criminal's telephone calls, it is done at the drop of a hat. Not so. There are only a specific number of "lines" available and the majority of these go to the security services, Special Branch and the Anti-Terrorist Squad, because of the threat to national security. In every case, including requests for more common-or-garden criminals' telephone calls to be intercepted, a report has to be made out, showing that an intercept is necessary in order to frustrate an impending and serious crime. Even then, the request may not be supported by senior police officers. But if it is, the report has to go to the Home Secretary for signing and then the warrant will be only for a specific period; it is very difficult to get that period extended. Of course, the whole thing is kept under wraps and, for many years, anybody under the rank of detective inspector was not even supposed to be aware of telephone intercepts.

So, when the use of telephone intercepts was suddenly aired in open court at Allen's trial, there was, as I have already said, considerable consternation. I believe that this daring gambit by the defence was made purely to shock the establishment to such a degree, that flushed with embarrassment, the director of public prosecutions would direct that no further evidence would be offered in the case. Well, if that was the case, they were wrong. All it did was to alert the jury to the fact that Allen was such a dangerous criminal that the Home Secretary had issued a warrant for his telephone line to be tapped. It was not as though what had been said on the telephone between Allen and his associates had been evidence; it would have been nice if it had been. And when Gillert simply answered that he could not "confirm nor deny" that Allen's telephone had been tapped, he was only saying what he had been instructed to say in that sort of eventuality.

What had caused Allen's defence counsel to ask the question? Well, I don't know, because I didn't take part in Allen's interview at the police station. But perhaps during the questioning Gillert asked, "Isn't it right that you asked a co-defendant this, that and the other?" Then, Allen might have thought to himself, "Yes, I did ask him those matters but surely it was all said on the telephone?" It would not be long before an even halfway intelligent criminal came up with the right answer, and Allen was a very intelligent criminal indeed.

Well, back now to Norwich Crown Court. It still had its fair share of mishaps to go. Following a submission to the judge, one of the defendants was acquitted. Two weeks later, the judge caused an enquiry to be held after it was alleged that approaches had been made to the jury; at the conclusion of the investigation, one of the jurors was discharged and the trial continued with just the eleven others.

Eventually, on 7 January 1977, after deliberating for fifty-one hours and fifty minutes, the eight men and three women members of the jury returned their verdicts. Allen was found guilty of both charges.

Telling him, "Your villainy has at long last been exposed," Mr Justice MacKenna sentenced him to concurrent sentences of seven years' imprisonment and ordered him to pay his own defence costs.

Two more of the defendants each received four years' imprisonment, another was sent down for three years, one was sentenced to twelve months' imprisonment, suspended for two years, and ordered to pay £2,000 prosecution costs and £5,000 defence costs, and one was acquitted.

And after eighty-three days, that was the end of the longest criminal trial that had then been held in an East Anglian court. The cost was estimated at £750,000.

The Allen enquiry spawned offshoots. In February 1976, I was investigating a long-firm fraud (one in which increasingly large orders are placed with a supplier of goods and settled promptly, until payment is evaded on an especially large one) in Lincolnshire; then I was searching a farm, making arrests for conspiracy to cheat and defraud, and for possession of a firearm; within days I was up in Leicestershire, staying at the Holiday Inn for a couple of weeks, to look at the activities of a gang of fraudsters; and then I went down to Dorset, in connection with a blackmail enquiry.

Everything that we did was recorded in maroon "Confidential" dockets, so when I went to the Yard that March, nattily attired to attend a board for selection to the rank of detective sergeant, I was taken aback when a crusty-looking old commander asked me:

"And what are you up to now, Mr Kirby?"

I gulped and replied, "I'm most awfully sorry, sir, but I can't tell you."

He frowned and looked at my papers, again. Suddenly, realization dawned. "Oh, my dear boy!" he cried. "I'm so sorry – I shouldn't have asked you!"

After that, everything went well; I was asked a few charming questions by the chairman of the board, Deputy Assistant Commissioner Ray Anning, and that was that – I was in and out of that board in record time – and more importantly, one month later (and having spent a bare three years in the rank of detective constable) I was promoted to detective sergeant. Better than that, instead of being posted off the Squad (as was quite normal following promotion), I stayed exactly where I was.

I flew to the Isle of Man to arrest a very disagreeable fellow for conspiracy to cheat and defraud. I remember that I had to speak to him quite sharply, but who he had conspired with, and who they were going to cheat and defraud, and what happened to them thereafter, I have no idea. There were so many enquiries being run, and I moved around, helping out on one, then going on to the next.

By then, I had been part of the Serious Crime Squad for a year and had thoroughly enjoyed myself. Everything tackled was top-level criminal investigation; the officers who staffed the Serious were top-notch and I'd hardly had a moment to draw breath. What happened next was going to transport me, for the first time, into the world of international organized crime. I'm going to tell you what I remember. It's difficult, because the enquiry was so vast. I didn't know the full picture at the time, and I'm not sure I do now.

* * *

It all started when we were given an East End gangster as a target. It was suspected that he was involved in fraudulent dealings with stolen and/or forged cheques, and he was kept under observation. He was followed from his home in the morning and usually he went to Prince Regents Lane in Plaistow, East London, where he had a scrap metal business. The business premises was kept under observation, and the comings and goings of his associates were photographed, noted and logged. From there, he would be followed, and who he met later would also be recorded and photographed. Some of these meetings took place in London's West End. And one of the watchers, Detective Sergeant Hilda Harris, noticed that he met a "funny, fat little foreigner". The following day, he met him again. And the next . . .

Before long, the foreigner became the subject of surveillance. He too met up with other foreign nationals. Long-distance cameras were used – over 5,000 photographs were taken – and bugging devices were utilized. That they were deeply involved in international fraud was clear. What also became clear was that we were not alone in observing them. One night, during an observation at one of the suspect's addresses, Detective Sergeant Trevor Cloughley had a word with one of our co-watchers; his explanation was neither satisfactory nor convincing and a huge row developed. It later transpired that the man was attached to MI5. They dropped out of the picture thereafter, and somebody unkindly remarked that the whole business was far too complex for them!

On one occasion, members of the gang left the country, taking with them a suitcase full of money. We were monitoring their every movement. There was a hiccup when they were searched by customs and the money was discovered. Customs and Excise were outraged when we told them to return the money and let them go – after all, this was a clear breach of the currency regulations in force at the time. But the word came from very high up; and they were allowed to continue on their way.

We had to pick them up upon their return, but this was

most difficult of all. Simply because they had produced return tickets to Paris, it did not mean that they were going to return from Paris; it could have been any airport in the world. Nor could we rely on circulating their passport details to the Immigration Officers; by now, we knew they were in possession of forged passports, in different names and allegedly issued from different countries. So what I had to do was stake out the whole of Heathrow and check *every single* incoming flight. This I did with a team from the Leytonstone office of the Special Patrol Group, who were really excellent. We started so early in the morning and finished so late at night, we never had any trouble with the traffic – and this was before the M25 had opened, remember. Between checking the flights, there were distractions; seeing Concorde take off was a staggeringly impressive sight, and also seeing Jacqueline Onassis step off an all-night flight from New York. She looked stunning.

But best of all was suddenly seeing the conspirators strolling towards immigration. I tipped the immigration officers the wink and they held them up long enough to photocopy their passports – they had used, of course, entirely different passports from the ones with which they had left the country. With the photocopies in my possession, we raced for our cars, and drove round to the terminal just in time to see them get into a taxi and set off for London. They were deposited at various addresses and that facet of the enquiry was over for us. I sighed with relief. If the gang had slipped in unnoticed, I would never have heard the last of it. Now, we could look forward to some much-needed sleep.

Not for long, though; we had heard by now that the gang had attempted to purchase some land in Torremolinos, Spain, by means of three banker's drafts, which totalled £1,300,000, on behalf of an Arab sheikh. In fact, the story of the sheikh was as phoney as the banker's drafts; and prior to handing these over, the conmen suddenly spotted an isolated error made by an otherwise perfect forger. The risk was too great. The conmen hastily departed and they lost out on their anticipated commission of £130,000, which the property developer would have been only too happy to give them.

The observations had gone on for months and there was a strain, both on finances and the constitutions of the officers carrying out the work. Finally, sufficient evidence was amassed to justify the gang's arrest.

In the early hours of 13 August 1976, there was a briefing in the gymnasium at Limehouse Police Station. Over a hundred police officers were present, including everybody attached to the Serious Crime Squad, officers from other departments at C1 and members of the Special Patrol Group. Everything depended on split-second timing. The entire gang had to be rounded up, all at the same time so that none of them could alert other gang members. All of us were given dockets for the targets. Mine was a German national, named Karl Lempertz. I had kept him under observation for so long that I felt as though we knew each other – when I arrested him, I would not have been particularly surprised if he'd said, "Hello, Dick!"

Lempertz (who was known as "Kärlchen" or "Charlie") was a playboy type, fifty-six years of age, tall, fit and tanned, with receding grey hair. He was always immaculately dressed, in a casual style which really would have suited a younger man – but with his fine physique and general air of *savoir faire* he carried it off quite well. We knew he had a police record in other parts of the world, but one piece of intelligence about him really had me on my mettle. He was supposed to be in possession of a fountain-pen gun, of the type favoured by secret agents during the Second World War, so when he was arrested I would have to move very quickly indeed.

At 6 o'clock in the morning, a small group of us gathered outside his bedroom in Mayfair's Berkeley Hotel. There was absolutely no reason whatsoever for me to suspect the girl on the switchboard of any impropriety, but I left an officer with her all the same, as we went upstairs with the manager; I didn't want there to be even the smallest chance of Lempertz being forewarned, resulting in me or any of my team getting ever so slightly shot. I quizzed the manager about the layout of the room, because once we went in, I wanted to be moving in the right direction, fast. The manager obliged by unlocking an identical, unoccupied room, so that I could see the position of the bed, the bathroom and the windows. Satisfied, I checked my watch. As the second hand swept past 6 o'clock, the manager quietly unlocked the door and in we went.

I could see two forms in the big double bed; I had identified which of the lumps was Lempertz, so I directed some officers to the other side of the bed. I nodded and as the other person in the bed was grabbed, I got hold of Lempertz's neck and whisked him right off the pillow and as he headed south, towards the floor, I flicked the pillow across the room; I'd reasoned that if he had the fountain-pen gun in his possession, it would be under there. It wasn't – nor was it anywhere else. Lempertz was handcuffed and if at that time I had been fluent in German, I would have laconically remarked, "*Also – Sie sind verhaftet!*" But I wasn't – so I merely stated, "Right – you're under arrest," and I've no doubt he knew what I meant.

Not so his twenty-five-year-old companion; she professed to know no English at all, although she appeared to find the whole business highly amusing. She was in possession of what appeared to be a quantity of quite expensive jewellery, so that accompanied her to the nick.

By the time I had got back to Limehouse, the prisoners were locked up and their property listed, and I found things were really moving. The head of the gang – the "funny, fat little foreigner" – had also been arrested. Originally we had known him as "Weisser", but now, as far as we could ascertain, the portly, balding little man was Henry Oberlander, aged fifty-one – but he might not have been. In his possession were found twenty-five forged passports, including diplomatic passports bearing his photograph, all in different names.

These passports, Oberlander would later say, were not used to perpetrate fraud. Oh no, they were an aid to avoid assassination! As a young man, he had been imprisoned in one of the Nazi concentration camps. Sentenced to death with other Jews, he had been machine-gunned in the legs, and, feigning death, he had rolled into a ditch with the dead bodies of his comrades, later escaping under cover of darkness. Shot in the legs, eh, while all the others had been killed? Right. And after that, he had devoted himself to helping other Jews to escape, a sort of a Scarlet Pimpernel character. And then he fled to Vienna and then Hungary, helping even more Jews escape from the Russians, following the uprising in 1956. But his overriding desire was to track down the Nazi killers. Why, he had tracked Josef Mengele, the "death doctor" of Auschwitz, to a ranch in Argentina – he was within shooting distance of him! Oberlander had wanted to kidnap Mengele but he was too well guarded; and now, here in London, agents from ODESSA, the organization for former members of the SS, were hot on his trail – hence the forged passports, to keep one step ahead of them.

This, as you will have probably already guessed, we considered to be complete and consummate bollocks.

Oberlander had a small, wire-haired terrier named "Napoleon". It couldn't be left behind, so it was brought in as well. It was put in the kennels at Limehouse and was generally petted by the officers who passed by. In the end, nobody knew what to do with it; I believe a PP voucher was put round its neck and it was sent off to the Prisoners' Property Store and was never seen again. Perhaps it was machine-gunned in the legs and managed to escape under cover of darkness.

Detective Sergeant Tony Goss had kicked in the front door of a flat in Vere Court, Bayswater. He had expected to arrest Francisco Fiocca, a forty-eight-year-old Argentinian, and so he did, but what he saw caused his mouth to hang open in amazement. He lost no time in getting on the telephone to Detective Chief Superintendent Len Gillert; and all he could say, repeatedly, was, "Fucking hell, Guv'nor! Fucking hell! You'd better come down here quick and see for yourself!"

Tony had discovered the ultimate forger's den. It was not just the printing press; the den was also stacked with 1,500 forged bank drafts, drawn on thirty-nine different banks and with a face value of almost £3 million, engraving equipment, rubber stamps for visas which had been stolen from embassies and consulates, 340 stolen airline tickets, credit cards, typefaces from different countries and a machine for printing in amounts on drafts. There were also birth and baptism certificates, travel documents and 120 forged passports. The enormous quantity of stolen and forged traveller's cheques took hours to count. And then there was four million pesetas, plus $50,000 in forged currency. There was also the gang's escape kit – bogus papers which would have enabled them to flee behind the Iron Curtain.

For someone of Fiocca's ability, the plan was simple. Hundreds of men and women from all over the world had their pockets picked, their handbags stolen, their jackets, left for a few moments over the back of a chair, rifled. Their passports, identity documents, traveller's cheques and airline tickets found their way to the gang who, because of their obvious connections with the country, became known as "The Hungarian Circle". The stolen goods were handed to Fiocca, who brilliantly forged them, using the right inks and papers. Banker's drafts, for relatively small amounts, were legitimately purchased; these too were copied. Just how brilliant these forgeries were will be seen.

The rest of the gang? André Biro, aged fifty-two, from Hampstead who, like Oberlander, was short, tubby and balding, and who often wore dark, horn-rimmed glasses, was the group's quartermaster. Born in Brazil, he had been taken to Hungary as a boy. Fleeing from the revolution in 1956, he had travelled to Argentina, and thence, illegally, to Britain in 1974. He had obtained the type, cheque machines and paper for Fiocca.

Romanian-born Jorge Grunfeld, aged fifty-five, was living at the same address as Oberlander. As a young man, he had gone to Budapest and then, in 1948, emigrated to Argentina. He described himself as an antiques dealer although, as I later unkindly pointed out to him, "You wouldn't have known a genuine antique from a fucking milk bottle." He also passed himself off as a property developer, buying genuine banker's drafts for Fiocca to copy.

We had originally known Emile Fleischman, aged fifty-seven, from Ladbroke Mews, Notting Hill, as "Vogel". It was one of many aliases that he used. He had been born in Hungary, educated in Switzerland, Sofia and the Sorbonne in Paris, and in fact his rather distinguished appearance, with his swept-back hair and dark glasses, did lend him a somewhat academic air. He added that he had been a French Foreign Legionnaire, although I did think this was stretching credulity a bit *too* far. If he had have been, he would have been entitled to French citizenship at the end of his service. Now, for whatever reason, he was stateless. He was also Oberlander's aide and he used false passports to pass forged banker's drafts around the world.

The East End gangster – who was later bound over to keep the peace for five years in the sum of £5,000 – and some associates were brought in too, plus some also-rans. And if the days following the arrest of Geoff Allen and his gang were considered frantic, these arrests would put Allen & Co. in the shade.

To start with, there was the immense volume of property. Then there were dozens of prisoners who had been brought in from the forty addresses which had been raided. The majority spoke good (if accented) English, but there were some who purported not to and some who clearly did not. Therefore, interpreters had to be brought in. One of the prisoners had demanded a Romanian interpreter, so one was located and was requested to come to Limehouse Police Station. 'Are you conversant with the Romanian language?" he was asked.

"Sir," he replied, proudly, "I can speak many languages." Unfortunately, Romanian was not one of them, because after a five-minute, one-sided conversation, the prisoner, who was looking more and more baffled, turned to us and said, "I haven't a clue what this cunt's on about. Come on, fuck him off out of it – I'll talk to you!"

I interviewed Lempertz's girlfriend. Where had the jewellery come from, she was asked. She shrugged. "Kärlchen" had given them to her. And where had he got them from? Again, she shrugged. In the end, there were no grounds for detaining her any longer, so she was released and returned to Germany, and I never saw her again.

However, that was not the end of her involvement in the case. We heard that Lempertz was suspected of being involved in a £900,000 jewellery robbery in Bonn, so we photographed the jewellery which I had found in the girl's possession and sent it to our West German counterparts, the *Bundeskriminalamt* (BKA) – the German Federal Police. Back came the answer – the pieces were positively identified as being part-proceeds of the robbery. We passed the details of Lempertz's bedmate on to the BKA, who had her placed under surveillance. The BKA's surveillance teams were second to none. For static observations, they recruited young mothers with babies and old-age pensioners. The latter were completely unobtrusive as they sat on the benches in a cemetery as they waited for the mobile surveillance team to follow Lempertz's girlfriend there, just as they had done on several occasions. She had spent quite some time at one particular graveside – in fact, it was her grandmother's – and after several such visits, she was detained and an explanation demanded. It was clearly unsatisfactory, so the BKA promptly started digging up the grave. Before the cadaver of her long-dead grandmother could be hoicked out of the coffin and frisked, it was discovered that there was a shallower and far more recent grave next to the main one. There they found the bulk of the jewellery from the robbery. It had been hidden there and a piece at a time had been retrieved to sell on. The young lady later had a tearful and uncomfortable encounter with the public prosecutor. The federal authorities, it seemed, had very unequivocal ideas about the misuse of consecrated ground, and probably considered it more serious than receiving a bit of stolen "tom".

2

Glasgow Crimefighter

Les Brown and Robert Jeffrey

Les Brown joined the Glasgow force hoping to be in line for some "real policing" – not simply to be pounding the beat – and he wasn't disappointed. Glasgow in the 1960s and 1970s was not yet the cultural hub we know it as today. The infamous post-war housing schemes in areas such as Castlemilk and Blackhill had been built with the best of intentions, and were a great improvement on the urine-soaked slums that had been cleared to make way for them.

However, their architects had planned little in the way of facilities and entertainment. Slowly, shops and even bars and bookmakers moved in. But in the beginning, residents were left with little to do, and this included a number of the city's infamous street gangs, such as the Cumby (named after Cumberland Street) who had been relocated wholesale along with their families. Against a background of poverty, routine drunkenness and random violence, robberies, safecracking and racketeering grew in frequency, as did street battles between gangs, or "rammys".

In this climate, Brown's talent for detection was recognized and his career progressed to membership of Glasgow's Flying Squad and Criminal Investigations Department. In his long career as a detective, Brown was in on the investigation of many of Scotland's most famous crimes, including those of Arthur Thompson Sr, Glasgow's infamous "Last Godfather", the "ice-cream wars", and the "Bible John" murders, the last of which still resonate, officially unsolved, today.

The following extract exemplifies the legal difficulties that can be created when plain-clothes detectives get close to an informer, especially when the "grass" is also a suspect! And yet a mere word from the street, which may have been second- or third-hand or even hearsay, has begun some of the most successful investigations in the history of policing. If a compassionate and straight-up copper like Brown can become mixed up in a case in which the defence can muddy the water with pertinent questions concerning the relationship between detectives and their source of information, then it gives a clue as to how fraught with legal difficulty the deployment of Covert Human Intelligence Sources can be, where the officer concerned may be sharing many aspects of everyday life with suspects, let alone information. For, merely by making use of an informant, Brown laid himself open to the mistaken interpretation that he and his staff had acted as agents provocateurs.

All careers have a defining juncture, something that transcends all that has gone before and that can cast a long shadow on what comes after. For me, it was the famous Albany Hotel drug trial in 1977. This complex, tortuous case had more twists and turns than a Hitchcock movie. In it, the Strathclyde CID and two members of the Strathclyde Drug Squad were pitched against each other. Drug dealers, out-of-town-couriers, shady characters much known about town and the biggest legal names of the day were all involved with a drugs raid in a luxurious hotel in the city centre. No wonder it dominated the headlines in the papers for weeks. It was, some say, the most controversial episode in the history of the force. I was at the centre of it – and I came out of it vindicated by the judge and jury, by my peers in the force *and* by the events that unfolded after the drama of the trial was long over. It was a period in my service that I will never forget – there were many worrying moments and many sleepless nights. For me, this was quite simply the mother of all trials!

The saga finally ended with a mysterious gangland death in a dusty ravine in Pennsylvania but it had all started back in

Glasgow many years before that bloody deed was discovered and it is wise to start this labyrinthine tale at the beginning and to remember that seemingly innocuous happenings, as the drama unfolded, would come to take centre stage at the eventual trial of David McHugh and Terence Frank Goodship.

In my Flying Squad days I was involved in a case of a David Cussins and some three hundred stolen car radios. Cussins was arrested for being involved in the theft but was found not guilty. However, I came in contact with him again when, some time later, we were hunting down a sex attacker in the Charing Cross area. Cussins lived locally and helped the Flying Squad by pointing out the house of a suspect – although he was subsequently eliminated from the inquiry.

In the following years, our paths crossed from time to time and I found it easy to talk to this relatively minor figure in the Glasgow underworld. I say relatively minor but he was a man who often knew just what was going on in his patch. To illustrate the sort of relationship we had, I will tell of a day at the races. I was on the course at Ayr, looking for a fugitive we suspected would be there, and Cussins was at the pleasant track down the coast to lose some money on nags that failed to live up to his expectations.

When we met that sunny day, he had the cheek to tell me he had done his cash in and ask for a lift home in a squad car. He had no chance of that but I did give him a fiver for the fare home. He repaid me a couple of days later by offering me tickets he had acquired for a World Cup football match in Germany between Scotland and Brazil. I was always wary of him, though, and careful about my relationship with him. So, when he offered me those tickets, it was not hard to say, "No thanks."

Cussins had by this time taken over a shop in Great Western Road. He and his family lived in the top end of Sauchiehall Street and, since his ear was usually attuned to what was happening on the streets of the town, I visited him and his family from time to time – but I never went without another member of the squad with me. When we were on night shift and there wasn't much doing we would pop into his shop, even as late as midnight.

The shop was in student territory and it was the sort of place that became busier as the night went on. It was a standing joke with the squad that, whenever we visited the shop, we would have a good look at the stock. One night, we thought he was overstocked with tins of instant coffee so we took one away and had enquiries made by the day shift to see if a consignment of coffee had been stolen. That was the kind of relationship we had.

It is vital to spell this out because, later, our relationship would be the subject of controversy. Cussins knew clearly that, no matter what, if he broke the law and we got to know about it, we would take action against him. It is also important to spell out that, despite what happened later, Cussins was not what could properly be described as a police informer, in the accepted definition of the term. We thought of him more as a likeable rogue who occasionally let slip something that could be a hint in police matters.

But the plot was beginning to thicken. In September 1976, I was on an inspectors' course in Ayr when Cussins phoned me seeking advice. We agreed he should come to Ayr for a chat and, the next day, he told me he was suspected of stealing a large sum of money from a flat in Roystonhill. The owner of the flat, one Thomas Paramasivan, knew where Cussins stayed and was well able to mount an attack on him or his family – and was likely to do so. He said that the theft of the money was being investigated by the Northern Division CID. I told Cussins I was returning to Glasgow the next day and would make some enquiries and speak to the officer investigating the case with a view to having a word with Paramasivan, who I knew, to let him know we were aware of the threats to Cussins. He seemed pleased and we agreed to meet the following day in a pub near his home.

The following morning I phoned Caroline Farmer, the officer in charge of the case, and received some surprising news. She told me that Cussins had attacked Paramasivan with a shotgun and she was looking for him on several serious charges. I told her of my arrangement to meet Cussins and told her of the agreed time and place. She went along with the suggestion that members of my squad and I should arrest Cussins and bring him in to her office. Joe Jackson, Brian Laird and I went to the pub as arranged but he was nowhere to be seen so we went to his house.

I told the guys I would knock at the door and, if Cussins was in, I would signal for them to join me. However, although Mrs Cussins was there, her husband was not at home. Mrs Cussins said she would contact David on his "Air Call" bleeper, a system of keeping in touch that was popular before everyone and his dog had a mobile phone. She made the call, gave a three-digit code number and said that he should phone home as someone wanted to speak to him. I didn't know it at the time but Cussins had a recently introduced, more sophisticated type of bleeper that could receive verbal messages. He would get the "someone wants to speak to you" message verbally with no need to contact anyone at Air Call. No sooner had the message gone out than I heard the noise of a bleeper going off nearby and this was followed, almost immediately, by the sound of a key in the door and in walked David Cussins accompanied by Joe and Brian.

I was furious with Cussins, who had broken our arrangement to meet at the pub, and he was immediately arrested for the attack on Paramasivan. The house was thoroughly searched and Cussins was taken to the Northern. As far as David Cussins was concerned, I thought, "Hell mend him." I went back to Ayr to complete my course.

On 5 October, I got a call from Mrs Cussins telling me that David wanted to speak to me in Barlinnie. What was said remains controversial to this day. I checked with Ms Farmer who had no objections to me talking to him. At no time in this meeting in the jail did Cussins ask me to get him on bail and at no time did I mention bail to Ms Farmer or to the Procurator Fiscal dealing with the case. But, despite there being no favours on offer from the police, this is what Cussins told me that day in the Bar-L.

According to him, the man behind most of the drugs coming into Glasgow was an Asian called Khan who lived in Pollokshields. I was told he had an associate called Ahmed who lived in Mount Florida, also on the south side. Another name was mentioned to me – that of Francis Wray from Govan. I wrote all three names in my notebook although, at the time, they meant nothing to me. Apparently, the drugs were coming into the country in specially adapted cars.

The day after this most significant meeting, I called into the Drug Squad's office after first going to the Scottish Criminal Records Office where I obtained a photograph of a man called Khan. I met with two extremely well-known cops: Jack Beattie, head of the Drug Squad, a former night fighter pilot and, according to his newspaper friends, the greatest master of disguise since Sherlock Holmes; and his right-hand man, Detective Sergeant John Brown.

We had a cup of tea and looked at the photograph. Beattie informed me, "You have the right name and address but the wrong photograph." Brown chipped in to say, "We know about Ali Khan and the drugs but you will have to go some to catch him." At this point, I told them where the info had come from and the temperature in the room dropped – this was clearly not what they wanted to hear. I was in the dark to the fact that Cussins had complained to the police that officers in the Drug Squad were giving students – many of whom he knew because of his shop – drugs provided the cops were given the names of the recipients. The complaint had been investigated and found to be false. Knowing the Drug Squad better than most, I would agree with that finding. But although Jack Beattie and John Brown had been investigated and cleared, they were aware that the source of the complaint had been Cussins. No wonder they responded the way they did to my info – to them anything coming from Cussins was to be treated with suspicion and, in the circumstances, who could blame them?

However, it is worth pointing out that, in January 1980, at Bristol Crown Court, nine men were convicted of illegally importing drugs into the UK in specially converted vehicles. Three were from Glasgow – Ali Ahmed Khan, Bashir Ahmed and Francis Wray – and they were all jailed.

On 27 October 1976, Cussins was released on bail and

during the first week of November Brian Laird and I visited his shop and found him sitting upstairs in a small office, ill at ease and obviously with something worrying him. We asked what was wrong and, after some persuasion, he told us he had become involved with "a right heavy mob". This transpired to be an invitation from a Glasgow "businessman" to go to London and negotiate a deal for drugs. Asked the name of the businessman, he initially refused to say but I said, "Tell me it all or tell me none of it!" and, after that, he said Eddie Topalion was the person involved.

A man well known in the city, Topalion owned the Ad Lib restaurant in Hope Street. Cussins said he was due to go south the very next day. He had known of the trip for about two weeks but had told no one about it. He asked me to go to London with him but, of course, I refused. I suggested he himself should refuse to go but he was told that, if he didn't go, they would just get someone else to do it. I didn't believe this and suspected he had made similar trips in the past. However, we agreed that he would go to London and contact me on his return.

On Friday, 5 November, Detective Sergeant John Corrie, then in the Criminal Intelligence Unit, received information that three men were coming to Glasgow on the Sunday and that they would be in possession of a "prize". They had apparently been in Glasgow before and had stayed at the Albany, one of the top places in town. Despite the classy nature of the hotel, they had complained that, for some reason, the room they had been given did not suit their needs. One of them was called Matt.

Around lunchtime on the same day, I received a call from Cussins saying he would take the 6 p.m. flight from London and asking if we would pick him up at Glasgow Airport. Brian Laird and I drove out to the airport, arriving just before seven, and we heard a call on the public address asking for me. It was Detective Constable Janet Grant at Temple. Cussins had phoned to say he had missed the flight and would arrive one hour later. Sure enough, when the eighty or so passengers appeared down the stairs from arrivals, Cussins was among them.

Later, when the whole saga came to trial, I was asked in court how I knew he had just come from London. The suggestion was that he could have arrived in Glasgow one hour earlier and got up to anything during that time before meeting us. It was true that we only had his word for it that he had missed the earlier flight but I didn't doubt him.

Once inside the CID car, Cussins handed me an envelope which I opened and found that it contained what appeared to be a small slab of cannabis. It was about half the size of a matchbox and gave off an extremely pungent aroma. Cussins opened up about his London trip and the anxiety he had shown before he left seemed to have been well merited. The "heavy team" he had talked of met him in a pub. Some were wearing shoulder holsters with the weapons on view. Two extremely well-dressed guys sat in a corner. Cussins remarked that they looked like cops and was reassured not to worry – "they're on our side." Not so far fetched considering some of the stories of what went on in the Met at that time.

We dropped Cussins at his home and drove to Police HQ where a police scientist, Campbell Stewart, confirmed that the substance in the envelope was cannabis – probably Moroccan gold, the top-of-the-range stuff. We left the HQ and made our way to the home of Detective Chief Superintendent James Binnie, head of the CID, who was aware what was happening as I had briefed him earlier. We showed him the cannabis and he jokingly said, "It would just about fill my pipe." I told him my intention was to give the cannabis back to Cussins as he might be required to show the quality to Topalion or anyone else for that matter. I asked for permission for our squad to be armed – such authorisation was required from someone above the rank of chief inspector – and it was given.

The cannabis was returned to Cussins at his house and he was told we would expect it back. He was unable to confirm exactly when the men from London would bring the drugs to Glasgow but thought it would probably be the Sunday. On Saturday, 6 November, Brian and I made another call at Cussins's house to discuss strategy should the couriers arrive the next day. We were inside the house when the phone rang at 12.40 p.m. and Cussins remarked, "This could be them." There was an extension to the main phone and I told Cussins to pick up the phone on the count of three and, simultaneously, I would pick up the extension. An English voice said, "Hello, Dave, it's Matt. I've been in touch with our friend and it's OK. We'll be coming through on Sunday about 5.30."

On a piece of paper I wrote, "Are you going to stay at the Albany?" – a question I wanted Cussins to ask this Matt. I gave the note to Cussins who asked the question and he was told, "I don't know – I'll let you know when I come through. Have you got the money?" David replied, "The money is OK." and Matt ended the conversation, saying, "See you tomorrow." On the money front, Cussins told us the London team had wanted £7,000 but he had knocked them down to £6,000 We asked Cussins about the cash and he said he hadn't collected it because he knew the drugs weren't reaching their ultimate destination. He didn't want Topalion involved. This made me worry about what would happen if the London team changed the plans and asked Cussins to meet them somewhere else and bring the money. We decided to stay with Cussins all day on the Sunday and, when the London team arrived – wherever that happened to be – we would pounce before they could change their plans. We were vulnerable and I knew it. Before we left Cussins's house, I reclaimed the cannabis sample and lodged it in a safe at the Temple Police Office.

On the Saturday night I went to the Albany and, with the assistance of the security officer, who I knew, ex-Chief Inspector Donald McCulloch, had a good look at the guest register looking for a Londoner who had been there two weeks ago. I asked if the manager was available, only to be told he had just gone on two weeks' holiday. But, at that point, in walked the manager. He had come back to the hotel to pick up something he had forgotten. He said he remembered the incident when a Londoner had demanded a room change. He could not remember the name but told me the guest had been transferred to room 1003. We soon discovered that a

Mathew Peters of 121 Agdon Street, London EC1 had signed in. I phoned the Met who told me there was such a street but the numbers did not go as high as 121. So we knew we had a man called Matt with a phoney address.

After the visit to the Albany, it was back to the office at Temple where I called a meeting to plan the operation next day – particularly what would happen at the hotel – and everyone involved attended. The Drug Squad were invited and John Brown did come along, but his boss Jack Beattie was obviously unwilling to attend and, considering his problems with Cussins in the past, I could understand his position. However, it is worth pointing out that, if there had been a serious murder inquiry that weekend, the whole business would have been handed over to the Drug Squad whether they liked it or not. A knife in some drunk's back on the Friday night could have changed the history of Strathclyde Police!

John Brown, the Drug Squad representative, made no comment on the fact that I, from the CID, would be the one to "write up the case". He knew that I did this from time to time depending on the demands faced by the team. If we had arrested anyone during the night, I would prepare the case on tape for the typist next morning. This assisted the day-shift officer and I would leave a note saying the case was on tape and in the typists' room. The day-shift man would then get on with other matters till around 10 a.m. when the typist would hand him the papers. He would read through them and then set off for the Sheriff Court to report the case to the fiscal. Not many of the detectives did this while on night duty but it was well known that I did.

Next morning, we moved to the Albany and I checked that there was no sign of "Matt" so far. Janet Grant was to take up a position behind the reception desk and Detective Inspector Jim Long would be in charge of the officers inside the foyer – one of whom was John Orr, later to become Sir John and the chief constable. Detective Constable Laurence Wilson, Detective Constable Donald Maule and Detective Constable Kerr Nelson occupied a vacant room on the eighth floor.

These officers carried .38 Smith and Wesson revolvers in
shoulder holsters. Detective Sergeant Joe Jackson and
Detective Constables Brian Laird and Joe Wood were patrolling the city centre in a squad car in constant radio contact
and ready to go where required. Detective Constable Graeme
Pearson and I were to spend the day with David Cussins so
that, if contact was made by Matt, we would be in a position
to take the appropriate action. At 3 p.m., the three of us went
into Heron House, the Post Office telephone exchange building, opposite the Albany. The other teams also took up
position at this time.

Inside Heron House, a few typists doing a bit of Sunday
overtime were intrigued with what was going on and fed us
tea and biscuits. We said we were expecting trouble at the
hotel and, when they left for the day, they asked us to be sure
to let them know what had happened. At that point, we didn't
know ourselves that the Albany raid would eventually fill television and newspapers for the three weeks while a major
drugs trial went on, with various factions in the police giving
evidence. At about six o'clock, I phoned across to Janet and
suggested everyone got a bite to eat as it could be a long
night. She laughed and said this was already in hand for the
folk on duty in the hotel. I suggested that great Glasgow
standby to Cussins, the ubiquitous fish supper. He declined,
saying he had to be careful what he ate because of a dodgy
stomach, and asked permission to phone his wife. He did so
and then turned and said, "That's our tea organized." His
wife had been instructed to put on three steaks. I told Janet
where we were going – Cussins's house was less than five
minutes away from the hotel – and told her to keep me
informed of what was happening.

I was just polishing off my steak when the phone rang to
say the suspects had arrived. I told Janet to tell Jim Long
to do what he had to do and not wait for us. We left Cussins
at home and arrived at the Albany three minutes after the
call. Janet told us that two men had booked in – one had
taken room 805 and one had room 809. Graeme and I went
up to the eighth floor and entered room 805 where we were

met by Jim Long, some of the other cops in the raid and a stranger. Jim showed me a black case which I examined and found it contained twenty-nine slabs of what was obviously cannabis – the smell was very noticeable. Jim said that the man beside him was Dennis Bryan from London. We moved to room 809 and it was a similar scene – some of the cops, Joe Jackson and a stranger. Joe introduced this stranger as Mathew Peters from London. He then handed me a hotel notepad with five telephone numbers:

> 041.12487.102
> 221.8991
> 334.4532
> 204.2303
> 204.3103

I was also handed a parking ticket number Kk417232 dated 7/11/76 which Peters said referred to a Rover (YOY 892) parked at Euston Station, London.

The next step was a call to the Drug Squad and a short time later Detective Constables Riddoch and McKinnon appeared and, after being given the suspect slabs to inspect, they confirmed that it was cannabis. I asked them to take the substance to the HQ for examination by scientists.

Downstairs, Janet had interviewed the receptionists and seized the cards filled in by the suspects who were then taken to Temple Police Station. Interrogated individually, their names and addresses emerged as Mathew Patrick McHugh, aged thirty-four, of 63 Patrick Common House, St Johns Street, London and Terence Frank Goodship, aged thirty-seven, 78 Eastcotes Road, Welling, London. They declined to give any information that would help trace the origin of the drugs. They were then taken to the Central where they were cautioned and charged – with the charge sheet reading, "That you did, on 7/11/76, at the Albany Hotel, Bothwell Street, Glasgow, have in your possession a large quantity of cannabis, a controlled drug, with intent to unlawfully supply it to another, contrary to Section 5 (3) of the Misuse of Drugs Act 1971."

The two men were searched by the station bar staff and
detained. The following morning, I prepared the case for the
Sheriff Court. The front sheet contained the names of
the accused, the charge and their personal details. Page two
contained a list of productions, including the cannabis, and
the total value. Pages three, four and five contained a
summary of the events that led up to the arrest. Page six was
a list of witnesses and, finally, there was a "back sheet" which
gave details of the accused and my details as officer in charge
of the case. At this stage, I did not mention the part played by
Cussins. Despite this omission, the facts, as supplied to the
fiscal, were accurate in every detail. McHugh and Goodship
were remanded in custody for further inquiry and this gave
me seven more days to prepare the case fully for the fiscal.
This would allow him to decide if bail could be granted. If
not, the Crown would have 110 days to complete the case
and that included the trial. A lot of work lay ahead but I didn't
foresee any problems. That was the biggest mistake of my
career!

The telephone numbers found in possession of the
accused were checked and we discovered the following:

041.12487.102 – no such number, obviously a real
    number disguised
221.8991 – Topalion's Ad Lib restaurant in Hope Street
334.5432 – home number of David Cussins
204.2302 – Air Call
204.3103 – number vacant at that time

The Ad Lib and Cussins house had been searched at the time of
the arrests but nothing was found. We knew Cussins was in with
a heavy mob, as he had told us, and the news that his house
had been searched might help take the heat off him in the after-
math of the arrests. After the prisoners had been through the
court, I spoke to McHugh. When I asked about the telephone
numbers, he told me that the owner of the Ad Lib used to work
beside him in the comedian "Cheerful" Charlie Chester's
club in London. He said Cussins's number – 334.5432 –

belonged to a casual acquaintance he knew only as Dave or David. He again declined to help trace the origin and said he was instructed to take the drugs to Glasgow where he would be contacted. The Flying Squad in London had checked the address given and told us that McHugh's father, who stayed there, said his son had moved out. The address given by Goodship was also checked out and found to be the home of a woman whose husband was doing time and the police had the feeling that Goodship was staying there unbeknown to the jailed husband.

The next few days were taken up with getting statements and doing further paperwork on the case. For his part, David Cussins was quite happy with the way the case had been handled and, indeed, he was appreciative of the fact that his house had been searched, knowing that it would help his position with the London mobsters. At this time, I told Cussins that I would have a word with the fiscal who was involved in his Paramasivan case. Despite what was alleged at the subsequent trial in the High Court, at no time was Cussins given or offered money. I can count on the fingers of one hand when I have paid an informant for information. This was not one of them.

On 8 November, I attended the Sheriff Court and was interviewed by Procurator Fiscal Depute Kowalski in connection with the Paramasivan case. I told him that Cussins had assisted the police in the Albany drugs case but he made no comment on this. I was then astonished to learn for the first time that the two other men alleged to be involved with Cussins in the assault on Paramasivan were still in custody. They had played a minor role yet they were in and Cussins was out. The fiscal told me that Cussins had been given bail because he had a fixed address and a business to run.

As all this was happening, I was, of course, involved in day-to-day serious crime investigations and the next episode of the Albany case came on 7 December when I was again interviewed, this time by Procurator Fiscal Depute Murray. Again, it was a question-and-answer session. I did not refer to Cussins's role and just repeated what I had said in my first statement. A few days later, I received a citation for the High Court to attend as a witness in the assault case against Cussins. This trial was to be on 11 January 1977 and, on the 7th, I met Cussins outside his house in a car. I suggested he should plead not guilty as there were mitigating circumstances. I noticed his hair had been cut very short and didn't guess why. He said, "Les, there is no way I can do time."

On the day of the trial, I spoke with the prosecuting advocate depute, Hugh Morton. We knew each other well and he was one of the most capable prosecutors on the circuit and a very genuine person. I told him of Cussins's participation in the Albany affair and that, in my opinion, he had prevented or at least delayed the setting up of a major drug ring in Glasgow. Mr Morton suggested I advise Cussins to plead guilty to the major part of the indictment and my comments would be considered. I was pleased with this response.

I didn't stay pleased too long. Minutes ticked by and there was no sign of David Cussins. The Crown asked me if I knew why he hadn't appeared. I had no idea but I would make enquiries. His wife confirmed my worst fears. No one knew where he was. He had "flown the coop" and a warrant was issued for his arrest. When I went to see Mrs Cussins, it was obvious she had been weeping. And I soon discovered that the whole business was about to get even more complicated. She confirmed that David Cussins had done a runner but she told me that he had written me a letter which she had posted after he had gone. She did not know the contents. On the following day, it arrived by the lunchtime post and I went home to collect the letter. I returned to Temple and opened it there. The L. Murray referred to is the famous Glasgow criminal lawyer Len Murray. This is EXACTLY what the letter said:

Dear Les,
   A brief epistle to put you in the picture. I am fully aware that there will be a great cry of "why on earth did he etc" but I am no use to anyone languishing in prison, particularly when most of the charges are to say the least

nonsensical – if only they had dropped the theft charges, or only if it were a lower court, if, if, if. I seem to have been caught between petty jealousies and envy between the S.C squad and the Northern CID and L Murray and Kowalski with the former in both cases being in the right. With L Murray talking in terms of 4, 5, 6 etc I feel that this is the only solution, and it is the hardest decision I have ever made in my life. To have to sacrifice my wife and two beautiful children, not to mention a prosperous business, nice house etc etc, but once again it gets back to what use am I in prison? Another factor which helped me make up my mind was having to call you to the stand. I don't think you would have liked it all that much and without your evidence what chance would I have? Don't misunderstand me Les, I am not suggesting for one moment that you would not have told the absolute truth which could of course only do me a great deal of good, but the mix, as it were, I feel was already in, A Simpson etc-reading between the lines. Also you could imagine the consequences regarding any connection between the two of us after recent events. This would have proved very difficult for me where I was going – and the way to fight fire is with fire – so in theory I could have got off with maybe 2–3 years and then either chibbed or stabbed or alternately doing considerable more porridge, either way not a very easy decision. Anyway it will soon be over, so think kindly of me, we could have been good friends if things had been different. I still think of you as a friend anyway. Now I would like to ask you a great favour, my wife, has obviously sufficient problems to cope with without getting a hard time, i.e. constant badgering by over zealous D.C.s every time they are passing so I would be greatly obliged if you would use your influence in this direction.

Anyway Les keep being a good person and have a drink to absent friends.

Yours aye

David

The postmark was Glasgow, 10 Jan 1977.

The letter was deposited in the Temple safe overnight and, on Friday, 21 January, I took it to Mrs Cussins. I told her the contents were as expected and that I would uplift the letter from her later. This was simply to put her mind at rest and, in any case, she knew as much about her husband's disappearance as I did. The following day, another trivial incident occurred – again it was something that was to have unexpected consequences. I was in Castlemilk with a couple of colleagues and decided to drive to the Cussins's home to pick up the letter because, by that time, she would have had time to read it and digest the contents.

On the way there, driving along Cathcart Road, we saw a well-known south-side criminal standing at the junction with Allison Street. He was holding a black bin bag stuffed full of something or other. I got out of the CID car on my own and approached him. On asking him what was in the bag, he went absolutely berserk – much to the amusement of my colleagues watching from the car. Eventually, they had to come to my aid and we looked in the bag and found that it contained nothing more significant than dirty washing. At this point, the man's wife appeared and a full scale "rammy" started with a crowd gathering to watch the fun. We did what we thought we had to do – arrested the man on breach of the peace charges and locked him up.

We continued with our journey to pick up the letter and, by then, it was around 6.30 p.m. I went into the house to collect the letter and the others stayed in the car in the street. After a little general chit-chat, Mrs Cussins told me that her husband was concerned that I might commit perjury on his behalf. I said to her, most emphatically, "If you or a member of the public committed perjury, you would go to prison for five years. If I or any other policeman committed perjury, we would go to prison for ten years."

She also told me that large sums of cash were available and, if the two Londoners lifted in the Albany got off, each member of their defence team would be given a new car of their choosing. She also mentioned that the lawyer, Ross

Harper, stood to gain £20,000. Knowing Ross Harper, I took all this with the largest pinch of salt available. Back in the car, I told my colleagues what had taken place including the talk of large sums available for a successful defence.

The following morning, I visited the fiscal in Govan to explain the breach of the peace case and suggested to him that I had acted as an agent provocateur. If I hadn't approached the accused in the first place, no crime would have been committed. The fiscal agreed and the charge was dropped. There was a brief lurch into normality after this but a big shock was on its way.

On Friday, 14 February, I was on the back shift and having a leisurely time of it when I picked up the *Daily Record*, the tabloid that was required reading for cops and robbers most days, and I was hit between the eyes by the front page. Arnott McWhinnie, a long-serving and much-respected reporter on the crime scene, had what the scribes call a "belter" of a story. The intro read, "Two top Scots detectives have been called in to probe claims that the police used a 'fixer' to set up a drugs haul." According to the story, the investigation began after a meeting between Lord Advocate Ronald King Murray and the leading Scots lawyer Mr Ross Harper. This led to Assistant Chief Constable Arthur Bell and Detective Superintendent Douglas Meldrum being drafted in to help. The story went on that Mr Harper claims that the fixer was used by the Strathclyde Serious Crime Squad. It was alleged that the so-called fixer was a criminal desperate for bail and that the police promised he would be given it but they had a price – they asked him to set up a £10,000 cannabis raid in a Glasgow hotel. Ross Harper was said to have investigated these claims for two months and had a dossier which claimed that that the informer travelled to London to set up a crime for the Scots detectives to "discover". A follow-up story along the same lines ran the next day.

After the second story was published, I was called to report to Mr Bell immediately. He told me what the *Record* had said was true – along with Mr Meldrum, he had been asked to investigate the allegations made by Harper with regard to the

arrest of McHugh and Goodship. I was given the option of
telling them the circumstances of the case or writing it all
down. Either way, it had to be done there and then so I wrote
it all down. Leaving nothing out, what I wrote ran to sixteen
sheets of foolscap. At one stage, Mr Bell left the room and I
took the opportunity to rest my hand and ask Mr Meldrum
how many allegations had been made. He replied that there
were twenty-one but that the main one was that I had planted
drugs on them. I felt better on hearing this – the defence
must be struggling to even suggest such a thing.

Mr Bell returned and I finished my statement and signed
it. I was told to discuss it with no one. I was comfortable that
Arthur Bell was on the investigating team rather than some
back-room pen-pusher with no street experience. My only
fear was that the chief constable would be conned by the
defence allegations into suspending me. However, all credit
to the chief, Pat Hamill, that he didn't fall for it. Had he done
so, it would have suited the defence strategy.

So, once again, it was back to work. This time it was a
brutal murder in Barrhead where the victim had been done
in by a thug wielding a brick. The accused was given life and
it did cross my mind, bearing in mind the investigation and
all the complexity of the Albany case, that, whatever else is
happening, life and death go on.

A few days later, I was back in Mr Bell's office. "What
were you doing on the 21st of January?" he asked. I referred
to my notebook and told him that I had arrested a man on
breach of the peace charges and locked him up in Craigie
Street Police Office. "Where were you at 6.30 p.m.?" he
asked. I told him about picking up the letter at Mrs Cussins.

Meanwhile, the solicitor for the defence, Ross Harper, had
been busy. He had recruited an ex-detective super, Willie
Prentice, to dig into my past career. Much later, Willie told
me that he had said to them that, if they were looking for
evidence to discredit me in the witness box, they were wast-
ing time and money. It seems that one of the reasons for the
defence case's suspicions and allegations about the way the
raid was handled sprang from the fact that McHugh's brother

had told a London police officer that McHugh and Goodship had been set up. The whole saga was further complicated when it emerged that, unbeknown to Ross Harper, someone in his office staff was passing information to a friend who had a police officer friend.

The info that came out was sensational. I never found out who this informant was and the information did not come to me directly. However, I heard through this source that Ross Harper had been at a shooting party in Ayrshire and that one of the other guests had been none other than Jack Beattie, head of the Drug Squad. It was said that Harper questioned Beattie on this occasion about the case and was told that the Drug Squad was not involved and that he could draw his own conclusions. At the suggestion of Jack Beattie, Ross Harper contacted Beattie's right-hand man, John Brown, who confirmed what Harper knew or suspected about the case. Beattie and Brown later went over the case with Harper and gave advice on several aspects of it. It is understating how I felt to say that it seemed strange to me that police officers from the Drug Squad, who had declined to be involved in the interception of two drug couriers, should be assisting the defence of the accused.

Much was made in the press of the so-called secrets of the shooting party but the fact that Beattie had discussed the case with Harper out on the moors did not really bother me. It only confirmed what Harper already knew. What did bother me was the possibility that Beattie or Brown named Cussins as the informer. That would have been below the belt. Certainly Harper was giving the defence everything he had. He also asked Jack Beattie to go with him to speak to the fiscal – apparently, with the intention of convincing him that the defence allegations had substance. And he also took the opportunity in a law lecture at Strathclyde University to refer to the Albany case under the heading of "Agent Provocateur". I reported this to Arthur Bell who responded that Harper would appear before the Dean of the Faculty of Advocates and be given "a slap on the wrist".

There was to be no slap on the wrist or any condemnation of me when, in advance of the trial of McHugh and Goodship,

Arthur Bell completed his report. The reverse was the case. The allegations had been reduced to four:

- that there was missing cannabis
- that I had fixed bail for Cussins
- that I had warned Cussins he was about to be arrested
- that the letter from Cussins to me was alleged to contain details of a cover-up.

Mr Bell reported the following:

- the cannabis resin production for the court was still intact
- the police played no part in Cussins's bail
- it was established that he was not warned
- the letter written to Brown by Cussins had been recovered and was found to contain what Brown had always said it did.

Mr Bell added that Ross Harper had been misled by Drug Squad officers and his report concluded that the prosecution should go ahead. It also contained information that the two accused were members of a criminal organisation that owned farms in Morocco where they grew cannabis and shipped it to Europe in two boats owned by them. He concluded that, if he had been in charge of the Albany drugs case, he would have handled it in exactly the same way it had been handled by the Serious Crime Squad – quite a compliment.

And now the stage was set for that mother of all trials.

Edinburgh Legal Luminaries and a Glasgow Detective under Heavy Fire in the Witness Box

Despite the flamboyance of legal dress – the wigs and the robes – the High Court in Edinburgh doesn't have neon lights over the front door advertising present or coming attractions. Nor does it take adverts in the papers to pull in spectators for the battles of the legal lions that take place behind its huge wooden doors. But, if it did, the events that began in that sombre, impressive arena on 5 September 1977 would have more than merited the phrase "all-star attraction". The cast was hugely impressive and it is worth listing some of the major players. Apart from David McHugh, Terence Frank Goodship, a certain Les Brown of the Serious Crime Squad and the late Jack Beattie of the Drug Squad, a copper nicknamed "The Flea" for his seeming ability to pop up everywhere, the legal line-up looked like this:

Lord Allanbridge: trial Judge
Mr J. G. Milligan: *(now Lord Milligan)*   Prosecuting Advocate Depute
Mrs A. Paton: assisting the prosecution
Mr J. P. H. Mackay QC: representing the accused Goodship *(now Lord Mackay of Clashfern)*
Mr R. E. G. Younger: assisting Mr Mackay
Mr N. H. Fairbairn QC: representing the accused McHugh *(later Solicitor General for Scotland)*
Mr Malcolm Rifkind QC: advocate assisting Mr Fairbairn *(later Minister of State for Scotland and Foreign Secretary)*
Mr J. Robertson: Clerk of the Court

Looking at that formidable line-up did beg a question – would two alleged drugs couriers from the east end of Glasgow have been so well represented? I think not. There was no question that all the members of the two legal teams were lawyers of the highest integrity but the fact was the accused could afford the best and that is what they got. When the guys in my squad were told the legal line-up, one remarked, "Christ, that's a bit heavy!" and another jocularly added, "It's OK – we won't be too hard on them."

As we waited for the trial to start, we just got on with the day-to-day job but thoughts of what was to come, within the august precincts of Edinburgh High Court, were never far from the minds of anyone who was to be involved. The day before the start, I convened a meeting in the CID room in the Central Police Office. I knew the defence were already aware that Cussins was the informant and I told everyone present that, if they were asked to name the informant, they could do so by writing his name on a piece of paper. The judge could then read it and decide who else could see it. There was tension and expectancy in the air but, again, routine matters like travel warrants to the capital had to be attended to.

Since Cussins and his involvement with us were at the core of the case, it is worth spelling out, in some detail, the guidelines, which are somewhat tricky, for officers involved with informants. Basically the situation is as follows:

1) The identity of the informant is to be kept secret.
2) The identity of the informant is not to be disclosed in court unless directed by the judge – even then the informant's name is to be written on a piece of paper and handed to the judge.
3) There has to be no guarantee to the informant that he or she is to be immune from giving evidence.
4) Participation by the informant is to be allowed only if it is essential to frustrate criminals.
5) Advice must be sought on this from someone holding the rank of chief superintendent or above.
6) The informant must not act as an agent provocateur.
7) The court must not be misled even to protect the informant.
8) There is to be no immunity for the informant.
9) The Procurator Fiscal need not be made aware of informant's identity.

There was plenty of room for dispute here – as we shall see!

If the all-star legal line-up was not enough evidence of unlimited funds for the defence, an amusing little happening underlined it before the trial had started. McHugh had been granted bail and the reception staff at Barlinnie were astonished when a female turned up at the prison with a holdall containing the six grand in tenners. She was directed to Ross Harper's offices in Glasgow where the niceties of paying bail money in Scotland were explained to her, the money was lodged with the defence and the appropriate cheque was made out to effect McHugh's release.

Despite the tension around the trial, we kept our sense of humour and, when the big day dawned at last, we took the 8.30 a.m. train from Glasgow's Queen Street Station to Edinburgh. There, a posse of press photographers lay in wait. There was a shout of "Which one is Brown?" and I pointed to Detective Constable Laurie Wilson who was then followed by the pack of snappers and photographed at every opportunity. It was not, however, so easy for me to escape the limelight when the proceedings got under way. Incidentally, we had been given a hint that a defence lackey would travel through on the same train and perhaps overhear something of interest. No chance – we passed the time playing cards.

When we clocked into the court, the prosecuting advocate, Mr Milligan, warned me I was going to have a rough time in the box and that he would leave me to nearer the end of the prosecution case in order that some loose ends could be tied up. The warning was not unexpected – I knew this would be a tough one – but I told him I would have no problem with my evidence since I was only telling the truth.

He also told me that Eddie Topalion, of Ad Lib, would not be called as he had sent in a doctor's certificate excusing him. I got Mr Milligan's permission to investigate this turn of events and we learned that the certificate had been obtained by telling the doctor it was a "minor" case where his evidence was not really crucial. That didn't wash and the guys back at Temple picked him up and brought him through to Edinburgh.

The bombshells were quickly being lobbed. McHugh and Goodship had hardly responded to the charges by saying, "Not guilty", when the clerk of the court read out a special defence, lodged by Fairbairn on behalf of his client McHugh. It read, "He states that the crime, if any, was committed by Detective Inspector Les Brown and David Cussins, a fugitive from justice, whose present whereabouts are unknown." What a start! The press bench and, no doubt, the editors back at the offices were metaphorically licking their lips at the feast of controversy that lay ahead. *This* was going to be good for sales!

Also in court were Chief Super William McMaster of the Police Discipline Branch and a shorthand writer. Their job was to listen to the evidence to ascertain whether any police officer had contravened police regulations or, for that matter, if they were guilty of committing a crime.

Detective Sergeant Joe Jackson was the first of our guys in the box and it was instantly obvious that the pattern of the defence would be to claim that everyone, other than the accused, was lying.

Fairbairn pitched in at Joe, saying, "My information is that Cussins received a call at the Bombardier Pub that the police were coming to arrest him."

Jackson said, "I did not know that."

Fairbairn suggested, "What happened was that you came into McHugh's room and put a parcel on the top shelf and said, 'What have we here?' McHugh said that you put the parcel there and that you responded with, 'Oh, no, it is yours and you are going down for that.'"

Jackson retorted, "That's a load of rubbish – no Scottish officer would use an expression like that." Joe Jackson was one hundred per cent right about that. I have never heard the phrase "You are going down for that" used by any Scottish policeman. That sort of B-picture crime language just isn't used up here. Anyway, what was being implied was that Joe had taken one of the slabs of cannabis from the other room and planted it in McHugh's room. Why would we need to do that? We had both accused "dead to rights". They had travelled up to the city together and booked into the hotel together. Joe was pretty sparky in the box and when he was asked about me and Graeme Pearson eating a meal in Cussins's house, just before the police pounced, he replied, "We have to speak to a lot of criminals and you don't get information about criminals at church socials."

During his turn in the box, Eddie Topalion admitted that he had known McHugh and they had worked together in Charlie Chester's club. He said that someone believed to be a major figure in the London drugs scene, a man not to be trifled with, had ordered him to visit McHugh in Barlinnie, which he did. While this was going on, I was sitting in the witness room like a man waiting for a dentist with no anaesthetics to call him in for some root canal treatment or worse. It was hard to keep my mind straight as my colleagues came in and out at regular intervals for their grillings. Of course, we did not discuss the case prior to my turn in the box but I was aware that Fairbairn was a skilled interrogator, infamous for interrupting a witness's concentration by throwing in a question or two that had no bearing on the case.

And that is what happened when John Orr was called. He had no trouble giving his evidence but, when Nicholas Fairbairn stood up to cross-examine him, he said, "Mr Orr, do you have a nickname?" Orr replied, "Not that I am aware of." Fairbairn persisted, "Do you not have the nickname 'Punk Rocker'?" Neither John nor anyone else in the squad had heard this nickname but Fairbairn must have got it somewhere. In any case, it was a ploy that didn't work with John.

My turn in the box wasn't to come until three days after the start of the trial. Before it did, there was a curious incident. I stood alone in the corridor, mentally preparing for what lay ahead, when I was approached by a well-known crime reporter. He offered me a sheaf of notes and remarked that they might help me as they told what my colleagues had said in the box. I swiftly said, "No thanks." I learned later that this reporter and a member of the defence team were friendly. I am not suggesting for a moment that the offer was orchestrated but I am well aware of what would have happened had I been foolish enough to accept the reporter's offer.

When my name was called and I walked across to the witness box, I was carefully watched by the defence team who were obviously making a visual assessment of how I would react to what was to come. I heard later that Nicky Fairbairn had been telling people that he "couldn't wait to get Brown into the box". Mr Milligan took me through my evidence slowly and precisely. There were no problems and, at the end of the day, I felt I had given a good account of myself.

The next day, I was back in the box at 10.25 a.m. and Nicholas Fairbairn QC, deadly interrogator, was about to get his wish. We had crossed swords before on several occasions at Glasgow High Court in murder trials, so I was well aware of the treatment I could expect. He rose to his feet and asked, "Do you know it is a criminal offence to have a drug in your possession with the intention of supplying it to another?" "Yes." "You committed a criminal offence by handing back the sample to David Cussins?" "By strict application of the law, yes."

Further questions were thrown at me regarding allowing Cussins to travel south to become involved in a drug deal. He then asked, "Is it correct that you did not inform the London Drug Squad of what was taking place?" This was tricky. There was no way I was going to reveal that, as we spoke, high-level investigations were going on in the south, by Detective Chief Inspector John Smith (who was later knighted and who became Deputy Commissioner of the Met in London), involving a racehorse owner and other matters.

To digress from the trial for a moment, I can explain that, in the run-up to the raid at the Albany, the informant in Ross Harper's office had let slip the name of a horse said to be the proverbial "good thing" running at Epsom. This nag, which incidentally won the race, was said to be owned by a Mr Big who had connections with the London drugs scene and the two accused. I made contact with the London Drug Squad boys who investigated and broke up a drugs cartel. The members were given long prison sentences. Because of this undercover stuff, I had to think carefully about the accusation that I had not got in touch with London.

The line of questioning was, however, cut short when the Advocate Depute shot to his feet to say to the judge, "My Lord, it might not be in the public interest for Mr Brown to answer that question." This in itself was an illustration of the complexity of undercover investigations as this intervention was to stop the court hearing that some of the London drugs officers were under investigation themselves. Whatever the rights or wrongs of this, it stopped Nicky Fairbairn going down that road.

He moved on by asking which senior officer had given permission for Cussins to continue to be involved in the case. I replied, "The assistant chief constable (crime), James Binnie." "Are you sure?" he asked and I replied, "Of course I am sure." The tide was turning in our favour.

The judge asked if Mr Binnie was a witness and was told he was no longer in the police service but he could be contacted quickly. Fairbairn started another question and answer session. To this day, I am convinced that he began the case thinking we were lying but I am also convinced that it suddenly came to him, as the trial progressed, that we were not. Very experienced in cross-examination, he knew one telltale sign that a witness is telling the truth is that he or she appears relaxed and doesn't delay any answers. He pressed on:

Mr Brown, you are not telling the truth.
– I am.
Mr Brown, you and I know that police officers sometimes, when giving evidence, withhold information that would help the defence.
– Not to my knowledge.
Mr Brown, you and I know of a case where police officers told lies – committed perjury – and, as a result, an innocent man went to prison on a charge of murder which he did not commit, didn't he?
– That is correct.

That shocked the court. The press stopped their note-taking in surprise, my colleagues sat bolt upright and even Lord Allanbridge seemed intrigued. Everyone had jumped to the conclusion that I was talking of Paddy Meehan and the Ayr bungalow case. Fairbairn, who played a major role in Meehan's trial, moved on:

Mr Brown for the benefit of this court, the ladies and gentlemen of the jury, the press, the advocate depute and myself, would you name the gentleman who was convicted of murder on perjured evidence and later set free?
– Yes, sir, it was Oscar Slater.

Fairbairn, as was his habit, had balanced his chin on his hand which was supported by the edge of the jury box. On hearing my answer his head slipped out from his hand. The judge gave a generous smile and nodded. Everyone in the legal profession and the police was aware of the case of Slater who was convicted of a murder in Glasgow in 1909 and subsequently cleared and released from prison. That was it for the day – a good one for the prosecution, I thought.

The next day Fairbairn started off with the fact that I had not originally named the informant and he said, "If it had not been for good detective work by Ross Harper, the informant's identify might never have been known." I wasn't going to let him away with that. I announced, "Cussins's name was given by Detective Chief Inspector Jack Beattie." (This goes back, as the reader will recall, to the shooting party on the Ayrshire moors where the Drug Squad officer socialized with a top man in the defence team and the subject of the trial came up. It seemed to me that, included in the conversation, would be the fact that Beattie was unhappy with the use of the informant but that was a matter for him. I didn't really have a problem with that for, after all, Harper could have got the name through other sources.)

The mention of Beattie annoyed Fairbairn who said I should not talk about that matter prior to that witness giving evidence. Astonishing as it may seem, Jack Beattie was scheduled to give evidence, for the defence, in a case where two London couriers were accused of bringing cannabis to Glasgow to sell on to another. Fairbairn then went on to speak about Beattie's position for at least three minutes before asking me if I would answer the question yes or no. I asked for the question which was, to say the least, vague to be repeated. The judge smiled but the question wasn't repeated. Little by little, it was going our way and a major turning point was coming up – the first really big mistake by the defence.

Where were you at 6.30 p.m. on 21 January 1977?
– Can you guide me as to what you are referring to?
On that date, at that time, you entered Cussins's flat in Sauchiehall Street to pick up a letter and, unbeknown to you, a man named Pearson was in the kitchen and wrote down, at the time, what you and Mrs Cussins discussed.

He then read out extracts from notes and it was obvious that someone had been there at the time specified because some of our conversation had, indeed, been noted. I asked to see the notes and the judge nodded that it was OK for me to do so. When I got them, I could not believe that what I was looking at was a photocopy. I turned to the judge and said so and asked if I could please see the original notes. I could hardly believe it when Fairbairn said, "There are no originals – these are the notes I am referring to." I pointed out to the judge that, if I was in the High Court giving evidence as a detective, I would not be allowed to use photocopies rather than originals. Lord Allanbridge asked me to accept that photocopies would be sufficient in this case but I had the bit between my teeth.

– My Lord, with respect, I must tell the court that Pearson was obviously in a position to overhear what was said but not everything that was said has been noted. Ross Harper's name was mentioned several times but it does not show in the copied notes. One of the reasons could be that Mrs Cussins told me Ross Harper stood to make a lot of money out of the case – each of the defence team would be offered a car of their own choosing if they were successful. (You will remember I told my colleagues of this allegation when I returned to the car that night.) That is why we are looking at copies of the notes – they have been edited to remove the name of Ross Harper.

At this, I felt that, somewhere in the court, I heard muted applause. I saw that my colleagues had smiles on their faces and even the jury looked impressed. The tide had turned. The explanation for the copies given by the defence was that Pearson had read from them and without warning had torn them up. Pretty lame stuff. Surely they could have been taped up and presented in that form?

While all this was going on, I glanced at Mr Mackay representing Goodship and got the impression he would rather have been elsewhere. He rose to his feet and asked me a few questions, more to the point than Fairbairn, got the answers and sat down. Then Mr Milligan asked a few more questions to clarify a point or two and, finally, Lord Allanbridge asked me to stand down and thanked me. It was the end of three days of intense interrogation but I still say, if you are telling the truth, such experiences are not a problem.

Next up was Brian Laird and, if you ever want a witness to follow you, Brian is the man. After him was Graeme Pearson who had shared the meal with me and Cussins on the night of the raid. He raised a laugh mentioning that, after his steak, he had bolted down "two puddings" before heading for the hotel.

The last witness for the prosecution was Assistant Chief Arthur Bell who told of his investigations into the Serious Crime Squad which had been prompted by the Ross Harper allegations. Late in February of 1977, Bell reported to the fiscal that he had completed his investigation and that, in his opinion, proceedings against Goodship and McHugh should go ahead. He then stunned the court when he said the two accused were part of a huge organisation which owned properties in Morocco from where drugs where shipped to the UK in luxury yachts and that the drugs were then sold to "the creatures of the street". It seemed like strong stuff but, as events were to prove, he was spot on.

That closed the case for the prosecution. As his first defence witness, John Mackay called his client Goodship who told the court that, for the past four years, he had worked as a property agent in Spain. He said he had never been to

Morocco. And the only reason he has assisted McHugh was because McHugh had asked him to. He said he had no idea what was in the bag they brought with them. Next on the stand was McHugh who, when questioned by his QC, said he thought the bag had contained blue movies.

Before the defence case had begun, Fairbairn had requested that the Serious Crime Squad be asked not to attend as, in his opinion, they presented a threatening influence on the defence witnesses. Despite my protests, most of the squad, including Joe Jackson, were told not to attend. When the business of the drugs found in McHugh's room arose, Fairbairn mentioned Joe and then added, "I see Mr Jackson is not with us today." The inference was not lost on me.

The next witness was Jack Beattie, whose high profile in the Drug Squad over the years and his friendship with some of the city's top newspapermen caused intense interest for those who worked in the city's papers as well as for those who avidly followed the crime stories in them. It was difficult not to feel sorry for him because, at this stage, he had been transferred from head of the Drug Squad to a uniformed position, still with the same rank, in Shettleston Police Office. I am in no doubt this was done to humiliate him but, in my opinion, he should have been left in his post until any complaints about his behaviour had been calmly investigated after the trial was over. As it was, the famous "Flea" found himself somewhat brought low and mortified in the midst of a controversial trial. That said, I could not believe my ears when he began to give evidence. He said I had told him about the drugs raid in October 1976 and went on to state, "It was not rational for strangers to come to the west of Scotland to distribute drugs – all of the drugs arrests in the west of Scotland tended to come from people with Glasgow connections."

What we discussed at that meeting, as I explained earlier, was the information about Khan and the other Asian. I wrote a note for the court officer to hand to the advocate depute. It read, "Ask to see Beattie's notebook – he wrote down some notes about the Khan connection in October 1976." In cross-examination, Mr Milligan did just that and Beattie's answer was as shocking as some of his earlier statements. "I have already reported that two notebooks and other items disappeared from my desk over the weekend prior to me leaving the Drug Squad," he said.

However, I felt the next defence witness, Beattie's sidekick John Brown, would at least clarify the position – after all, he had been at the meeting when I passed on the information on Khan. But no one will ever know what Brown would have said because the defence declined to call him to the witness box.

About this time, the defence dropped their special defence of blaming me. It was good, if not unexpected, news and I heard of it in an odd way. I had been in the High Court in Glasgow as a witness and arresting officer in a murder case and had gone to the canteen in Police HQ for lunch. I heard two typists, in the queue in front of me, talking about the Albany case and one simply remarked, "I see they've dropped the special defence."

Back in Edinburgh, the defence closed its case and Mr Milligan began his final address, asking for convictions. Mackay followed, on behalf of Goodship, and was characteristically short and to the point. Fairbairn was more flamboyant, as was his nature, and he started off by telling the jury:

> To provide a knock for the valuable services of Brown, a complete bogus crime was set up. It would not matter if it was McHugh, one of you, Mickey Mouse or the Prime Minister – anyone would have done. If this is how convictions are to be obtained, where are your liberties now?

On Tuesday, 20 September, Lord Allanbridge addressed the jury and reminded them, at the end of his summing-up speech, that they had the choice of three verdicts – guilty, not guilty or not proven. And he pointed out that, to bring in a majority verdict of guilty, at least eight members must agree.

The jury retired to consider almost three weeks of claim

and counterclaim. They left the courtroom at five minutes to noon and returned just under three hours later, finding the case against Goodship not proven. But, for McHugh, the guilty verdict was unanimous.

Lord Allanbridge said, "Terence Frank Goodship, in view of the verdict of the jury, I discharge you from the dock." The advocate depute then moved for sentencing and informed the court that McHugh had some minor previous convictions but, in December 1964, he had been imprisoned for a year for robbery. Malcolm Rifkind then rose with a plea of mitigation (Fairbairn was not in court) and said:

Cannabis, as compared to other drugs, is reckoned to be a soft drug. This particular drug is not one, according to the medical profession, the use of which is likely to cause major damage to the health of those taking it. McHugh can be considered one of the small fry in the drug scene so far as it operates.

Lord Allanbridge seemed unimpressed – the so-called small fry got six years for his trouble.

3

The Informer: The Real Life Story of One Man's War Against Terrorism

Sean O'Callaghan

Before today's globalized landscape of multinational crime gangs and international terror, the years that comprised the height of The Troubles in Northern Ireland – from Bloody Sunday to the Peace Accords – witnessed one of the most intense environments of undercover policing, informing and soldiering in human history.

Certainly Columbia's drugs cartels (with whom the provisional IRA sought to form allegiances), and today, tragically for its home-loving and spiritual people, Mexico's, have "surpassed" even The Troubles in their disproportionate ruthlessness, to say nothing of the body count. Gangs from the former Soviet Union, with their portfolio of products to traffic from Caspian-Sea caviar to stolen phones and indentured people, exceed anyone else in their global reach. But The Troubles were possessed of a unique intensity and an atmosphere of mutual mistrust that was heightened by their very localism.

Between Ireland's Garda; the loyalist-leaning and at times unhelpfully partisan Royal Ulster Constabulary; and the UK's security services together with the regional UK police forces (with whom MI5 had an occasionally fractious relationship and who came into play whenever the PIRA conducted its "campaigns" on the mainland), there was a troublesome, triangulated relationship which meant that human intelligence – the arms-shipment details, the death warrants whispered in sleepy pubs – from whichever side occasionally disappeared into the cracks between them. More than once, this was a source of frustration to Gardai inform-ant and republican penitent, Sean O'Callaghan.

The following extract concerns such an occasion: during 1985 and 1986, the IRA was in receipt of huge arms ship-ments from Libya, about which O'Callaghan informed his handlers. Aside from misty-eyed Irish Americans of the kind satirized in Richard Bean's play *The Big Fellah* (who proba-bly had little conception of the historical complexities of the Irish Free State and the original IRA's fight with it), Gaddafi's Libya was the PIRA's chief patron, and one reason why younger members of the republican movement, broadly, continued to take a socialist view of what the politics of a united sovereign Ireland should look like.

A self-confessed republican killer from Tralee in County Kerry, O'Callaghan gave himself up to British police in 1988, receiving an infeasibly long prison sentence (539 years) two years later. In 1996, however, he was released by royal prerog-ative: O'Callaghan had been an active member of the IRA since his teens – and for around two-thirds of that time, he had been informing to the Garda, foiling operations – includ-ing the planned assassination of Britain's Prince and Princess of Wales (evidently not the Queen of Irish Republican Hearts) – without blowing his cover, responsible for the arrests of many provisionals. Born into a community natu-rally sympathetic to republicanism who even recruited his childhood friends to the IRA, he boasted an authenticity and heritage that no covert cop could ever match. As a former informer, O'Callaghan seems to have an expert's take on the politics of personal identity: that if you allow it to be deter-mined by blood, blood tends to be spilled . . .

In the latter part of 1984 I was asked to find eight or nine men to go to Libya. It was explained that they should be from a rural background and be comfortable handling cattle; I was not told why they were needed. From my point of view it was the first serious indication that the Libyan connection had been reactivated.

Obviously it was important to choose carefully, so I deliberately picked a fellow who was over six feet, had long very blond hair and thick-lensed glasses. I reckoned that even the dumbest policeman couldn't fail to pick him out. Some months later, in early 1985 I learned that Gabriel Cleary, IRA director of engineering, was also in Libya. Kevin McKenna – ever cautious – told me that there were expectations of "lots of modern gear". His grand scheme was that with such gear the IRA could create a "free zone", running along the Clogher valley from Tyrone to Fermanagh – an area the security forces could enter only in strength and with helicopter backup, a similar situation to that existing in South Armagh. It was a plan that had obsessed him for years.

Shortly after that, when I was up in Dublin one day, I got a message that Joe Cahill wanted to see me. I went along to the Sinn Fein offices where he normally lurked. Cahill reminded me of a certain businessman, a keen sailor who owned a boat, and who had been an IRA sympathizer. During the seventies he had acted as liaison for Brian Keenan when Keenan was running the IRA's bombing campaign in Britain. Cahill wanted to know if he was still sound. I replied that I believed he was. Cahill asked me to arrange a meeting, so I approached the businessman, who was more than agreeable, and I arranged to see him at his home. On the agreed date I met Cahill in Dublin and we drove there together. I was more than curious to know what was going on, but Cahill wasn't going to tell me and I wasn't going to ask. I did, of course, suspect that the sudden interest in the businessman had a great deal to do with his boat – and Libyan weapons – but I could not be sure. Or not yet.

My Garda contact told me to be cautious; he was worried that, coming so soon after the *Marita Ann*, this might be a set-up. I felt that was unlikely. It was all too complicated in its way and such a set-up would not, I felt sure, be McKenna's style.

Cahill and the businessman went upstairs to talk while I remained below. When Cahill returned he looked very pleased and it was obvious that things had gone well. When we were in the car he confirmed that, saying, "Your man is still very sound."

A week or so after that Cahill was back in touch. He told me that McKenna wanted him to have a further meeting with the businessman within two days. For such sensitive contacts, rather than telephoning I travelled to his home, spoke to the businessman and returned to Dublin to tell Cahill the meeting was on for the next day.

On the way back Cahill told me that we were meeting a couple of people at a hotel en route and that they would be coming with us to meet the businessman. When we got to the hotel car park there were two men sitting in a car. I recognized one of them; Malachy McCann was the IRA's director of purchasing, the man in charge of buying and importing weapons. Since Joe Cahill, the IRA's senior finance person and member of the Army Council, and Chief of Staff Kevin McKenna were both also involved, I figured there could be no doubt why they were interested in the businessman. I passed all this information on to my Garda contact, some of it before Sean Corcoran was murdered, some after.

Sinn Fein work was beginning to take up a lot of my time. Local elections loomed and the IRA insisted that I stand as a candidate in the Tralee area. Throughout this period Corcoran's murder was constantly on my mind and, though busy, I began to spend much more time at home in Kerry with my girlfriend. I felt dispirited by the terrible turn events had taken, and my previous motivation had all but disappeared.

In spite of this, some of the Sinn Fein National Executive meetings became very interesting during the period from April to June 1985. Sinn Fein and John Hume had recently had some public exchanges, as a result of which Adams proposed at a National Executive meeting that Sinn Fein publicly invite John Hume to a meeting. "We may have nothing to say to John Hume," he said. "The probability is that we do not. But northern nationalists will never forgive our refusal to talk."

Adams's proposal was carried unanimously, but immediately afterwards there was a moment of high farce. Having propelled his proposal through the meeting, Adams appeared to adopt the persona of an international statesman. He announced that he also wished to invite other groups, such as People's Democracy, at which stage Danny Morrison laughed out loud and said, "You don't mean that bunch that fall around drunk at the Rock Bar every Saturday night?" "Just invite them, Danny," replied Adams. "I'm not inviting that bunch of idiots," retorted Morrison, before turning to his copy of the *Irish Times*. Adams was obviously very angry. I found it hard to keep a straight face. Adams finished the squabble by regaining his temper and saying in a soft voice, "We'll talk about this later, Danny." He knew that Morrison had poked fun at him in front of every leading member of Sinn Fein. He also knew that he looked rather silly. No invitation was ever sent to the People's Democracy.

John Hume responded publicly to the invitation by saying that there was no point in meeting with Sinn Fein as long as it was controlled by the IRA. A meeting was therefore arranged between the IRA and Hume. To my certain knowledge the IRA delegation consisted of Seamus Twomey, J. B. O'Hagan and one of the Maze escapees. On the night in question I was in Sligo to see Jimmy Jones, but that meeting was cancelled because Jones had been drafted in to help organize the Hume/IRA summit. The meeting was a failure, in any case, ending after only a few minutes when Hume refused to allow the IRA to videotape the proceedings.

All of this was set against the backdrop of the behind-the-scenes diplomatic activity that eventually resulted in the Anglo-Irish Agreement of 1985. For years Sinn Fein/IRA had kept up a steady tirade against the SDLP, describing them variously as domestic cockroaches and the Stoop Down Low Party. But Adams was gradually coming to realize that John Hume was hugely influential within the nationalist movement – if not indeed its dominant figure – particularly in the politically influential circles of Irish America. Adams's immediate challenge was to work out ways of co-opting Hume's influence and harnessing his respectability.

The Anglo-Irish Agreement was sold to Margaret Thatcher on the basis that it would bolster support for the SDLP to the detriment of Sinn Fein, and would result in improved cooperation on security from the Irish Republic and also, it was believed, a tougher line there on the IRA. None of that materialized to any significant degree, except that in the short term the electoral rise of Sinn Fein was indeed halted, and in fact reversed.

Sinn Fein/IRA opposed the Anglo-Irish Agreement because they recognized that it was a gift to the SDLP. They also believed that it institutionalized partition. But under the surface, Adams in particular was viewing things in a different light. Though of course opposed to the Agreement, he learned two valuable lessons from it: that the British government would ignore the wishes of unionists if it suited them; and that John Hume was a much bigger political player than were the republicans. In that recognition lay the beginnings of the IRA/Sinn Fein peace strategy. Over the coming months and years IRA/Sinn Fein's outward stance towards John Hume and the SDLP began to soften. All of this was obvious to anybody attending the meetings that I was attending, particularly if, as I was, you were interested in examining the nuances of republican plotting and language.

The local elections took place on 20 June 1985, and I was elected to Tralee District Council as Sinn Fein candidate. One of the reasons why I have always distrusted most politicians is that I understand how easy and effective it is to be insincere and dishonest. I didn't want to be a Sinn Fein candidate, nor even a councillor, talking about and proposing things I did not believe in. In fact, in most cases I held the opposite view from the one which I was forced to propound. I did what I could, but it was at best faintly irritating having to go along with half-baked policies that would have been greeted with laughter at a meeting of the Flat Earth Society. The irony was that by the June 1985 I was OC of the IRA's

Southern Command, a member of GHQ staff, a member of Sinn Fein's National Executive and a local councillor – as well as being a high-level informer for the Irish police. A bizarre existence, if ever there was one. And through all of this time the murder of Sean Corcoran remained uppermost in my mind. In spite of my responsibilities I still could not, at that time, summon any enthusiasm for my work.

Throughout the summer of 1985, I acted as the contact between the boat-owning businessman and the IRA. One day, after bringing him another message of yet another meeting, he asked me if I knew what was going on. I replied that I didn't, nor must he tell me. He replied that he was only prepared to go ahead if he could work with me, to which I replied that he must sort that out with Joe Cahill.

I knew that plans involving him and the IRA were steaming ahead, but I hadn't been made privy to them. I knew the idea in essence and that was enough. I was happy not to be officially involved: if it ever came to anything I would be in the clear. Although I was OC of Southern Command, this did not automatically make me aware of any or all arms shipments into the Irish Republic. Information in the IRA is compartmentalized; this was an Army Council operation, and McKenna, Gabriel Cleary and others were going to tell no one about it who did not need to know.

On 27 June our daughter was born – but I was exhausted and stressed, and felt I was beginning to lose control, as if everything was coming unglued, and I was dangerously close to not caring.

At the end of August I resigned from the Sinn Fein National Executive and shortly afterwards stood down as OC of Southern Command, giving the excuse that I wanted to spend more time at home. There was resistance. Gerry Adams initially refused to accept my resignation from the National Executive and at one stage Pat Doherty came to my home and offered me the position of national organizer for Sinn Fein. It was an important job: the abstentionist issue still hadn't been resolved, but the leadership was determined to bring it to a head, and the Army Council had decided that making political progress in the Irish Republic was the main task facing the movement at the time. The national organizer would play a key role. I turned the offer down. From that point I dropped very much out of the public frame. I still had access to an enormous amount of information from different sources, which I always passed on, but in truth I'd had enough.

I also became aware around October that a small number of people were beginning to oppose and perhaps even distrust me. I knew for certain that Maurice Pendergast had suspicions that he could not articulate. Luckily for me he seemed unwilling to act on what was obviously a highly honed instinct. Once I ceased to be in absolute control it left a gap into which other people moved, and some began to question my way of doing things. For quite some time I had had the sort of control – certainly locally – that allowed me to set the pace and provide cover for my real activities. Once that control had gone, it was inevitable that eventually people would begin to wonder why certain things were done in certain ways.

In November I made up my mind to leave Ireland, along with Louise and our daughter. By that time all I was really doing in terms of republican activity was attending council meetings and keeping in touch with people like Pat Currie. I told my Garda contact. I think from a personal point of view he was glad to hear it. We had both known that this double life could not go on for ever. And perhaps after Corcoran's murder he understood that it was only a matter of time until I ended up the same way. But I don't think that fear was the reason I felt I had to get out. I was simply tired from the crushing emotional and mental pressure of the life I had been living. Louise wanted to return to England too. She had never really spoken about it, but I knew it was in her mind and I went along with it. The biggest sadness would be leaving my son. He was now six years old and I had seen a lot of him throughout those years.

Making arrangements to leave without anyone's knowledge was difficult. I had to tell my ex-wife Liz that I was leaving but I told no one else except my Garda contact. The Gardai made a token attempt to make me stay, but I think they knew that there was simply no point in pursuing it. My mind was made up.

We left Tralee under cover of darkness on the evening of 6 December 1985. With the help of a friend we had quietly sold most of our possessions. We couldn't afford to have any visitors in the last couple of days. One glance would have shown that we were moving and had word leaked out it would have been very bad news for us. It was an emotional event for me, as it was for Louise, who had by now made many friends in Ireland. I had said goodbye to my son a couple of hours before we were due to leave and he had been very upset. He didn't know exactly what was happening, of course, but he knew that I was going away and that he didn't want me to. How can you explain any of this to a six-year-old? I didn't know whether I would ever see him again, whether I would ever speak to or see my parents, brother or sister, or indeed old friends from childhood and schooldays. What would happen to Louise and our daughter? How would we live? I didn't have an answer for any of these questions. Driving out of our house, past the familiar windmill and the canal at Blennerville, I felt sadness mixed with relief. I really loved this place and I determined then that one day I would return.

We made our way to Cork, where we intended to get a flight to Heathrow. The Garda had already asked me if I would be prepared to meet the English police once I arrived at Heathrow and I knew that someone from Special Branch would meet me at the airport.

By the time we reached Cork, however, my girlfriend had been taken very ill and was suffering from severe abdominal pain. We quickly drove to a local hospital, where she was admitted for tests. I was now in a difficult position. We had been extraordinarily lucky that no one had come to visit us at home during our last couple of days there; I couldn't push my luck by going back now. We had very little money and I could not afford to stay in a hotel for long. Most republicans in Cork would know me by sight, so it wasn't safe to hang around for very long. The tests revealed that Louise had acute appendicitis, which had gone untreated for some time; she was extremely ill and would require an operation and a longer than normal period of recuperation. She was feeling very low and I badly wanted to stay and visit her, but after a couple of days it was clear that that would be too dangerous, and that our daughter and I would have to go to England ahead of her. My daughter was just five months old at the time. I knew that the moment I disappeared the IRA rumour mill would spring into action. As the plane took off I wondered if I would ever see Ireland again.

It was a bitterly cold evening when we arrived at Heathrow. I was holding our daughter in a little carrycot, waiting for my luggage, when a couple of stewardesses began to play with her. Suddenly I heard this voice beside me saying, "Get rid of them! Get rid of them!" Everybody else heard him as well. It was my introduction to the policeman from Scotland Yard who had been assigned to look after me.

Over the next month or so I would learn that he was far from the best choice: he proved to be inefficient, a racist and a bigot. For now we walked to a car and drove to a guesthouse close to the airport, where we waited outside for quite a long time until the owner arrived and let us in. I didn't discuss anything with the owner, but it was obvious that he knew my escort was a policeman. I was Irish, carrying little in the way of luggage, and I had a young baby with me. It wouldn't have taken much to work out that I was in some kind of trouble.

At this stage I had only £4.04. I had left several hundred pounds with Louise, which is what remained from the sale of our possessions. My daughter and I stayed at the guesthouse for several days, during which time I met my very own police-man a number of times. Even the most simple dealings with him were nearly always pointless. Once, when I asked him to get some disposable nappies for my daughter – the smallest size available – he came back with antiseptic wipes.

Four days or so after we had left Cork, Louise signed

herself out of the hospital there and flew to Heathrow, where she got a bus to where we were staying. Her condition was poor and she really should have been in hospital, but being away from our daughter in such strange circumstances had proved too much for her to handle.

Strange as it might seem, she still did not question me about my work. She obviously had an idea, though, and was glad that we were leaving Ireland. She assumed that the guesthouse owner was a friend of mine from my past.

She phoned her parents, who lived near by, and told them to expect us. That evening we took a taxi to their home. She appeared confident that we would receive a friendly reception, but I was not nearly so sure. After all, they hadn't seen their daughter for four years. They knew about their grandchild but hadn't met her, and their daughter and I weren't married. To cap all of that, we were landing at their home in a taxi in the snow, with very little luggage and even less explanation. To say that it all looked odd is hardly overstating it.

Her parents did greet us in a friendly, if reserved, manner. My girlfriend, her mother and our daughter rather quickly went upstairs, leaving me alone with her father, a quiet, somewhat withdrawn man. For perhaps an hour and thirty minutes no words were spoken. Eventually he said, "Be careful of the shower in the morning. The water comes on very hot." Then he went back to doing his *Daily Telegraph* crossword puzzle.

We stayed with her parents for a week or so and throughout that period they asked very little about our situation or future intentions. We told them that we were moving to Bristol, where I would work in my uncle's business. No such uncle existed, but we had to tell them something to buy time. While we were there I wrote a letter to Pat Doherty, which I sent by way of my Garda contact, to be posted in Dublin. In it I outlined my "anger and frustration" at having been the subject of local gossip regarding my integrity and loyalty to the cause, and my decision to leave the movement rather than remain and create further problems for them. Rumours would have escalated to such a degree by the time the letter arrived with Doherty that its contents would have appeared entirely plausible. And so, to my satisfaction, it proved. I later learned that Doherty, McKenna and O'Neill would not countenance the notion that I was an informer, and though they were still keen to talk to me to clarify matters, the necessity to do so was perhaps less urgent.

By now I had also been introduced to another policeman, Graham, who was of far superior quality to his predecessor in every respect. He attempted to debrief me, but he lacked the background and it wasn't entirely successful. I was also in constant phone contact with the Garda and they were aware of my dealings with the English police.

When we left Louise's parents' home we went to stay briefly with an old schoolfriend of hers who had once visited us in Ireland. Then we moved back near her parents, where we shared a house with another of her old friends. I had no idea what I was going to do. I knew from my Garda contact that discussions were taking place between the Garda and the British security services about how best to give me a comprehensive debriefing.

Early in January I received word from Graham that "other people" wanted to speak to me. I checked with the gardai – they knew about it and were happy for me to go ahead. Even though I was concerned that too many people might get to know about me, I realized that by this stage I had no real alternative. I went to London – to Liverpool Street station – where I reacquainted myself with my first policeman, who proceeded to get us lost as he tried to find the hotel where we were due to attend the meeting.

When we eventually found it I was introduced to a tall, fair man in his late thirties or early forties, who looked as if he had spent considerable time in the army. The policeman left as soon as very basic introductions had been completed. I turned to "John", as he called himself, and said, "Does this mean that I'm not going to have to deal with that halfwit any longer?" He laughed loudly and said, "Yes, Plod is a bit tiresome, isn't he?"

Strangely, in all of my dealings with the security forces over the years, that policeman is the only person I found it impossible to deal with. But I felt that the security service's disregard, sometimes even contempt for "Plod" was uncalled for.

During my first conversation with "John" I explained that the most important thing I had to tell him was about the boat-owning businessman and the Libyan connection. He listened carefully to what I had to say and then asked me if I knew where any shipments would be landed. I replied that I didn't, and he said, "Arklow, off the coast of County Wicklow." I didn't reply; it seemed to me that they already had the information they needed. The next thing I told him, however, produced an instant reaction. It concerned Sean Meehan, brother of well-known Ardoyne republican Martin Meehan. The IRA already knew that Sean Meehan was an RUC Special Branch and MI5 agent, because a rogue member of the security forces had fingered him. Meehan had been lucky to escape the clutches of the IRA. I had found out from Seamus Twomey that the IRA believed that Meehan was in Fort Worth in Texas. I told this to John. The look on his face told me all I needed to know. In fact I was able to tell him that the IRA had sent a man to Texas to investigate and that they believed Meehan ran a small haulage business there. John confirmed or denied nothing, but he was obviously very interested.

We arranged to meet again after lunch. Only at that point did John explain that he didn't work for the police, but for another "agency". I told him that I had more or less grasped that. I also said that I was in regular contact with the Garda and would be bound by what they said. The information was not too well received, but I didn't care. This was how it had to be.

John told me that they wanted to conduct a full, professional debriefing, which would be cleared at a high level with the RUC and the Garda. I was quite agreeable, especially as the Garda had already mentioned this before I left Ireland and were keen for me to comply as they lacked the facilities for such an operation outside Ireland. He further explained that I would have to live outside Britain for this to happen

– somewhere in Europe – and that I would have to leave the country within two days. I wondered why this had to be, but to be honest I didn't give it a lot of thought. I explained that I would be taking Louise and our daughter with me, but he seemed to have no opinion about this.

I really didn't know what Louise was going to make of my telling her I wanted to move to some place on the continent, but she trusted me and had long ago taken the decision not to ask questions. Before I left, John gave me £300 to cover the cost of travel and told me that "Plod" would give me a further £1,700 to cover relocation costs, accommodation and so on, once I had actually left the country. I went home and told Louise that we were going to live in Europe for a while. Her passport was out of date, so I would have to go first and find a place for us to live, and she would then follow with our daughter once that was sorted out. She was relatively happy and appeared to have confidence in me, which helped her to overcome her fears and uncertainties about the future.

Two days later I met with policeman "Plod" and we travelled by train from Victoria to Dover and then by ferry to Calais. On the ferry he told me that if the police ever became aware that I was in Britain after this day they would have to arrest me. He also muttered something like, "Maybe it will be different in a year or so." Beyond registering that, I took little notice. Only later would I realize that what he said that day on the ferry was indeed of some importance. In effect, I was being escorted from the country and told not to come back.

Once we got to Calais we had a drink and he went off back to London. Before he left he gave me the £1,700. Good riddance, I thought to myself. I stayed in Calais that night and travelled on to Paris the following morning. I spent a couple of days there but decided that Holland would suit us better, so I took the train to Amsterdam and booked into a hotel near the centre. I had a phone number for John and used it. Throughout this time I was in constant contact with Louise. After a couple of days in Amsterdam I rented a flat, or at least paid the initial deposit. It wasn't in the best position, being too central, and even though it was relatively expensive it wasn't best suited to a couple and a young baby.

I had been in Amsterdam for about a week when a further meeting was arranged with John. Like many meetings that followed, it was arranged in a tortuous, almost comical way. I would phone a number in London, which was always answered by the same woman, who then gave instructions usually on the lines of, "Turn left, proceed eastwards for five minutes, on coming to a named landmark turn right, next left, second right." I had some good fun trying to spot who, if anyone, was monitoring me as I followed the convoluted instructions.

Our first meeting in Amsterdam took place on the day when Louise and our daughter were due to fly in. John was quite adamant that Amsterdam was not a good place for me to live. It had a large Irish community, many of them from Belfast, and a substantial core of IRA sympathizers. I was aware of this but perhaps did not really appreciate how well organized they were there. He suggested that I move to Haarlem, a town relatively close to Amsterdam. We spoke for some time that day and he outlined how he would like the debriefing to develop. He proposed to see me at least once a month; after these meetings he would liaise with the RUC and Garda and together they would formulate the questions and follow-on for the next session. I was quite happy to help in any way I could. Helping to inform democratic governments about IRA terrorism and possibly helping to save lives seemed to me to be a decent thing to do.

Later that day I went to the airport to meet Louise and our daughter. I had given up the flat in Amsterdam, and we stayed the night in a small hotel in Haarlem. The next day we booked into fairly cheap self-catering accommodation, from where we spent a week or so investigating the area until we chanced upon Zandvoort, a seaside resort on the North Sea, a short train ride from Haarlem. Because it was still February and well out of season there was plenty of accommodation at relatively cheap rates. We rented a small house from a young married couple who lived next door. It suited us just fine and Zandvoort was a lovely place at that time of year. The people were friendly and easygoing, and we had the sea to enjoy and wonderful nature walks near by. We were happy, and for the first time since our very early days Louise and I were spending a lot of time in each other's company. I even wrote the bulk of a long novel.

On top of the initial relocation allowance of £2,000, MI5 paid me approximately £500 a month, which, after rent, meant that we lived on slightly less than £40 a week. It wasn't possible for me to work without a permit, although I was writing all of the time. The lap of luxury it was not.

Once every three or four weeks John would come over and we would spend a day together going through whatever areas were of interest to him. He handled these sessions in an extremely professional manner, asking questions that were coherent and intelligent, which meant that little time was wasted. We usually met fairly early in the morning. I would phone London from an agreed callbox and would follow the directions given. Somewhere along the route John would appear and we would go to a hotel room that he had booked. The session would continue all day with a break for lunch in the room. Our dealings were always amicable, but we tended to stay away from our personal lives and political views. I didn't want to discuss with him my motivation, my personal views or my relationship with my girlfriend. John often asked to see a section of the novel I was writing but I always refused.

Before our meetings began John always made it clear that he did not wish me to admit to or discuss specific activities I may have been involved in in Northern Ireland. Then one day, after about four of these sessions, he said to me, "It won't be possible to get you a pardon." I looked at him in some amazement. The subject had never come up before and I had certainly not raised it. He went on to explain that it was impossible for someone in my position to get such a pardon. He gave the example of Anthony Blunt, who had in 1964 been granted immunity from prosecution in return for telling the security service the full story of his spying activities for the

Soviet government. It had caused considerable controversy at the time and wouldn't be allowed to happen now.

John told me that the RUC believed me to be responsible for the murder of Detective Inspector Peter Flanagan, but that they had no proof. He also mentioned that Sir John Hermon, Chief Constable of the RUC, was willing to let the matter drop. Trevor Forbes, head of Special Branch, said that I should be rewarded for the work I had done, but Michael McAtamany, Deputy Chief Constable of the RUC, said I should be pursued to the ends of the earth. That is what I was told, without my asking any questions. I have no way of knowing if these stories were true.

At this stage John raised the question of whether I would be prepared to lecture to the SAS and junior intelligence officers. He also asked if I would agree to questioning by RUC officers in Holland, and told me that provided I admitted to nothing they had not one shred of evidence against me. I replied that I was quite prepared to do whatever he wanted. Neither of these matters was ever mentioned again and I can only presume that he and his agency were unable to find a way around the obvious difficulties of my situation.

We continued with the debriefing until September 1986, when it came to an end. John had told me some months previously that September was the likely cut-off date, and he made it clear to me now that if I returned to Britain, and the RUC found out, I would be arrested. He reaffirmed that there was no evidence against me. Before we finally parted he handed over £4,000 with a suggestion that Sweden might be a good place to live. I asked him two questions. "Do you believe that I have told you the truth?" He replied that he did. I then asked him what he thought I would do next, and he said, "I think you will return to the British mainland and that the RUC will get their claws into you." It was a pretty prophetic answer, as things turned out.

When the time came to say goodbye I don't think that there was any sense of loss on either side. I had been more than happy to help and the relationship had remained professional. John was capable and played his part cleverly and subtly. My intention had been simply to make sure that I helped people to understand the true nature of the Provisional IRA and to that end I was prepared to work for the benefit of either the British or the Irish government.

Throughout my stay in Holland I had remained in touch with my Garda contact and had occasionally been able to help him; but now, for the first time since 1979, I was free of any official contact with anti-terrorist agencies. Misguidedly, I felt that for the first time my life was my own. I was to be quickly disabused of this assumption.

In November 1986 I returned to England, aware that I had to maintain a low profile to avoid attracting police or IRA attention. For financial reasons it was almost impossible for us to remain in Holland; I had no work permit and could at best get only a low-paid job in the black economy. In addition, Louise had continuing health problems which meant that she had to go to hospital in London every four weeks for tests and monitoring. To do so in Holland would have meant going private and we simply could not afford it. Consequently England seemed the only viable option for us.

We settled in Tunbridge Wells, partly because Liz, her partner and our son had moved there and it meant that I was able to see the boy again. We rented a three-bedroomed semi-detached house in a quiet part of town. I had no idea whether I could work in my own name, and thus any work I got during that period was either part-time or temporary – labouring, shelf-stacking in supermarkets, and so on, where few questions were asked. Before long Louise was well enough to return to work, at first part-time and then full time.

Life was relatively happy, and for some time I was quite content to let the days go by in an easygoing way without dwelling too much on the past or the future. We both felt unfulfilled, though; the future seemed empty and a bit bleak. Of course, my involvement in Ireland was missing from my life, and I felt its absence. Every now and again something would happen that would push Ireland, or more specifically the IRA, into the forefront of my mind.

In autumn 1986, just after the end of my debriefing with John, the republican movement split. An IRA convention held in Navan in October of that year – the first since they became operational in 1970 – voted by a large majority to abandon the traditional republican policy of refusing to allow Sinn Fein candidates to take their seats in the Irish parliament if elected. Once the IRA had taken such a position, Sinn Fein's rubber stamp was inevitable. The Sinn Fein ard fheis which took place soon after, on 1 November, overwhelmingly endorsed the decision of the IRA convention.

Ruari O'Bradaigh, Daithi O'Connaill and the group of traditionalists aligned to them walked out of the ard fheis in a planned move. They were supported by those IRA members who were opposed to the new policy, and together this group immediately announced the formation of Republican Sinn Fein. They were warned by the IRA that any attempt to establish a military wing would be met with an immediate and severe response.

Meetings did, however, take place across the country, and this led to the formation of the Continuity Army Council. To avoid any further split in the republican movement the IRA agreed that its members could also be members of RSF, providing they gave full allegiance to the IRA's armed struggle. Of course, as long as the IRA was engaged wholeheartedly in the armed struggle there was no real opening for the Continuity Army Council, but once the IRA moved into ceasefire mode things were rather different. Indeed, in recent times the CAC has gone on to engage in occasional bombings and attempted bombings, probably with some degree of support on the ground from disgruntled IRA supporters.

Following the emergence of Republican Sinn Fein, the Provisional IRA stepped up its campaign on the ground to prevent their support seeping away to RSF: this was, of course, facilitated by the arrival of the huge Libyan arms shipments in late 1985 and early 1986.

Of even more concern to Adams and McGuinness had been the signing of the Anglo-Irish Agreement in November 1985. They knew that if the Dublin government

fulfilled its obligation under the Agreement to improve security cooperation, then the pressure on IRA logistics and
planning would increase dramatically. Quite clearly, the
Agreement was also designed to damage Sinn Fein in its
electoral battle with the SDLP for control of northern
nationalism.

But although the IRA was implacably opposed to the
Agreement, with good reason, Adams – that pragmatic politician – was still examining it in terms of how republicans
could turn it to advantage in the longer term. Some of the
National Executive felt that it should be left to the unionists
to destroy the Agreement, or if not destroy it then succeed in
damaging their own credibility by engaging in confrontation
with Thatcher. Since she had refused to give in to the hunger
strikers, some judged it unlikely that once the Agreement
was signed she would backtrack, no matter what pressure was
brought to bear – especially since its political impact would
be confined to Northern Ireland.

This was the political backdrop in 1986, when the Provisionals
ended abstentionism. No one at the time was aware of the
massive shipments of weapons that had recently been imported
from Libya. I knew later from two people who were present that
the call from the floor of the IRA convention was, "Give us the
gear to finish the job." Few of them knew then that much of the
"gear" was either already available or on its way.

I had thought from my conversations with John that the
security forces were well aware of the details of the Libyan
connection and on top of the situation. On 1 November 1987
I learned that the French authorities had seized a massive one
hundred and fifty tons of arms and ammunition, including
twenty surface-to-air missiles bound from Libya to the IRA
on board a coaster called the *Eskund*. My first thought was,
"Bullshit." Surely the capture was not down to the French
but was the result of intelligence cooperation and surveillance dating back to 1985? My delight was quickly to turn to
disbelief and anger as it became clear that the IRA had in fact
already succeeded in landing three shipments. How could
this have happened after all the information I and others had

provided? It is difficult to say, but I suspect that internal rivalries within the different security agencies in both jurisdictions had much to do with it. I had told the Garda, Scotland Yard and MI5 that the shipments were due and MI5 were aware of where they would be landed. And yet the historical fact remains that such shipments still successfully made their way into the country.

With such material at their disposal the IRA very probably had the military hardware to keep the campaign going for many years to come. More importantly, they had achieved a significant psychological victory. The most important function of the security forces was to try to deprive the IRA of money and material; with the Libyan connection the IRA had demonstrated its effectiveness by importing, distributing and dumping vast quantities of weaponry. It was a huge aid to the morale of the organization – it also provided the IRA with the wherewithal to continue their activities indefinitely.

I could hardly believe that such a security disaster was possible. The key person captured on the *Eskund* was Gabriel Cleary, the IRA's director of engineering and the man most responsible for its range of very effective home-made weaponry – from mortars to sophisticated long-delay timing devices. Over the coming weeks the Irish government carried out massive searches to try to find the Libyan weapons from the three previous shipments – with some success, it must be said. During that time I kept in regular touch with my Garda contact, who was certainly helpful in reminding and prompting me about individuals and areas where such amounts of weaponry might be held.

4

Murder in the Métro

Gayle K. Brunelle and
Annette Finley-Croswhite

A grisly murder though it was, to our modern tastes there is something almost quaint – or at least, stylish, the stuff of fiction – about the time, place and circumstances of the death of young Laetitia Toureaux. A genuine "locked-room" mystery from the days of art deco and Agatha Christie, the case reads like something from a cosy-crime novel, taking place as it did on a train, and featuring the death of a demure *demi-mondaine* who had gone undercover to gather information for the French police.

Her story, however, is as real as death itself, taking place as the shadows of fascism spread across Europe. Early in the evening of 16 May 1937, Toureaux's corpse was found stabbed in the neck in an otherwise empty first-class compartment of Paris's Métro. Witness testimony established that the murderer had little over a minute between stations (Porte de Charenton – home of the asylum in which the Marquis de Sade had once been incarcerated – and Porte Dorée) in which to accomplish the brutal task, and in that time no one was seen entering or leaving the train at either station, or passing through the carriages.

Europe in the 1930s was obsessed with the ideological threat posed by communism from the east, together with the socialism of organized labour movements in general. Hitler had succeeded in placing the blame for Berlin's Reichstag fire with Germany's communists; Britain had its black-shirted Union of Fascists;

Franco was gaining the upper hand in Spain and Mussolini was an ally of the French Cagoule – the popular name for the Comité Secret d'Action Révolutionnaire, which translates, somewhat masonically, as something like "the hooded ones". The Cagoule aimed to overthrow the Third Republic and replace it with an authoritarian regime with the help of its Italian ally.

It did not stop at fomenting terror to achieve this end, posing a threat to public safety. Toureaux was tasked by the French police with infiltrating this dangerous group.

We think of honey traps today as the stuff of espionage – dissident Israeli nuclear scientist Mordecai Vanunu, for example, was spirited home to face trial following his seduction by a Mossad asset. Undercover police work by contrast must be clearer as to its boundaries, as it aims to place credible, uncompromised evidence before a court. But no such distinction existed in the 1930s, and Toureaux not only succeeded in insinuating herself with the Cagoule, but in seducing one of its leaders, Gabriel Jeantet.

Toureaux received an eight-inch stiletto buried to its hilt in her neck for her pains. Her killing bears the hallmarks of a premeditated assassination – in its silent professionalism and effectiveness, together with the lack of any evidence of a sexual motive or attempt at robbery. In all likelihood this operation cost Toureaux her life.

The Cagoul was no mere bunch of cranks, and claimed to have around 132,000 men ready to fight. By 1937, Cagoulards had already been responsible for a host of crimes and threats to public order, including the murder of two arms dealers who had attempted to cheat them on price; other political stabbings; the murder of two Italian antifascists in order to curry favour with Mussolini; the blowing up of iron-workers' union buildings (and an attempt to blame this, Nazi-misinformation-style, on communists); the sabotaging of planes bound for the Spanish Republic, and the attempted infiltration of republican Spain's International Brigades.

Jean Filliol, considered for a long time to be the chief suspect in Toureaux's murder, has form for these previous stabbings. After her death, in November of the same year, police raided the Cagoulards and found them to be in possession of several anti-aircraft or anti-tank guns, well over a hundred rifles and sawn-off shotguns, five hundred machine guns, sixty-five sub-machine guns and two tons of high explosive. Some of the guns were Italian- or German-made. Did Toureaux's work contribute to this haul? The following extract aims to shed light on the true character and motives of this enigmatic undercover operative.

By way of an interesting historical footnote to the Cagoule, the links between fascist regimes and the world of big business has often been noted, and authoritarian governments have frequently been analysed as a kind of corporate state, in which totalitarianism is harnessed in the service of increased profits and inflated contracts. It might be flippant to suggest that when it comes to the French would-be equivalent, a perfumier would have to be involved, albeit a large one: for the Cagoule was started by Eugène Schueller, founder of cosmetics firm L'Oréal. After spending World War Two as a high-ranking collaborationist in Limoges, Filliol, the chief suspect in Toureaux's killing, fled to Franco's Spain and found work at L'Oréal's subsidiary company there.

The seemingly impossible mechanics of the audacious murder comprised only part of the police's dilemma. Motive, too, was extremely problematic at first, because there seemed not to be any. On its surface, Laetitia Toureaux's life resembled closely that of many other young women in 1930s Paris. She was born 11 September, 1907. Her parents separated in 1920, when her mother moved to France with Toureaux, her sister, and her two brothers, while her father, a construction worker and farmer as well as a World War I veteran, remained behind in the Valle d'Aosta in Italy. The family, minus the father, spent some time in Lyon before they migrated to Paris, joining the burgeoning Italian immigrant community drawn to the French capital in search of work.

The police naturally found it odd that Toureaux's entire family had relocated to France, leaving the head of the family behind in Aosta. Toureaux's mother explained that she and Laetitia had migrated to Lyon in 1920. When they were quickly able to find factory work, Laetitia's siblings joined them in Lyon. Laetitia's father remained in Italy, her mother claimed, because he loved the simple life and had a horror of big cities. Subsequent police investigation suggested, however, that the Nourrissat couple was estranged, as Madame Nourrissat evidently took a lover in France, a M. Guiseppe Chatillard, with whom she lived for eight months. Only after she had broken with Chatillard in 1925 did mother and children relocate to Paris.

Of all the children, only Laetitia remained close to her father, Henri Jean-Baptiste Nourrissat, despite his objections to her marriage. Like his daughter, Nourrissat père cobbled together a living, in his case primarily from farming and construction work. When interviewed after her death, Toureaux's father praised her to the skies. "She was my darling daughter, whom I loved more than all the world, my only joy in life anymore. The others [Toureaux's brothers and sister] have abandoned me, for seventeen years now. Only she came to visit me every year. She was happy, sincere, intelligent." Her mother, Marie Dauphine Nourrissat, also professed to adore Toureaux, declaring that "she was for me a spirit of joy". Toureaux was also close to her sister and two brothers. Riton told *Détective* magazine that he was her "true friend" and spoke of how radiant and happy she was on the day of her death. Toureaux was widely known for her kindness; she doted on her young niece (her sister's daughter), looked after poor children who lived on her street, and flashed a smile even at passing acquaintances in the neighborhood. She was a member of two respectable public service organizations, the Union Valdôtaine et Mont Cervin Réunies and the Ligue Républicaine du Bien Public, both of which required sponsors to attest to the good character of prospective new members. In fact, during the first days after Toureaux's murder, the police could hardly find anyone in her circle of family and friends with a bad word to say about her, let alone a motive to kill her.

The police quickly followed up on Toureaux's note arranging a meeting with the unknown Jean, which they had found in her purse, and the amorous letters stored in her desk. Perhaps a disappointed lover had killed her? They discovered that the correspondence came from two young military men, one of whom had clearly been romantically involved with the victim. René Schramm was a soldier stationed at Longwy, a fortification on the Maginot Line. He had met Toureaux at a *bal musette* called Le Tango in June 1936, and the two quickly became lovers. Schramm, a plumber in civilian life, enjoyed waltzing and doing the java with Toureaux, and the two even talked of marriage before Schramm was called up for military service, joining the 149th Infantry. The other suitor, Jean Martin, was a sailor stationed in Toulon. An apprentice mechanic, he too met Toureaux as a civilian and in a *bal musette*, L'As-de-Coeur. Like Schramm, Martin was drafted, ending up in the navy. It was this Jean that Toureaux had arranged to meet the night of her murder, after the dinner party for the Union Valdôtaine. Hoping to be able to steal a night away in Paris during the long holiday weekend, Martin had arranged for his brother to give Toureaux his note confirming their appointment. Schramm's and Martin's commanding officers affirmed, however, that neither man had managed to obtain passes to leave their posts on 16 May, and thus neither could be suspected in the murder. Nor did the police learn anything from their interrogations of the two men, other than the fact that Toureaux had an active love life. Martin insisted that he had just met Toureaux and that nothing physical had transpired between them, but Schramm freely admitted that they were sexually involved and had met regularly for sexual encounters, either at her apartment or at a hotel in the suburb of St Antoine.

Since both Martin and Schramm had an alibi, they proved to be another dead end in the investigation. Still, it was becoming clear that, at the very least, Toureaux was a flirtatious woman who enjoyed manipulating her many admirers, most of whom she met at various *bals musette*. While it is possible that Toureaux supplemented her income with occasional prostitution, like many working-class women who danced with men for money and were reputed to be *entraîneuses* (seductresses), the police never turned up any evidence that Toureaux had actually charged for sex. Rather, they discovered that she had been deeply in love with her husband and by all accounts was faithful to him during their marriage. After he died, however, friends and colleagues indicated that she had been driven by sheer loneliness to a string of lovers with whom she had enjoyed an active and exciting sex life. In late 1935, a year after Jules's death, she met a young man named Pierre Émile Le Boulanger at the *bal musette* Le Lotus, located in the Latin Quarter. Le Boulanger went by the sobriquet Petit-Pain. Within weeks they were lovers, and she went often to his room at 75 rue Pigalle to engage in lovemaking. Once Petit-Pain left Paris for active military duty, she took up with a buyer for Renault who often had business in Paris. This affair with Maurice Lamoureuse in March 1936 was brief, and while Lamoureuse later testified that he had found her elegant, he considered their sexual affair nothing but a "petit flirt". By the summer of 1936, she had met Schramm; she also had a brief affair with a fellow Italian named Giovanni Gasperini, a married barman whom she met at the *bal musette* Chez les Vikings, on the rue Vavin. Gasperini was known to the police because he belonged to the Italian fascist party that operated in Paris. He and Toureaux met on several occasions and had sex "en plein air" at the Bois de Boulogne and the Bois de St Cloud. As Toureaux's relationship with Schramm intensified, her affair with Gasperini ended, although he claimed they remained friends. Nevertheless, Toureaux considered Schramm too immature for her, and by 1937 the couple was known to have had loud public disagreements. Letters found in Toureaux's apartment indicated that at one point they fought over Leonie Devouillon, who Schramm had apparently flirted with at a *bal musette*. Devouillon was known to police as an occasional prostitute. By 1937, it seems that Toureaux had set her sights on men of higher station, or at least the police had reason to suspect that sometime in 1936 she took a wealthy lover. Le Boulanger, Lamoureuse, and Gasperini, moreover, all had solid alibis on the day of Toureaux's murder, as did most of her friends and acquaintances from the world of the *bals*.

One reason why Toureaux went so often to L'As-de-Coeur was that she had a second job there tending the cloakroom several evenings a week. Her dancing also turned out to be a source of income. Toureaux was paid to circulate among the male guests without partners and dance with them for money. This was a common practice in pre-World War II European dance halls, which often employed both men and women who were attractive and cut a good figure on the dance floor to make sure any guests who wanted to dance had a partner. The tie to L'As-de-Coeur seemed suggestive for another reason. One of the two stores where Toureaux's killer could have bought the murder weapon was located on the rue Pastourelle, less than two hundred metres from the rue des Vertus.

But police interviews with M. Fageon, the owner of L'As-de-Coeur, and patrons of the *bal* led nowhere. While the police doubted that Toureaux's murderer hailed from the milieu of the dance halls or that, despite her reputation as a flirt, her killer was a jealous lover, official procedure required them to follow up all possible leads. Accordingly, they set about hunting down known violent criminals with whom she might have crossed paths. In an example of such a trail, Georges Albayez, a police inspector, interviewed Gustave-Jules Milhomme, a thirty-four-year-old "mechanical" dentist who lived in Paris on the rue de la Réunion. Milhomme declared that while he was living at 166 boulevard de Charonne, a friend of his named Henri Sicres came by from time to time, accompanied by a man with the descriptive nickname "Gros Louis". Gros Louis supposedly worked as a handyman and bouncer at L'As-de-Coeur. According to Milhomme, one day Gros Louis boasted that a criminal acquaintance of his named Jo L'Algerois had killed Toureaux for one thousand francs. Albayez tracked down Sicres, who was a forty-year-old waiter at a café, although he was in prison when Albayez found him. All Sicres was able or willing to tell the police was that the real name of Gros Louis was Louis Le Louarn and that in May 1937 Le Louarn seemed to have had more money than usual, despite the fact that (like much of the French workforce) he had been unemployed for some time. The police never caught up with Jo L'Algerois, but they couldn't find any motive or evidence linking either him or Gros Louis to Toureaux anyway. As is typical in police work across the ages, the detectives had to follow up on scores of similar dry leads as they struggled to solve Toureaux's murder.

Meanwhile, rumours flew in the press about Toureaux's secret life. Her work at L'As-de-Coeur did not seem to be wholly innocent; a guest of the establishment claimed to have caught her riffling through the coat pockets of at least one of the guests. The police busily combed the newspapers for leads, where journalists asserted that Toureaux's expenses exceeded her salary. At 1,500 to 1,800 francs per month, she earned more than average for a factory worker, but not enough to pay for her lifestyle. Nor could the little she earned in tips at L'As-de-Coeur have supplied the difference. Had she found a sugar daddy among her lovers, or was she supplementing her income in more nefarious ways? Furthermore, although Toureaux had joined the Ligue Républicaine du Bien Public on 20 November, 1936, her novice membership did not yet entitle her to wear the Ligue's signature red pin with black trim that she sported the night of the murder, and upon which the bus driver and ticket-taker had remarked. How did she obtain it, and why had she chosen to wear it? Did she want to be picked out of a crowd, and if so, by whom? The people she was supposed to be meeting that evening – her brother and, later, Jean Martin – already knew what she looked like. Did she have another appointment, perhaps with her assassin? Was she murdered to prevent her from keeping this secret rendezvous? It seemed that the deeper the police dug, the more mysterious a figure she became.

On 22 May, the newspapers and weeklies revealed the most

sensational information of all about Toureaux: the police had discovered that she was a private investigator whose under-cover name was Yolande. "We are raising the veil on the strange life of Laetitia Toureaux" ran the subtitle to the cover story of *Détective* on 27 May 1937. Exposing Toureaux as "a sleuth in skirts" (*"un limier en jupons"*) who worked for the private detective agency known as the Agence Rouff, the politically neutral *Paris-Soir* concluded, "The life of Laetitia appears each day to be more and more adventurous." For journalists, "Le Crime du Métro" had now become "L'Énigme du Métro", with the focus fixed squarely on Toureaux and her secret escapades. The papers disclosed that Georges Gustave Rouffignac, head of Agence Rouff, had recommended her for a job opening at the Maxi factory. In the wake of the strikes in the summer of 1936, M. Dalit, the factory's director, needed an employee to replace a female union activist whom he had fired for stirring up trouble in his factory. He wanted someone who was not sympathetic to the communists, someone who not only would be a dependable worker but would also keep an eye on potential union activists. He thus had requested that the police recommend a capable candidate for an informer. The police in turn contacted Rouffignac, who offered them Toureaux. Rouffignac and a police inspector, M. Cettour, had also sponsored Toureaux for membership in the Ligue Républicaine du Bien Public. Rouffignac seems to have had a much closer relationship with Toureaux than he had been will-ing to admit to the police or the press. The police offered no explanation as to how Toureaux and Inspector Cettour had become acquainted. Could Toureaux have been hired to infil-trate the Ligue, an organization on the political left, as well as the Maxi factory?

As Michael B. Miller points out, "Spy fiction between the wars was never as good as fact." French cities, especially Paris, swarmed with undercover agents and adventurers in the 1930s, and nowhere were the spies thicker than in the Italian immigrant circles, where pro-Mussolini and anti-fascist agitators carried their covert battles into France. The political tensions of the era, the conviction that the interwar period was a breathing space but not a permanent peace, and the strides professional espionage had made during World War I all meant that European governments placed a high premium on intelligence. The Italians had begun infiltrating their emigrant communities in France even before World War I, and they stepped up their activities in the interwar period. The French police, fearful as they were of both communists and fascists, also habitually used Italian immigrants to spy on their compatriots. By the same token, the French police relied heavily on paid informants, many of them women, to help them solve crimes, especially crimes committed in the underworld society to which the police had little access. And both the public police and private companies hired workers to infiltrate factories and other workplaces.

The French government, even under the socialist Popular Front, lived in terror of violent popular riots, such as those of 1934, and of mass general strikes, like those that paralyzed France in 1936. With the world economy mired in the doldrums, the political cleavage between left and right growing ever wider, and the threat of another world war on the horizon, the government wanted to prevent further street fighting and strikes at all costs. Moreover, paranoia and subterfuge seemed to have a grip on the popular psyche. The police archives are replete with letters, many of them unsolicited and only rarely useful, from informants ratting on employers, friends and family members. The police received quite a few anonymous letters in the Toureaux case, most of them spurious. Interestingly, Toureaux seems to have come by her penchant for spying honestly; evidence in the police files reveals that either Toureaux's mother worked as an informant in 1929 or that Toureaux had already begun acting as an informant while still in her teens.

But how seriously should Toureaux's sleuthing have been taken? Was she really an experienced professional, liable to embroil herself in the kind of cases where her employers, their clients, or her quarry might have been willing and able to murder her? The dilemma of French journalists was that the men most likely to know – her boss at the detective agency, Georges Rouffignac, and the police commissioner in charge of the case, Charles Badin – seemed unable to make up their own minds on this issue. On 22 May Rouffignac stated, "I had the impression that she [Toureaux] was well acquainted with the detective profession well before she began to practise it in my service." He elaborated, "When this young woman presented herself at my establishment, I immediately perceived that I was not dealing with any debutante in the profession. I had the impression that she had learned somewhere other than my place how to follow a trail." In an interview with *Détective*, Rouffignac continued to praise her sleuthing prowess. "She was a model employee," he explained, "a real expert in all of her duties. I gave her delicate surveillance work and difficult investigations and she always did a great job." *Paris-Soir* also quoted Rouffignac as saying, "Effectively, as I looked back on this affair, one of my collaborators confided to me that Mme Toureaux boasted to him about two months ago that she had been at the Alcázar [probably meaning the Alcázar of Toledo, an important stronghold of the Spanish Nationalists during the Spanish Civil War] with a card [a calling card affording her entry to the building] signed by a political figure."

Yet Rouffignac contradicted himself repeatedly and at times drew a less flattering image of Toureaux. On 25 May, describing her demeanor when she first went to work for him, Rouffignac told the conservative newspaper *Le Matin* that when he offered her his best counsel and advice, assuming that he was dealing with a novice, Toureaux had smiled and replied, "I'll figure it out." On 22 May in *Paris-Soir*, Rouffignac characterized Toureaux as being even more confident about her abilities as a spy. He claimed that she declared, "Don't take the trouble, I know how to do it [detective work]," when he had offered to instruct her on the ins and outs of sleuthing. He also said that when he asked her if she wasn't afraid to work at L'As-de-Coeur, she replied, "No, I'm used to that." Yet Rouffignac averred that her work was mostly to tail other women and was not dangerous at all. And when a journalist asked, "Didn't you have the impression that this [kind of] work was nothing new for her?" Rouffignac changed course completely, replying, "Not in the least. Look at this, for example. In filling out her surveillance reports, she floundered lamentably. On this account, I was obliged to teach her the ABCs of the profession." For that reason, he insinuated, he didn't employ her all that often and she spent much of her time idle, collecting unemployment. Rouffignac was not alone in his willingness to disparage Toureaux's work. The police seemed to have concluded that she was inept at her profession. "An examination of her notes and papers," stated a police communiqué, "shows conclusively that Laetitia had little aptitude for this type of vocation and that her reports had a childish character." The same day Commissioner Badin himself expressed in an interview with the press his conviction that "Laetitia Toureaux, an inexperienced detective, could not have inspired hatred sufficiently powerful to legitimize the hypothesis [that her murder was a crime] of vengeance."

Rouffignac and Badin both appear to have been disingenuous with the press on this issue. Despite the sloppy, thin reports that she supposedly prepared for Rouffignac, and the rarity with which he claimed that he called on her (only six cases, he told the press), Rouffignac admitted elsewhere that he had hired Toureaux for no less than sixteen assignments over several months, thus at a rate of about one a week. Five of these jobs involved surveillance of adulterous spouses, while the rest entailed the less challenging task of verifying addresses. For all this work, Rouffignac claimed to have paid her a total of 1,035 francs, 35 sous, less than a month's salary at the Maxi factory. Why did he continue to give her jobs if her performance was so unsatisfactory? Moreover, he recommended her to M. Dalit, the director of the Maxi factory, not only as a good worker, but also as a subtle sleuth well able to keep an eye on her co-workers without any of them suspecting anything. Dalit certainly had no complaints about her work. Nor did most of the people who worked with Toureaux at the Maxi factory suggest that she was anything other than a well-liked colleague, although a couple later confessed that they had had their suspicions.

That Rouffignac was less than forthcoming despite his vaunted cooperation with the authorities is not surprising, as he was rather a shady character himself. A rotund man with a small moustache, and a dapper dresser who sported straw hats at the beach and bowlers in town, he strongly resembled Agatha Christie's fictional character Hercule Poirot. Although he was a Frenchman, it was rumoured – probably because of his thick southern French accent and dark hair – that he was actually Italian, perhaps even a spy. Born in 1895 in Marsac, in the Charente region of France, Rouffignac married in 1919 and was the father of a teenage boy in 1937. Although he claimed that his detective agency mostly performed routine surveillance, he clearly also provided spies for the police and for private industry.

Rouffignac never seemed to know quite how to play his relationship with Toureaux to the press. On the one hand, he denied any culpability in her death, insinuating that she was a seasoned detective with many espionage irons in the fire, of which her job with the Agence Rouff was only one. On the other hand, he disparaged her sleuthing abilities and minimized her work for him, exculpating himself by claiming that it was her rank amateurism that got her killed. It seems that he may have been trying deliberately to blacken Toureaux's reputation. He insinuated in his 22 May interview with *Paris-Soir* that she was a welfare cheat who took government handouts while working both for him and L'As-de-Coeur. Moreover, it emerged that the "guest" of L'As-de-Coeur who claimed to have seen Toureaux searching customers' coat pockets was none other than Mme Paulette Vicarini (née Léonard), Rouffignac's secretary. According to Rouffignac, as soon as Vicarini informed him of Toureaux's unseemly behaviour, he passed the information along to police, and he declared that neither he nor his secretary had the slightest idea why Toureaux would have done such a thing. It certainly wasn't in the course of a job for the Agence Rouff, and must have been related to her own private affairs.

Eventually the police learned that Rouffignac had arranged for Toureaux to work in the cloakroom of L'As-de-Coeur as part of her sleuthing work for him. The cloakrooms of *bals musette* were often used in the 1930s as depositories for mail too sensitive to send through the regular system, and it appears that Toureaux facilitated such transfers. In this vein, an interrogation of one of Toureaux's friends revealed that she tried to arrange for other women to work in the *bals* for Rouffignac as part of his private surveillance force. In October 1936, Toureaux brought her eighteen-year-old friend, Yvonne Cavret, to meet Rouffignac in anticipation of securing a job in the cloakroom of a *bal* near the Place Pigalle. The young woman's fiancé, Victor Riou, later explained to Badin that Rouffignac had made it quite clear that Cavret would be part of his private investigative staff. Ultimately, Rouffignac found Riou too young and did not engage her. Riou later insisted that once she understood she would be spying for Rouffignac, she lost all interest in the position.

The police also concluded that Rouffignac was correct that Toureaux had performed detective work for another employer in 1936 and 1937. According to Riton, Toureaux, in her campaign to improve his fortunes, had tried to induct him into the espionage business by giving him a few simple tasks to perform for her. In particular, she sent him to three addresses, all in the 18th arrondissement. Unfortunately, Riton proved to be an inept sleuth and was unable to fulfill his missions to Toureaux's satisfaction – an indication that she did have experience and professional standards in this line of work. She paid him the cost of his transportation to the addresses, but informed him that in the future she would do the jobs herself. Rouffignac denied giving Toureaux any assignments that involved the 18th arrondissement, however, which led the police to conclude that she "consistently worked as a private detective for a third party, other than Rouffignac". They proved unable to ascertain who that person or persons might have been; nor did they admit the possibility that it was one of the branches of the police.

The mystery surrounding Toureaux's death deepened still further when witnesses came forward claiming that the seemingly confident, carefree adventuress was in fact well aware that she was in over her head in the days and weeks preceding her murder. Not all of their stories were credible; there were numerous inconsistencies in the statements that Toureaux's acquaintances, friends and family offered to the police and to the press. There was, for example, the so-called "mystery of the green outfit". According to the newspapers, people accustomed to seeing Toureaux on a daily basis – such as Mme Marie Quiniou, who sold tickets at the Métro Philippe-Auguste, the station nearest the rue Pierre Bayle where Toureaux lived – were astonished to see her sporting a new green suit and freshly tinted blonde hair on the day of her murder. They claimed that they had never seen her wear anything other than widow's weeds since she moved into the neighbourhood after Jules's death. Riton, in contrast, saw nothing surprising in her decision to wear the green outfit; he claimed that Toureaux's mother had just made it for her, and as Toureaux was lunching with her mother that very day, it stood to reason that her mother would have expected her daughter to be wearing the new outfit. By the same token, the testimony of Rouffignac's secretary Mme Vicarini that Toureaux showed up on her first day of work at the Agence Rouff in a stylish grey suit and hat trimmed with mauve indicates that Toureaux did indeed wear colours other than black in the two years between Jules's death and her own. Still, journalists made much of her seemingly suspicious decision suddenly to change her wardrobe and hair colour on the day she was killed.

The witnesses from the Métro marvelled that Toureaux had travelled in first class on 16 May, as they swore that in all the time they had known her, she had purchased only second-class tickets. Yet Toureaux's mother said at one point that because Toureaux was often dressed in her finest on Sundays, she sometimes treated herself to first-class seating. This did not stop the press from speculating about her decision to upgrade her fare on 16 May, placing herself alone and vulnerable in one of the usually deserted first-class cars and thus providing her killer the opportunity he needed to strike. Were her changes in habits merely coincidence, or were they signs that she sought to disguise her identity because she sensed the net closing in around her? Had someone unknown to the police instructed her to take the fateful first-class car as a rendezvous point?

Another odd piece of the puzzle surfaced. According to her friends Suzy Fiancette and Joseph Chatrian, Toureaux had feared for her life at the hands of a powerful and obsessed lover whom she could not shake, and even went so far as to consult a psychic for guidance. The psychic, a Mme de Romanellas, claimed that Toureaux asked her to use black magic to rid her of this unwanted lover.

Even more suggestive, was the testimony of M. Émile Martin, the station chief of Philippe Auguste. He and the other regular workers at the Métro station had good reason to be familiar with Toureaux, as she ordinarily took the Métro three to four times a day; around 7:15 a.m. on her way to work at the Maxi factory, around 6:00 p.m. when she returned home, at about 9:00 p.m. when she went to work at L'As-de-Coeur, and again on her way home if she returned before the Métro closed around 12:30 a.m. M. Martin, Mme Quiniou, Mme Louise Leclercq (the night clerk), and Mme Alice Jhoupin (the newspaper vendor in the station) were all used to seeing Toureaux pass, flashing them her radiant smile. Sometimes she stopped to make small talk if she wasn't in too much of a hurry. According to Martin and Leclercq, on the evening of Thursday, 13 May, only three days before her murder, Toureaux told them that she had been attacked by a man who had tried to knife her as she left the Métro station. She was able to drive him away by slapping him in the face. "In that case, aren't you frightened?" asked Martin. "No," she replied. "But now I take my umbrella to defend myself." Martin offered to walk her to the Métro exit, but she refused. "If someone attacks you again," he said, "cry out loudly this time." "Will do," she replied, with a laugh. Then she shook his hand and went on her way.

Mme Marie Chartrian offered a different version of the story. Toureaux and the Chartrians were good friends, as she and Joseph Chartrian came from the same region of

Italy. Joseph worked in a café near the Agence Rouff, and he and Rouffignac both testified that it was Joseph who recommended Toureaux to Rouffignac when the latter was in need of a female sleuth for certain cases. His wife testified that Toureaux told her that the attack on 13 May took place not at the Métro station, but in front of the door of her building on the rue Pierre Bayle. According to Mme Chartrian, Toureaux said, "I was returning home very late one night in a car with a [male] friend. I had gotten out at the angle of the boulevard Charonne and the rue Pierre Bayle. I was just about to ring the doorbell so that [the concierge] could let me in when a man got out of a car who evidently had been following us, and approached me in a menacing manner. I was about to attempt to defend myself when the door opened. I was able to go in and shut it behind me. But I was terrified." The police gave the impression that they did not take the incident too seriously. Badin doubted that the attack on 13 May was related to the murder and suggested that Toureaux's assailant that night probably was "an enterprising stalker or a criminal who was after her pocketbook".

By mid-June, in the absence of any obvious progress in the case on the part of the police, the Parisian newspapers were grasping at any straws, no matter how far-fetched, to keep the story alive. Much of what they wrote was a combination of rehashed information from stories that had broken in the first week after the crime, new and questionable testimony from people ever further from Toureaux's circle of close family and friends, and outright speculation. Every now and then, the police would get a false confession, such as that from Jean-Émile Goderoy, who claimed that he had shared a prison cell with Raymond Leblanc, whose sister dated the assassin. It turned out, however, that Goderoy's friends considered him a "bit crazy" and that Leblanc had no sisters. But the police investigation was making little progress, and journalists suspected that the turgid pace was deliberate. As the communist daily *L'Humanité* asserted on 27 May, "Quietly they are smothering the Laetitia affair."

In one sense, *L'Humanité* had it right. On 25 May, the newspaper stated in its daily story on the Toureaux case that the police had possession of "considerable correspondence" between Toureaux and her "protector", who the paper asserted was "a well-known politician of the right". Why, complained *L'Humanité*, was no one discussing this? Further revelations appeared on 28 May in *Paris-Soir*: "My daughter was charged with delicate missions and she feared vengeance," Toureaux's father supposedly proclaimed. These "missions" were for the police, and she continued with them despite her fears because she "loved this work", as it kept her from dwelling on her "unhappiness", and in particular the loss of her husband. She had accepted the job in the cloakroom of L'As-de-Coeur precisely because it helped her with her detecting, and, when she realized that she was quite skilled at detection, she began to work for several different agencies. She knew that her life could be threatened, but the rewards made the risk worthwhile. This testimony was very similar to what Toureaux allegedly told her friend Mme Chartrian, who stated that Toureaux declared that she loved her detective work because it afforded her the opportunity to forge relationships with people in "high places" and to "make something of herself".

The judicial police remained mostly silent in the face of accusations that they were deliberately dragging their feet, in part probably because they were used to such complaints from the press and public. In the recent Stavisky and Prince affairs, the press had kept up an insistent drumbeat of reports that the victims in fact had been assassinated and had harshly criticized the police for their inability or lack of will to solve these "political crimes".

On 26 May the judicial police did issue a statement that attempted to quell the wilder journalistic rumour-mongering. The inquiry so far had established, the police declared:

1. That Laetitia Toureaux was employed from June to November 1936 exclusively by M. Rouffignac, a private detective, to shadow people suspected of infidelity in

six different cases involving individuals of no great importance. She was never charged with any other mission. The examination of the notes and papers furnished [by Rouffignac] on this subject demonstrated peremptorily that Laetitia had little aptitude for this type of mission and that her reports had a childish character. She never worked in a detective agency other than the Agence Rouff.

2. No one knows of any protector as such of the victim. She did have several flirtations. Her style of life was modest, her lodging, which was composed merely of one room and a small kitchen, was appropriately and nicely furnished with furniture derived from her marriage. Her means of existence were the fruits of her labour at the House of Maxi and the sums she earned as tips working in the cloakroom of L'As-de-Coeur, which in winter could be as much as thirty francs an evening, and in the summer up to twenty francs. Having fairly elegant taste, she often made the clothes which she wore herself. She had absolutely no other source of revenue and her lifestyle corresponded with her income.

3. The judicial police have established no relationship between the affair of the Porte de Charenton [Toureaux] and those of Fontainebleau or Morangis [other unsolved murders]. By the same token, Inspector Cettour continues to work in the section [of the police] relating to public theft and has never changed his branch of service.

The last sentence of the statement is particularly curious, because it implies that the press suspected, correctly, that there was something odd in Cettour's sponsorship of Toureaux for the Ligue Républicaine du Bien Public. This suspicion lay behind the false rumour that Cettour had been transferred to a job outside of Paris, perhaps to put him out of reach of the press. Overall, the communiqué should be taken with a grain of salt because there is ample evidence that Toureaux was a much better detective than either the police or Rouffignac wanted to suggest. And the police themselves concluded privately that Toureaux had in fact worked for another detective agency besides the Agence Rouff, although they were not able to track down which one. Possibly the police wanted to avoid tipping off the murderer, if he was connected to a job she had done for another employer, before they got the opportunity to follow up on that angle of the investigation.

Another reason for the police reticence to discuss their progress with the press may have been that *L'Humanité* was getting uncomfortably near the truth. Toureaux had, it seemed, formed some decidedly odd political alliances for a lowly factory worker and part-time cloakroom attendant. On the one hand, the Ligue Républicaine du Bien Public, for which Rouffignac and Inspector Cettour had sponsored her membership, was a fairly high-profile organization on the French political left. Founded by two prominent socialists in 1935 as the heir to an older antiroyalist organization, its mission was to oppose the spread of fascism in France. On the other hand, the police found in Toureaux's apartment a postcard from someone attending a conference called the "Rassemblement Universel pour la Paix" (Universal Assembly for Peace), held in Brussels in July 1936. This person, who signed the card only "I. CH", expressed fervent rightist opinions, which, the police deduced on the basis of other correspondence found in her apartment, Toureaux shared. I. CH informed Toureaux that he would be returning to France in September 1936. The police were unable to identify who had sent her the card. This evidence suggested that there might well have been a political dimension to Toureaux's murder. But what sort of politics, right or left? Without more evidence, the police had no way of knowing which of the plethora of political groups sprouting like mushrooms in the increasingly tense political climate of 1937 France might have been involved in the crime.

Thus, despite the dogged police investigation and the journalistic frenzy, Toureaux's case remained unsolved as the summer and autumn of 1937 wore on. There was now an ample list of suspects who might have wanted her out of the way, but no concrete evidence linking the crime to any of them. Although the police seemed to have run into a dead end or were at least unwilling to tell all that they knew, journalists continued to report on the case. The closest they came to the truth in the days immediately following Toureaux's murder was in an article published on 23 May in *Paris-Soir*, which asserted, "But Laetitia Toureaux, who knew well the Italian milieus and who made many voyages (although less frequently than some have asserted) between France and Italy, could have been employed as an informant either by the national police, or by private organizations or groups."

Might her work as a private detective or a police informant have led to her death? "It could well have been a drug trafficker from the circle of Toureaux's closest associates, a friend of the unfortunate woman, who decided to take it upon himself to put an end to her unpleasant police activities," speculated an evening paper, *L'Intransigeant*, in June. But could journalists ever confirm this hypothesis? Not if the police had anything to say about the matter. They seemed determined to keep a lid on the whole affair. Other newspapers, especially *La Liberté* and *Paris-Soir*, were more *au courant* regarding the progress of the case, perhaps because they had cultivated better contacts within the police. Police reports indicate that some of the inspectors assigned to her case were aware of Toureaux's work as a paid informer at the time of her death. They eventually concluded that an extreme right-wing terrorist organization called the Cagoule may have had a hand in the murder. As yet the judicial police knew very little about the Cagoule, beyond rumours from their informants that the group was highly secret with a penchant for violence. They were not eager to publicize what little they had learned, since doing so might have compromised their ongoing probe of the Cagoule. Moreover, competition and mistrust within various divisions of the police force, as well as political pressure from the government, made the inspectors at the Sûreté reluctant to divulge any information on Toureaux and the Cagoule, even to their colleagues in the Paris prefecture. As a result, the judicial police got no further breaks in the Toureaux case until near the end of 1937.

5

Chief Inspector Fabian Searches for a Raincoat

(from Famous Stories of the Murder Squad)

Leonard Gribble

We may think of the 1940s as mannered – an age when, if an inspector called, he would remove his homburg in the hall. In reality, life for many in Britain was lived in desperate conditions, once the euphoria of wartime victory had died down. Rationing – on food and other essentials – continued until 1954, with some members of the political class, such as Sir Stafford Cripps, even thinking of it as a potential means of social engineering, of narrowing the gap between rich and poor and reducing malnutrition.

In reality, the law of unintended consequences applied: sexual favours were swapped for prime cuts of meat, bringing smiles to the ruddy faces of provincial butchers. Petrol for official use was siphoned off for private customers with the right contacts, ensuring that even the most socially upstanding were corrupted. As is ever the case with prohibition, a thriving black market was created for many products. Soldiers returned home, suppressing their wartime traumas with customary silence on the subject, while the more rootless or feckless were now well trained to turn to robbery and other kinds of crime. Forged or stolen documentation was commonplace.

In Britain at the time, it seemed that nearly everyone was running "a fiddle", and many felt they couldn't have survived without one. The chaotic state of the railways and roads enabled easy access to freighted merchandise for the spiv – the new breed of middleman who retailed products acquired cheaply from these sources "on the QT" to members of the public frustrated with waiting for times of plenty to return. Even the temperamentally honest were psychologically exhausted enough to go along with the endemic corruption of the age, which contained within it the seeds of how, commercially at least, we were to lose the peace to Volkswagen and Mitsubishi.

Donald Thomas outlines a typical scam in his fascinating book, *Villains' Paradise: Britain's Underworld from the Spivs to the Krays* – "The railways were scarcely an area of life where the spiv had much to fear. The chaotic state of the goods network enabled customers to combine with workers in supplying the black market. A Clapham High Street tailor was in the habit of sending parcels by way of Clapham Junction goods depot. The parcels clerk would agree to label them incorrectly, re-routing them to the tailor's shop. The tailor would then claim for the loss against the railways, in whose labyrinthine processes the clothes had been allegedly mislaid or stolen. The claim was paid. The tailor meantime had sold the clothes to the black market, coupon-free, at a considerably higher figure than he would have got legally. He was richer, his accomplice in the parcels office was rewarded, and the spiv who retailed the clothes could boast of contented customers."

Gents' apparel is also central to the following extract which, allowing for the detail of time and place, in parts feels surprisingly contemporary, with its tale of how a famous robbery-murder case was solved with the aid of Scotland Yard's Murder Squad's plain-clothes surveillance (in this case of known dealers of stolen property) and painstaking detection techniques. It would seem, for example, that the detective's tactic of parading an accomplice past a suspect being interviewed about a serious crime is as old as it's universal.

For all this, British society was of course more mannered than it is today. One change for example, perhaps not for the better, concerns the working lunch: it's observed as worthy of note that Inspector Bob Fabian "didn't wait to collect his dessert and coffee before giving his first instructions". If it was considered unusual for a detective working a murder case to interrupt his lunch on receiving news of a break-through, a hard-working editor who routinely skips his own to get a book to press might reflect that progress isn't always all it's cracked up to be!

Four years after the hanging of the wigwam murderer, on a sunny April day in 1947, murder was enacted on a London street corner in the open. This was a crime that was to have several repercussions. It was also one that gave the post-war Murder Squad a great deal of publicity. It also brought considerable publicity to Chief Inspector Robert Fabian, who later became well-known as Fabian of the Yard.

On that sunny April morning in 1947 he was on the threshold of what is probably his most celebrated case.

But there would have been no murder case if that morning a black Vauxhall saloon car had not been moving up from Oxford Street to a street corner in Charlotte Street, which runs parallel with Tottenham Court Road, and at the same time a young man on a motorcycle had not been making in the same direction towards his appointment. The motor-cyclist was some distance away from the three men, all younger than himself, seated in the Vauxhall, on a collision course. But like them he was making for Charlotte Street.

The Vauxhall drew up outside a jeweller's shop which was on the corner of Tottenham Street and Charlotte Street. It parked in Tottenham Street, pointing towards Charlotte Street.

Like the man on the motorcycle still some distance away, the young men who got out of the Vauxhall had come from the southern side of the Thames. They paused for a moment outside the jeweller's shop, which had the name "Jay's" over the plate-glass window, glanced up and down each way outside, and then crossed the pavement and walked inside.

At this precise moment the man on the motorcycle was preparing to thread his way up Charlotte Street, which would take him past the site of a butcher's shop, where in November 1917, on a night when German Gothas were bombing London, Louis Voisin murdered Emilienne Gérard. The motorcycle wove in and out of the traffic, chugged beyond 101 Charlotte Street and the ghosts of a bygone crime, and approached the corner with Tottenham Street.

The time was half-past two. The lunch hour in the area around Tottenham Court Road was over. Suddenly a muffled shot rang out. The man on the motorcycle could have heard it. He certainly heard the vibrant ringing of a burglar alarm which began pealing stridently. He glanced in the direction of the sound and saw three young men run from the jeweller's. They had handkerchiefs tied across their faces, and he saw them throw themselves into a parked Vauxhall. One of them ground on the starter, but the engine failed to start. The man in the driver's seat was still trying desperately to start the engine when a van drew into the kerb in front of the stationary Vauxhall, and the way ahead was blocked.

The three young bandits who had run from the jeweller's sprang from the car as a man staggered from the shop and collapsed on the pavement with blood pouring from a head wound. They now ran towards Charlotte Street and darted across it as people on the pavements shouted. But they didn't have a clear crossing. The man on the motorcycle had reached the same stretch of road at the same time, and he swung his machine and braked to block their way. He, too, shouted, for he had seen enough to judge that a robbery with violence had taken place in the shop called Jay's. He waved an arm.

There was another sharp report, and then the motorcyclist was falling in the afternoon sunshine.

The runners continued past him towards a short dead-end street called Charlotte Mews. There they bunched together before doubling back from the cul-de-sac, and one of them dropped a silver cake-stand he had grabbed inside the shop as he ran out. They ran past Whitfield Street and on towards Tottenham Court Road.

As they vanished people gathered round the shot motor-cyclist, who was dying. He murmured brokenly, "They got me. Get them."

His eyes closed and he lay unconscious until an ambulance arrived and he was borne swiftly to the Middlesex Hospital, which was not very far. Before it arrived the motor-cyclist was dead. His name was Alec de Antiquis. He had been murdered at point-blank range by a young thug who was one of the first of a new post-war breed of criminals to bring violence to the streets of Britain.

When the word of a shooting in a London street in daylight reached Scotland Yard there was only a brief interval before the additional message informed the head of the CID that the victim was dead. His body lay in the mortuary at Middlesex Hospital. Also in that hospital was the man who had collapsed bleeding from a gun battering on the head. He was being bandaged and waiting to tell a Yard man the little he knew about a raid on the shop where he worked which ended with his falling unconscious in Tottenham Street.

From the Yard sped Bob Fabian, his chief assistant Robert Higgins, and a crew of forensic experts. Fabian was taken to see the wounded man who had been allowed to leave now that he had received attention.

"I'd like to know anything at all that you can tell me, Mr Stock," said Fabian, who had cut his teeth on hard crime investigation when he had been chief of the Yard's Flying Squad.

The wounded man explained how just before half-past two that afternoon two young men had entered the jeweller's shop through a side door giving on to that part where customers could pawn articles. Another young man entered the main shop, where jewellery, watches, gold and silverware were on display. The three met in the main shop, and at once drew knotted handkerchiefs up over their faces. They then produced firearms.

"I looked up when I heard steps," Ernest Stock told Fabian, "and found myself staring at three levelled revolvers."

He explained that several of his assistants were young

women. They stood frozen into silence by the menance on the other side of the counter.

One of the armed and masked raiders said, "This is a stick-up. Get back and keep quiet." He waved his weapon and at the same time reached for a tray of rings that was on the counter. That was when Ernest Stock moved to prevent the theft, and was at once smacked across the head with the gun in the young man's right hand.

"I fell down," he told Fabian.

Immediately a shot rang out. This was followed by a stool being thrown across the shop by one of the assistants, who was only seventeen. The assistant also sprang for the burglar alarm and set it off. A bandit threw his gun at the assistant before running for the door. The other two followed him. By this time Ernest Stock was on his feet, blood streaming from his head wound as he too made for the door. But he couldn't make it across the pavement.

To Fabian it was obvious that the bandits had not carefully prepared the raid and timed their moves. The fact that the driver had switched off the engine of the getaway car, instead of staying in the car and keeping the engine running, revealed the criminals as amateurs. They were dangerous, but without skill, either in their planning or in dealing out violence. He hoped they would be equally careless in achieving their getaway.

Fabian's men began taking fingerprints. The gun that had been dropped by one of the fleeing trio was recovered and tested for them, as was the silver cake-stand recovered from Charlotte Mews. But the resulting prints were not on record with the Criminal Records Office. One of the forensic experts placed over the steering wheel of the bandits' Vauxhall a false steering wheel, which enabled the car to be driven to the Yard for a full examination without destroying any fingerprints left by the last driver.

But by this time Fabian had been informed that the Vauxhall was a stolen car. It had been taken by the bandits from where it had been left in Whitfield Street. The check with the owner proved that the car had been stolen barely five minutes before the raid was carried out.

Fabian now knew that the violent criminals who had resorted to murder were not only careless, but hurried. They might be hard to find because they were obviously not known and experienced villains. Had they been, they would have planned with greater care and collected what they had gone after without resorting to shooting when they met opposition.

A "forty-five" bullet was dug from the shop's wall and another of "thirty-two" calibre from the dead de Antiquis's head. They were sent for examination by Robert Churchill at his establishment in the Strand. The following hours were a busy time for Superintendent Fred Cherrill, the chief of the Yard's Fingerprint Bureau, who had many fingerprints to check. For all his work and the time it took, the only progress he could report was of a negative nature. He wasn't able to name any of the three bandits.

Fabian had his men work methodically through the Charlotte Street area, asking questions and checking with passers-by who had been in the street at two-thirty p.m. At the same time Fabian had extended the manhunt and dozens of detectives began making calls on hotels and boarding houses and youth hostels. Other detectives covered railway stations and questioned bus crews who had been anywhere near Tottenham Court Road at half-past two. Lorry and van drivers were stopped and questioned. While this work progressed information was systematically fed to provincial police forces as it was obtained, together with a request for cooperation and additional information if available. Within a few hours London and the Home Counties were a vast police trap that might be sprung by any careless bandit on the run.

Bob Fabian was never a man to wait patiently when he knew a certain course of action might get what he wanted. He was not put off by being unable to establish the criminals' identity through their fingerprints. He had the Criminal Records Office hand-sorted for known car thieves and armed bandits, work that today would be speedily accomplished by a computer. As a result a number of men with records of violence were surprised to receive a visit from CID detectives with questions to be answered. One of those questions concerned their whereabouts at two-thirty on the afternoon of 29 April.

Word reached Fabian that there was growing resentment at the wide ripples his tactics were creating in the underworld. He sent back a succinct message: "Finger the killers and the pressure will be off."

When the only response was silence he knew that the trio he sought were not professional criminals. Indeed, they were unknown to the professional criminals with whom Bob Fabian had been rubbing shoulders for years. He made a report to a special conference at the Yard headed by Ronald Howe, the chief of the CID, who decided to step up the hunt for the wanted men in the Metropolitan Police area. Fabian gave fresh orders as soon as the conference broke up. It is said that his first news of the case came while he was in the middle of his lunch period on that memorable 29 April. He didn't wait to collect his dessert and coffee before giving his first instructions.

That was how Bob Fabian operated. The job came first. Not surprisingly the results he achieved in a remarkable career were unique.

On this case it took him three days of continuous inquiry to find a taxi driver who at half-past two on the twenty-ninth was taking a fare up Tottenham Court Road. A man suddenly jumped from the pavement and landed beside him on the near side.

"Engaged," the driver yelled, pointing to the lowered meter flag under the man's nose. The man muttered a few words the driver couldn't distinguish and dropped back on the pavement, having gained about a hundred yards. The driver saw him disappear across the pavement and inside a large building.

The driver couldn't describe the man except to say he had a bandage round his jaw. It could have been the handkerchief used as a mask in the jeweller's. But he was able to describe the building into which the man had vanished. It proved to be a large block of offices named Brook House.

Everyone employed in the building was questioned and a

youth recalled seeing two men run into the entrance shortly after the time of the murder and jump into the lift. The youth also saw them when they came down in the lift. One had gone up wearing a raincoat, but had come down without it. Brook House was searched by detectives from basement to roof, and a car ignition key was found. A short while later Fabian knew he had the key of the stolen Vauxhall.

There was an empty office on the top floor of Brook House. In here the searchers came upon a cap and scarf and a pair of gloves, also a triangular mask with knots at the ends. But, as was to prove most important, they also found a discarded raincoat, a worn and stained garment of a make that had been distributed widely to multiple clothes shops. It looked like a few thousand other coats.

At least, until Fabian had the seams unstitched, and found what he was looking for in the lining of the coat's armpit. This was a number on a special label sewn into the garment as a record of its manufacture.

The number on the distinctive label was in red marking ink. It was 7800.

There was no let-up in the manhunt while Fabian switched his personal inquiry to raincoat manufacturers throughout the British Isles. In what now seems a surprisingly short time he had a report from Leeds. No. 7800 had been stiched into a raincoat made in that city. The manufacturer's ledgers were gone through, and a consignment of garments that included raincoat No. 7800 was shown to have been dispatched to a warehouse in south-east London.

At that time, two years after the war, clothing was still rationed in Britain. Fabian did not believe a garment that had been checked to the London warehouse would have ended up on the black market. He began checking with shops that had taken stock from the warehouse, and after a good deal of further inquiry decided the coat could have arrived at one of three particular retail shops. Past raincoat purchases from those shops were checked, and Fabian received the names of customers who had surrendered clothing coupons for such purchases.

When he came to one of those names he paused. There seemed to be something about it that rang a faint bell in his mind. The name was Vernon George.

The ringing of that mental bell did not become clear until he turned the name round – George Vernon. He recalled then that there was nothing the police had against George Vernon, who had apparently bought the raincoat from a shop in Deptford on hire purchase. But Vernon was known to be related to a young man who was violent and had a police record.

Fabian called at the Vernon home and spoke to Mrs Vernon, who told him that her husband had lost that raincoat several weeks before. Fabian left. So did the woman shortly afterwards. She was followed to the home of a family named Jenkins. One member of this family was a young man with a record of violence. He was Charles Henry Jenkins, who had once broken a policeman's jaw.

Now the Criminal Records Office provided Fabian with something he had not previously been able to find without a name. Charles Henry Jenkins had been released from prison as recently as 23 April, six days before the Charlotte Street murder.

Fabian realized that the really vital clue was the raincoat, owned by a respectable working man named George Vernon, against whom there was no suggestion of being involved in the raid that had ended in murder. But Mrs Vernon was Charles Jenkins's sister, and it was possible that her brother could have come into possession of the raincoat in some ordinary and easily explained way. He could have borrowed it without telling anyone.

Only Jenkins could explain how he came by the raincoat. He was picked up, and Fabian arrived to question him only to be offered an alibi. The young man who had once served a term in Borstal seemed quite confident and unshaken by Fabian's interest.

He was asked to sign a statement and released. A disappointed Fabian began doggedly to go over the known crime events of that April, and he found himself considering a report about armed men who had broken into a jeweller's shop in Queensway, Bayswater. On that occasion, too, the raiders had worn masks. The date was 23 April, the same day that Charles Jenkins had been released from prison.

Detectives were now given orders to keep a close watch on the establishments of certain known fences, or dealers in stolen property. One such character in Southend coyly agreed that he might have purchased articles unknowingly that had come from the Bayswater break-in. He told the police the name of the man who had sold him these articles.

Within a short while this man was picked up in the Woolwich area and taken to the police station in Tottenham Court Road, where Bob Fabian, looking grim, was waiting to start a new round of questioning. It continued for a long time, but eventually two names were mentioned in response to Fabian's probing. Both were in connection with the Bayswater raid.

The names were Jenkins and Geraghty.

The Yard man now believed the alibi he had been given by Charles Jenkins was one that could be broken if rigorously tested. He saw the Bayswater raid as a rehearsal for the raid on Jay's. Only the rehearsal had not included the intervention of a brave and public-spirited citizen named Alec de Antiquis.

Charles Jenkins was the next man brought to face fresh questions asked by Fabian at Tottenham Court Road police station. When he tried out the alibi again it broke down.

Fabian then asked Jenkins where he was at half-past two on 29 April. Jenkins tried to appear confident, but his act was far from convincing. He said he wasn't prepared to explain just then. This wasn't good enough for him to be released a second time. He found himself sitting on a bunk in a cell while Fabian's men set forth to round up Geraghty. They brought a cocky young man to Tottenham Court Road police station and Fabian had them take Geraghty for a walk past Jenkins's cell. When Geraghty saw Jenkins his step slowed and he stared at the face beyond the bars of the cell door as though he couldn't credit his eyes.

However, Geraghty did his best to keep a bold face to his

adversaries when his own questioning time began. He did not crack until he had been verbally manoeuvred by Fabian into a position where he had to lie or tell the truth, with no middle ground left where he could escape to safety. Jenkins had already admitted borrowing the raincoat found in the search at Brook House from his brother-in-law, but had said he had lent it to a friend. Fabian had insisted that he name this alleged friend, and in desperation Jenkins had given the name of the man who had also been named by the Southend fence, who had mentioned the names Jenkins and Geraghty to the police. It all had a bad smell in Fabian's nostrils, and the Yard man knew something unshared with Geraghty. This was that the named third man had admitted to tricking his other two partners in the Bayswater raid. He had got away with most of the proceeds, and so to Jenkins and Geraghty the robbery had been largely a failure. This might have been responsible for the raid on Jay's so soon afterwards. The pair had empty pockets.

Geraghty sensed that Fabian knew something unmentioned and guessed that someone had talked too much. So when Fabian asked who had shot down the motorcyclist Geraghty realized that a lie would be worse than useless and would go down on the record of any statement he made.

He said, "I didn't mean to kill him. I fired at him to frighten him."

It was the break Bob Fabian had worked for. Geraghty had come up with the hoary excuse of so many murderers who pretended they hadn't meant murder when they fired a gun and shot dead someone who was unarmed. But Fabian still wanted the name of the third partner in the Jay's raid. Having admitted to shooting Alec de Antiquis, Geraghty now named the other man in the trio. He was a youth of seventeen, who had been recruited to replace the man who had accompanied Jenkins and Geraghty on the Bayswater raid and later double-crossed them. Fabian had now in his possession the names of each of the trio who had invaded Jay's when masked and brandishing a firearm.

By this time Geraghty was in a desperate plight and

realized as much. It was his feeling of desperation that urged him to claim that the lad of seventeen was responsible for the shooting.

"If he hadn't panicked," he asserted, "there wouldn't have been any shooting."

Like various other statements he had heard recently, this didn't sound convincing to the Yard man.

Geraghty was put in a cell and the third member of the youthful gang was found and arrested. He was obviously scared and also intimidated by the speed with which retribution seemed likely to overtake him. He offered neither pretence nor excuse, but frankly admitted to being on the Jay's raid.

Fabian felt it was time to go back to the eldest member of the trio, Charles Jenkins. He was a more hardened young criminal, and when again confronted by Fabian refused to admit any participation in the raid or the shooting. He produced a nervous swagger and tried to act the tough guy.

"I'm no grass, copper," he is said to have sneered.

He maintained the same intransigent attitude when he duly appeared before the Marlborough Street magistrate some time later, on 20 May, and found himself remanded for trial at the Old Bailey. If Jenkins had his hopes buoyed up by the knowledge when he left Marlborough Street that the guns had not been found he was due to be disappointed and disillusioned within a few days.

The weapons had been tossed over the Thames Embankment instead of being thrown from a bridge to fall in mid-river. They were found by children playing on the foreshore of the river at low tide. The guns were sent for forensic and ballistics tests to Robert Churchill, who established that one was the weapon Geraghty claimed to have fired, which killed Alec de Antiquis, and the other was the gun that had fired the bullet found in the jeweller's shop.

At last Bob Fabian could relax, for the material he had would provide the Director of Public Prosecutions with a watertight case, proving the guilt of the three awaiting trial. The trial opened in July of that year before Mr Justice Hallett.

Like most trials of young men who have been charged with murder, it created a sensation, and for the first time the general public heard of the brilliant detective work undertaken by Bob Fabian and his chief assistant on the case, Robert Higgins, himself to become a detective superintendent before his retirement.

The story was told in court of how the three criminals had stolen pistols and ammunition from a gunsmith's near the Borough Underground station, bought tickets at Goodge Street station two days before they were required for a getaway, and how a mistaken interpretation by the youngest robber of a waved hand had precipitated disaster.

There was a piece of harsh irony in the case, as Robert Higgins pointed out later. At the time of the raid Geraghty was in employment. He had secured a job in a paint shop almost opposite Tottenham Court Road police station and on several occasions before his arrest he had watched from the shop's window the detectives arriving and leaving on an investigation he had thought would never find him. But when the Murder Squad team of Fabian and Higgins were sent in pursuit the odds had moved sharply against the criminals.

The Old Bailey jury found the defendants guilty, and Mr Justice Hallett duly sentenced the elder pair to death. Charles Henry Jenkins was twenty-three and the only one of the trio to go into the witness box, where he claimed his already exploded alibi before a dozen jurors who obviously did not believe him. Christopher James Geraghty, the actual killer of Alec de Antiquis, was two years younger. Terence Peter Rolt, who was little more than a boy, was sentenced to be detained during His Majesty's pleasure.

The next day a national newspaper declared, "No murder investigation of modern times has enhanced the reputation of Scotland Yard to a greater degree than the de Antiquis case."

It had been a special triumph for the Murder Squad team, and Robert Higgins has recorded that "During the twenty days that elapsed before we finally caught our men, Fabian and I were engrossed in our investigation day and night. Every other aspect of our lives went by the board. Our relentlessness gained us several official commendations, and during our inquiries the assistant commissioner, Mr Ronald Howe (later Sir Ronald), paid us a special visit to compliment us."

But there is another harsh piece of irony about the case. Annually the Metropolitan Police recommend to a member of the general public the Binney Medal for an outstanding piece of bravery in helping the police. In 1947 the medal was awarded posthumously to Alec de Antiquis, who left a widow and six orphans. The medal takes its name from Captain Ralph D. Binney who was killed when trying to prevent smash-and-grab raiders getting away three years earlier. He tried to intercept the raiders' car near London Bridge just after the raid. One of the raiders that afternoon on 8 December 1944 was named Thomas Jenkins, who had a brother named Charles Henry.

6

Serial Killer Investigations

Colin Wilson

Soviet psychology, no stranger to politicisation since the days of Stalin's purges and show trials, held that serial killers were a product of western capitalism's decadence; the effects of a culture of endless aspiration on the weaker, less self-possessed mind. As such, the orthodox view was that the Soviet Union did not produce them.

And yet, as the ever-reliable Colin Wilson details in the following extract, the police force of the Rostov Oblast did arrest one hapless suspect on the basis of a previous sex-crime conviction, who was eventually mistakenly executed for one of Andrei Chikatilo's killings, leaving the monster (no hyperbolic description of this unhappy, bullying cannibalistic wretch) free to kill again.

This was not the only way in which the investigation of Chikatilo was a profoundly frustrating blend of inspired surveillance work – which did eventually lead to his capture, this time for good – and official obtuseness that more than once let Chikatilo slip the net. Soviet cops, it would seem, were not in general of the more empathetic type portrayed in Martin Cruz Smith's novel *Gorky Park*.

Interrogation techniques that must have owed something to Moscow's Lubyanka prison produced false confessions from a number of youths with learning difficulties, while heavy-handed tactics led to the suicides of three gay men. Bodies, however, continued turning up.

That said, three episodes of methodical surveillance work led to the killer's capture. In September 1984, after Chikatilo's fifteenth killing of that year alone, he was observed by an undercover cop making serial attempts to lure young women away from a bus station in Rostov-on-Don. Sadly, on that occasion, he was released, despite being in possession of an abduction kit featuring ghoulishly incriminating contents such as rope and a knife. Viktor Burakov, a cop who had been involved in the case since 1982, hatched the masterful, systematic surveillance plan detailed in Wilson's extract, which was not implemented until October 1990. Using a combination of conspicuous, uniformed officers and a team working undercover in plain clothes, Burakov intended to drive the predatory Chikatilo towards train stations at which only the undercover teams were present – and it worked. Chikatilo was seen acting suspiciously at Donleskhoz station, scene of the killing of a young boy only ten days before the operation started, on 6 November. In fact, he had just killed a twenty-two-year-old woman but, sadly, was once again not picked up.

Nevertheless, the report of the incident, along with one in which Chikatilo had been observed with a young man who had later been found dead, did at least allow police to piece together his movements and ascertain that they dovetailed perfectly with the murders about which they knew. A further surveillance operation was mounted, this time on Chikatilo alone. On 20 November, six days after this observation began, he was observed attempting to pick up young people once again. If one of them broke off the conversation, he would move to the next. Plain-clothes police picked up Chikatilo, this time for keeps, as he left a café.

It is thought that Chikatilo may have been scarred by the stories and lore of cannibalism that arose during a childhood spent amidst the famine and devastation in the Ukraine caused by Stalin's collectivization of agriculture. The young Chikatilo had been told by his mother that his brother Stephen had been killed and cannibalized by starving neighbours. But such Freudian analyses, unqualified by the observation that not every Ukrainian who suffered such deprivation went on to become a serial killer, cannot be the whole story and are perhaps even a little insulting to those other survivors who did not go on to kill or maim. Chikatilo, like many serial murderers, found he was compulsively attracted to those weaker than himself – young women, or children of either sex – whether or not he knew this was the reason. But it would be ironic if, far from western decadence, it had been a Soviet great leap forward that had in fact woken the monster in Chikatilo.

In the autumn of 1990, a year before the dissolution of the Soviet Union, Ukrainian police were hunting a serial murderer who had been killing for at least ten years, and who was one of the worst sadists and sexual perverts in human history.

One of the main reasons the police found him so difficult to track down was the Soviet policy of giving little or no publicity to murder. While a wave of serial killings was taking place around Rostov-on-Don, the Soviet press continued to insist that Russia's crime rate was virtually nil. So Russian women or children who might otherwise have thought twice about accompanying a strange man to some lonely spot had no idea that they might be in danger.

To the police, the Rostov Ripper was known as the *lesopolosa* killer, or Forest Path Killer, because so many of the victims had been found in woodland. He killed children just as readily as adults, and boys as readily as girls. He preferred to pick up his victims on trains, or in public places such as bus stations, and then take them to some quiet place, where he strangled or stabbed them to death, performed horrific mutilations, and sometimes cooked and ate parts of the body.

As far as Major Mikhail Fetisov, the head of the Rostov CID, was concerned, the murders had begun on 12 June 1982, when a thirteen-year-old girl, Lyubov Biryuk, disappeared on her way home from an errand in the village of Donskol. Thirteen days later, her body – reduced to little more than a skeleton by the heat – had been found behind some bushes. She had been stabbed twenty-two times, and chips of bone missing from around the sockets suggested that the killer had even stabbed at her eyes. Her state of undress indicated a sex crime. Because Lyubov was the niece of a police lieutenant, the case aroused more attention than it might otherwise have done, and Fetisov investigated it personally. From the fact that the killer had taken such a risk – the main road was a few yards away – Fetisov deduced that he was driven by an overpowering sex urge, while the number of stab wounds indicated a sadist for whom stabbing was a form of sexual penetration.

Thirty-four-year-old Vladimir Pecheritsa, a convicted rapist, was hauled in for questioning – he had been at a nearby venereal clinic on the day of the murder. Russian interrogation techniques, developed by the secret police, were designed to extract a confession in the shortest possible time. But instead of confessing, Pecheritsa went away and hanged himself, the first of five men who would end their lives after becoming suspects.

With Pecheritsa's death, Fetisov hoped that the case was closed. But before 1982 was over, two adult female bodies – reduced to unidentifiable skeletons – were discovered lying in woodland near Rostov. Both victims had been stabbed repeatedly, and stab marks around the eyes made it clear that these killings were the work of the same person as the others – the Forest Path Killer. Fetisov organised a special squad of ten detectives to hunt the maniac. It would later develop that the Forest Path Killer had killed another four victims that year: Lyuba Volubuyeva, fourteen; Oleg Pozhidayev, nine; Olga Kuprina, sixteen; and Olga Stalmachenok, ten.

Many of the murders took place near the town of Shakhty, not far from Rostov. The newly formed "Red Ripper" unit therefore began by dispersing police over a wide area, hoping to come upon the murderer by chance.

During 1983, the Forest Path Killer kept up a steady pace of slaughter: 18 June, Laura Sarkisyan, fifteen; 8 August, Igor Gudkov, seven; 8 August, Irina Dunenkova, thirteen; and 27 December, Sergei Markov, fourteen. By the next year, however, the killer seemed to be butchering in a frenzy. On 9 January he killed seventeen-year-old Natalya Shalapinia. On 22 February he killed a forty-four-year-old vagrant named Marta Ryabyenko, in Rostov's Aviator Park. Ten-year-old Dmitri Ptashnikov was found near Novoshakhtinsk on 27 March. In early July, police found evidence of a double murder in woods near Shakhty – a woman whose skull had been smashed in, and a ten-year-old girl who had been beheaded. In late July, another woman's body as found in woods near Shakhty. On 3 August, it was a sixteen-year-old girl named Natalia Golosovskaya, found in Aviator Park; on 10 August, seventeen-year-old Lyudmila Alekseyeva, in woods near the Rostov beach; on 12 August, a thirteen-year-old boy named Dmitri Illaryonov, who had been castrated; on 26 August, an unidentified woman in woods 30 miles east of Rostov; on 2 September, eleven-year-old Aleksandr Chepel; on 7 September, twenty-five-year-old Irina Luchinskaya, again in Aviator Park. Twelve murders in eight months.

The police had one important clue. Semen found on the clothes of many of the victims revealed that the killer had blood type AB, the rarest blood group. Unfortunately, this clue would mislead investigators more disastrously than any other during the long investigation.

On a hot evening at the end of August 1984, Major Alexander Zanasovsky, one of the "murder squad" watching the Rostov bus station, spotted a tall, well-dressed man with a briefcase and thick glasses talking to a teenage girl. When she caught a bus, he moved on to another. Zanasovsky decided to ask the man to step into the police office on the station. There the grey-haired suspect produced his identification papers, which showed him to be Andrei Romanovich Chikatilo – not a typical Russian name. His credentials seemed to be impeccable: he was a graduate of the philological faculty of Rostov's university, a married man with two children, the head of the supply department of one of the city's main factories, and – most impressive of all – a member of the Communist Party. He explained that he lived in Shakhty, and was about to return home. He had once been a teacher, he said, and enjoyed talking to kids. His story sounded reasonable, and Zanasovsky let him go. The soft-spoken man certainly did not look like a serial killer.

Zanasovsky asked the girl if Chikatilo had tried to persuade her to go with him; she said no, he just asked her about her studies.

But when, two weeks later – on 13 August – Zanasovsky again spied Chikatilo approaching two teenaged girls in succession at the bus station, he decided that it might be worth following him. When Chikatilo boarded an airport bus, Zanasovsky was right behind him, together with a plainclothes colleague, and they watched him trying to catch the eye of female passengers. Two stops farther on, Chikatilo got off the bus and boarded another on the other side of the road. Here again he tried to engage female passengers in conversation – not with the irritating manner of a man looking for a pickup, but casually and kindly, as if he simply liked people. When he had no luck, he climbed on another bus. In two and a half hours he switched buses repeatedly, after which he tried to approach girls outside the Central Restaurant, and then sat on a park bench paying particular attention to female passers-by. At three in the morning, he was in the waiting room at the mainline railway station, attempting more pick-ups. Finally, when the station was almost deserted, he succeeded with a teenage girl in a tracksuit, who was lying on a bench trying to sleep. She seemed to agree to whatever he was proposing, and he removed his jacket, and placed it over her head as she lay in his lap. Movements under the jacket, and the expression on Chikatilo's face, revealed that she was performing oral sex on him. After that, at 5 a.m., Chikatilo took the first tram of the day, and got off in the central market. Zanasovsky decided it was time to make an arrest, and placed his hand on the man's shoulder. Chikatilo recognised him, and his face broke into sweat; but he made no protest when Zanasovsky told him that he would have to accompany him to the nearest police station.

There the contents of the briefcase seemed to justify Zanasovsky's belief that he had arrested the Forest Path Killer. It contained a kitchen knife with an eight-inch blade, a dirty towel, some rope, and a jar of Vaseline.

Chikatilo's story was that he had missed his bus to Shakhty and was merely killing time. The knife, he said, was to slice sausage and other comestibles. He also agreed to take a blood test.

Zanasovsky was amazed when the test showed Chikatilo to be innocent. His blood group was A, not AB as was the semen found in the bodies. He was held, nevertheless, on an unrelated charge relating to the theft of a roll of linoleum that had vanished when Chikatiko was in charge of supplies to a factory. Three months later, he was released.

The murders near Rostov had stopped, but when a woman's corpse was found with similar mutilations near Moscow, there was fear that the killer had moved there.

In fact, it soon became clear that the killer was still in the Rostov area when, on 28 August 1985, another mutilated corpse was found in the woods near Shakhty – an eighteen-year-old mentally retarded vagrant named Irina Gulyaeva.

In retrospect, her death was a turning point in the investigation. In Moscow, the authorities decided that the case must be solved at all costs. The murder team was increased substantially with additional detectives and legal experts. And a new man had to be placed in charge of the new "Killer Department". He was Inspector Issa Kostoyev, known as one of the best detectives in Russia. It was Kostoyev who finally had the satisfaction of hearing the confession of the Forest Path Killer.

At the start of Kostoyev's investigation, all was frustration. The murders ceased for almost two years. But between May 1987 and November 1990 the body count rose by at least eighteen. During that time, Fetisov and Buratov used their greatly increased manpower to keep a watch on railway stations, bus stations and trains. There was evidence that the killer had lured victims off trains at fairly remote stations – for example, two victims had been found in Donleskhoz, in the middle of a forestry commission area. Was there some method of persuading the Forest Path Killer to choose such a station, rather than Rostov or Shakhty? Suppose, for example, they placed uniformed policemen at all the large stations? Would that not encourage the killer to use the smaller ones?

The huge operation required 360 men, mostly placed prominently on large stations. But on three smaller stations – Donleskhoz, Kundryucha and Lesostep – there would only be a few discreet plain-clothes men.

On 12 November 1990, Fetisov reached a new low point in morale. Yet another body – this time of a young woman – had been found near Donleskhoz station, in spite of the plain-clothes surveillance. Her name was Svetlana Korostik, twenty-two, and she had been disembowelled; her tongue had also been removed. She had been dead about a week.

But, said the nervous and stammering plain-clothes man, they had been taking names of all middle-aged men on the station during that time. They had a pile of forms which they intended to send to Rostov very soon . . .

When the promised paperwork at last arrived, Fetisov ran his eye over the forms, noting the names. Suddenly, he stopped. He had seen this name before – Andrei Romanovich Chikatilo. He turned to Burakov. "Have you ever heard of this man?" Burakov had. He recalled that Fetisov had been on holiday when Chikatilo was arrested in 1984. Now he was able to tell his superior that Chikatilo had been cleared because he was of the wrong blood type.

But Fetisov then recalled an interesting piece of information issued to all law enforcement agencies from the Ministry of Health in 1988: police should no longer assume that a sex criminal's blood type was the same type as his semen. Rare cases had been found of men whose blood and semen types differed. Both Fetisov and Burakov felt that Chikatilo had to be the man they were looking for. The first step was to find his address. It seemed that he no longer lived in Shakhty, but in Novocherkassk, and that he worked in a locomotive repair works in Rostov.

The entire investigation now focused on Chikatilo.

Fetisov learned that his job had once allowed him to travel widely, and that this was the period when victims were found over a wide area. When his job confined him to the Rostov area, the victims were found there. As a schoolteacher, he had been dismissed for child molesting. He had been dismissed from the Communist Party. And while he had been in prison for three months in 1984, the murders had stopped abruptly.

Now that they were almost certain, it was tempting to shadow him and try to catch him in the act. But that entailed the obvious risk that he might kill before the tail could stop him. It would be safer to place him under arrest. Kostoyev, told of this development, agreed. He also agreed to allow Fetisov to conduct the preliminary interview.

At 3.40 on the afternoon of 20 November 1990, three plain-clothes men in an unmarked car drove to Novocherkassk, and waited at a point where – they knew from the surveillance team – Chikatilo would soon be passing. In fact, Chikatilo halted outside a café. The policemen approached him, and one asked his name. "Andrei Chikatilo." "You're under arrest." Without speaking, Chikatilo held out his wrists for the handcuffs.

The man who was brought into Mikhail Fetisov's office did not look like a mass murderer. He was tall – about six feet – and thin, although obviously muscular, and his face had a worn and exhausted look. He wore glasses and certainly looked "respectable". His shoulders were stooped, and he walked with a shuffle, like an old man. The only sign of degeneracy was the mouth, with its loose, sagging corners, suggesting a weak character.

Chikatilo was subdued and politely uncooperative. He never looked Kostoyev in the eye. At first all he would say was that he had been arrested for the same crimes before, and had been released as innocent.

But Kostoyev had received a piece of information that left him in no doubt that Chikatilo was the Forest Path Killer. Comparison of his blood type and his semen – he had been masturbating behind a newspaper in his cell and left traces on his underpants – revealed that he was indeed one of those rare males who blood type differs from his semen. His blood type was A, his semen AB – like the killer's.

At the third interrogation, Kostoyev spoke to him kindly, and asked about childhood problems. Suddenly, Chikatilo asked if he could write a statement. In this, he spoke of having deranged sexual feelings, and "committing certain acts". The remainder consisted of self-pitying complaints about how he had felt degraded since schooldays, how everyone jeered at him, and how later employers had treated him with contempt. His "perverted sex acts", he said, were an expression of his fury at all this mistreatment. "I could not control my actions."

The next day, all the ground seemed to be lost as Chikatilo went back to fencing and evasions.

Time was running out. They had ten days to question a suspect before charging him, and this allotment was nearly up. Chikatilo did not take well to Kostoyev's approach – the approach of a top Soviet official who is accustomed to authority. And as it became clear that the ten days would not bring the confession they expected, Buratov made a suggestion – that Kostoyev should give way to someone with a "softer" approach. A local psychiatrist, Alexander Bukhanovsky, had already written his own detailed psychological portrait of the Forest Path Killer. He was now called in, and his more sympathetic approach soon produced results. As Bukhanovsky read his own words aloud, Chikatilo listened with a silence that had ceased to be hostile or noncommittal, and was obviously moved by the psychiatrist's insights into the lifetime of humiliation and disaster that had turned him into a killer. Soon he was holding back tears. Next he was telling the story of his life as if he was lying on a couch. Towards evening, he suddenly confessed to his first murder.

It was not, as Bukhanovsky had expected, that of Lyuba Biryuk in 1982, but of a nine-year-old child named Lena Zakotnova, and it had taken place four years earlier, in 1978. In that year, Chikatilo explained, he had bought a dacha – hardly more than a wooden hut – at the far end of Shakhty.

Three days before Christmas 1978, when night had already fallen, he saw a pretty little girl dressed in a red coat with a furry collar and a rabbit-fur hat standing at a tram stop. He asked her where she had been until such a late hour, and she explained she had gone to see a friend after school. As they talked, she found his friendly manner irresistible, and was soon admitting that she badly needed to find a toilet. Chikatilo told her that he lived just around the corner, and invited her to use his.

Inside the hut, he hurled her onto the floor, and with his hand over her mouth, tore at her clothes. His intention was rape, but he was unable to summon an erection. He ruptured her hymen with his finger – and immediately achieved a violent orgasm at the sight of the blood.

It was, he admitted to Bukhanovsky, a revelation. Now he suddenly understood: he needed to see blood to achieve maximum excitement. Still gripped by sexual fever, he took out a folding knife, and began to stab the screaming child in the stomach. It was then that he discovered something else about himself – that stabbing with a knife brought an even greater delight than normal sexual penetration.

He carried the girl's body and her clothes to the river, and hurled them in. They drifted under a bridge and were not found for two days.

Chikatilo was an immediate suspect. He was taken in for questioning nine times. Then he had an incredible piece of luck. Not far from his shack lived twenty-five-year-old Alexander Kravchenko, who had served six years in prison for a rape-murder in the Crimea. The police transferred their attention to Kravchenko, "interrogated" him, and soon obtained a "confession". Kravchenko was executed – by a pistol shot in the back of the head – in 1984.

From then on, Chikatilo admitted, he knew that his deepest sexual satisfaction could only come from stabbing and the sight of blood. But the unpleasant memories of the police interrogations made him cautious, and for almost three years he kept out of trouble. Meanwhile, he had been made redundant as a schoolteacher, and begun working as a supply clerk in Shakhty. This involved travelling all over the country, and offered him new opportunities. On 3 September 1981, he fell into conversation with a seventeen-year-old girl, Larisa Tkachenko, at a bus stop in Rostov. She was his favourite kind of pickup – a rebellious school dropout with a taste for vodka, and would offer sex in exchange for a meal. She agreed to accompany him to a local recreation area. There his control snapped. He hurled her to the ground, bludgeoned her with his fists, rammed earth into her mouth to stop her screams, and then strangled her. After that, he bit off her nipples and ejaculated on the naked body. Then he ran around the corpse, howling with joy, and waving her clothes. It was half an hour before he hid the body under branches.

And now he had crossed a kind of mental Rubicon.

He knew he was destined to kill for sexual enjoyment. Before he had finished, Chikatilo had confessed to fifty-three murders – a dozen more than anyone had suspected. He never admitted to cannibalism, although the fact that he took cooking equipment with him on his "hunting expeditions" leaves little doubt of it.

In mid-December 1990, the Russian public finally learned that the Forest Path Killer had been caught when Kostoyev called a press conference. Before the coming of Gorbachev and glasnost, the news would have been kept secret. Now this horrific story of a Russian Jack the Ripper quickly made headlines all around the world. This was the world's first intimation that the Soviet Union was not as crime-free as communist propaganda had insisted.

The trial of Andrei Chikatilo began in the Rostov courthouse on 14 April 1992. In any other country but Russia, it would have been regarded as a circus rather than an administration of justice. In any Western country, its conduct would certainly have formed grounds for an appeal that would have led to a second trial, and even possibly overturned the verdict.

Chikatilo, his head shaved and wearing a 1982 Olympics shirt, was placed in a large cage, to protect him from attacks by the public. This was a real possibility, since the court was packed with angry relatives, who frequently interrupted the proceedings with screams of "Bastard!", "Murderer!", "Sadist!"

Chikatilo confessed to all the crimes except the very first, that of the murder of Lena Zakhotnova. Kostoyev had no doubt that this was because pressure had been brought to bear; he had actually succeeded in obtaining a posthumous pardon for the executed murderer, Kravchenko, but the legal authorities obviously felt that it would be better to let sleeping dogs lie.

On 14 October 1982, as Chikatilo received individual sentences for fifty-two murders, the court was filled with shrieks that often drowned out the judge's voice.

Sixteen months later, on 14 February 1994, Andrei Chikatilo was executed by a single shot in the back of the neck, fired from a small-calibre Makarov pistol.

PART 2

HEAVY MANNERS: Tackling corruption in the UK and USA

Another Brick in the Law: Met. Detective Sergeant Challenor, Building Up Evidence

Chris Barber

When cops break the rules, it may not always be a case of corruptibility, they may also be acting out of an excess of zeal, a different kind of character flaw altogether in which they're convinced of the rightness of their own actions. Plain-clothes detective "Tanky" Challoner was just such a man, but it may be a little kind to say that he lost his grip, his perspective, merely. Despite Challoner's own insanity defence, war record and social status he was, quite simply, bad to the bone.

To paraphrase the old graffiti'd joke – with Challoner about, you didn't have to go to a tailor to get fitted up. In fact, Challoner at one point fitted up a tailor himself. In his stand-ard issue brown raincoat, he "ran" 1960s Soho as firmly as any gang leader in an Italian suit. His patch was his turf. But whereas a gang leader is sadistic as a means to an end, even if, like Reggie Kray, they're not exactly averse to the cuttings, shivings and terror brought about, Challoner's bullying was an end in itself. He was a not-for-profit inducer of anguish, in the service of the Crown, as he saw it, and his own sadistic nature.

As Chris Barber's essay outlines, Challoner's image in the press gave us the social stereotype of the corrupt, plain-clothes cop of the period, an apposite place to begin any talk of bad cops. To discuss police corruption is not to seek to make especially political or partisan points. We need "the thin blue line". But there's good and bad in every institution. Cops are only human. For all the derring-do and the Dixons of Dock Green, there's bound to be a few Inspector Knackers. Their presence can only, in the long term, increase social alienation. Which makes them a threat to law and order in themselves.

> *CHALLENOR: You're fucking nicked, me old beauty . . . Don't say please to me, my old darling.*
>
> 11 July 1963

> *TRUSCOTT: You're fucking nicked, me old beauty. You've found to your cost that the standards of the British police force are as high as ever.*
>
> Loot by Joe Orton, 1966

Detective Sergeant (Second Class) Harold "Tanky" Challenor, of West End Central (Savile Row) constabulary, was something of a local hero around his home turf – London's Soho, in the early 1960s. The press frequently applauded his vigilant crusade against crime in lurid headlines. His superiors and colleagues in the Met admired his record-breaking number of arrests and convictions. The judiciary praised his courtroom banter, homespun rapport, and ability to cajole juries. None forgot his distinguished war record, tactically gained behind enemy lines with the SAS. No one questioned the methods he employed to achieve his extraordinary success. When circumstances finally conspired, forcing the government to examine Challenor's unique policing methods, a dozen innocent people were pardoned and released from prison. Parliament demanded public inquiries, policemen were jailed, and the Establishment closed ranks; while Challenor ended up in the madhouse – at Her Majesty's pleasure.

The Challenor case represents either a landmark or watershed in the annals of British justice. Yet the scandal that brought about Challenor's demise was only the tip of the iceberg. Challenor's wartime exploits earned him the nick-name Tanky (of tank corps). Unfortunately for Tanky, his real name inspired the pejorative colloquialism "doing a Challenor" – Metropolitan Police slang for taking bribes or acting mad to avoid prison. Whether Tanky "did a Challenor" among his many misdemeanours remains contentious. Allegations were made but dismissed by official inquiry – or cover-up. Basically, Challenor earned his reputation as a super crime-stopper by planting weapons on suspects to secure convictions where real evidence was lacking; he also routinely beat up and intimidated suspects. But he finally blundered when he planted a weapon on Donald Rooum, a member of the National Council for Civil Liberties (NCCL, now Liberty). Playwright Joe Orton based his "nasty cop" character, Truscott, on Challenor in his West End stage hit *Loot*. Another Tanky eccentricity was his persecution complex, inspiring him to compare himself to Oscar Wilde!

CASE ONE: GANG WARFARE
(Pedrini, Oliva, Ford, Fraser, Cheeseman)

On the evening of 21 September 1962, twenty-two-year-old Riccardo Pedrini left his parents' house in Bloomsbury to meet his mates for a drink in the West End. Riccardo had grown up locally and worked in the family-owned restaurant.

He met Alan Cheeseman (a fellow homeboy, aged twenty) in the Lorraine Club/Bar, and danced with another friend, Josephine Jennings. Other pals arrived later. At 11 p.m, Riccardo and Alan left the club with four acquaintances. They strolled along Old Compton Street, seeking fast food and cabs home. As they passed the Phoenix Club (strip joint), Riccardo and Alan lagged behind.

Suddenly two cops burst out from the shadows, grabbing Pedrini and Cheeseman. The other lads were nowhere to be seen as the bewildered friends were piled into a police van that sped off to West End Central police station. Duty PCs Legge and Wells were accompanied by Phoenix Club propri-etor Wilfred Gardiner, who had pointed them out to police.

Upon arriving at the station they were dragged into the charge room and ordered to empty their pockets on to the desk. "Why did you bring us here?" Cheeseman asked.

"You'll find out soon enough," replied Legge, grinning. A well-built, clean-cut, plain-clothed man with dark hair appeared from the corridor, arrogantly smirking with over-bearing authority. His name: Detective Sergeant Challenor.

"Do you know Oliva?" he demanded menacingly.

"No," says Cheeseman.

Pow! Challenor whacks him in the face, ranting frantically about protection rackets. "You know what I'm talking about. Don't go to sleep, my darling. I'm coming back!" He marches off, leaving Cheeseman speechless with shock.

Moments later, Challenor returns, now clutching handfuls of dangerous weapons. He drops an iron bar on Pedrini's property (on the desk), and a flick-knife on to Cheeseman's bits 'n' bobs. "Sign for it, it's yours . . . better for you if you make a statement." An adjoining cell door is flung open and Pedrini staggers out, his nose bleeding profusely.

Both prisoners are charged with possessing offensive weapons (despite their strenuous denials). They are held overnight and, next morning, they're joined in the cells by Johnnie Ford – one of their acquaintances the night before – who was arrested on Shaftesbury Avenue. Another inspector was on duty when he was brought in, so Ford was only charged with demanding money with menaces. Not until three o'clock the following afternoon does any cop bother to inform their parents of the arrests.

A couple of days later, Joseph Oliva was nicked by Challenor and PCs Jay and Laing. As Oliva was dragged from his car, Challenor searched it. According to the arrest-ing officers, Oliva was carrying a knife and a home-made petrol bomb, both of which were discovered in his car. Initially Oliva maintained both weapons were planted by cops but, fearing this wouldn't stand up in court, he later claimed the knife was dropped by a friend, but insisted that Challenor had brought the bomb.

Johnnie Ford lived next door to the Pedrinis and was

casually acquainted with the whole family. Ford was engaged in a long-running feud with Gardiner (the Phoenix Club owner) that started when Ford applied for a bar job at the Phoenix and Gardiner refused to employ him. They were also in dispute over a girl working in the club. Whenever Ford and friends (Joseph Oliva and James Fraser) passed Gardiner's clubs, there was much macho posturing and taunting between Ford and Gardiner, which sometimes led to scuffles. In one incident, Gardiner's car was damaged, threats were exchanged, and both sides called the police. Another time, Ford wanted to press charges against Gardiner. The police escorted all parties to Savile Row but, en route, Gardiner (a police snitch, according to "Mad" Frankie Fraser) harangued Ford, causing him to withdraw the charges.

Gardiner claimed the final "gang member" was James Fraser. He was arrested, searched and charged, apparently in possession of a razor; again, he began insisting it was a police set-up, but bottled out in court.

On 6 December 1962, "the gang of five" appeared in court together, charged with conspiring to obtain money with menaces. Further, Fraser, Pedrini and Cheeseman were charged with actually demanding money. Four of the five men were also charged with possessing offensive weapons. The trial lasted two weeks at the Old Bailey.

Challenor was in his element for his court appearance, conjuring up his Soho beat as a twilight world of warring mafias, sexual degenerates and drug-crazed, spiv street gangs. Judge, jury and the media must have known better but chose to applaud Challenor's immaculate performance, accepting his vivid accounts as gospel. The prosecution case rested solely on evidence from Challenor, Gardiner (who presiding Judge Maude referred to as "a ponce") and Gardiner's mistress, Elizabeth Evans. Gardiner claimed the Ford gang regularly threatened him in the street, and that Pedrini sliced his ear with a knife on the night of their arrest. In his defence, Pedrini's dance partner (on that night) testified he wasn't carrying a weapon when they smooched.

The verdict is guilty. Fraser is sentenced to fifteen months (for the lesser offence), while of the other four, for possessing weapons and demanding money with menaces, Pedrini gets seven years; Cheesmen, three years; Oliva and Ford each take five years' incarceration.

WHO DARES WINS

Harry Gordon Challenor was born on 16 March 1922 in a slum district of Bradley, Staffordshire. His father was, "not to put too finer point on it, a bastard – a mean, cruel sadistic tyrant who terrorized his family", prepared to take a swing at his wife or son, whenever the mood took him. In his memoirs, Harold admits to nurturing a deep-seated hatred of his old man. His schooling was elementary and Harold took jobs as a male nurse, lorry driver and motor mechanic before turning twenty, when he enlisted in the army. He soon distinguished himself as a model soldier, winning selection to the SAS (Special Air Services).

During the war, Challenor was part of an elite commando force parachuting behind German and Italian lines on clandestine sabotage missions. He was renowned for his tactical ability and camaraderie when in the firing line. But, eventually, a mission into Italy went wrong, leaving Challenor a lone survivor. He was captured and tortured, but engineered his escape. Linking up with the Italian partisan resistance, Challenor was in his element, vigilantly charging around incognito, blowing up troop trains and wrecking enemy communications. Upon returning, he achieved the rank of company quartermaster sergeant and was awarded the Military Medal.

After leaving the army he joined the Flying Squad and, following several years' service, was promoted to Detective Sergeant Second Class and appointed to West End Central police station in 1962. One of his duties was to select, subordinate and train young PCs as potential tyro detectives.

CASE TWO: 'ELLO, 'ELLO, 'ELLO . . .
(Wallace Gold)

Wallace Gold had a small dairy outlet in Soho and rented out an unused room over his shop. On 1 November 1962, Challenor appeared on his doorstep, asking after a tenant. Gold invited him in but Challenor eyed Gold suspiciously, referring to him as "my old fruit". It transpired that Gold's tenant had been involved in a recent heist of cigarette lighters. Challenor was shown the rented room, invited to search it, and allowed to wander freely around Gold's own rooms. Tanky instigated two prolonged searches of the building, without Gold objecting. Bingo! In the tenant's chamber, Tanky finds a crate of the stolen lighters. He then wanders up to Gold's rooms, and is noted twiddling with a pack of Gold's cigarettes on the sideboard. Then he wanders out without saying a word. Next thing, Challenor's back, straight over to Gold's sideboard and "'ELLO', 'ELLO, 'ELLO, what's all this then?" From Gold's fag packet, Tanky produces one of the lighters.

Gold is nicked and interrogated in custody for several hours before being allowed to phone a solicitor – by which time it is 8 p.m. and too late. When he finally sees a solicitor after a night in cells, Gold protests his innocence. The solicitor tells him the court will not believe him and he should plead guilty, for a lenient sentence. Eventually Gold agrees, appearing at London Sessions in January 1963, and receiving nine months for handling stolen goods. Incidentally, later that day, Challenor escorted the tenant into the same court, where he owned up to purloining the lighters, without implicating Gold. Double whammy – Tanky gets the real thief knocked up as well!

Rumour has it that Challenor suspected Gold knew more about the lighter theft than he was telling. So Tanky decided to teach him a lesson.

COP DRAG ACT

Challenor was a workaholic and determined to top his military achievements with vigilant and unorthodox policing methods:

> *On one occasion he persuaded a small-time crook to take him to a criminal's pub so that working villains could be pointed out to him. Since the man was not prepared to be seen with a policeman, Challenor got hold of a woman's wig, borrowed one of Dorris's [his wife's] longest skirts, a roll-neck sweater, high-heeled shoes, nylon stockings and a cloak-like coat and handbag. Heavily made-up, he sat nursing his gin and tonic while the villain nodded at the professional heisters and hoisters present. Challenor's cover was nearly blown when he entered the gents by mistake and told a startled drinker: "I've recently had a miscarriage and must still be a bit light-headed." He was even propositioned and rescued by his "boyfriend" for the night, who kept up the deception and called him a "silly old cow".*
>
> *The Underworld* by Duncan Campbell

After such excursions, Tanky sounds like a jovial eccentric. But from his earliest days at Savile Row, he *weren't acting right*! He lived with his wife in the Kent countryside – and every night after work in the West End, he insisted on walking home. Further, he frequently complained of deafness in one ear (usually as an excuse for his spoilt-child-like temper rages, which frequently intimidated suspects).

CASE THREE: GAMBLING WITH THE LAW
(Lionel King and David Silver)

Challenor had enjoyed the media limelight of being portrayed in the press as London's top gangbuster, a self-styled Eliot Ness, leading The Untouchables. But by 25 April 1963, the attention was fading, so Tanky arrested Lionel King – an employee of a Soho gambling chain – along with David Silver, a friend of King's, who happened to be in his car when Challenor pounced.

Sometime prior to King's arrest, Challenor had approached him to become a police informer, hoping to cash in on King's rapport with notorious Soho villains who used his bookmaking service. King laughed at Tanky, and declined. Challenor was furious at his rejection and flew into a rage, promising King trouble. When King parked up, Tanky was waiting with PCs Jay and Etheridge, who pulled the driver and passenger aside for questioning, while Challenor suspiciously fumbled with the car-seat cushions . . . Surprise! His efforts uncover explosive detonators, hidden under a cushion.

Both King and Silver were charged with possession of offensive weapons. The only prosecution witnesses at the trial were three corroborating police officers, but the case hit the headlines shortly after a series of gang-related explosions hit Soho's bookmakers, arousing the public's fascination in gangland wars. The defence claimed the detonators were planted, but the jury decided the suspects were guilty. King got a two-year prison sentence, and Silver six months.

CRAZY HARRY CONTRA MONDEM!

"Your Uncle Harry . . ." was Challenor's preferred introduction to prisoners. When it came to interrogating suspects, Challenor played good cop and bad cop, a one-man show, oscillating between intimidation and rapport, usually addressing his prisoners as "my old beauty" or "my darling".

He developed his own concept of justice and methods of detection. This involved ignoring the traditional system of following up crime reports in favour of getting out and searching for culprits. Having selected and arrested his villain, he would return to HQ, where he'd amassed an impressive selection of weapons (in his drawer or locker), one for every occasion. These were dropped in front of prisoners with his customary punchline, "That's yours, sign for it."

In his memoirs, *Tanky Challenor*, he recounts:

> *I arrested more criminals in my period of service than any other officer. None of it was accomplished by unlawful acts, but*

by the cultivation and use of informants. They trusted me and knew I would never let them down. The men of violence were my target.

But he admits:

I think it was Wilde who said that all men kill the thing they love, and I certainly did that ... I accept that my illness may have resulted in me approaching my work with a crusading zeal ... If I feel an attack coming on I take my pills ...

CASE FOUR (and more):
THE RIGHT TO REMAIN SILENT
(Ernest Pink, Robert Brown, Frederick Bridgeman, William Francis and friends)

These four were arrested at Soho's Establishment Club on 25 May 1963 and charged with the usual – possessing offensive weapons. Pink was deaf and dumb, and Brown was deaf. All four of them tried to join a Soho club and were admitted by the doorman. When it was realised they weren't members, someone panicked and called the cops to eject them. Tanky was there in a flash, accompanied by a dozen officers, catching the four lads on the stairs. Challenor would claim in court that he confronted Pink, ordering him to take his friends outside. Pink apparently ignored the instruction and made "offensive signs with his hands". So, under Challenor's orders, the boys in blue returned "offensive signs" with their boots. Dragged into the street, the four were searched and, low and behold, Pink was carrying a razor, Brown had a flick-knife, Bridgeman possessed a stiletto, and Francis was concealing a hatchet. All denied possessing weapons and all the prosecution witnesses were cops – six of them. Quite why none of the gang had used the weapons during the struggle was not considered at the Old Bailey. Pink (the only one with a previous criminal record) got three years, the other three each got one year.

During their preliminary hearing at Marlborough Magistrate's Court, four of Pink's pals turned up to offer moral support. Braggins, Matthews, Ireland and Steel were also deaf. During proceedings, Challenor noticed them in court and claimed they were making "threatening signs". So they were nicked and charged with conspiring to pervert the course of justice. All were refused bail. Steel got sixteen days, Braggins and Matthews got seventeen days a piece, while Ireland landed three weeks inside.

BLOWING THE WHISTLE ON TANKY

Gangland Soho may well have offered Challenor an ideal location to appeal to the public imagination with his creative embellishments. The metropolitan public – even judges and magistrates – who piled into Soho to chill out on jazz, eat in the world's finest restaurants, or be seduced by spectacular stage shows, were either lacking brain cells or knew, deep-down, that the sleazy porn merchants and gangland gamblers only represented a tiny contingent in the bohemian heartland. But that actuality was too obtuse; people wanted Soho to evoke danger and excitement, a subterranean criminal empire. So they chose to patronize Challenor's sense of drama. Thus it was Challenor and his crime-busting cohorts in the Met who were believed in court; not the numerous young, sometimes foreign and usually working-class lads, who insisted they were set up. But Challenor was about to utilize his tried and tested methods in an alternative setting – a political demonstration – and his first victim was going to blow the whistle on his unorthodox approach to policing.

CASE FIVE: BRIC-A-BRAC
(Donald Rooum, John Apostolou,
Ranald Ede, Gregory Hill)

In July 1963, Her Royal Majesty Queen Frederika of Greece hit London on a high-profile state visit. Greece was seen as a very dodgy place at that time: authoritarian, autocratic, corrupt, oppressive . . . In particular, its police force largely comprised corrupt, neo-fascist thugs, employing violence to control and coerce the poverty-stricken majority of citizens. Human rights were dirty words; trade unionists, democrats and social reformists frequently "disappeared" or had accidents in police custody. Many Greeks had split, preferring to live in exile in other European democracies – including London (renowned for its justice, fairness and honourable police force!).

So when a Greek head of state was welcomed in the UK, she was pursued by hordes of demonstrators protesting against everything she represented. Her presence at Claridges Hotel on 11 July attracted a large crowd of protestors, essentially peaceful, but shouting insults, waving banners and creating a harmless nuisance in the surrounding streets. One of these people was Donald Rooum, a professional cartoonist and NCCL/Liberty activist.

The police were out in force, intent on preventing protestors from expressing themselves in the royal presence. Extra officers had been drafted in for duty with nice overtime bonuses. Among them was Detective Sergeant Challenor, posted with three other detectives to keep an eye out for rambunctious protestors. Being an arch-royalist, Challenor regarded protest against a queen as a personal affront. He hadn't a clue about Greek politics and clandestine police agendas; he didn't need to, he had his own programme and tactics.

Rooum certainly wasn't an obstreperous demonstrator; he held back by the police line, quietly clutching his home-made paper banner, which read "LAMBRAKIS RIP". Suddenly, four plain-clothes cops were upon him, snatching his banner. "Can I have my banner back?" he asked politely.

"You're fucking nicked, my old beauty," replied the officer in charge, as Rooum was grabbed by the collar and jostled into a parked van. Back at West End Central, Rooum was escorted upstairs with clouts to his ear and was knocked to the floor, then frogmarched into the detention room, where Challenor continued to assault and insult him. Next,

Challenor produced a package from his own pocket, wrapped in crumpled newspaper. Unwrapped, it revealed a piece of brick.

Meanwhile, Challenor was having a field day, returning sharpish to the demo and nicking a few more "beauties" before the day was out – including two minors (under sixteen) whom he kindly provided with a bit of brick each. John Apostolou was arrested first, then two juveniles together, Ranald Ede and Gregory Hill.

All four were charged with possessing offensive weapons (bits of brick, supposedly to chuck at the royal). Each strenuously denied the charge from the start, claiming they were fitted up at the police station. The PCs assisting Challenor making the arrests were Baites, Oakey and Goldsmith. The same officers also arrested another four suspects – another (unnamed) juvenile, Colin Derwin, and John and Ronald Ryall. (Likewise they were charged with possessing bits of brick, which they maintained were planted by the cops.)

Poor Ede and Hill, it really wasn't their day. They had nothing to do with the demonstration when they were arrested. They were playing tennis that afternoon, and their family homes happened to be near Claridges. They were surprised to find police roadblocks halting their usual short cut home but, rather than taking a longer route, they decided to try to pass the police cordon with a group of protestors; not that such incidental details ever bothered Challenor in the course of his duties. Because they were under sixteen, they faced proceedings in a juvenile court (and the press was prohibited from revealing their names, adding to confusion) when Challenor's exploits hit the media, prior to completion of their hearing. Just as well, because after preparing a vindictive case against them, the prosecution advocated its intention not to pursue it.

Despite Challenor's excessive physical and psychological violence while interrogating Rooum, the cartoonist refused to sign a statement claiming the brick was his. For once, Challenor's punishment (or accidental oversight) meted out to the suspect turned out to be a blessing in disguise. Challenor neglected to bail Rooum, leaving him to spend the night in a cell. When Rooum was finally allowed a phone call, he rang his wife, who promptly contacted the NCCL, ensuring a top-notch solicitor appeared at the cells next morning to represent him. Mr Stanley Clinton Davis sorted bail at £10, escorting his client from police custody and immediately insisting on a change of clothes, taking possession of Rooum's suit, worn since the demo. Davis then phoned the Metropolitan Police forensic laboratory, asking them to test the suit for brick dust. (It's rare, but not unheard of, for police forensic scientists to prepare evidence for defence cases.) But Davis had second thoughts, realizing that Challenor would have to take the suit to the lab himself. Instead, Davis carried the clothes to an independent laboratory.

This attention to detail established an airtight alibi and cast-iron defence case. When Rooum's barrister, Mr Michael Sherrard, was briefed, he had the crucial results of a rigorous scientific analysis of Rooum's clothes on the day of his arrest. The report concluded Rooum could not possibly have been carrying the said brick bit in that suit pocket without it crumbling and leaving dust traces. But there were no such traces. What's more, the scientist – Mr K. F. Kayser – realized that the type of brick concerned (from Marston Valley Brickworks, trade dealers) would necessarily strain the suit-pocket lining, causing scratches in the material. There were absolutely no such signs in the pocket, nor brick grains or fibres. Further (as Kayser would later testify at the trial), dust particles he retrieved showed it was not possible that any dust had recently been removed or any attempt made to clean the garment.

Rooum had an advantage over Challenor's preceding victims: he was a middle-class professional and well connected with the NCCL. The circumstances of Rooum's case were coincidentally fortuitous for the NCCL, because Challenor's activities had already reached their attention. Friends and relatives of prisoners, who maintained their innocence against

Challenor's evidence, had contacted the organization for help. Despite NCCL's attempts to have these cases reviewed, the Home Office consistently declined to take action, claiming insufficient evidence. Here was the opportunity Liberty had waited for.

Rooum's hearing was set for 19 July. However, Challenor was conspicuously absent from court, forcing the prosecution to ask for a recess (Challenor being the main prosecution witness). The magistrate complied, scheduling the case to be resumed on 8 August. While leaving the court, Rooum's disappointed council bumped into Challenor, heading for another case. They pleaded with him to visit the magistrate and ask him to resume the case immediately. Challenor became agitated, refusing outright to cooperate.

Three weeks later, Rooum's case resumed at Marlborough Magistrate's Court, with Kayser giving defence evidence as an independent forensic scientist. As a further precaution, the defence put Challenor through a gruelling cross-examination. But the finest defence stunt was held back for their summing up. In a spectacular display of courtroom drama, which outmatched any of Challenor's dramatic tirades, the defence produced before the court two further lumps of brick: one being the prosecution evidence from Ede's case; the second was apparently found in Hill's possession. These were placed alongside the brick supposedly from Rooum's pocket. Hoop-la! The three separate lumps matched together exactly, producing the complete brick.

The magistrate, Mr Robey, surveyed his courtroom while fumbling with the brick bits, noting the incontrovertible fact of their crumbling in his hands at the slightest touch. "Not guilty, case dismissed!"

Mr Robey went on to refuse Rooum costs for expenses. What's more, he later presided over John Apostolou's case, facing the same charge and based on evidence of the same Detective Sergeant, in the same court, with almost the same brick bit as the prosecution's evidence. And Robey found Apostolou guilty as charged, fining him £10.

DOING A CHALLENOR

After August 1963, the repercussions of Rooum's brick case (and seven other Challenor "brick bit" arrests from the protest) were finally attracting attention and embarrassing the Home Office. The NCCL pursued other unsound convictions pertaining to Tanky, and Rooum claimed damages. The media were asking questions. Police from outside Challenor's jurisdiction were ordered in to investigate. Tanky was given sick leave from September and, weeks later, suspended from duty. Yet he continued to drop into the police station and frequent his usual Soho haunts – doubtless returning to the scenes of his crimes! In December, believing himself to be invincible, he apparently leapt out in front of a moving vehicle (with no serious injury).

Eventually, crown prosecutor Mr John Mathew prepared a case against Challenor and his cohorts, PCs David Oakey, Frank Battes and Keith Goldsmith (who were under Challenor's charge). The charge was all too familiar to Tanky: conspiring to pervert the course of justice, specifically regarding the eight brick-bit busts. Proceedings started in March 1964 at Marlborough Street Magistrate's Court. Tanky had regularly appeared there in the witness box. Now he was in the dock, facing his former magistrate/fan, Mr Robey.

Rooum was called as a prosecution witness – despite his protestations that, on principle, he did not want to help send anyone to jail (regardless of what Challenor had done to him). Now the pressure was mounting on Challenor, who collapsed during proceedings and was escorted from the courtroom by a doctor. When the case resumed, all four cops were sent to the Old Bailey.

Come May, Challenor was still considered unfit to appear, so Mr Justice Lawton granted the prosecution request for a medical examination. When sessions resumed on 4 June, Dr William Calder testified that Challenor was mentally unfit to stand trial, backed by an independent doctor. Doctors claimed Challenor was a paranoid schizophrenic, and had been mentally unstable and potentially dangerous for some time. Tanky was sent to a mental hospital for treatment, held at Her Majesty's pleasure.

Police officers coined the expression "doing a Challenor", henceforth used to refer to bent coppers. PCs Oakey and Goldsmith were each banged up for four years (reduced to three on appeal) and Battes got three years.

It was alleged that Challenor took bribes. Although not substantiated by investigation, it was not rigorously refused. Cheeseman's father claims he paid Tanky £50 for not opposing his son's bail. Apparently Challenor later phoned papa Cheeseman, demanding another £50; this was refused. Also, Fraser alleges he paid Tanky £100 not to reveal evidence concerning his apparent involvement in the conspiracy (with Pedrini etc.).

CASE SIX: BLACK MALE (Harold Padmore)

Padmore was an immigrant to the UK, born in Barbados; he had lived here many years, trouble free. He was once a renowned cricketer, but by July 1963, he was a London Transport shunter. His neighbour, Patricia Hawkins, worked in Soho "sex bars" and had a reputation for fleecing customers.

When a Swiss tourist complained he was robbed by a couple of prostitutes, who took his cash and refused to have sex, the police arrested Hawkins (and her friend Jeanne Brown), installing them in cells at West End Central. Upon hearing this news, Padmore strolled over to the station and offered to post bail. Unfortunately, Tanky happened to be on duty.

Before he knew what hit him (literally), Padmore was beaten by Challenor and dragged up to the charge room by bobbies, bleeding from a broken tooth, while Tanky bawled "coon", and similarly tiresome clichés, between swigging gulps from a bottle of whisky. Other duty officers stood by, smirking. Challenor was probably inebriated and chanted racist rhymes like a soccer lout. When he tired of chanting and acting tough, he had Padmore banged up in a cell for the night, returning at 7 a.m. to turf the prisoner out after confiscating his diary and ordering him to return to the station at 7 p.m. for further questioning.

Twelve hours later Padmore dutifully showed up, accompanied by his solicitor. Tanky met him with two other officers, accusing Padmore of "obviously taking part in a conspiracy". Harold P. was informed he would be detained, until Challenor could be bothered to charge him. Padmore motioned to his solicitor to take his wallet, causing Tanky to lurch at him and forcibly curtail the transaction. Held overnight in a cell, Padmore heard an inspector enter the charge room, suggesting to Challenor that he might charge the prisoner, but was bluntly told he was "too busy". Next morning, Challenor rudely awakened Padmore with a left hook (a charge Challenor later denied); but it so happened on that morning that another prisoner remembered glancing a black man who worked for London Transport in an adjacent cell, with blood pouring from his nose. The observant prisoner was Donald Rooum.

On 8 January 1964, Padmore appeared at the Old Bailey with Hawkins and Brown. The prosecution alleged Padmore had conspired with the women, in a Soho "clip joint" rip-off scam, brought to police attention by a Swiss victim. Padmore insisted he had nothing whatever to do with the club; he was just a friendly neighbour trying to do a good turn. This time, the jury could not agree a verdict, so a fresh trial was ordered. By the time this was scheduled, it was Challenor that the media and public wanted to see in the dock. The prosecution tactfully chose not to pursue the case and Padmore was acquitted (and later awarded £500 damages).

PARDONS ALL ROUND

By late 1963, thirteen convicted prisoners claimed they had been framed by Challenor and his PCs. Cases were taken up by Liberty and lawyers, who lobbied Parliament and the Home Office, and appealed for appeals. Martin Ennals was a prominent NCCL activist, while prisoners' determined friends and families fought for justice. Then there were the eight brick-bit arrests, including juveniles, fairly claiming they were set up, having charges against them dropped during proceedings, or having already served jail sentences.

Rooum issued a writ against Challenor, claiming damages for assault and wrongful arrest, false imprisonment and malicious prosecution; he was awarded £500.

Henry Brooke, the Home Secretary, finally made a statement on the Challenor cases on 2 July 1964, claiming, "by excessive devotion to duty and overwork in the police service", Challenor had suffered a mental breakdown. Further, he named twelve convictions secured by Challenor where gross injustices *may* have arisen: King, Silver, Ryall, Ryall, Derwin, Pedrini, Ford, Cheeseman, Oliva, Fraser, Louciades and Gold, announcing five free pardons, five referrals to the Court of Criminal Appeal, and two cases where no further action was intended. Confronted with a barrage of questions and insults from MPs, Brooke stated his intention to open two official inquiries into the affair.

CASE SEVEN: THE TAILOR'S NEW CLOTHES?
(Andreas Louciades)

Andreas Louciades was a local, prize-winning tailor with a distinguished clientele, but a few of his regulars were wealthy crooks and gangsters. In 1959 and earlier, he's known to have occasionally passed information to the police, helping their enquiries. But by 1963 he felt he had done his bit for "justice" and wanted out with his cop associates. Tanky had planned to use him to obtain information on some dodgy deals going down and was infuriated by his refusal to help. "You're in my territory now . . ." he warned Louciades. The tailor was unmoved by the cop's threats and, besides, Andreas wasn't planning to spend much time in Soho now; his sartorial reputation meant customers were prepared to travel to him.

By the evening of 17 August 1963, Louciades had avoided Soho, and Challenor, for some time. He met one of his customers in a Balham pub, the man owing his tailor cash for a suit. Another friend accompanied the customer, and the three of them sat in Louciades's car in the pub car park to discuss payments.

They were astonished when cops surrounded the car. Next thing, they were in custody, at West End Central. Louciades implored Challenor to explain why he was arrested. Tanky murmured he was in the company of a felon in the car. Clearly, thought Louciades, a misunderstanding had arisen, and he proceeded to explain the situation to his custodian with a relieved sigh. The disinterested cop suggests it's not that simple, because his car had been searched and a sack of housebreaking implements had been discovered in his boot. What's more, the chap owing him suit money was wanted "very badly" for something, and that if Louciades were released, they would have to drop charges against the "wanted" man as well. No, best if they all appeared in court together, charged with housebreaking.

And so it goes . . . Louciades appeared at London Sessions in September alongside the other two (despite their insistence Louciades was not involved with them) and was duly sentenced to two concurrent eighteen-month prison sentences.

THE BROADER IMPLICATIONS

One genuine crook acquainted with Tanky is ex-Richardson gang henchman Frankie Fraser, who says in *Mad Frank's Diary*:

> *I'd known Challenor . . . he came sniffing round, but . . . we sent him on his business. Challenor had been going mad for months, if not years, and he thought he was a one-man campaign to clean up Soho. When he was in court he made it sound like Chicago in the days of Al Capone and what was worse everyone believed him . . . in them days who was going to believe a young kid against a war hero?*
>
> *Challenor got all the praise from the press . . . and what's worse he got a licence to go round fitting people up . . .*

And Challenor went on and on. He did all this in front of other officers, who didn't stop him.

... he was found unfit to plead and had a short spell in hospital. After that I heard he'd got a job as a solicitor's clerk over South London.

The Challenor Case exposed not only the police, but the whole British legal establishment (judges and magistrates, court process and juries, the Home Office and legal apparatus) to serious re-examination.

The number of pardons for wrongful imprisonment has soared in recent years. If there were any significant changes after Challenor, it was too little, too late. Tinkering with the system by successive regimes has not delivered. Only a complete and radical overhaul of the whole caboodle might restore faith in justice (like Bertrand Russell's suggestion, that Britain needs a second police force, whose sole function is to prove the innocence of suspects). This just isn't going to happen. But there's an alarming warning for us all in this highly flawed criminal justice system. Fitting up innocent people for unsolved crimes could happen to anyone, from school kids playing tennis, to deaf mutes watching a public trial ... to *you*.

8

Investigating Officer X: Operation Countryman vs. the Metropolitan Police

Martin Jones

The value of undercover policing is of course very great when it comes to investigating the police themselves, and the internal-affairs divisions who police the police, logically, have the best cover available – being cops already. Investigating the police is not a matter of creating new identities, but of keeping the *actual* investigations on which they are working, covert. As seen in Part 1, Chapter 1, Britain's Flying Squad has a proud history of keeping the public safe, especially since armed robbers have developed in daring, ambition, scope and firepower, and a notable heritage, with busts such as the Kray twins on their books. In August 1993, an armed robbery at a Barclays Bank in Blackfen, Kent was the first time that the Sweeney was fired upon with machine guns. Facing risks like these, they often work with SO19 and CO19 firearm squads, for example in foiling the Millennium Dome raid in November 2000, arresting five men who had set out to rob the flawless Millennium Star diamond, valued at two hundred million pounds.

In the 1970s, however, their own star was looking tarnished: close ties with the criminal underworld have always been crucial to the Sweeney's system of intelligence-gathering, but at times it seemed that the "F" in "Flying Squad" was silent. The Sweeney were coming in for public criticism and commentators were asking credibly if the tail had not long since begun to wag the dog. Several scandals of bribery and corruption were seeing the light of day, and in July 1977, Flying Squad commander Detective Chief Superintendent Kenneth Drury was convicted of five corruption charges and jailed for eight years. Twelve other officers were convicted along with him, and many gave their resignation or took early retirement, in order to avoid further investigation perhaps.

The scandal led to a massive internal investigation into the Metropolitan Police and the City of London Police, two forces who had for years passed bucks and, in the days of Jack the Ripper, bodies between them. (In the fetid streets of nineteenth-century London, it was known for each force to move corpses, upon discovery, into the other's jurisdiction!) In a sly nod to the Dorset Constabulary that was to conduct the investigation, it was code-named Operation Countryman.

The following extract and the one after it concern events following this operation, and *Investigating Officer X* represents a clear, brief summary of the labyrinthine events of Countryman. It does, however, read a little over-suspiciously of Arthur Hambleton, Dorset police's Chief Constable, for stating publicly that his investigation was not being hampered and then admitting to a BBC documentary team that there was evidence that it was, not long after. This would seem to be a logical decision – it was crucial to the success of the investigation not to tip off targets that they were being investigated – providing the opportunity to destroy evidence, bribe witnesses or otherwise take evasive action, but there was no harm in so doing once events had made it clear those targets were aware. This, rather than any sword-to-the-chest, hocus-pocus Masonic conspiracy, would seem a sufficient explanation of Hambleton's logical, even justifiable course of action . . .

Central London in the mid 1970s. Over the course of three years, three violent crimes take place in the city north of the River Thames:

- May 1976 – At the Fleet Street headquarters of the *Daily Express*, four gunmen steal £175,000 in employee wages.
- September 1977 – A security van delivering money to the Williams & Glyn City bank in Birchin Lane is ambushed by six masked gunmen. One guard is shot in the legs. The gang escape with £270,000.
- May 1978 – After a security van has been locked inside the loading bay of the *Daily Mirror* offices, three gunmen – two disguised as employees – attack it. The van's driver is shot at point-blank range and dies on the way to hospital. The robbers get away with an estimated £200,000 in wages.

No one was ever charged with the *Daily Express* robbery. After the Williams & Glyn job, eight known London criminals were arrested, but all of them – including Tony White, George Copley and Francis Fraser Junior (a relation of "Mad" Frankie Fraser) – were freed on bail, and the following year every charge related to that case was dropped due to lack of evidence. Tony White was arrested again in June 1978, two weeks after the *Daily Mirror* robbery, along with one Billy Tobin. White made bail and subsequently had charges dropped against him. Tobin was later acquitted.

It seemed to all concerned that these three successful robberies were the work of a gang outside London. But, in the years immediately following the crimes, some would have you believe that the brains behind them were deep in the heart of the city, right at its lawful centre: anonymous, high-ranking police officers embroiled in criminal complicity and conspiratorial dealings. It was the "Square Mile" robberies that were more or less directly responsible for the formation of the internal investigation known as Operation Countryman. An expensive and ultimately fruitless gesture, Operation Countryman was created ostensibly to dig out claims of corruption within the Metropolitan Police Department in the late 1970s. By its closure all the investigation had achieved was a few unrelated convictions, a deep mistrust between certain individual officers, and more fuel for the rumour mill it had uncovered.

ALL POINTS BLOCKED

Formed in 1829 through a Parliamentary Act enforced by the Home Secretary Sir Robert Peel, the Metropolitan Police force has not been without its share of internal dirt. Hardly surprising, considering it has 99 per cent of Greater London – and most of the suburbs – under its jurisdiction: an area of some 786 square miles (2,036 square kilometres). The Met's most infamous scandals appeared at either end of a hundred-year span: in 1877 conmen William Kurr and Harry Benson enlisted the services of bribable inspectors and lower ranks to act as "early warning systems" for their crimes. In 1977 the Flying Squad subdivision – or "Sweeney" (rhyming slang: Sweeney Todd – Flying Squad) – became the subject of investigations over officers taking cash gifts from Soho porn shop owners. Throughout the 1960s and 1970s, the Metropolitan Police Department appeared to be staffed by hard-drinking, morally indifferent officers who thought nothing of taking cash from the highest, or lowest, bidder. After the Soho scandal, there was barely a chance for the Met to breathe before another incident surfaced to tarnish its already damaged reputation.

Following accusations made by criminal informers, in July 1978 the Commander of the Flying Squad, Don Neesham, filed a report to his superiors citing what he believed to be a "corrupt association" between the armed men who had undertaken the Square Mile robberies and the City of London Police. A shortlist of officers' names was drawn up as evidence. Peter Marshall, Commissioner of the City force, asked New Scotland Yard to conduct an investigation into the claims; but, after obtaining further information, the Met's Complaints Investigation Bureau (CIB) decided that a force independent of London was needed to continue the process.

Marshall contacted the Home Office and, with the consent of the Home Secretary Merlyn Rees, invited Assistant Chief Constable Leonard Burt up from Dorset Constabulary to undertake the investigation. Burt brought with him a team of thirty officers and was appointed under Section 49 of the Police Act 1964. With headquarters set up in Camberwell Police Station (south of the Thames), his brief was given by the City force to investigate a number of specific complaints relating to alleged malpractice by City officers in connection with recent serious crimes. Operation Countryman was born.

A few weeks into the investigation, it became apparent that Metropolitan officers might possibly be involved alongside their City colleagues. The Deputy Commissioner of the Met, Patrick Kavanagh, asked Burt to extend his brief in order to look into the allegations. An unrelated scandal in 1970, after which the Met was rumoured to have closed ranks against outside investigators, was still fresh in Kavanagh's mind, and he was determined as much as the newly appointed commissioner Sir David McNee to erase this image, eager to have his force portrayed as open and willing to cooperate. But, despite the free hand offered by their hosts, it appeared that Burt and his superior, Chief Constable Arthur Hambleton, had different ideas as to where the Countryman investigation should take them. Hambleton, in particular, began to take an increasingly prominent role in the investigation.

From the start, they seemed to make things difficult for themselves: Met officers nicknamed the team "The Sweedey", a tag that played on the provincial stereotype and doubts that they could cut it in the City (the official name of the investigation was chosen by Hambleton); and they gathered no allies by beginning a series of complaints about "obstructions" made during the course of their work, the first of which being the allegation that there had been an attempt to interfere with records at their Camberwell HQ. Burt requested that his team be moved to a station outside the Metropolitan Police district. With the cooperation of Sir Peter Matthews, the Chief Constable of Surrey, Countryman was moved to Godalming Police Station, 30 miles (48 km) outside the capital. It was seen by senior officers as a terrific waste of time: staff now had to travel to and from London to Surrey, and a shorter working week was created due to having to go home on Friday afternoon and return on Monday morning.

But the Met stayed fast in their help; Kavanagh was still sensitive to his force's image, and let Countryman's autonomy ride for a while, neither asking for nor receiving any reports. Countryman's initial investigations were well publicized but hardly inspiring: they collected word-of-mouth accounts from criminals and "supergrasses", but did not take any written statements at that point, an action that would come back to haunt them later. Because of the investigation's high profile, Countryman officers also began to receive many complaints against the Met and City forces that were unconnected with Leonard Burt's original brief. For reasons known only to himself, Burt did not pass on these complaints to the relevant forces for separate investigation, but decided to keep them within the net of Countryman. It was obvious to some observers that Burt saw the operation as an anti-corruption squad that he would sweep through the London forces, cleaning up in style. But, for all intents and purposes, the original aim had disappeared in Burt's eyes and he was now overwhelmed with evidence from all quarters. Instead of returning to the City brief, he – with the support of Hambleton – increased his team to eighty officers. This meant that provincial forces all over the south of England were depleted in order for Burt to cast his net wider.

Every complaint the team received was investigated, which did nothing more than push the original target further away; and not everything received could be called solid evidence: every criminal with an axe to grind, a grudge to sate, an officer to get one over on seemed to turn up at the Countryman HQ. Because of so much information streaming in, Burt requested a computer to store it on, an expensive matter in the 1970s. With an eye on the mounting cost, the Met provided them with one. Although every decision was made through Home Office consultation, the Met was still granting requests, worried about potential claims of interference.

At some point during the early stages of the investigation, Hambleton steered Burt towards the Flying Squad and its subdivision, the Robbery Squad. Further complaints arose when it was discovered that Countryman detectives were muscling in on supergrass informers, the Robbery Squad's main vein of information. Enraged by this interference, Don Neesham – who had set the whole investigation rolling in the first place – made a complaint in November 1978 about their dealings with informers. Neesham's main problem with Countryman was the fact that they had been known to offer "soft" options to informers, thus undermining the Robbery Squad's authority, knocking down any trust individual detectives had spent years building up.

As complaints were received from a small number of Sweeney officers over Countryman detectives approaching their informers, both Peter Marshall and David McNee wondered why they were being kept in the dark. They were not the only ones. In July 1979, Sir Thomas Hetherington, the Director of Public Prosecutions (DPP), met with McNee and Kavanagh to express his concern over the length of time Countryman was taking: he had his doubts over the expertise of Burt's team, and of their ability to provide any solid results. This was something McNee agreed with but, like Kavanagh, he knew it was no basis for interference from the Met. Instead, he diplomatically offered to lighten the burden of the Countryman team by taking away cases not related to the original brief. Burt refused the offer, on the grounds that all complaints and information had been passed to the team under the strictest confidence. It seemed that in his quest to drive out corruption, Burt saw all around him as potentially corrupt.

Elsewhere, the DPP found other problems: one of his officials, Kenneth Dowling, denied a request by a Countryman sergeant to interview a suspect in prison. The sergeant went ahead anyway, and the suspect, George Copley (one of the men arrested in connection with the Williams & Glyn robbery), surreptitiously taped the interview. The tape was later produced at trial, showing that the sergeant had offered him a reduced sentence in return for admitting to the robbery and providing evidence of corruption among certain Met officers.

By October 1979, Kavanagh still could not see what Countryman had achieved, or where the investigation was heading. He told Hambleton and Burt as much, but all Burt could offer was that the DPP had hindered him by not making a decision on a Countryman report submitted twenty-two weeks earlier (McNee later heard that this was because the report had been inadequate). Burt resented the suggestion that he was hoarding information and running with enquiries that were far removed from his original brief. Hambleton acted as mediator and it was agreed that Kavanagh would regularly be kept up to date. But by the next month, neither Kavanagh nor McNee had received any new information on Countryman's progress. This led McNee – who, as Commissioner, was supposed to remain impartial – to write a letter of complaint to Hambleton.

In reply, Hambleton and Burt met with McNee, Kavanagh and the DPP at New Scotland Yard. Hambleton brought with him progress reports, with, he said, the rest to follow within a few days and the promise of regular reports from thereon. He also agreed that Countryman would not take on any new lines of enquiry without prior consultation. As a gesture of goodwill the DPP offered to provide a member of his staff to Countryman full time.

Within less than two weeks of the meeting, a report appeared in the *Sunday Times* stating that Burt was unhappy with the "obstacles" being placed in the way of Countryman by the Met and DPP. Angered by this rejection of his good-will, on 7 December 1979 Kavanagh, along with the DPP and Ernest Bright (Assistant Commissioner of the City force), held a meeting with Hambleton. He was told that if he or Burt continued to make complaints about obstruction he would have to resign as head of the investigation. Unwilling to do this, Hambleton offered his cooperation in a venture that would put the investigation back on track. Together the four of them drew up a press statement to be released on the same day by Dorset Police, under Burt's name.

Among the seven points laid out, Burt was required to admit that some of the complaints investigated had been proved unfounded, that during the inquiry regular consultations were made with the DPP, and that accusations of obstruction were completely without grounds, with Countryman receiving full cooperation from the DPP and both Commissioners. "My detectives are working extremely hard," he stated:

> *They are dedicated and have the will to succeed; they are undaunted by some reports that have appeared in the press and other media. Events in the future will prove that the Countryman team has been more than adequate for its task and that any difficulties they have encountered have been overcome.*

But this did not hide another point made on the statement: after over a year of investigations, only five Metropolitan officers had been suspended from duty, with only four subsequently made subject to further proceedings by the DPP. In the City force, only one officer had been charged. McNee called the claim made later by Hambleton on the *World In Action* television programme (broadcast 20 July 1981) – that Countryman would have folded if he hadn't agreed to the contents of the statement – "nonsense". Kavanagh told McNee that at the time of the statement Hambleton had alleged that Don Neesham had been "unhelpful" towards his team; but Hambleton produced no evidence to support this. Nevertheless, still determined to have no blemishes on his force, McNee saw that Neesham would be moved to other duties. Instead, Neesham took early retirement and resigned, leaving with more complaints against Countryman. The Commissioner must have wondered at what price his actions were placed, especially when he and Kavanagh visited Countryman HQ:

> *I was not impressed. It seemed to me that the name of any police officer mentioned to members of the Countryman team, in conversations with criminals and others, was being fed into the computer. Wholly innocent officers were accordingly going into the pool of suspects, often only on the world of rogues. Far too much attention was being given to compiling a mass of*

intelligence, much of it of doubtful quality, and I was convinced
that the team were being sidetracked from their primary objec-
tive. No arrests after many months of inquiry was not my idea
of success.

But a natural end came to Hambleton's reign when he
announced that he was to retire at the end of February 1980,
although he did not leave without difficulties. Hambleton
took it upon himself to conduct an almost exclusive vendetta
against the DPP. The most serious incident came when
Countryman finally made its first arrest of a Detective
Inspector from the City force, although the charge was
unconnected to the original brief. In blatant disregard for
procedure, Leonard Burt bypassed the DPP and, with a
Dorset solicitor, brought the case before a court in
Hertfordshire. Magistrates there granted an application for
the accused officer to be remanded in custody for three days
and he was taken down to Dorset for the duration. On 18
February 1980, a representative of the DPP had to attend
court to request that the prosecution be withdrawn due to
inadequate evidence. With this one "success" snatched away
from him, Hambleton claimed that the whole of Countryman
would be discredited, despite the fact that he had become a
law unto himself when it came to running the investigation.
He also claimed that the DPP was obstructing their progress,
but again could offer no convincing examples. In a move
strange for such outsiders in the capital, Burt ordered the
DPP's representative at Countryman HQ to leave.

The representative stayed, but Hambleton left on 29
February, and Sir Peter Matthews took over responsibility for
Countryman. Burt continued as its head until he too returned
to Dorset in May 1980. With these two antagonists gone,
Matthews quickly took charge: he cut the operation down to
the terms of the original brief and passed all unconnected
matters on to the Met CIB or the City force. He also brought
in Deputy Assistant Commissioner Ron Stevenson, who had
lengthy experience of corruption within the force, being a
former head of the CIB. Eventually, eight Met officers were

indicted, but none were convicted by the courts. Three were subsequently dismissed as a consequence of disciplinary proceedings taken by the Met, which had found them guilty of tampering with suspect interview records (one of the dismissed, Inspector James Jolly, had been separately tried and acquitted for attempting to frame one of the *Daily Mirror* robbery suspects, Billy Tobin), one resigned, and four resumed duties. But it was too little, too late. On 30 June 1982 Metropolitan Police involvement in Countryman officially ceased. The eventual cost of the operation came to £4 million.

Later, three senior officers on the original list of suspects were separately investigated by the CIB in regard to other offences, and this led to the conviction of two of the officers; but how these convictions came about adds another layer to the disordered workings of Operation Countryman.

OUTSIDERS ON THE SQUARE

On 1 June 1978, the day after the *Daily Mirror* robbery, Detective Chief Superintendent John Simmonds left the Met to become head of the Criminal Investigation Department at the City force. He was now in charge of 830 officers. Formed in 1839, the City force patrols the Square Mile of the capital on the north bank of the River Thames. Simmonds was a morally sound officer, and also a Freemason, but he walked into his job determined to keep quiet about his affiliation. He was well aware that the force was rife with the "Brotherhood", and did not want to be accepted among his men purely on that basis. His superior, Peter Marshall, was a non-Mason, but both men had enough sense to realize that the City force, because of its independence and relatively small reach, was essentially inbred and closed to other forces. Simmonds suspected that this led to criminal cooperation among some of the officers, taking as an example the recent Square Mile robberies: three violent crimes executed successfully on City turf, and not one conviction between them.

For a while Simmonds maintained his bluff, until one day

in September 1978 when City Detective Chief Inspector Phillip Cuthbert met a non-force friend of Simmonds at a Masonic gathering, and inadvertently learned of his boss's ties with them. When Cuthbert confronted his superior, Simmonds admitted his membership but stated that he wanted to keep it to himself. This had no effect on the garrulous Cuthbert, and soon enough Simmonds detected a more relaxed atmosphere among his new colleagues. DCI Cuthbert was Master of Lodge No. 3475 (Waterloo), but there was a reason beyond Masonic business for his ingratiation into Simmonds's world: Cuthbert had discovered that *his* name was on the shortlist of officers put forward by Don Neesham in relation to the Square Mile robberies. It was time for the Brotherhood to do him some favours.

Bypassing police rank, Cuthbert approached Simmonds "on the square"; that is, as a fellow Mason bound by the same rules of secrecy. Cuthbert wanted to unburden himself of something, and Simmonds agreed to meet up in a pub a few days later. But the lawman in Simmonds suspected a deeper agenda behind this, and so he told Commissioner Marshall about the meeting, who in turn contacted Operation Countryman. Together they agreed that Simmonds should go to the meeting wearing a concealed tape recorder and microphone. The "wire" recorded a three-hour conversation involving Simmonds, Cuthbert, and two of his associates: Irving Shire (a solicitor's clerk) and Paul Davis (a solicitor). The finished tape would not be used until 1982, when Cuthbert and another officer appeared at the Old Bailey on bribery charges, the result of the CIB's investigations post-Countryman.

The Masonic links holding Operation Countryman up are hard to ignore. This is not to claim that Masons were under every stone on the investigation's path, but connections have been made between the two by numerous writers. Arthur Hambleton was also a Freemason but, like Simmonds, he fully understood the influence Freemasonry had on the police and refused to let it interfere with his Countryman quest (he did not join a lodge in Dorset until after he had retired from that force). According to Martin Short in *Inside The Brotherhood* (the follow-up to the late Stephen Knight's *The Brotherhood*):

> *It was later alleged that Freemasonry was not only involved in the corruption that Operation Countryman was investigating, but had later caused its overall failure by sabotage.*

But Short goes on to state – rightly – that just because many crooked (and lawful) officers were Masons, it did not mean that the Brotherhood was behind it all. But, then again, absence of evidence does not mean evidence of absence. Stephen Knight's earlier book traces the root of Operation Countryman back to one man: the Commissioner of the City of London Police between 1971 and 1977, James Page. It could be seen as a tenuous link, but Knight was a fervent man with a nose for conspiracies (his 1976 book *Jack The Ripper: The Final Solution* is one of the most convincing in that field), and Page's history adds more than a few pieces to the crimes that sparked Operation Countryman, the crimes that Hambleton quickly forgot in his own particular crusade.

After it was announced that the current Commissioner of the City Police, Arthur Young, was retiring, Chief Superintendent James Page was made Acting Commissioner in November 1969. Up to that point, Page had worked his way steadily through the ranks of the Met. Originally hailing from the Blackpool City force – which in the 1960s was under the command of the venal Chief Constable Stanley Parr – Page transferred to the Met as a Commander in 1967. Two years later he was promoted to Chief Superintendent. On the eve of his temporary Commissioner promotion, Page was visited by an anonymous, high-ranking officer. The officer warned him about two City officers – Knight calls them "Oates" and "Tearle" – whom he knew to be taking bribes off criminals in return for altering charges. With good humour, Page ignored these warnings; after all, it was addressed that the best way he worked with his men was on a grass-roots level: he liked to be known by everyone as "Jim", and was an enthusiastic social drinker, with a reputation for turning up at even the smallest gatherings. Freemasonry must have seemed like a dozen hospitable doors opening to Page, and he was eventually admitted in the summer of 1971 to City Livery Club Lodge No. 3752. Around the same time he won the Commissioner's position, ahead of the other shortlisted – and favoured – candidate, the Deputy Assistant Commissioner (Metropolitan Training) John Alderson.

Page's promotion surprised many, especially when there had been better-suited candidates. Despite a number of professional achievements, and his popularity within the lower ranks of the force, Page was seen as unsuitable for the job: mainly because of his constant drinking, but also because the position was far above his abilities as an officer. Knight underlines the fact that Page's first allegiance was to the Masons, which perhaps goes some way to explaining how he got the job: the Brotherhood appealed to Page's nature on a surface level, i.e. if you were a police officer and a Mason then you were a good officer because Freemasonry was a benevolent organization. Page drank with "Oates" and "Tearle", who were also – obviously – Masons. Within his own lodge, "Tearle" was Worshipful Master, and so superior in rank to Page. Both "Oates" and "Tearle" were promoted a number of times under Page's guidance. This, it seemed, was the way the Masonic pyramid worked: influence and advantage trickling down from higher levels.

But some who caught the flow were not always made of the same material as men such as John Simmonds. According to Knight, "Oates" and "Tearle" had played a part in all three of the Square Mile robberies. They assisted with the *Daily Express* job, and helped set up the Williams & Glyn and *Daily Mirror* jobs. Masonic police shared out the proceeds between them, including around £60,000 from one job alone. Knight reasons these actions thus: if Page had *not* been a Mason, he would *not* have promoted "Oates" and "Tearle". But they, and others, *were* (he concludes with the information that "Tearle" remained in the force but "Oates" left, possibly as the one officer who resigned after Countryman's closure). If the two officers were corrupt *and* trusted, that would lead to more complicity than among non-Masons. The problem, it seemed, stemmed not from these directly involved officers, but a superior such as James Page, whose lax attitude was the root of the problem, albeit unwittingly. Page, like Phillip Cuthbert, was a thorn in the side of Countryman, purely because of his Masonic connection. But Page was perhaps oblivious to what went on beneath him, whereas Cuthbert was using Freemasonry to dig himself out of a deep hole.

The significance of the connections between Masonry, Page and Cuthbert are that the Brotherhood's bonds of secrecy tend to rise above the common laws of England. Felony, however, is one of the acts these bonds do not apply to, so John Simmonds rose above *that* and decided that someone needed to be told. Meanwhile, Masons like Cuthbert and Page just sunk deeper into the arms of their corrupt brothers, with the latter forced to make an ignominious exit from the force in 1977, moving on to the Home Office (the late Page's family made complaints over his "unfair and inaccurate" portrayal when *The Brotherhood* was published). As Short records in *Inside The Brotherhood*, Simmonds's decision to expose his criminal fellow Mason resulted in his ostracism from the Brotherhood: for other policemen, it was easier to turn a blind eye to what was happening within their own force.

A MEANS TO A LOOSE END

Where Countryman failed, the CIB succeeded. An unconnected conviction still had threads leading back to the original investigation brief but, by that time, it was too late to restart such a costly operation. DCI Phillip Cuthbert and Detective Sergeant John Goldburn were the two men successfully convicted. The trial began in June 1982 at the Old Bailey, and would hang Cuthbert up as an example, perhaps to cover the dead ends that had gone before him.

Simmonds's taped conversation with Cuthbert became the main evidence in the trial. He had dangled a microphone down into the Masonic depths of the Met and City forces and then plucked it out for the courts to listen to. At their pub meeting, Cuthbert took Simmonds into his confidence almost immediately, due to their Masonic connections. Cuthbert told him that an unnamed senior officer (hereafter called "Officer X"), at the time working on the Regional Crime Squad, was the mastermind of the *Daily Express* robbery, pocketing at least £20,000 from it. Cuthbert called him "one of the greatest unhung villains" in London, and alleged that this officer had also taken a bribe (or in police slang, "a drink") from the Williams & Glyn robbery, despite having no direct involvement in it, legitimate or otherwise. The amount from that job to change hands within the force was, according to Cuthbert, between £60,000 and £90,000. When Simmonds questioned why the senior officer had received the bribe, Cuthbert explained:

> *Because he was [Officer X] and because he worked with all of us, and, you know, he was in a position of power up there on the fucking Regional Crime Squad and covered things, same as all the blokes on the Robbery Squad had a drink out of it, going right up to the fucking top of the tree . . .*

Discussing the Williams & Glyn job, Cuthbert admitted he had some involvement in it, but nothing direct. All his actions were guided by Officer X: Cuthbert was just the man who handed over an envelope. And everyone profited, even a little. The curve of distorted evidence ran, it seemed, from the bottom to the top. And this was not Cuthbert's only crime: the tape revealed that he had given insurance reward money to various Scotland Yard commanders over the years.

As well as the tape, the court heard a statement from a junior officer who said that Cuthbert had paid him bribe money after the Williams & Glyn robbery, and also from criminal Alfie Sheppard, who had acted as middleman in negotiations between Cuthbert and the underworld concerning bail bribes and the watering-down of evidence connected with Williams & Glyn. Sheppard said that, on behalf of the

Williams & Glyn suspects, he had handed over thousands of pounds to Cuthbert in a restaurant opposite Bishopsgate Police Station. But it was the tape that sent Cuthbert down, not just for his criminal – though tenuous – involvement with the Square Mile robberies, but also for the fact that he had taken bribes continuously over his fifteen-year career, unconcerned by any potential consequences, sheltered by the wing of the Brotherhood.

When Cuthbert gave evidence, he claimed that he was drunk at the time the recording was made, but this didn't hold up in trial. The still-unnamed-in-court Officer X responded with a written statement saying that all the allegations made by Cuthbert were totally unfounded, but that he was obliged to apologize for inaccurate evidence he had given in the case. On 20 July 1982, after a six-week trial, DS John Goldburn was sentenced to two years in prison. DCI Phillip Cuthbert was found guilty of taking up to £80,000 in bribes during his career; to secure bail, overlook past convictions, and not to gather evidence against the eight men who had been charged with the Williams & Glyn robbery. He was sentenced to three years.

On the tape recording, Cuthbert told Simmonds that Officer X was trying to make him a fall guy for Operation Countryman. In the mess of tangled ends that the investigation left behind, it seemed that someone had to be thrown to the lions: there were too many questions left unanswered. And even in its wake, there were too few answers for too many questions: the subject of police corruption highlighted by Countryman was taken up by Liberal Party MPs David Steel and Stephen Ross; and as late as March 1998, questions were asked in Parliament regarding the release of Countryman's findings. Even James Page's one-time rival John Alderson took up the cause, appearing on the same *World In Action* programme as Arthur Hambleton, despite being unconnected with the original investigation. In a strange turn of circumstance, Granada Television, the makers of that programme, had to pay out £20,000 to a Metropolitan detective constable in 1985 because the officer had been caught on film exiting a police station while the programme's voice-over talked of CID officers taking bribes from criminals.

In the end, Operation Countryman highlighted the fact that, despite criminal proceeds dripping down to the lowest level, police corruption was the work of established, well-paid officers high in rank – the Officer Xs who flitted like blurred shapes through the investigation.

9

Bent Coppers: The Inside Story of Scotland Yard's Battle Against Police Corruption

Graeme McLagan

In Thailand, travellers may be mystified to find dusty decals of Al Pacino gracing the mudguards and bumpers of trucks and taxis. Pacino, in his bearded, Jesus-like incarnation as Frank Serpico, the straight-batting NYPD cop whose unease at his fellow officers' corruption led to them mounting an attempt on his life, has become a symbol for Thai drivers of their opposition to once-endemic police corruption, and a warning symbol to said cops that the driver won't take a "request" for a bribe lying down.

A look at top BBC journalist McLagan's comprehensively researched *Bent Coppers* will give the reader the idea that for some Londoners in the 1970s and 1980s, a Pacino-like symbol of their own would not have been out of place. In the wake of the concluding trials of Operation Countryman (Part 2, Chapter 8), provisions were made for the establishment of a "Ghost Squad" – a team of cops who would work undercover within the police to gather information for further prosecutions of those cops who had been corrupted, whether by a pattern of being subsumed into a pre-existing culture among their colleagues, or individually seduced by the power they wielded within the community. Bent coppers really came to believe in their own untouchability – whether fitting up the innocent, thieving property or cash, or selling information, whether accurate or not, to one side or another in a court case.

From the beginning it was important not to confirm that there was even such a thing as a squad investigating corruption, which for most coppers at that point was a matter of rumour only. "Shadow Squad" might have been a better phrase, because these undercover cops were very real and, thanks to convincing cover stories that could explain their presence to even the most suspicious, able to become virtually inseparable from their prey.

As Sir Paul Condon, Met Police Commissioner, said, "I do have a minority of officers who are corrupt, dishonest and unethical. We believe, sadly, that they commit crimes, they neutralize evidence in important cases, and they betray police operations and techniques to criminals. These bad officers sap the morale of their honest colleagues and they do immense damage to public confidence. Because of their training they are aware of the tactics we use to try and catch them. They are cunning, they are experienced, they are surveillance-conscious."

Condon alludes to the difficulty of infiltrating people who have been trained to spot when they are being watched, and indeed are schooled watchers themselves. Not wishing to put a damper on the very activities they had been tasked with investigating, it was important that their targets did not twig that a member of the undercover "Ghost Squad" could even have been one office desk away.

"We recognize that a small number of officers either through bad behaviour or corruption can have a disproportionate impact on our reputation. We want them to be in constant fear of exposure."

Sir Paul Condon, Metropolitan Police Commissioner
(1996)

By the end of 1996, the secret ghost squad had been in existence for well over two years. As outlined in Chapter 8, it had taken time before its officers had been able to get down to their main task of trying to assess the extent of corruption, its nature and how to tackle it. Recruiting more than twenty officers for such sensitive work had taken far longer than expected. Many of them had to undergo special training in carrying out highly skilled surveillance work. Finding suitable premises for the unit away from police stations had been difficult, and there were continuing problems over their cover story – that they were working for a newly formed company in the communications business.

Other problems surfaced only when the squad was up and running, but centred on a simple question. How can you investigate when you don't exist? The ghost squad could not even carry out their own checks on the PNC, the Police National Computer. Instead, they had to channel such enquiries through Roger Gaspar or his number two at CIB. The need for secrecy meant that those carrying out physical surveillance, although well trained, were limited in what they could do. Normally Scotland Yard's surveillance officers, and those working undercover, could rely on a huge backup operation to follow up their information, but this was not the case for ghost squad members, and it led to an inordinate amount of time being spent on researching relatively simple intelligence. Sometimes, follow-up checks were not made at all.

If, for instance, a suspect was followed into a bank where he carried out a transaction at the counter, the "normal" surveillance officer could either make immediate enquiries with bank staff or arrange for it to be followed up later. But the ghost squad watcher could do neither. He did not exist, and the backup machinery was virtually non-existent. Similar problems occurred at police stations. Ghost squad members could get inside a police building using their false police identities, pretending, for example, that they wanted to check with the station's collator of intelligence on a local criminal's associates. But how did they find out at which desk a suspect officer usually sat, so they could plant a bug there? How did they find out when the officer was next due on shift? Asking even simple questions could arouse suspicion and lead to a suspect finding out that he was under investigation.

Further problems arose over electronic surveillance. By law, police need the prior permission of the Home Secretary to intercept calls on telephones in private premises. Because the ghost squad wanted its operations kept secret, it rarely applied for permission to tap officers' home phones, preferring to monitor their calls in police stations, which did not require official outside authority. The ghost squad also had sophisticated technical equipment. They used very sensitive bugging equipment, favouring the "probe", because this meant there was no need to gain physical entry to premises. Installing a probe involved silently drilling a tiny hole in a suspect's home, usually in a window frame or through the wall of an adjoining property, and the insertion of a microphone-transmitter so conversations in a room could be picked up and recorded near by. Where the difficulties for the ghost squad lay was in the huge amount of time needed to listen to and study all this recorded material. Police tapes of normal criminals' conversations would be sent to an outside agency for transcription, but the need for secrecy meant that this option was not available to the squad. Listening to and transcribing tapes was kept "in house", and because both tasks were boring, very time consuming and often fruitless, they were approached in a disorganized manner, with some recordings remaining unplayed altogether.

Maintaining the unit's secrecy had taken precedence over all other work and there was a clear need for it. There was evidence that those the investigators termed the "enemy", the corrupt officers, were trying to find out what was going on, so that they could stay one step ahead of any anti-corruption inquiry into their activities. The ghost squad's head, Detective Chief Superintendent Roger Gaspar, was playing two other roles. He was also in charge of CIB operations at Tintagel House, but as part of his cover story he had another secure office on the eighth floor of the building. From there, he was supposed to be in charge of a special unit carrying out a hush-hush inquiry into corruption in a provincial force, far away from London. This was a lie. There was no such inquiry. It had been invented, and word of it allowed to spread in order to provide cover for his secret work running the ghost squad.

Proof that the strategy was working came from listening to

the telephone calls of one of the officers being targeted for corruption. He had been told of the "provincial inquiry" that was taking up so much of the CIB chief's time, and he remarked: "That's good to know. We've been trying to find out what's going on in that room." He then went on to say something to the effect that if a provincial inquiry was all Gaspar was involved in, then he and other corrupt officers had nothing to worry about. In fact, the secret anti-corruption group trusted virtually no one, not even senior CIB officers at Tintagel House. Even they were fooled by the deception, because Gaspar heard he was being criticized by some of them for spending too much time away on the provincial investigation, neglecting his duties with the Metropolitan Police as head of CIB2.

Those working under Gaspar at the secret location in west London were all leading double lives, pretending to be employed by a commercial company while working for the ghost squad. This led, perhaps inevitably, to confusion and mix-ups. Gaspar had more than one identity. He used different names for different occasions and had separate credit cards and identification documents for them all. On occasions even he forgot who he was supposed to be, leading to embarrassing moments. Once, correctly using a credit card in his false name to pay for a hotel room, he signed the payment slip with his own name. Realizing the mistake seconds later, he apologized and asked the hotel receptionist for the slip back. She said it did not matter, tore up the paperwork, threw it into a rubbish bin and made out a new form. Gaspar signed it with his false name, but he was worried that not retrieving the original slip, even though it had been torn up, could backfire in some way and expose his double identity. He again asked for the slip back, but once again the receptionist said it was unnecessary. Becoming irritated, he had to insist on it being returned to him before the woman eventually retrieved it, totally mystified by his performance.

Working for the ghost squad, away from former colleagues, led to other unforeseen problems. The strains involved in leading double lives away from colleagues and normal police work resulted in staff falling out with one another, and to arguments, with "inappropriate" language being used. Luckily, the stresses caused were never serious enough to warrant major disciplinary action – a move to another mainstream police department or even dismissal. "Imagine if we had had to sack someone from a unit so secret that it didn't exist," Gaspar said to me.

Sorting out all these problems meant that much less had been achieved after two years than had been anticipated when the ghost squad had been formed. As head of CIB2, Gaspar had also been forced to spend a great deal of his time on two totally separate inquiries. One of these had been into leaks to newspapers of details of the police investigation into the mysterious death of the Conservative MP Stephen Milligan, found trussed up with ropes with an orange in his mouth. The second investigation was into allegations of a huge conspiracy involving corrupt police who were all Freemasons. Gaspar and other senior officers, experts in corruption investigations, all play down the significance of any Masonic influence, taking the view that the fact that some police officers are Masons and get together at Masonic functions does not mean that they are part of a large-scale corrupt conspiracy.

In terms of the ghost squad's performance, the intelligence-gathering side had gone fairly well, with further information obtained about corrupt detectives involved in all the areas originally targeted by the squad. These included Stoke Newington in north London, the south London bases of the South East Regional Crime Squad, and sections of the Flying Squad. But there had been difficulties in turning this intelligence into evidence strong enough to mount prosecutions or take disciplinary action. Part of the problem lay with CIB itself.

When Gaspar took over in 1994, he found a department in which most of the senior officers were nearing retirement, and unwilling to put themselves out or take risks. As an example of this tired attitude, he outlined a case where a prostitute had complained late one afternoon of having to pay protection money to an officer whose next visit was to be in the morning. The woman was happy to cooperate with CIB, agreeing to have her room bugged. The job was given to a senior CIB officer, who went home, declaring that it was too late to set up a surveillance operation. It was left to a more junior officer to try to sort something out. He managed to install recording equipment in time for the morning meeting and everything went smoothly. The corrupt sergeant arrived at the prostitute's premises and was recorded demanding £300 from her in protection money.

"With me looking after you, you're not going to get any hassle," he said. "The alternative is I can bust you, and you go down. Now, not only am I offering you protection, I'm also saying we ain't going to do you."

Prostitute: "So, well?"

Sergeant: "Three hundred. Not too steep."

"Sorry?"

"Three hundred, not too steep?"

"No, that's not too steep at all."

"Well, don't say that because I might raise it."

"Don't do that, please."

CIB officers monitoring the "shake-down" conversation then burst into the room and told the startled officer. "We're from CIB. You've been videoed. You are under arrest for corrupt practice." Subsequently Sergeant Ian Vale was convicted and given an eight-year prison sentence for corruption and gross misconduct.

Other inquiries could have been handled better by CIB2, but there were limitations on what could be achieved with few staff, most of them inexperienced in proactive work and lacking up-to-date equipment. One early case Gaspar oversaw involved a Turkish woman who was a drug dealer and heroin addict, and had turned police informant. Given the pseudonym "Gina Flowers", she made a series of complaints against one of her handlers, a SERCS detective sergeant. Her allegations ranged from him, along with other officers, stealing four kilograms of heroin to his sharing in her police reward money and pestering her for sex, which she claimed amounted to rape. A full-scale operation could have been mounted against the officer and his colleagues to prove corruption, but lacking the resources for this the CIB chose to concentrate on the sex allegations. Evidence here would be easier to obtain because his demands for sex were continuing, and the woman agreed to cooperate with CIB2. A protected witness, Gina had been moved to a safe house in Essex, and this represented a problem for the anti-corruption officers. The plan was to put a bug in the woman's bedroom to record the conversation between her and the detective, while CIB officers waited outside the property, ready to move in and arrest him if he forced himself on the woman. The operation was potentially dangerous, as no one knew how the detective would react or whether he would be with anyone else. If the safe house had been in the Metropolitan Police area, there could have been backup. Help could have been obtained from Essex, but there was concern that word of what was planned could leak out if an official request was made. CIB decided to go ahead on its own.

The observation team was exposed. If they encountered trouble, they had only old radios on which to call for help, and there was no certainty that they would function properly at all times outside London. There was also another unforeseen problem. Although the bug worked, and the suspect detective arrived at the flat, the waiting CIB officers could hear from the conversation between him and the woman that he was not interested in sex. He said he was "feeling knackered". Although the woman had been briefed to behave normally, she, in fact, was making all the running, asking the officer to go to bed. For the apparent benefit of those listening outside, she then gave a commentary on what was happening, referring to him "penetrating" her. She then told him to stop, but he replied that he was not doing anything. If he was not physically aroused, it appeared that his suspicions were, because he asked why she was acting strangely. At that stage, the CIB officers burst in and arrested the detective.

A report went to the CPS, setting out what had happened in the bedroom and setting out evidence of other alleged wrong-doings. But eventually the CPS decided that a prosecution was impossible. There had been no rape and there was little or no evidence against the detective for any of the other alleged offences beyond the word of the woman herself, and she was likely to be viewed as unreliable in any court because she was a drug addict. Interestingly, both she and the detective had known that her heroin use would cause just such a problem. She had related a particular conversation with him when first interviewed by the CIB officers, prior to the sting operation. She told them that she had threatened the officer with exposure for rape: "I said, 'I'll have you. I'll go down to the police station, and have you done for rape.' I said it many times. He said to me, 'Who are they gonna believe? An ex-junkie with a boyfriend in prison, or me, a detective sergeant? I'll say you wanted it.'"

Three years after he was arrested and suspended, disciplinary action was finally taken against the SERCS detective for interfering with a protected witness. The officer had been on full pay the whole time, and this continued as he frustrated the disciplinary process by declaring that he was sick. Eventually he was sacked, and it is believed that he retained his pension rights.

Gaspar likened a corruption inquiry to a murder investigation, where the first twenty-four hours after the crime are by far the most important for gathering evidence. "I had to push all the time," he told me. "CIB just didn't understand that we had to win the mental battle. CIB argued that officers had to be properly interviewed and it would take time to prepare for such interviews. I said that was nonsense as it was known they were going to say nothing. Just get them and tell them they'd been caught doing so and so. They're not going to say anything."

As well as "dinosaur attitudes", there was another associated problem in trying to turn the ghost squad's intelligence into evidence, eventually recognized by Gaspar. "You couldn't gather evidence and stay secret at the same time," he told me. "The idea that you could simply drop in our secret intelligence to operations wasn't always working. Questions would be asked about where the information came from. How did anyone know it was reliable? It was difficult to answer such questions without revealing our existence."

However, a different complexion was put on the problem by another senior officer who later became involved in the anti-corruption drive. Critical of this area of Gaspar's operation, he said: "Years ago, evidence for investigations would be gathered secretly, and then the executive arm would be called in and they'd work on the material and then make arrests. That way the baddies never knew where the stuff was coming from. Gaspar and company started doing the same, but they were five years behind the times. The rules and regulations had changed. They were floundering."

In addition to CIB investigators' natural curiosity about the origin of the intelligence information given to them, major changes to the law meant that prosecution evidence in court cases had to be fully sourced in order to withstand defence challenges over its veracity. This meant, for instance, that it was no longer enough simply to produce a tape recording or a bank statement in evidence. The officers making the recording or obtaining the statement could be required to appear in court. Giving evidence in legal proceedings had been causing MI5 and the Special Branch problems in Irish terrorist trials. Most of the work of these agencies was done covertly, and the security service did not want to have secret techniques made public or made available to "the enemy" through pre-trial disclosure. Undercover officers who had penetrated Irish groups and MI5 informants were at particular risk, unable to give evidence because their lives would be in danger. Even simple confirmation of the existence of a well-placed intelligence source could result in a flow of information being stemmed, and to secret operations being aborted.

The original idea had been that ghost squad intelligence would be drip-fed into CIB for further action. But CIB2 was still essentially a reactive organization, geared up to act only in response to a complaint or a crime that had already taken place. Not only was it not up to the job of properly developing intelligence information, but any requirement that its

evidence be sourced could lead to the secret squad's existence becoming known. The implications of this horrified
Gaspar. It would have meant the end of the ghost squad.

The Scotland Yard hierarchy that had authorized the
setting up of the secret operation faced stark choices. Millions
of pounds had been spent on it over two years, but on the
surface there was little to show for all the expenditure. Strong,
useful intelligence had been gathered which showed that
there could be two hundred corrupt detectives in the London
area. But because so much time had been spent on forming
the squad and maintaining its secrecy, it had not delivered on
the second of its original important aims – an effective way of
tackling the bent cops. It had made two big breakthroughs
into a murky world, but both were unresolved. Investigations
into Geoffrey Brennan's allegations that he had paid £50,000
to two officers had come to nothing. Speculation that he may
have manipulated Gaspar's team for his own ends was to
receive some confirmation early in 1997 when he withdrew
his allegations and complained about CIB. The other example concerned investigations into Flying Squad wrong-doing.
After nearly two years there appeared little prospect of
anyone being charged over stealing some of the proceeds of
the £1.5 million security van robbery. Corruption appeared
to be flourishing.

Although Operation Countryman, the last big corruption
inquiry, enjoyed only limited success in the early 1980s as far
as prosecutions were concerned, publicity about it had at
least caused enough of a stir to deter corrupt detectives for a
time. But nothing similar had occurred as a result of the
ghost squad's operation because the measures taken to
preserve its secrecy had been totally successful. Only a handful of very senior officers outside the unit knew of its
existence, let alone what it had been looking at. CIB officers
were still viewed by corrupt detectives as sleepy and ineffec-
tive. Far from being deterred, some of those aware that they
had been under investigation in 1993 were still "at it" a
couple of years later.

In 1993 the BBC's *Panorama* had exposed corrupt

dealings by John Donald, a detective in the South East Regional Crime Squad. He took bribes totalling at least £20,000 from a drugs dealer for help in collapsing a prosecution against him and also for police information on other drugs investigations, including one into the notorious gangster Kenny Noye, now serving a life sentence for a road-rage murder. Donald himself was given an eleven-year sentence. It was this programme which helped kick-start the whole secret probe into Metropolitan Police corruption.

The *Panorama* programme also gave rise to another important corruption inquiry, the first major investigation into the workings of NCIS, the National Criminal Intelligence Service. As a measure of its seriousness and sensitivity, the then Chief Constable of Northumbria, John Stevens, was brought in to superintend it. Stevens at that stage was a rising police star, having conducted two investigations into claims that members of the Northern Ireland security forces provided loyalist paramilitaries with intelligence files. Stevens was called to London during John Donald's Old Bailey trial in 1995 after a serious breach of security. Transcripts of intercepts – phone taps – had been produced in court. This was not only against the law, which states that such material should not be used in evidence, but there had also been a clear breach of security at the sensitive NCIS headquarters, from where phone tapping is supervised. Direct verbatim transcripts of intercepts are not allowed out of the building. Detectives engaged in investigations involving the tapping of criminals' phones are allowed into NCIS headquarters at Spring Gardens in Vauxhall, south-west London, but they can only make notes from the transcripts in specially issued and logged notebooks. These notes must not themselves be copied, according to the strict rules applying at NCIS. They have to be handed back after a very short time period.

The Stevens investigation lasted a year, and the report he presented in January 1997 was devastating to NCIS's prestige. He found that nine hundred of the special notebooks had not been returned. Some were lost. Although many officers insisted that they had given them back, there were no records to support their claims. Other officers still had note-books, and explained that they had not understood that they should have been returned. Stevens found procedures a shambles. He made ninety recommendations for change, all of which were accepted by NCIS. Later, after a spell as Her Majesty's Inspector of Constabulary, Stevens became the Met's Deputy Commissioner, which, among other things, put him in charge of corruption and disciplinary matters. In 2000 he became the country's top cop, taking over as Commissioner after Sir Paul Condon's retirement.

With corruption still rife at the end of 1996, Scotland Yard decided to launch the second part of its new anti-corruption strategy and to shake up CIB. Although to an extent disorganized, the ghost squad had largely completed the first part of its job in assessing and gathering intelligence on the level of corruption. Part two, tackling and rooting out the cancer, would now be got under way. Sir Paul Condon warned of what was to come in the summer of 1996. In "London Beat", the Met's strategy for the new millennium, he said that under-cover squads were being set up to target crooked officers, adding: "We recognize that a small number of officers either through bad behaviour or corruption can have a dispropor-tionate impact on our reputation. We want them to be in constant fear of exposure." As part of the new crackdown, the Met later set up an internal confidential telephone system called Right Line which officers and civilian staff could call if they suspected any wrong-doing on the part of colleagues and were uncomfortable about telling senior officers. Somewhat disingenuously, the Deputy Commissioner, Sir Brian Hayes, said: "This is not in response to any major problem we perceive in the Met of corruption, but there are always cases cropping up in a service as big as this. We need to make sure we are in there quickly, nipping them in the bud before they become a problem."

The ghost squad's work would be incorporated into CIB and its intelligence information used to target suspect detec-tives. But instead of conducting retrospective investigations, they would now be proactive. Rather than using bugs, probes and intercepts to gather evidence on officers' past crimes, the same tools would be used to catch them in the act. If the suspects were too clever to be heard discussing anything of significance, then temptations would be put their way. If necessary, sting operations would be initiated against them, just as they were sometimes mounted against major criminals.

His job largely done, Detective Chief Superintendent Gaspar was told that he was to be transferred to one of two posts. He was either to take over as head of Scotland Yard intelligence or become commander in south-west London. Eventually he was told he would go to south-west London, as the boroughs wanted commanders with major crime experience rather than uniformed bureaucrats. Gaspar had wanted to stay working centrally, but admitted he was feeling burned out with the stresses and strains of leading a double life, and with handling such sensitive work. He had suffered in other ways too. Professionally he had been greatly respected, and that had been reflected in the number of Christmas cards sent to him by colleagues. He reckons that each year he used to receive about eighty cards. But after he had been heading CIB for a couple of years, the number sent to him had dropped to six, itself a reflection of the depths of ill feeling and resentment of what was viewed as CIB's unnecessary work. Gaspar says semi-seriously that those six Christmas cards were probably from people unaware of his move to CIB. This social shunning would have been even more severe if colleagues had known of his other role, heading the secret anti-corruption squad. Later in his career he returned to a key police role, becoming number two at NCIS.

The officer chosen to take over as overall head of CIB and transform the intelligence-gathering squad into a proactive operation was Commander Roy Clark, later to become Deputy Assistant Commissioner. He had been the man most directly responsible for persuading Sir Paul Condon to set up the secret squad in 1994. Clark then became head of the South East Regional Crime Squad in the aftermath of the John Donald corruption affair. He had kept in close contact with

DCS Roger Gaspar, giving him information about suspect SERCS officers, much of which he obtained late at night, when, in relative safety, he scoured empty offices, looking through drawers and files. Through Gaspar, Clark kept abreast of developments and problems arising out of the secret inquiry. This meant that he already had answers when the then Deputy Commissioner, Sir Brian Hayes, handed him Gaspar's final report and strategic assessment and told him, "You're in charge now. How are we going to tackle this?"

Like Gaspar, Roy Clark was a hard-working police officer, at his desk in Scotland Yard every morning by eight o'clock at the latest, staying until well into the evening. Dedicated to the job, he was not above telling the occasional white lie, especially when it meant preserving the secrecy of anti-corruption operations. While head of SERCS he wrote a memo to staff saying they should expect shocking publicity when John Donald came up for trial at the Old Bailey for corruption. However, his memo continued by saying that Donald was a "one-off" and SERCS would recover. While the latter part of the statement may have been true, Clark knew that Donald was far from being a lone rotten apple in SERCS. Not only did Clark know at the time of writing that those closest to Donald at his Surbiton base were still under investigation and would remain so for some time, but he also knew there were suspect pockets of corruption at neighbouring SERCS bases. When asked later about this contradiction, Clark responded that circumstances forced him to write such a memo. If he had told the full truth he would have blown the secret inquiry and the already low morale within SERCS ranks would have sunk even further.

Clark began phase two of the anti-corruption strategy by starting the process of transferring the ghost squad's information to CIB headquarters at Tintagel House, close to the HQs of both the National Criminal Intelligence Service and the National Crime Squad. Later, another office was used at Jubilee House in Putney, also in south-west London. To act on the intelligence, a new secret proactive CIB unit was set up, the forerunner of a new department, known as CIB3.

Experienced senior detectives were drafted in. All were known to be of the highest integrity, and all had either made some kind of stand against corruption in the past or had been directly involved in actual operations against bent cops. Despite those earlier experiences of this murky world, these officers were shocked on reading and being briefed about the extent of corruption uncovered by the secret squad. Some of them were to face personal problems. To their apparent surprise, they learned that some of their long-standing friends had been targeted as corrupt. For example, an officer who was godfather to one senior anti-corruption officer's child was later charged with corruption; similarly with the best friend of another officer. These new CIB detectives would have to minimize contact with these suspect officers, without their suspicions being raised. Questions were to be raised later about these relationships. How could these "whiter than white" CIB officers have such close friends or colleagues without knowing what they had been up to?

The first of this new intake was Detective Superintendent Dave Wood, who took over as operational head in December 1996. He had not wanted the job. He knew of CIB2's reputation, and he had been very happy working for SERCS in south London, close to his family home. But the Deputy Commissioner told him he had no choice. Wood was joined early the following year by Detective Chief Inspectors Chris Jarratt and John Coles. All three were shocked on learning of CIB2's lack of resources and expertise. Wood, a bespectacled, avuncular man who had been a DCI under Roy Clark at SERCS, put it diplomatically in an interview with me. He said that CIB did not attract experienced, career detectives at that time:

> It attracted another type of police officer who may do their job very well, but these investigations into dishonest and corrupt police officers are the most complex and difficult investigations that can be done. The people employed there, generally speaking, didn't have the skills or experience to tackle such work. They did reactive investigations where

you take statements and interview officers about what the statements allege. But that's what I would describe as the dorsal fin. There's a shark below the surface that hadn't been seen. There was a small number of corrupt officers and the extent of their criminality was quite astonishing.

Asked why officers became corrupt, he replied:

It's a very difficult question to answer because there are all sorts of reasons. There's greed. There's exposure to large sums of money. Some of these officers are going into houses where there might be half a million pounds in cash, which has just come from a drugs deal. If the officer was to walk away with that half a million, the person is not going to complain. They'll be delighted because that's major evidence against them and it's going missing. These are the sort of temptations that Met police are faced with fairly regularly. Some officers will succumb to that temptation. Thankfully, ninety-nine per cent will not.

Those that did succumb, he continued, developed a certain arrogance.

The very corrupt ones tended to be very experienced detectives who'd worked on regional crime squads or other squads like that. They were aware of the strategies the Met was using to investigate complaints. They were aware the people they were stealing from, or had corrupt relationships with, were not going to complain against police. And even when there was a complaint of any shape or form, the people who were going to interview them or try to investigate them had poor experience compared to the corrupt ones. So that gave them a confidence to go about their activity and, indeed, an arrogance about the way they went about it.

Wood was also to find that some of this arrogance came from corrupt officers' friendships and contacts with CIB2 officers. He suspected information was leaking from CIB, some of it deliberate. Wood had asked one CIB2 detective to make covert enquiries about a particular officer, but the detective had declined, offering the excuse that he was already over-worked. The following evening, Wood's frustration with officers with little or no commitment to the job turned to fury when he attended a social occasion at a police sports club. As he parked his car, he saw the same CIB2 detective talking behind some bushes with the very same officer he had been asked to make enquiries about. The next day, Wood challenged the CIB2 detective. The officer said he had simply been having a social chat, but Wood was having none of that. Why were they talking in a secluded place in the car park? Wood called him corrupt and reported him. The officer was sent home on the police equivalent of civil service 'gardening leave'. He retired shortly afterwards.

The new men came under some pressure to produce results. Under Roy Clark's supervision, Wood set in motion what was to be the huge task of transferring the intelligence data compiled by the ghost squad to a newly created unit, the Complaints Investigation Branch Intelligence Cell, CIBIC for short. Much of this intelligence information had never been fully analysed. It included tape recordings from bugs and intercepts which had never been properly listened to, if ever actually played.

The secret squad had already cost several million pounds, and with some of London's best detectives being drafted in for its second phase in 1997, there were murmurings of dissent from the London boroughs and senior officers in the area specialist squads. They asked what was going on. Why were they being stripped of their best men? When told that the anti-corruption squad was being beefed up, they queried whether it was necessary, some disputing that corruption had reached a level that justified more money, resources and expertise being slung at it. Those high up in Scotland Yard knew from the ghost squad's intelligence that corruption had again taken hold and was increasing. But without revealing the secret squad's achievements, they had no immediate way of reassuring the doubters. The new-look CIB was asked to try to come up with a big case in which the evidence was so strong it would demonstrate that corruption was again at a very serious level.

Superintendent Dave Wood was in charge of new operations, with DCI Chris Jarratt heading CIBIC and looking after intelligence-gathering. The pair saw that the retrospective investigations had not progressed far, so they concentrated on trying to make use of some of the information gathered by the secret squad. They worked through the material collected over the previous two years, prioritizing it, picking out what looked most promising. What were called "intelligence packages" were produced and handed on to experienced operational detectives to develop. These "packages" could consist of only two or three items. There might, for instance, be information about a suspect officer gleaned from tapping a telephone. This could be supported by surveillance on the officer which showed him meeting a criminal or another suspect officer, away from police premises. Sometimes the ghost squad had itself followed up such sparse material. But much of it was untouched. Either way, it was rare for any of it to have been used in prosecutions. It was up to the experienced detectives to develop it and obtain sufficient evidence to mount court cases.

According to one of the senior men drafted into CIB, much of this ghost squad material was flawed.

> I don't want to be too critical, because they had been doing their best, but quite frankly, some of the jobs the secret squad had worked on were in a mess. They had a lack of resources, so hadn't developed some of the intelligence material at all. These jobs had gone stale, so we were trying to play catch-up, which is always very difficult. And some of the jobs that they had worked on had been developed by them in the wrong way, making it impossible to get evidence which would stand up in court. If we had had the same raw intelligence, we would have pursued it in different ways.

The best way forward for the new team was seen to be the proactive targeting of the suspect officers judged most likely to be tempted by sting operations. Their vulnerabilities would be worked on, and if entrapment was successful, the aim would be to turn the corrupt officers into super-grasses, to provide evidence against their suspect colleagues. But the new team was not going to waste precious resources mounting sting operations against individual suspect detectives thought to be acting on their own. They aimed to tackle squads in which corruption was believed to be endemic and systematic.

The measures taken, used routinely against major criminals, were unprecedented against police officers. The new men selected the Flying Squad for further targeting. Ironically a Home Office report at that time was applauding the Squad's use of proactive measures to catch robbers. The report, *Armed Robbery: Two Police Responses*, compared the Flying Squad's approach to that of the South Yorkshire force, which was largely reactive. It praised the Flying Squad and its ability to cultivate and handle informants, and urged other forces to set up databases similar to the Flying Squad's of all known and suspected robbers, with detailed offender profiles. "The information held should include details on patterns and styles of offending, linked to trade marks of different offenders," said the report. It was exactly this kind of information which had been produced by the secret ghost squad. It was now to be developed for use against the Flying Squad, and, in particular, against Detective Constable Kevin Garner.

The thirty-five-year-old Garner was one of the detectives allegedly involved in stealing up to £200,000 of the proceeds of the £1.5 million security van robbery in January 1995. But that was not the only reason why he became a suspect – there were other reports of his corrupt activities after this robbery. Garner came to CIB notice after making two checks on the Police National Computer. It turned out that these had been done on behalf of a criminal called Michael Taverner, who was under investigation for dealing in stolen cars, sending them abroad with false registration details. Taverner was also linked to the two robbers who had carried out the security van raid with Bobby Freeman. In fact, unknown to any anti-corruption detectives at the time, Garner's corrupt relationship with Taverner had started shortly after the robbery on the security vehicle, when he had bought counterfeit currency from him and switched it with real money seized by the police from criminals.

The team handling the stolen car inquiry visited Garner early in 1996 to ask why he had made the PNC checks. He explained that he was trying to develop Taverner as an informant, and to help that relationship had carried out what he claimed were "harmless" checks for him on the ownership of two cars. Undeterred by the car squad's visit, in April 1996 Garner bought a stolen Mercedes from Taverner, registering it in the name of his partner, Jackie Coote, also known as Jackie Buisson. He believed his cover story had worked. Such was his confidence that he started discussions with Taverner over a plan for him and another detective to take part them-selves in a robbery modelled on the security van "tiger kidnap".

What Garner was proposing was serious corruption – police officers were actually conspiring to commit an armed robbery with criminals. Garner developed his plan after being part of a team investigating another security van robbery earlier in the year. He had visited the robbed guard's home and found him a weak and vulnerable character who was short of money and required little persuasion before agreeing to cooperate in another robbery. Garner planned to fit him with a dummy bomb and microphone, copying what had been done to the security van driver-guard the year before. Taverner introduced another apparent criminal into the scheme, someone known to Garner only as Irish Mick. This mystery man was to play a key role in the Garner saga at a later stage. But in April 1996 the plan was that Irish Mick and Taverner would carry out the robbery while Garner and his trusted detective colleague would make sure that they were crewing the Flying Squad "crime car" that day, ensur-ing that the robbers would make a clean getaway. However, unknown to the conspirators, they were under surveillance by anti-corruption officers, alerted to Garner by the stolen car squad officers.

The robbery plan left the CIB investigators in a quandary. Much of their information had come from phone taps which could not be used as evidence in court. So if they arrested the four men prior to the raid on the security vehicle they would have little usable evidence against them, and a prosecution would almost certainly fail. It would also have the effect of blowing open the whole covert investigation into alleged Flying Squad corruption. An alternative was to let the robbery go ahead and then make arrests. But such a strategy held greater potential risks. There would be a public outcry if some innocent person was shot, or even killed, as police moved in on the robbers, knowing beforehand that other police officers were involved. Anyway, the anti-corruption investigators simply did not have the resources, facilities or manpower to mount what would be a huge operation, monitoring and moving in on the robbers. Instead, it was decided to disrupt them, to frighten them into calling off the robbery. Such tactics were sometimes used for various reasons by other specialist police squads. It was known that if the Flying Squad, for instance, heard of plans to rob a bank but did not have resources that day to mount an ambush, they would deter the robbers by parking a marked police car close to the bank. A similar tactic was used to stop the Garner-Taverner robbery, but it was more subtle. The plan was that a surveillance team would deliberately "show out" to Taverner, so he would realize that he was being watched and be forced to abandon the robbery. The ruse worked perfectly.

As Taverner changed a number plate on a car in the street outside his house, he heard the loud click of a camera shutter coming from bushes near by. Realizing he was being watched, he stopped what he was doing, telephoned Garner and told him the job was off as the police were "all over him". Garner was worried too. If police were on to Taverner, it was for two possible reasons. Either they were continuing to investigate him for stolen car dealing or they knew something of the robbery plot. Garner decided to take no chances. He knew he already had a reputation among some of his colleagues for odd behaviour, which had started after he had left his wife. This had deepened when he spent time trying to penetrate a gang of hit-men who had carried out contract killings. He had also been attacked in a pub and hit over the head. Garner decided to go sick. Over that weekend he met a former colleague, Keith Green, who had moved on to the National Criminal Intelligence Service and retired on grounds of mental ill health following a shooting incident; he was mounting a civil claim against the Yard. Garner pumped him for information about how he had gone about making his claim. The following Monday, Garner went sick, never to return to the job. Later he was allowed to retire. But the intelligence operation against him continued. He was to become the key to providing evidence for use by anti-corruption officers investigating Flying Squad corruption.

DCI Chris Jarratt, in charge of intelligence operations, assessed what had been learned and made further enquiries into Garner. He took the view that Garner was weak and vulnerable and, if caught, would "roll over" and confess. Jarratt himself had a reputation for being a hard man, dedicated to the job. He was given the nickname "J. Rat" by his detractors, those he was hunting down. Unlike other senior detectives, he does not recall encountering corruption early in his career, probably, he says, because he had always taken a hard line over gifts and favours, believing that while an officer is on duty even a cup of tea should not be accepted without payment. Confirmation of this high-minded attitude comes from his vivid recall of an incident years before and his continued questioning of whether he had acted correctly over it. He had been on a day out in Brighton in a fish restaurant with his wife and children when some youths started causing trouble. Jarratt intervened and the youths disappeared. The restaurant owner was so grateful that he refused to accept payment for the family's meal. Jarratt persisted in trying to pay, but the owner was adamant and Jarratt finally gave up. He still wonders whether the owner guessed he was a police officer from his actions and was trying to curry favour, or whether his generosity was simply out of gratitude for a kind act. Jarratt's first encounter with real corruption was not until the late 1980s, when a shotgun seized during one of his operations went missing from a police station.

During the autumn of 1997, Jarratt and the other senior CIB officers assembled teams capable of surveillance work and intelligence-gathering and able to take part in complicated sting operations. The notion of strict "sterile corridors" was introduced, so that each of the different units would not know what the other was doing. Everything was to be run on a "need to know" basis. "The corrupt officers we were targeting had great abilities, through what they had learned from their training and their various postings," Jarratt told me. "To work for us, we had to take in people who were totally untainted, so they couldn't be a mole to the other side, wittingly or otherwise. For example, if they had training as detectives, they could have been in contact with the quarry. We looked at people's postings, social meetings, etc. Clean people were needed, like the IRA needed for some of their operations here. They had to have integrity and ability, and, if necessary, an ability to be trained up to the job. That can be assessed in an interview, whether they're free thinkers, lateral thinkers." For the sting operation to be mounted against Garner, Jarratt chose officers he knew who had worked with him in south London. He trusted them, and they were less likely to know Flying Squad colleagues of Garner.

Exact details of how the sting was set up are unclear. The officers involved are reluctant to give away the secrets of a successful operation because they may have occasion to use the same techniques again. Even Garner himself is unsure which of two criminals set him up, and he still does not know whether either of them was cooperating with anti-corruption police or whether what they did was done unwittingly. Garner was by then retired and working as a chauffeur and "gofer" for a foreign embassy. But it was known from the intelligence operation against him that he was saying he wanted to get involved in the drugs trade, and he was still mixing with

Michael Taverner and Irish Mick. CIB decided to give Garner
what he wanted – drugs. Information that a large amount of
cannabis was for the taking in an east London flat was fed to
him. The information came from Taverner, who was then on
bail for dealing in stolen cars, having been arrested and
charged in April 1997. Did the police put him under pressure to betray Garner? There are clues as to what occurred in
events following Taverner's prosecution. He had also been
charged with possession of an automatic pistol and ammunition, but these charges were eventually dropped after he
pleaded guilty to the theft and handling of a large number of
stolen vehicles. Was the relatively low prison sentence he
received because of a favour he had done for the police, or is
the more likely candidate for setting the sting in motion the
mysterious Irish Mick? The answer may be that it was both of
them, with Irish Mick playing the more devious role. This
Irishman's full identity remains a mystery. The police are
determined to keep it that way.

Although it is only speculation, a version of events with an
authentic ring of truth was given to me by a detective source.
He told me that Irish Mick was an undercover officer, brought
to London especially for work with CIB. The thinking was
that if an undercover officer posing as a criminal was introduced to Garner as being from London or anywhere else in
England, checks could have been made on his origins, with
the risk that his pose would be seen through. But because he
came from Northern Ireland, it would be impossible for any
suspicious corrupt officer to penetrate his "legend". The
detective said:

> Imagine what would happen if anyone with a London or
> English accent started making enquiries about a criminal
> from across the water, with all its terrorism and criminality.
> They'd get nowhere. It was the perfect cover. The police
> persuaded Taverner to introduce Irish Mick to Garner and
> to vouch for him. What did Taverner get out of it? He got
> a lighter prison sentence. Sure, nothing was said when he
> was being sent down. But these things can be fixed behind

the scenes. Even his own lawyers don't have to know anything of the background. And where is Irish Mick now? Who is he? What's his full name? He's disappeared and probably still acting undercover now. My bet is that no one will ever find out what his real role was.

What is not in dispute in this intriguing story is that the flat chosen for the sting was 4A Albert Road, in Silvertown, east London, close to the old Royal Albert Dock and near the much newer City Airport. It had been rented by another undercover officer using fake documentation. He had spun a story to local estate agents to the effect that he wanted a flat for his brother and some mates who were coming to London from Australia for a visit. Having paid a deposit and a month's rent upfront in cash, the undercover officer handed the keys over to other squad members for the sting's next phase. CIB's technical experts moved in to install tiny video cameras and microphones in the flat. One camera was hidden inside a dummy electric socket screwed to a wall close to the floor. It pointed down the stairs, to the front door, so that anyone coming in would be filmed. Another was hidden in a light fitting in the bathroom. Outside, police set up an observation point, an OP, in offices next to the Tate and Lyle sugar factory across the railway line running parallel to Albert Road. From the OP, the flat's front door could be seen, but it was too distant for accurate, clear video images, especially at night. So another small video camera was fitted at the top of a lamp-post standing on railway land, across from 4A. It could swivel, remotely controlled by officers in the OP with monitor screens. The pictures obtained from all three cameras were sharp.

On 2 December 1997 eighty kilograms of best Moroccan cannabis, taken from a Metropolitan Police warehouse packed with drugs seized in raids, were planted in the flat. The load was divided into bags and stuffed into a cabinet under a basin in the bathroom. The drugs had been specially marked. For evidential reasons, photos were taken of the stash in the bathroom cabinet the next day. With the trap set, it was then a question of the officers at the observation point waiting for the police thieves to arrive. CIB was so short of trusted staff that those chosen to man the OP had to work thirty-six hours at a time. Although the information about the drugs was aimed at Garner, it was not expected that he would pick them up alone. The information fed via Taverner and Irish Mick suggested that the flat was occupied, and the anti-corruption detectives believed that Garner would ask for help from his corrupt former Flying Squad colleagues, because they would be able to obtain a search warrant to make the raid on the flat look official. CIB was confident that someone would turn up to steal the drugs. The unknown factors were when that would be, and how many would be involved.

Chris Jarratt, the officer in charge recalled:

> The area was like Gotham City, dripping with atmosphere, especially at night. There were bursts of steam coming out of a big sugar factory and noises from the trains going by. I've been involved in some stings before and the whole thing about this one was that it looked right. It wasn't one where the target would think, "There's something's wrong here." It was absolutely spot on. It was an area where you'd engage in criminality. The area and the flat were right for a level-two drugs dealer, someone likely to have a few sacks, and eighty kilos was the right amount to put in. If it had been twenty kilos, for instance, it wouldn't have been enough to make it attractive for Garner.

Told of the drugs stash by Taverner and Irish Mick, Garner prepared to steal the drugs from 4A Albert Road late at night on 4 December, and he would indeed not be alone. He had contacted two trusted colleagues who had been with him in the Flying Squad. Terry McGuinness, still a serving officer, had agreed to take part. Garner had tried to get another detective, another Squad officer, to join in to act as a "heavy". But the detective was on police duties elsewhere, so Garner enlisted another former Flying Squad officer, Keith Green, to act as lookout. The trio met up at a police station where McGuinness was on duty, on night shift. They drove in two cars and parked round the corner from Albert Road. Like common criminals, they were "tooled up", ready for any eventuality.

The anti-corruption officers in the observation post watched developments from the monitor screens in front of them. The camera opposite the flat picked up the trio standing in a huddle on the pavement outside number 4A. As the tall and beefy Green kept watch, looking up and down the street, the other two broke in using a jemmy. Garner told Green to stay on the doorstep. The camera inside the flat at the top of the stairs then picked up McGuinness and Garner climbing up to the first floor, McGuinness carrying what looked like a search warrant. An ex-boxer, nicknamed "Meathead", he looked tough and ready for business as he passed in front of the camera lens. Next up the stairs was Garner, and he was followed a little later by an equally tough-looking Keith Green, carrying a big wooden truncheon. They had come prepared to meet resistance. One of them shouted, "Anyone in?" Having established that the flat was empty, they began to search for the drugs.

In the CIB observation post, there was a mixture of excitement and worry. There was relief that the intelligence had been right, and that all the resources put into the job and all the hours of waiting had not been in vain. People had turned up at the flat, and the fact that their faces could clearly be made out resolved another possible problem. It had been decided beforehand that if the thieves were masked then they would be arrested as they left the flat. That tactic was now unnecessary, as the thieves could easily be identified. But the trio were not recognized by the officers in the observation post. The operation had been mounted on a need-to-know basis, and it had been thought unnecessary to tell the CIB officers anything about Garner. This meant that they were virtually completely reliant on the video recording equipment working properly. Although the pictures on the screens were clear and sharp, if the recording equipment had broken down, later identification of the villains would have been very difficult, or even impossible. So there was worry about the equipment and worry that the trio in the flat would be unable to find the drugs. One of the detectives in the observation post told me: "As we watched and heard them moving about the flat, we weren't saying to ourselves, 'Go on, go into the bathroom – that's where the drugs are.' We weren't exactly willing them to go there, but we were very relieved when one of them was seen by the second hidden camera going into the bathroom and bending down under the basin." Garner was then heard shouting to the others: "Here you are. It's here!" Just three minutes after breaking in, the trio emerged carrying the bags, heavy with drugs. They walked calmly to their cars, as though this was everyday work.

The secret watchers were jubilant that all their planning had worked. Jarratt was not there, so he was paged with the simple message "Happy Birthday". He knew what it meant and started telephoning, setting in motion the sting's next phase. The identities of the three were not positively established until the next day, when a group of anti-corruption detectives assembled to study the videos. Jarratt recognized Garner immediately. Others identified the other two. It had been decided beforehand that, whoever they were, no one should be arrested immediately, the thinking being that an experienced, well-trained detective could come up with a convincing story if arrested too quickly. Garner could say he had just been tipped off about the drugs being there and had taken them, seeking a reward. He could add that there had been no time to alert the police at that hour of the night, but he had fully intended to take the drugs to a police station at a later stage. The secret squad knew that any such false explanation would not hold water if the three failed to report what had happened within a reasonable length of time.

Further precautions had been taken to make sure the sting worked properly, but to the end it was a high-risk plan, with no certainty about what would happen to the drugs once they had been taken from 4A Albert Road. Sometimes, in operations against ordinary criminals, electronic tracking devices are hidden in the drugs so police or Customs can monitor their movements afterwards. But this was not done on this occasion because it was feared that Garner, a trained and experienced detective, would search the drugs for just such a device, and if he found one the sting operation would be blown. Instead, each kilo slab of the cannabis had been given a distinctive mark with a special pen which would only show up under fluorescent light. But would Garner do as he had been told by Taverner and Irish Mick, and take all the drugs to the designated lock-up garage, or would he skim some off, telling the pair that there had been less than expected in the flat? The CIB team had decided not to follow Garner as they did not want to run the risk of being seen. Given such a situation, Scotland Yard had accepted that some of the drugs could go missing. There was no honour among thieves, even if they were police officers. The possibility that drugs would be lost was to become a reality.

Garner took the haul to the lock-up, then met up with Taverner and Irish Mick and handed over the keys. At a second meeting the next day, the former officer was told by his fellow criminals that there was not as much cannabis as they had expected. They suggested that Garner had taken some of the drugs himself before putting them in the garage, but Garner denied it. He was promised £20,000 from the sale of the drugs, which he was supposed to share with McGuinness and Green. Taverner had meanwhile rented a house in Peterborough Road, Leyton, in east London, and he moved the drugs there. When police raided it several days later, they found only fifty-four kilos. About a third of the cannabis was missing. Who had taken it, and at what stage, remains a mystery.

There was a further hiccup when CIB went to arrest Garner, McGuinness and Green on 8 December. Their three homes were to be raided at the same time, 7 a.m., rather than the visits being staggered, so none of them could be alerted and disappear. Garner and Green were in, but there was a hitch over McGuinness. He was not at his family home. He had gone to a girlfriend's after work and was arrested there later. Garner's arrest was dramatic. Eight officers with a dog handler smashed their way into his house at Brentwood in Essex. They were led by DCI Jarratt, who shouted, "Police officers." With his partner Jackie shouting, Garner was grabbed by one officer, and, when he resisted, Jarratt put an arm round his neck, wrestled him to the ground and shouted: "You're under arrest." Garner refused to put his hands behind his back for handcuffing, and continued struggling, so Jarratt put his foot on his head, pinning him to the floor while another officer managed to handcuff him. A search of his home revealed what looked like a sawn-off shotgun, and there was a crowbar in his car. Twelve bullets and a knife were found at McGuinness's home address. When arrested at his girlfriend's home, he went quietly, as did Keith Green, at whose home were found shotgun cartridges, a knuckleduster and a truncheon. Although he had retired from the National Criminal Intelligence Service, he had what looked like an NCIS identification card and also a police-style warrant card.

The sting had worked perfectly. CIB had got their main target, Garner. McGuinness and Green were unexpected bonuses. But there was apprehension about the next phase. Would the three confess, not only to their own corruption, but to other Flying Squad wrong-doing too? Garner was potentially a huge supergrass, and there were also rumours about McGuinness, who after leaving the Flying Squad had transferred to normal CID duties at a police station. Certainly he had been under investigation by CIB for other wrong-doing. It had been alleged that he had accessed the Police National Computer for a national newspaper in order to get the home address and details of someone who had won the national lottery. He had also tipped off a newspaper about the whereabouts of an east London publican who had fled to Spain with £20,000 of money raised for victims of the Dunblane shooting massacre. Less was known about Keith Green, who had moved from the Flying Squad in 1993 after nearly being shot in the chest by McGuinness while arresting two robbers. Suffering from stress and other mental problems, he transferred to NCIS, and was allowed to retire on grounds of ill health in 1996.

The new CIB team had thought long and hard about attempting to turn officers into supergrasses. They recognised that the supergrass system had fallen into disrepute in the 1980s and since then had been used rarely. Wood and Jarratt looked at its failings and how criminals who had become supergrasses had been able to manipulate their status for their own benefit. The CIB officers decided on strict new safeguards to prevent abuse. Rather than using the harsh term "supergrass", participants would be called "resident informants". They would be held separately from other colleagues who had also turned informant, and there would be a "sterile corridors" policy for the police investigators too. One supergrass's debriefers would have no direct contact with another's questioners or with the teams of detectives who would be following up the information and leads coming from them.

The first task, however, was to find a means of turning arrested officers into supergrasses without offering them inducements that could be challenged in court. The prospect of a supergrass's evidence being thrown out at trial because he had been given promises or shown favours inducing him to talk was appalling. Such a scenario was unlikely to happen in this case, however, as the suspects were experienced detectives who knew the rules for informants. They did not have to be promised light prison sentences if they informed on their colleagues. They already knew that this would be their due. But CIB also had to cope with restrictions imposed by the Police and Criminal Evidence Act, PACE, which included the recording of any questioning about the offences committed by the arrested person. The anti-corruption officers got round this by introducing what they called "intelligence interviews". These would usually occur in the cells before or during questioning. The arrested officers would be told in general terms that there was a huge amount of evidence against them, but that they could help themselves by considering giving evidence against their colleagues. One tactic was to talk about "meat-eaters" and "grass-eaters", terms originating in the 1970s during corruption inquiries in New York.

Officers described as "meat-eaters" were vicious predators who instigated corruption while "grass-eaters" were grazers who had simply gone along with their colleagues as part of the herd. CIB detectives could tell arrested men that they believed them to be simply grass-eaters, and that it was wrong that they should suffer while the meat-eaters escaped. Because these were "intelligence interviews" the exact words used were not recorded, so a court would have no evidence on which to judge whether or not inducements had been offered, or whether there had been other malpractice.

The three former Flying Squad officers arrested for stealing the drugs were interviewed separately and the first indications were not encouraging. Green vehemently denied knowing that drugs were being stolen. He said he had been doing what he thought was a favour for his old friend Garner, who had told him he needed help in repossessing office equipment belonging to his then employer, the Argentine embassy. While Green stuck to his story, the other two were totally uncooperative, answering "no comment" to even innocuous questions from the anti-corruption officers. Superintendent Dave Wood started his interview with McGuinness gently, asking him whether it was correct that he'd been with the police for eighteen years.

McGuinness responded: "No comment."
Wood: "During your eighteen years' service you've been posted to various police divisions, mainly as a detective, and spent five years on the Flying Squad. That's correct, isn't it?"
McGuinness: "No comment."
Wood: "During your time, I understand you've had lots of dealings with drug cases. Is that correct?"
McGuinness: "No comment" . . .

On and on the interview went in the same vein, until Wood eventually called a halt.

Detective Chief Inspector Jarratt was faring little better with Garner, but he felt he could break his silence and persuade him to talk with the help of his girlfriend Jackie Buisson. Garner said he wanted to talk the situation over with her. The pair met early the next morning, and Garner later told Jarratt that he was willing to assist. Before there was a chance for him to change his mind, Jarratt took him to an interview room, switched on the tape recorder, and three minutes later, after the formalities were over, asked Garner: "Can you tell me in criminal terms how many people you think you can give evidence against?"

> Garner: "I've been thinking all night and things kept coming into me head. It's somewhere between twenty and thirty."
> Even Jarratt was taken aback by these numbers, and at first could only manage to respond with the words "All right". Then, to make sure that Garner was talking about bent cops, he asked him, "Twenty to thirty police officers?"
> Garner: "Yeah."
> Jarratt: "How many of those officers are serving now?"
> Garner: "Um, well, the majority of them . . . they're mostly SO8" (the Flying Squad) . . .

Garner had "rolled over", and was to confess over the next few days to a series of corrupt acts in which he and many others in the elite squad had been involved. McGuinness followed him in turning supergrass, estimating that he could name between ten and twelve detectives as corrupt, including two chief inspectors, two inspectors, sergeants and constables. Between them, the pair were talking about massive corruption. Police had planned robberies, stolen huge amounts of money and fitted people up.

CIB's delight that the operation had worked and that Garner and McGuinness had turned supergrass was shared by the Metropolitan Police Commissioner, Sir Paul Condon, as events seemed to confirm and validate what he had told the House of Commons Home Affairs Committee on 4 December, the day of the sting operation. "I do have a minority of officers

who are corrupt, dishonest and unethical . . . These bad officers sap the morale of their honest colleagues and they do
immense damage to public confidence."

Sir Paul had continued by attempting to get the problem
in proportion:

> Clearly corruption is about human frailty and opportu-
> nity. The opportunity is at its greatest in the big city
> environment. That is where huge sums of money can be
> offered to suborn officers from the straight and narrow. It
> has to be accepted that the excesses of police malpractice
> are at their most pronounced in big city environments
> around the world because that is where the most serious
> criminals operate, that is where huge sums of money can
> be thrown at officers to suborn them. A small provincial
> force is not going to encounter the magnitude of the prob-
> lem we have in London . . .

Although the Garner case was shocking, the Commissioner
and those close to him would use it to great effect in two
ways, helping to silence their critics, at least for a time. First,
they said it demonstrated how big a problem corruption
represented, with the video film taken at 4A Albert Road
providing apparently incontrovertible proof for those asking
where the evidence was. Second, the Met was now seen to be
starting to crack down on the problem, and would be justified in seeking further resources to tackle it even more
effectively.

"It was a groundbreaking sting – a defining moment," one
senior officer told me. "It proved to the police and to the
outside world that we had big corruption. Together with
the inquiry into the Stephen Lawrence murder, the whole
course of policing was changed, not only in the Met, but
throughout the country."

10

Crime Beat: True Stories of Cops and Killers

Michael Connelly

The following complex tale sheds light not only on plain-clothes LA policing in the wake of the Rodney King scandal, but on the workings of the California justice system and the way in which the momentum of a hugely controversial case, hearing-to-hearing, can peter out amid technical arguments concerning dry questions of civic liability which had never-theless been triggered in the first place by the most frenetic, dramatic police activity, by plain-clothes power given licence to act off the leash and become judge, jury and executioner.

Whether intended by its original legislators or not, there's no doubt that sustained legal action, even when conducted on behalf of plaintiffs who believe they or their loved ones have been the subjects of heavy-handed policing, acts to dilute public anger with delay, and mollify calls for further investigation into allegations such as evidence-tampering until the plaintiffs are exhausted, even with an ambitious, hot-shot lawyer plighting their case, and the public fatigued and desensitized – it's the fog of law.

Compelling and successful serial thriller writer Connelly was an LA crime reporter (an established career path, it seems, for American thriller authors) before he became known as the creator of detective Harry Bosch. His reports for the *LA Times* on the following case of an alleged LAPD undercover "death squad", laid out in their order of publication from February 1990, tell their own, at times squalid, story.

POLICE SURVEILLANCE UNIT
KILLS 3 ROBBERY SUSPECTS

LOS ANGELES TIMES

February 13, 1990

Three suspected robbers were killed and a fourth was wounded early Monday by nine officers from a controversial Los Angeles police squad who watched the suspects force their way into a closed McDonald's restaurant in Sunland and rob its manager at gunpoint.

Shortly after the suspected robbers climbed into their getaway car – and one pointed a gun at the officers, police said – the officers fired 35 shots into the late-model bronze Thunderbird. No officers were injured during the 2 a.m. confrontation in front of the deserted Foothill Boulevard restaurant. The manager, who had been tied up by the robbers and left behind, also was unharmed.

Police said the officers, who are members of the police department's Special Investigations Section, a secretive unit that often conducts surveillance of people suspected of committing a series of crimes, watched the robbery take place but did not move in because of safety reasons.

After the suspects, who were believed to have been involved in a string of fast-food restaurant robberies, got in their car, the SIS officers pulled up, shouted "Police!" and opened fire upon seeing one of the men point a gun at them, police said.

Three pellet guns that appeared to be authentic handguns were found in the car and on one of the suspects after the shooting. Police said it did not appear that any of the pellet guns had been fired.

The police shooting was being investigated by the department's officer-involved shooting unit. Lt. William Hall, head of the unit, said the officers did not violate a year-old department policy that says officers should protect potential crime victims even if it jeopardizes an undercover investigation.

The police was instituted after police officials reviewed the procedures of the SIS. A *Times* investigation in 1988 found that the 19-member unit often followed violent criminals but did not take advantage of opportunities to arrest them until after robberies or burglaries occurred – in many cases leaving victims terrorized or injured.

Police said the officers involved in Monday's shooting are SIS veterans with an average of 19 years of experience with the Los Angeles Police Department. The officers were identified as Richard Spelman, 39; James Tippings, 48; Gary Strickland, 46; Jerry Brooks, 50; John Helms, 40; Joe Callian, 31; Warren Eggar, 48; Richard Zierenberg, 43; and David Harrison, 41.

The gunfire early Monday echoed throughout the commercial and residential area where apartment buildings sit alongside restaurants, convenience stores and small service shops.

"I woke up hearing many, many shots," said Alejandro Medina, whose corner apartment overlooks the shooting area. "I got up to see and then there were more shots. I hit the floor."

Although SIS officers had watched at least one of the men off and on since the beginning of the year, Hall said the suspects were not seen breaking any laws before they forced their way into the McDonald's at 7950 Foothill Boulevard.

"At the times the surveillance has been on the suspects, (police) saw no crimes," Hall said. "To stop them they needed a reason. That had not occurred. Once (the suspects) went up to the restaurant, maybe they crossed that threshold."

Hall said the officers, however, then decided they did not want to risk the safety of the restaurant manager by attempting to burst into the McDonald's and arrest the robbers.

"The decision was made that, since there never had been any injuries involved in any of these robberies, rather than try to force entry into the building, they would wait and let the suspects exit," Hall said.

The names of the three dead men were not released Monday. The wounded man was identified as Alfredo Olivas,

19, of Hollywood. He was in a serious condition, suffering from two shotgun wounds, at Holy Cross Medical Center in Mission Hills. Police said that when he recovers, Olivas will be arrested on a murder charge because, under California law, he can be held responsible for any deaths that occur during a crime he allegedly committed.

Police began their investigation of the suspects after the robbery of a McDonald's in downtown Los Angeles in September, Hall said. Because detectives and McDonald's security officials believed the robbers had knowledge of how the restaurant operated, several employees were questioned and given lie-detector tests.

One employee was fired after failing the polygraph examination but there was no evidence to arrest him, police said. The downtown robbery was similar to at least six others – five at McDonald's restaurants and one at a Carl's Jr. – in Los Angeles since August, police said. In each case, the robbers had knowledge of the business's operations and forced a lone manager at gunpoint to open a safe after hours, police said.

SIS officers began to follow the former employee in early January and, on Sunday night, the officers watched as he met with three other men in Venice and drove with them to Sunland in a bronze Thunderbird belonging to one of the men, police said.

The four men arrived at the McDonald's as it was closing at midnight and watched it from the Thunderbird parked across the street, police said. At 1:36 a.m. when only night manager Robin Cox, 24, was still inside, three of the suspects got out of the Thunderbird and approached the restaurant.

Hall said one man remained in front while two others attempted to break in a rear door. Cox heard the break-in attempt and called police. Patrol units were not dispatched, however, because SIS officers were watching the restaurant.

Hall said the officers held back on arresting the suspects because the suspects were too spread out. As the officers watched, the two suspects at the rear of the restaurant moved to a side door and forced their way into the McDonald's.

All four suspects then entered the restaurant. Cox was tied

up and threatened at gunpoint until she opened the restaurant's safe. Several thousand dollars was taken, police said.

The suspects came out of the restaurant half an hour later and walked across the street to the Thunderbird. After they were in the car, four unmarked cars containing eight officers pulled up from behind and one officer ran up on foot.

Hall said the officers identified themselves and were wearing clearly marked "raid" jackets that said "police" on the front and back.

"When they approached the vehicle they saw one of the suspects with a handgun point it toward their direction," Hall said. "One of the officers said, 'Watch out, they've got a gun.'

"At that time we had several officers fire into the vehicle. The passenger in the front exited and fled into an open field. He was carrying a handgun and several officers fired at him. All the shots were fired in just a few seconds."

Hall said that after the firing stopped, two officers approached the car and fired four more shots into it when they saw "two of the suspects were moving around, reaching down to a floorboard where a gun was."

A total of 23 shotgun blasts and 12 shots from 45-caliber handguns were fired by police at the suspected robbers, Hall said.

Several residents in the area said they were awakened by the gunfire and shouts of the police officers.

"My husband yelled to me to call the police," said Ronda Caracci, whose apartment also offers a view of the shooting area. "I looked out the window and said, 'Hey, it is the police.'"

ATTORNEY CALLS SPECIAL LAPD SQUAD "ASSASSINS" AS CIVIL RIGHTS TRIAL OPENS

Courts: Case will focus on tactics of Special
Investigations Officers who fatally shot three robbers.

January 10, 1992

Members of a controversial Los Angeles police squad who fatally shot three men after a 1990 robbery in Sunland were called "assassins with badges" Thursday by an attorney representing the families of the dead men in a civil rights lawsuit.

Attorney Stephen Yagman made the allegation during opening statements in a U.S. District Court trial that will focus on the tactics of the police department's Special Investigations Section, a 19-member surveillance unit that targets suspects in serious crimes.

The families of the three men killed in the Feb. 12, 1990, shooting, along with a fourth robber who was shot but survived, charge that the SIS is a "death squad" that follows suspects, allows them to commit crimes and then frequently shoots them when officers move in to make arrests.

"What they do is attempt to terminate the existence of the people they are following,"Yagman told the 10 jurors hearing the case.

Deputy City Atty. Don Vincent countered that the officers acted properly and that the SIS is a valuable police tool. "This is a necessary organization that most police departments have," he said. "It is even more important in Los Angeles, a city of 365 square miles . . . where the criminals are just as mobile as the police."

The trial before Judge J. Spencer Letts is expected to last at least two weeks. The suit names members of the SIS, Police Chief Daryl F. Gates, Mayor Tom Bradley, the Police Commission and all former commissioners and chiefs during the unit's 25-year existence. Yagman says officials have allowed an environment in which a "shadowy" unit such as the SIS can operate. The shooting in front of a McDonald's restaurant on Foothill Boulevard occurred after a lengthy investigation into a series of restaurant robberies. Police said that in late 1989 investigators identified the suspects – Jesus Arango, 25, and Herbert Burgos, 37, of Venice and Juan Bahena, 20, and Alfredo Olivas, 21, both of Hollywood.

SIS officers followed the four intermittently for three

months before they watched them break into the McDonald's where manager Robin L. Cox was working alone after closing for the night.

After they tied up, gagged and blindfolded Cox, the robbers left the restaurant with $14,000 from its safe.

When all four were seated in their getaway car, SIS officers moved in on foot and in cars. Police said two of the men pointed guns at the officers, who opened fire, killing three and wounding Olivas in the stomach. Police said they recovered three pellet guns that resembled pistols.

Officers later explained that they could not make arrests before the robbery because the four men moved too quickly and were too spread out around the restaurant.

Whether the men in the car were armed at the time of the shooting will be at issue in the trial. Yagman said they had no weapons and were shot in the back.

Olivas, the first witness to testify, said that the robbers stored their weapons in the trunk of the car before getting in. The shooting started a few seconds later, said Olivas, who is serving a 17-year prison term for the robberies.

Vincent in his opening statement sharply disagreed, saying two of the robbers drew the police fire when they pointed their weapons at the officers. "Officers have a right to self-defense," he said. "They don't have to wait for someone to shoot them."

FBI PROBES SLAYING OF ROBBERS BY LAPD

Police: Existence of inquiry came to light
in suit over SIS unit's killings of three men
who had robbed a Valley restaurant.

January 16, 1992

The FBI is investigating the killing of three robbers in Sunland by a controversial Los Angeles police squad, and the Justice Department apparently has taken the case before a federal grand jury, court documents showed Wednesday.

The investigation surfaced when the U.S. Attorney's Office mentioned it in asking a U.S. district judge to throw out a subpoena for an FBI agent called to testify in the trial of a lawsuit filed over the shooting.

The request indicated that the shooting by the Special Investigations Section had been under investigation for nearly a year.

The FBI agent, Richard Boeh, was subpoenaed to testify in the civil rights suit filed after the Feb. 12, 1990 incident, when nine SIS officers fired at a getaway car used by four robbers who had just held up a McDonald's restaurant in Sunland. They killed three and wounded the fourth.

The survivor and relatives of the slain men are suing the city and the police department, alleging that the SIS squad violated the robbers' civil rights by executing them without cause.

Police have contended in testimony in the week-old trial of the lawsuit that the robbers were shot because they pointed pistols at the officers. Weapons found at the scene were discovered to be pellet pistols, similar in appearance to firearms.

Stephen Yagman, the attorney representing the plaintiffs, summoned Boeh as a witness, saying the federal agent has information that could be vital to proving the suit's key contention – that the robbers had placed their pellet guns in the trunk of the getaway car before getting into it, and therefore were unarmed when the SIS officers surprised them and opened fire.

Yagman said the FBI investigation dates from early last year, when Boeh interviewed the sole surviving robber, Alfredo Olivas, now 21 and serving a 17-year prison term for robbery.

"It would be a perversion of justice for the jury to deliberate this case without hearing what the FBI has found," Yagman said outside of court.

But the U.S. Attorney's Office filed a motion to quash the subpoena for Boeh. In a declaration contained in the motion, Boeh said he has been investigating the police shooting since

April 1991 and indicated that he has provided testimony to a grand jury investigating the incident.

"If called to testify, my testimony would violate the rule of secrecy relating to proceedings before the grand jury," Boeh said.

Boeh said that if he testified he would also have to reveal the identity of informants and other details of the federal investigation.

"To my knowledge, the information from the informants and the identity of the informants is known only to the government," Boeh said. "My testimony would reveal facts relating to the strategy of the government in the investigation."

Assistant U.S. Atty. Sean Berry, who is seeking to block Boeh's testimony, did not return a phone call seeking comment. The U.S. Attorney's Office routinely withholds comment on grand jury proceedings, which are secret.

Los Angeles Deputy City Atty. Don Vincent, who is representing the police officers and other defendants in the civil rights suit, including Police Chief Daryl F. Gates and Mayor Tom Bradley, could not be reached for comment after the trial recessed Wednesday.

Judge J. Spencer Letts has not yet ruled on whether Yagman will be able to call Boeh to testify.

In trial testimony Wednesday, a parade of former top managers of the police department testified briefly about their roles in running the department – some going back to the early 1960s.

Yagman called 13 former members of the civilian Police Commission and three former police chiefs in an attempt to bolster the lawsuit's contention that the SIS, a secretive unit that places criminal suspects under surveillance, is a "death squad" that has operated for 25 years because commissioners and chiefs have exercised little control over the department.

According to testimony, the unit has been involved in 45 shootings since 1965, killing 28 people and wounding 27.

Most of the former commissioners testified that they considered the appointed post a part-time job, and four testified they never knew of the SIS while they were members of

Michael Connelly

the commission. Former Chief Tom Reddin, who held the top job from 1967 to 1969, said in brief testimony that he had known of the unit's existence but had never investigated its activities.

Roger Murdock, who served as interim chief for six months in 1969, said he thought the SIS unit was formed to investigate the assassination of Sen. Robert F. Kennedy.

Yagman did not ask Sen. Ed Davis (R-Santa Clarita), who was police chief from 1969 to 1978, about the SIS. Instead, he asked how Davis viewed the role of the Police Commission during his time as chief.

"I might have been wrong but I always thought they were my bosses," Davis said. "They were tough bosses. . . . I danced to their tune. I wanted to keep my job for a while."

Note: FBI Agent Richard Boeh refused to testify about his investigation of the SIS and was held in contempt of court. The agent immediately appealed and the contempt order was reversed by the 9th Circuit Court of Appeals. The trial then resumed after a month's delay without his testimony.

CHRISTOPHER REPORT: IT CUTS BOTH WAYS

Courts: The findings of the city-commissioned panel could work against L.A. when jurors rule in police brutality suits.

February 4, 1992

As Mayor Tom Bradley sat in the witness chair, a thin smile played on his face. He was facing an uneasy situation that he and the city may have to get used to.

Bradley was testifying in federal court last month as a defendant in a civil rights trial. And he was repeatedly saying, yes, he fully agreed with the conclusions of the Christopher Commission, the independent, blue-ribbon panel that last year investigated the Los Angeles Police Department and found problems with management, excessive force and racism.

"You have no reservations about your agreement with

those conclusions?" the plaintiffs' attorney, Stephen Yagman, asked.

"No," Bradley told the 10 jurors.

Bradley was testifying in a civil rights case in which police officers are accused of killing three robbery suspects without provocation. Police managers and Bradley are also accused in the suit of tolerating excessive force and many of the departmental problems cited by the commission.

In effect, the mayor was being cut with his own sword; after all, he was a main force behind creation of the commission. Now, the commission's findings could prove pivotal when jurors decide if the officers acted improperly and their supervisors – right up to Bradley and Chief Daryl F. Gates – are responsible.

While the trial is the first in which the report has been brought up by plaintiffs against police and city officials, it most likely will not be the last.

Yagman, a civil rights attorney who specializes in police-related lawsuits, said he has clients with five more cases set for trial this year. He plans in each case to introduce the commission report as evidence of a police department that he says is out of control. Other civil rights attorneys said last week that they plan to do the same.

"It is paradoxical and sweet," Yagman said of having such a key document essentially prepared for him by the city that his clients are suing. "The effect of having this report is like putting whipped cream on a malt."

Meantime, Deputy City Atty. Don Vincent, in charge of defending the city against police-related lawsuits, said his staff is developing strategies to deal with the report when it comes up in trials. He conceded that his task may only be beginning.

"It is a valuable tool for all civil rights attorneys," Vincent said. "I am sure we will be facing this for several years to come."

Though the report has been discussed at length in front of the jury in the trial, Vincent hopes to block inclusion of the 228-page volume as evidence in the case. Though pointing out that the report makes many favorable conclusions about the police department, Vincent said its damaging claims are largely hearsay and opinion – not evidence.

The current case arose from a shooting on Feb. 12, 1990, in which nine members of the police Special Investigations Section opened fire on four suspects who had just left a McDonald's restaurant in Sunland after a holdup. All four men were hit by police shots and only one survived.

The families of the dead men and the survivor, who was later imprisoned for robbery, filed suit against the officers, Bradley, Gates and the Police Commission alleging that the robbers' civil rights were violated because the police opened fire without provocation. The lawsuit also alleges that the SIS is a "death squad" that has been created and fostered by an environment of lax management, brutality and racism in the department.

More than a year later, the Christopher Commission, formed by Bradley after the outcry that accompanied the Rodney G. King beating, delivered a report highly critical of management of the department and concluded that the police force had problems with excessive force, racism and a "code of silence" among its officers.

Yagman said in a recent interview that many of the report's conclusions mirror the allegations in the lawsuit spawned by the McDonald's shooting.

He unsuccessfully sought to have Warren Christopher, who chaired the commission, testify as a witness. However, U.S. District Judge J. Spencer Letts has allowed Yagman to use the commission's report to question witnesses such as Bradley, Gates and police commissioners.

Letts is expected to rule later whether the report will be accepted as evidence and whether jurors will be able to refer to it during deliberations.

Regardless of the ruling, the report and its conclusions are already a large part of the trial record. So much so that at one point during Bradley's testimony, Letts interrupted and cautioned the jury that they were not deciding a case on the incident that prompted the report.

"Don't get confused," Letts said. "Rodney King is not here."

Outside of court, Yagman has told reporters that his questioning of witnesses has covered "every single chapter" of the report.

But how important the Christopher Commission report will be to the case and others that follow cannot be determined until verdicts are returned.

Jurors in the McDonald's case have heard conflicting testimony over the report. Bradley said he agreed with the report's conclusions, while Gates testified that he believes many of them are untrue or exaggerated.

And even in testifying that he accepted the report, Bradley sought to repair any damage to the defense by stressing that the report targets only a small portion of the force. He said that, overall, the city has the finest big-city police department in the country.

But Yagman and other attorneys said the commission report will automatically lend a strong degree of validation to claims made in lawsuits of police abuse.

"This is not a wild-eyed civil rights lawyer saying this, it is a blue-ribbon panel appointed to fairly evaluate the LAPD," attorney Benjamin Schonbrun said. He plans to introduce the report as evidence in two upcoming trials against the Los Angeles police.

"I've been saying these same things for years," Yagman said of the report's conclusions. "Everybody now believes it."

Other attorneys specializing in police misconduct litigation said the effect that the report will have on how they prepare lawsuits against the Los Angeles police will be significant, and possibly expensive as damages are assessed.

"By all means, it is terribly important," said Hugh R. Manes, a civil rights lawyer in Los Angeles for more than 35 years. "I think it is a very important tool against the LAPD. It is based upon their own files and records going back 10 years and thus shows a pattern of misconduct."

Manes said the report's broad coverage of the department's problems will mean that at least portions of the report will be relevant, and admissible, in almost all LAPD-related cases.

Veteran police litigator Donald Cook has a federal suit pending against Gates and the city that also alleges misconduct by the SIS.

"And guess what I am going to use as evidence?" he asked recently.

He said that, like Yagman, he will attempt to introduce the commission's report as evidence of the department's poor management and condoning of excessive force.

"It is a great piece of evidence – really trustworthy, credible evidence of what we have been saying for years," Cook said of the report. "It is ironic that we are validated by the city. It is really ironic.

"I think the city is getting a dose of justice."

Vincent, the deputy city attorney, has yet to mount the city's defense in the current case. Though he declined to reveal specifics about his strategy, he said his task is to clearly separate the report from the facts of the shooting that is the basis for the lawsuit.

"We are going to stick to the facts of the case," Vincent said. "Our opinion is like the mayor's. It is still the finest police department in the nation."

He said that almost all documents used as evidence in lawsuits against the police come from police-shooting reports, policy statements and disciplinary records. So facing the commission report is not a totally unfamiliar situation. Still, Vincent said, its impact may be the most difficult to deal with.

"I think it is significant," he said. "It has certainly gotten recognition and prestige.

"But I think it is something we will effectively deal with. We think some of it is flawed. It gives a skewed view."

That view comes from the report's focus on problems within the department without a full reporting on positive aspects of the force, Vincent said. The report's conclusions are too broadly drawn, he added, and jurors will be unable to ascribe them to the officers involved in the McDonald's shooting because neither they nor their unit is mentioned in the report.

"This type of information should never be used," Vincent said. "It has come into this case to prejudice officers that are not even named in it."

Still, Vincent is resigned to having that task of deflecting the effect of the report in trials to come.

"I am not sure of all the ways it can be used against us," he said. "So we are thinking about it.

"We are just going to take it one case at a time."

L.A. DETECTIVE TELLS DETAILS OF FATAL SHOOTING

Civil rights: The officer is testifying as a defendant in a suit alleging the Special Investigations
Section killed three unarmed robbers.

March 5, 1992

In testimony lasting nearly three hours in federal court Wednesday, a Los Angeles police officer described in grim detail the shooting in which he and fellow officers fired 35 times at four robbers outside a Sunland McDonald's, killing three and wounding the fourth.

Detective John Helms said he fired six times with a shotgun and three times with a pistol after seeing one of the bandits flee the getaway car with a gun and a second man brandishing a gun inside the car.

Afterward, police discovered that the weapons used by the robbers during the Feb. 12, 1990 incident were pellet guns that were replicas of real firearms.

During the shooting, Helms said: "I was looking for any indication that these men were trying to submit to arrest. I saw nothing that indicated surrender."

Helms' testimony came in the months-long trial of a civil rights lawsuit filed by the surviving robber and the families of the men killed.

Their suit contends that the nine officers who opened fire did so without warning or provocation and that the use of excessive force violated their rights. The suit says the officers, all members of the department's Special Investigations Section, are part of a "death squad" that specifically targets criminal suspects for execution.

The surviving robber, Alfredo Olivas, testified earlier that the bandits had stowed their pellet guns in the trunk of the car after the robbery and therefore were unarmed when fired upon. Several officers later testified briefly that they saw guns being brandished, prompting the shooting.

Now, in the defense phase of the trial, the officers are testifying at length about the incident and why they opened fire.

Seemingly choked with emotion during some of his testimony about the shooting, Helms told jurors that, because of tactical and safety concerns, the officers could not move in to arrest the bandits until the thieves left the McDonald's after robbing the lone employee inside.

When the four men were in their car, which was parked on the street, four SIS cars moved in to block their escape. Two of the police cars actually hit the getaway car, "jamming" it behind a parked truck.

As officers jumped out of their cars, Helms said, he heard one officer shout "Gun!" – a warning that he saw a gun in the getaway car. Helms then heard shots being fired and shouts of "Police! You're under arrest!"

"Things were going on simultaneously," Helms said. "I saw a man get out . . . and I saw a gun in his right hand. I saw him start to run."

Helms said that, because the robbers had used guns during previous crimes, he believed the men still inside the car were also armed and that the officers surrounding the car were in danger.

"I started directing fire at the back," Helms said. "The next thing I saw was one of the handguns being brandished through one of the holes in the rear window."

Helms fired again, emptying his shotgun of shells. In the meantime, other officers shot the man who had run from the car when he allegedly turned and pointed a pellet gun at them.

"I knew I was out of ammo on my shotgun," Helms said. "I put it in my car and took out my .45."

Helms then described how he and his partner approached the car to make sure the three robbers inside were no longer a threat. He said that when he looked into the car one of the men in the backseat was reaching for a gun on the floor. Helms said he yelled for the man to stop and fired twice when he did not comply. Helms said the other man in the backseat then reached for the weapon, and Helms fired at him as well.

Helms said he did not know how long the shooting lasted. "When I believe my life is in danger, I am not a good estimator of time," he said.

During cross-examination of Helms, the plaintiffs' attorney, Stephen Yagman, pointed out that the weapon the officer claimed to have seen in the car was an unloaded pellet gun. Yagman has said that the jury will have to decide whether it is plausible that the robbers would have pointed or attempted to reach for pellet guns when confronted by nine officers with shotguns and .45s.

GATES WANTS TO BE "JUDGE, JURY, EXECUTIONER," LAWYER SAYS

Courts: Attorneys make their closing arguments in the trial stemming from a February 1990 shooting in Sunland in which officers killed three robbers.

March 25, 1992

The Los Angeles Police Department is a "Frankenstein monster" created by Chief Daryl F. Gates, who has allowed a squad of officers to operate as "assassins," a federal jury was told Tuesday in a trial over a police shooting that left three robbers dead.

But the allegations made by an attorney representing the robbers and their families was rebutted by the city's attorney, who defended Gates and said members of the police squad – the Special Investigations Section – use tactics designed to avoid shootings.

The statements came during closing arguments in a three-month trial stemming from the Feb. 12, 1990, shooting outside a McDonald's restaurant in Sunland.

"The police have gone too far in Los Angeles by using excessive force," plaintiffs' attorney Stephen Yagman said.

"The LAPD and Daryl Gates have ruled this community for 14 years by fear," Yagman said. "He does and has done as he pleases. The LAPD is his Frankenstein monster. It is something that has gone beyond all bounds. . . . He wants to be judge, jury and executioner."

Gates and nine SIS officers are defendants in the lawsuit filed by the families of three bandits who were killed by police and a fourth who was shot but survived. The lawsuit contends that the officers used excessive force and fired on the robbers without cause. The 10-member jury is expected to begin deliberations today.

Deputy City Atty. Don Vincent countered Yagman's claims by telling jurors that evidence presented in the case clearly shows the nine officers opened fire when they sensed they were in imminent danger. He defended the firepower – 35 shots from shotguns and handguns – as being an appropriate response when the officers saw the robbers brandishing weapons. The weapons were later discovered to be pellet guns resembling real handguns.

Vincent cautioned jurors not to confuse the superior firepower of police with excessive force, noting that each officer feared for his life and had reason to fire. "This is not the Old West where you get out on the street and have a shootout at noon," Vincent said. "They are not the sitting ducks of the public."

According to trial testimony, the officers opened fire on the bandits after they watched them break into the closed McDonald's, rob the lone employee inside and then return to their getaway car. The shooting started almost immediately when officers converged on the car.

The plaintiffs contend that the bandits had put their unloaded pellet guns in the trunk of the car and therefore were unarmed when the shooting started.

Noting that U.S. District Judge J. Spencer Letts ruled earlier that the police had probable cause to arrest the four suspects before the robbery, Yagman argued that the officers allowed the crime to take place and orchestrated the stakeout in such a way that the shooting was "inevitable, inescapable." He said the special police unit has a long record of using tactics that often end in shootings.

Yagman said police took the pellet guns from the trunk after the shooting and "planted" one inside the car and one on the body of a robber who had run from the car before being shot by police. He said police photos show the gun inside the car in different positions, indicating police tampered with the evidence.

He said that while the claim that guns were planted might be "hard to digest," the alternative – the police story – defies common sense.

"What person, when faced with nine officers with shotguns, would point an unloaded, inoperable pellet gun at them?" he asked. "What does common sense tell you?"

In his closing argument, Vincent denied that Gates condones excessive force. He also said an extensive department investigation cleared the officers of any wrong-doing.

He recounted police testimony that the gun was indeed moved. Vincent said the gun was photographed as it was found by officers and then removed from the car but later replaced so additional photos could be taken. But the original photographs are clearly marked, he said.

Vincent noted that the weapon allegedly planted on the body of Herbert Burgos was the same weapon the survivor, Alfredo Olivas, testified that Burgos used during the robbery. Vincent asked jurors how the officers could have known on which robber to plant which weapon.

"Nothing was planted in that car," he said. "It would mean that it was happenstance that they placed the right gun with the right body."

Vincent said the explanation for why the robbers pointed unloaded pellet guns at the police will never be known. "They might have thought it was someone else and raised the guns to scare them," he said.

COUNCIL SUED OVER FATAL POLICE SHOOTING

Attorney offers to drop members as defendants
if they make Gates pay damages assessed in same
incident. Officials angrily charge extortion.

April 2, 1992

Los Angeles city council members were sued Wednesday over a police shooting that left three robbers dead, but the attorney who filed the case offered to drop them as defendants if they make Police Chief Daryl F. Gates personally pay for damages assessed against him this week for the same shooting.

Council members familiar with the new suit and a city attorney who defends the city in police-related cases reacted angrily to the offer from civil rights attorney Stephen Yagman, which was contained in a letter to the council that accompanied the new $20-million suit.

"Sounds like extortion, doesn't it?" said Deputy City Atty. Don Vincent, head of the city's police litigation unit.

Councilman Zev Yaroslavsky, who favors making Gates pay the damages from his own pocket, said he was nonetheless disturbed by Yagman's letter.

"Nobody likes to be threatened," he said.

Councilwoman Joy Picus, who is undecided on the issue of whether Gates should pay, said Yagman was using tactics of intimidation and harassment.

"The nerve of him," she said. "I've dealt with attorneys who have tried to extort and threaten me before. I'll be damned if I'll be intimidated by him."

Yagman denied his offer to the council was improper or threatening.

"Everybody has a right to ask people in the government to do or not do something, and to say if you do it the way we want we will take action or refrain from taking action," Yagman said. "That's not extortion. That is trying to settle the lawsuit."

The lawsuit filed Wednesday in U.S. District Court against the council and numerous police officers and officials is the latest twist in the case that has followed the Feb. 12, 1990, shooting outside a McDonald's restaurant in Sunland.

The shooting initially spawned a lawsuit on behalf of four family members of three robbers killed by members of the police Special Investigations Section and a fourth robber who was shot but survived.

The plaintiffs, represented by Yagman, contended that the police used excessive force and fired on the robbers without provocation. Gates was named as defendant because the suit said he was ultimately responsible for the officers' actions and condoned the use of excessive force.

After a three-month trial, a federal jury returned a verdict in favor of the plaintiffs Monday and awarded punitive damages of $44,042 against Gates and nine members of the SIS. Jurors said the damage award was purposely set low because they believed the chief and his officers should pay it out of their own pockets. Gates was to pay $20,505 of the award.

The verdict touched off a debate this week among council members over whether the city should pay the damages anyway. The council has routinely picked up the tab for punitive damages assessed against police officers for incidents that occurred while they were on the job.

On Wednesday, the new lawsuit further added to the controversy. The new suit is identical to the first one but was filed on behalf of two-year-old Johanna Trevino, daughter of Juan Bahena, one of the robbers police killed.

Yagman said Trevino was born six days after Bahena, whose real name was Javier Trevino, was killed and can file the lawsuit under a federal precedent set last year in another case involving the SIS. In that case, in which Yagman is also the plaintiff's attorney, a federal appeals court held that a child who was not yet born when a parent was killed by police may still sue for damages over losing a parent.

The new lawsuit names 20 SIS officers, Gates, Mayor Tom Bradley, 17 former police chiefs and commission members and all City Council members in office at the time of the shooting.

In a letter enclosed with the suit to the council, Yagman said:

"If the council votes not to indemnify Gates for the punitive damages in this case, then all of you who make up the majority so voting will be dismissed voluntarily as defendants in this new case."

Vincent, the city attorney, said he could not comment on the lawsuit until he received it. But of Yagman's letter to the council, he said, "I have never heard of an attorney doing anything like that at all."

Council members who received it Wednesday also reacted strongly.

Councilwoman Joan Mike Flores said the lawsuit and Yagman's tactics were an outrage.

"I will not be intimidated by these types of tactics," she said in a statement.

Yaroslavsky said the letter Yagman sent could hinder efforts by council members who believe Gates should pay the damages awarded by the jury.

"I don't think Yagman's letter advances that cause at all," he said. "I think it's unnecessary and inappropriate. My inclination is not to pay for Chief Gates. . . . I will come to a final conclusion based on the facts, not a threat."

But Yagman said his letter was an effort to make the council abide by the wishes of the jury that heard the McDonald's shooting case.

"We are just saying that if they refuse to indemnify Gates, we will drop the case," Yagman said. "It might be wrong to threaten to sue them. But we haven't done that. We have sued them and said, 'If you act in a responsible way we will consider dismissing you from this lawsuit.'"

ATTORNEYS AWARDED FEE OF
$378,000 IN BRUTALITY SUIT

Courts: The ruling could lead to more sparks
between lawyer and the city council.

August 5, 1992

A federal judge has awarded $378,000 in legal fees to civil rights attorney Stephen Yagman and his partners for their work on a successful excessive-force lawsuit against former Los Angeles Police Chief Daryl Gates and nine police officers.

The ruling released Tuesday sets up another potential conflict in a running legal battle between Yagman and the city council over the council's financial support for officers defending themselves from civil suits alleging brutality.

Yagman outraged city officials earlier this year when he submitted a bill that asked for nearly $1 million in fees for himself and two partners who handled the lawsuit over a 1990 police shooting that left three robbers dead and one wounded outside a McDonald's restaurant in Sunland.

City attorneys, who had argued that the fee award should be about $216,000, said they considered it a victory that Yagman received much less than he asked for, but Yagman said he was satisfied with the amount. A decision has not been made by the city on whether to appeal the decision. After a three-month trial, the surviving robber and the families of the three dead men won a $44,000 damage award against Gates and the nine officers, all members of the department's Special Investigations Section. The plaintiffs maintained that the officers violated the robbers' civil rights by opening fire on them without cause, and that Gates' leadership fostered such excessive force.

The determination of legal fees by U.S. District Judge J. Spencer Letts on Friday could widen the battle between Yagman and the council over who will pay the lawyers' fees. Although the jury had urged that Gates and the officers pay the $44,000 damages personally, the council earlier this year voted to pay the awards from the city treasury.

Yagman said Tuesday that the legal fees awarded in the case should also be personally paid by Gates and the officers. Under federal law, an attorney who brings a successful civil rights case to trial must be paid by the defendants, with a judge determining the amount after hearing arguments from both sides.

"We have no judgment against the city,"Yagman said. "We have a judgment against nine SIS officers and Gates. They should pay it. Why should the taxpayers pay?"

Yagman said that if the council pays the $378,000 from city coffers, it will provide him with new ammunition in another lawsuit stemming from the same police shooting.

The second case, filed on behalf of a daughter of one of the dead robbers, names council members as defendants as well as the police. Yagman argued that council members should be held responsible for the officers' actions on the grounds that their decision to pay the damages in the first case in effect condoned the police misconduct that the jury found.

Yagman has contended that each time the council members vote to shield police officers from personal financial penalties in civil brutality suits they strengthen his argument that they are promoting police brutality and should also be personally liable for damages.

The second case has not yet been scheduled for trial. But Letts last week refused to dismiss the council members as defendants, rejecting the city attorney's argument that they are automatically immune from civil liability for their official actions.

Deputy City Atty. Annette Keller said council members don't have a choice over whether to pay such fees.

"It is part of the legal obligation of the city to defend employees sued for action taken in the course and scope of their employment," Keller said. "We are obligated to pay any judgment for attorney fees. It is not an issue for the council."

Yagman said his proposed fee was simply a "wish list" and that he was pleased with Letts' ruling. "This is a lot of money and I am happy to get it," Yagman said. In a 24-page order outlining his decision on fees, Letts praised Yagman for taking on the case that he characterized as "peculiarly undesirable" because the plaintiffs were a convicted robber and the families of robbers.

A *Times* investigation of the SIS four years ago spawned criticism that members of the unit trailing people with long criminal records often watched violent crimes take place without making a move to stop them so that the criminals could be arrested on the most serious charges possible, carrying more severe sentences.

In the McDonald's case, members of the unit followed the robbers to the restaurant and watched as they broke in and robbed the lone employee inside. She was left physically unhurt but is also suing the officers, claiming that the incident was handled negligently.

PART 3

POLICE AND THIEVES: Undercover in North America, Australia and Online

11

The French Connection: A True Account of Cops, Narcotics and International Conspiracy

Robin Moore

Simonson: "Buddy, here's the warrant. The court order's in there for the wiretap, the judge gave you sixty days on it. Tell Doyle that Mulderig and Klein will sit in for the Feds. They'll make all the buys. Be sure you keep them informed of everything that goes down."

Doyle: "Look, I say we keep sitting on Boca!"

Simonson: "Jimmy, give it up. Give it up, it's all over with. If there was a deal, it's gone down by now. We blew it, we blew our warrants, and we blew our cover."

Doyle: "Listen, I know the deal hasn't gone down yet. I know it! I can feel it, I'm dead certain."

Most famous for having inspired the hugely successful 1971 thriller directed by William Friedkin and starring Gene Hackman and Roy Scheider, the French connection was an entirely real international heroin-smuggling network believed responsible, during its period of operation, for practically the whole of the US's supply of the opiate. (A sweeping and unverifiable claim, but entirely possible in times more straightforward than our own, before South American gangs began to "supplement" their main cash crop, cocaine, with the cultivation of "Mexican Brown".)

The movie, of course, is full of action and spectacular – a tense hostage situation on a train, plenty of collateral casualties from among the general citizenry (the likelihood of which, in reality, would have caused any responsible police force to have called off a pursuit), and car chase scenes second only in their thrills and spills to those in *Bullitt*. The police do not ordinarily, of course, put the public at risk in these ways. But otherwise, the film is not unfaithful to the reality as told in Robin Moore's book, on which it was based. Eddie "Popeye" Egan was the basis for Hackman's character, the bigoted but brave Popeye Doyle, and even has a cameo in the movie as Doyle's boss, Walt Simonson. His detective partner, Sonny "Cloudy" Grosso, becomes Buddy Russo in the film.

Today, we're used to the idea that drugs may travel more than halfway around the world. But at the time the French connection was an audaciously global scam, albeit one that required the might and ruthlessness of existing organized crime to handle its distribution arm.

Until the Turkish government agreed to ban the cultivation of opium poppies in 1971, opening the way for Afghanistan's farmers to fill the void, the country was the world's leading supplier of heroin, having surpassed Indochina in this regard. Heroin labs were discovered in Marseille as early as 1937, controlled by the Corsican gangs. This cosmopolitan port city was the perfect location from which to supply their buyers via shipments to the Eastern seaboard. From there, the drug was distributed throughout the US by many notable gang and Mafia leaders including Lucky Luciano and colleague Meyer Lansky. Buying from the French, it seems, was not a partisan issue between the rival crime families and gangs of the USA.

The CIA (and the French equivalent, the SDECE) had developed links with the Corsican crime bosses following World War Two in an attempt to counter the influence of left-wing labour unions among the port workers. As American agents had done with the Sicilian Mafia as part of the war effort – Lucky Luciano in particular received some quid pro quos from the US justice system, it is alleged, on account of his organizational role in Operation Avalanche, the Allied invasion of Italy). So the film gives a misleading impression only in presenting the operation run by the suave Jean Jehan and TV presenter Jacques Angelvin as a one-off.

Tough-talking Doyle appeals straight to that strand of American culture that's suspicious of urbanity, especially on the part of the French. (Could it be that the French male's stereotypical ability to mix interests that, to the American mind, are often unmanly and effete with a sexual insouciance and a seemingly conquering charm confounds the Darwinian pastiche of jocks and cheerleaders prevalent in US high-school culture and beyond?)

A war veteran and Harvard-educated East-Coast blue blood, Moore's other books included bestselling Vietnam-War non-fiction, *The Green Berets*. He even penned the lyrics to "The Ballad of the Green Berets" (the number-one selling US single in 1966 – the year of the so-called British Invasion of the pop charts by The Beatles, Rolling Stones and others). More controversially, he also wrote *The Crippled Eagles*, unpublished as it stood and later issued as *The White Tribe*, a book about the American Vietnam vets who fought with the Rhodesian security forces during the Rhodesian Bush War, to whom Moore gave house room and who eschewed their description as "mercenaries", maintaining that they enlisted in the regular ranks. So we can safely assume what square-jawed aspirations the author's conception of masculinity entailed, despite the daring short shorts sported by Rhodesia's army at the time.

The French Connection begins when Egan and Grosso decide to tail Pasquale "Patsy" Fuca, proprietor of a humble news-stand, whom they've seen hanging out at the Copacabana Club, a high-rolling night spot, flashing money like it's newspaper, in the company of known gangsters. This leads them to buyer and distributor Salvatore "Sal" Boca . . .

Egan has switched to following Patsy Fuca, acting on a hunch that the heroin has now been received from Jehan. The feeling that he's acting along the right lines are confirmed when his car is boxed in by that of one of Fuca's connections, Solly "the Brass" diBrasco. As soon as he's free, Egan races to Anthony's Auto Shop on East Broadway, where the drugs have been hidden inside the body panels of a car that was waiting for Patsy – the cops hope. Running down his haunts, they see Patsy chatting at a bar. He drives off in an unfamiliar Oldsmobile, which they follow to Patsy's parents' home in Brooklyn . . .

Sonny Grosso and Frank Waters were among the dozen or so bleary-eyed officers staked out around 137 Henry Street. It was a dreary street, crowded on both sides by three-, four- and five-storey tenements, weathered storefront shops and auto-repair garages. Detectives slouched in unmarked cars at either end of the block in which Patsy had last been seen entering the store where the gambling was going on; other cars were scattered on side streets through the area, which, Egan was reminded, was but a few blocks from Blair's Pike Slip Inn and the section where, back in November, he and his comrades had futilely chased Patsy in the Canadian Buick.

Sonny and Waters had parked on Pike Street, around the corner from Henry Street and within view of Blair's, six blocks east towards the river. Egan climbed in with them and fell on the rear seat with a grunt. "So what else is new?" he asked hoarsely.

His partner eyed Egan. "You look terrible."

"What the hell, I been sitting in a gin mill all night, while you guys were out getting the air."

"They gave us the air, all right," Waters cracked.

"Frog One is safe and sound, huh?" asked Sonny.

"With the amount of booze he put away tonight, he oughta sleep for a week. He's probably got a good case of blue balls, too."

"Yeah, what happened with the blonde?" Waters grinned.

"Nothing. A big zero. Poor Jehan. *I* came closer to getting laid than he did."

"With his blonde?" Sonny exclaimed.

"No. Some chippie tried to pick me up at the bar. A big

leaguer all the way. We fooled around awhile, then she had to go take care of a customer. I was supposed to meet her at four o'clock."

Waters glanced at his wristwatch, eyes twinkling. "Well, it's almost five now. Where you been for the last hour?"

"Christ, I couldn't get it up now with a jack. Man, I'm whipped. So, is Patsy still playing cards with his *paisans*?"

"We *hope* he is," Sonny said. "He went in there, and nobody seen him come out yet."

"He could've gone out the back way, huh?"

"Who knows? All we can do is wait and see. But as long as Jehan is on ice . . ."

Egan yawned loudly.

"Why don't you go log some sack time?" Sonny suggested. "You've been out like three nights in a row."

"I oughta stick around here with you guys."

"Popeye, the area is covered," Waters said. "Sonny and me, we've had a chance to relax. Go on, grab a couple of hours. You may have to relieve *us* by then."

Egan thought it over sluggishly. Finally he muttered, "Okay," and heaved himself from the car. Even the click of the door as he closed it behind him gently seemed to echo in the deserted street. "I'll catch up with you guys later," he said.

In a fog, Egan drove his car not up onto either the Manhattan or Williamsburg Bridges which would have taken him home to Brooklyn but, by some reflex, back uptown on the East River Drive.

The black rim of the sky far to the east was being smudged with grey as he realized that he'd driven almost to midtown. He swerved off the three-lane drive at 42nd Street, thinking he'd have to go back downtown half a dozen blocks to the Midtown Tunnel in order to get back to Queens and Brooklyn. But then he thought of what a drag it would be hauling out of his own bed only a few hours hence and driving into Manhattan again. Why not stay at a hotel? He turned up First Avenue, broad and almost desolate at five-thirty on a Saturday morning, past the towering United Nations. He turned left at

49th Street and, three blocks west, found himself at the corner of Lexington Avenue waiting for a light, facing the Waldorf-Astoria. Why *not* the Waldorf? Could the city begrudge him a little indulgence for once? Screw the city, anyway. He knew security officers at the Waldorf.

When Detective Eddie Egan finally crawled into a soft, crisply fresh bed in the Waldorf-Astoria about 5:45 a.m., Saturday, 13 January, it is debatable whether he would have roused even had he been aware of the identity of the handsome visitor from Paris, France, sleeping somewhat fitfully in a large bed-sitting room upstairs in the same hotel. Egan had never heard of the French television star Jacques Angelvin. But they would meet four days hence, and that introduction would transform despair into sunshine for the New York Narcotics Bureau.

Egan awoke after only four hours, and he couldn't get back to sleep. His wristwatch on the night table said it was nine-forty. Slowly Egan hauled himself upright, and sat on the edge of the bed in his underwear, staring morosely at the green carpet. He reached over and called in to base. On the phone they told him the force still was zeroed in on Jehan at the Edison. Frogs Two and Three still had not returned to their hotels, and as for Patsy, he'd finally left 137 Henry Street around 7 a.m. without incident and gone to his home in Brooklyn. Sonny Grosso and Frank Waters had also gone home and would be in later.

What now? Egan went into the bathroom for a glass of water and decided to take a shower. All we can do is stick to Frog One. They've got to contact him. He shaved with the toiletry kit he had brought from his car, then dressed in his rumpled, slightly soiled shirt and suit, and left the Waldorf without checking out. He drove across 49th Street, parked in a lot near Seventh Avenue and stopped at a drugstore for orange juice and coffee. Then he walked to the Edison Hotel.

It was 12:30 p.m., and, because it was early Saturday afternoon, the theatre district was quiet and unhurried as Egan approached the main entrance of the Edison on 47th Street. He saw no one he recognized on either side of the street.

Egan paused a moment at the revolving door as a man started to push through from the interior. Then he stepped into the moving glass entranceway and was just emerging into the lobby when he froze. The man who had spun past him out into the street, an elderly, distinguished-looking man in black, was Jehan: *Jehan?* Nerves suddenly taut, Egan looked quickly about the quiet lobby to see only a few old people reading newspapers or just daydreaming. A couple of women were getting into an elevator, and he saw two bellmen chattering near the empty front desk.

Holy Mother! The sonofabitch just walked out the door, and there must be twenty of our guys around here somewhere, and nobody's on him! Egan whirled and slammed out through the revolving door, to find that Jehan had almost reached the corner of Broadway. Egan desperately searched 47th Street for some sign of police awareness that Frog One was calmly strolling out of the picture, but he spotted no one. Taking a deep breath, Egan started after the man.

Jehan appeared little the worse for wear after his long Friday night. He was walking easily south on Broadway towards Times Square. Egan was confused and angry. How could so many supposedly professional police officers blow one old bastard who stands out like a giraffe in a field full of cows?

Jehan continued to amble without apparent purpose along the "Great White Way", which by daylight was dingy and pallid. Pedestrian traffic was minimal, so Egan was able to keep a clear view of the tall grey-haired figure in black. When Jehan paused at a shop window near 46th Street, Egan, at the corner of 47th, took another moment to look around him once more for assistance. A man and a woman were entering a cab in front of the Edison, but still he saw none of *his* people – until he recognized two hatless, overcoated men lounging at a soft-drink stand on the opposite corner of 47th Street: Detectives Frank Meehan and Roy Cahill.

Egan whistled sharply, and as the two officers looked up he jerked his thumb viciously in the direction Jehan was going. The Frenchman was just moving away from the shop window that had caught his attention and had resumed his leisurely pace. The two detectives, looking very surprised, downed their drinks and stepped out behind Egan.

At 43rd Street, in Times Square, Frog One strolled to the BMT subway kiosk and descended the stairs. Not once in the four blocks, so far as Egan could make out, had the Frenchman so much as glanced back nor otherwise indicated any suspicion of being observed; and now he had gone straight down into the subway as though he knew exactly where he was going. Egan enjoyed a flush of elation: the Frog must be making a meet; maybe our luck *is* changing. But then, he thought, surely this guy, this cool one, must know by now that the operation had been burned, that the other Frogs had faded? And he must have guessed that he himself was carrying a tail? So why the subway bit all of a sudden on a Saturday afternoon?

Underground, Jehan did not go to the BMT trains. He headed for the crosstown shuttle, the short subway line that plies back and forth between Times Square and Grand Central Terminal. With Meehan and Cahill right behind him now, Egan bought a token and cautiously followed the subject through the brightly marked passageway from the main subway station to the shuttle platform. Unlike the streets above, the underground complex was crowded. Tourists goggled at the dreary, noisy, impersonal efficiency of New York's vaunted transportation system. New Yorkers from outlying sections of the vast city, many with children, streamed glumly to and from Manhattan weekend excursions. Egan had to press forward to keep Jehan in view.

Both tracks of the shuttle run were unoccupied, and the platform on one side was filled with citizens waiting for the next train in from Grand Central. Egan figured he had three or four minutes to call in and alert base radio. Catching the eyes of the other detectives he threw a nod towards Jehan, who was standing easily behind a cluster of people, appearing as unconcerned as a headwaiter on his way to work. Meehan and Cahill moved separately to an edge of the crowd at either end of the platform, keeping their undivided attention on the tall Frenchman.

Egan found a public telephone cubicle, also within sight of

Jehan, and dialled base. "I'm sitting on Frog One," he began. The voice at the other end droned, "Yeah, we know, we got the Edison covered like a tent." It was Agent Ben Fitzgerald.

"The Edison? Balls! I got him down in the subway at Times Square. He's about to take the shuttle to Grand Central. You got any men over there? Send some more over. What the hell's going on? I make him coming right out of the hotel, free as a bird. Not a soul around. If I hadn't run into a couple of cops at a snack bar, it'd be a real sweat." The two-car shuttle train clanked into the station and began to unload its packed cargo. "The train's in. I gotta go. Have those guys stake out Grand Central!"

Jehan had boarded the second car as Egan came up behind the last knot of passengers edging through the doors. Meehan and Cahill had seated themselves at each end of the car. Jehan sat near the middle, close by the centre door. Egan waited until all passengers were in, then quickly pushed into the now crowded car. Taking pains not to look toward Frog One, he shouldered his way toward the front end of the train, where he stood with his red-haired fingers grasping a chin-high hand grip, staring at the advertising in front of him.

His mind's eye, however, was scanning what could happen when they reached the Grand Central end of the half-mile trip. Base had advised that several detectives were already in the terminal keeping close watch on the banks of storage lockers. Frogs Two and Three had loitered in Grand Central the previous night before losing their tail, so there was still some suspicion that the load might be stashed there after all. And now, presumably, other officers in cars would be speeding to the terminal area to help Egan.

Egan's only possible plan was to get off the train first and let the Frog catch up and pass *him*. From there, he and the other detectives would just have to play it carefully, with Meehan and Cahill keeping a sharp eye out for fellow cops. When the train lurched to a stop, Egan made his way to the forward door and, on the crowded platform, proceeded slowly towards the tunnel corridor connecting the shuttle with the main station.

Several minutes passed, and the crowd streaming past Egan from behind him became a trickle, but Jehan had not appeared. Egan chanced a glance back. No one else was coming from the train now – no Jehan, not even Meehan and Cahill! Shucking caution, Egan bolted towards the two-car train he'd just left, now almost filled with return passengers. He marched grimly through both cars, checking every occupant. Nothing. Oh, good Christ Almighty! He jogged back along the passageway to the main 42nd Street subway station. Neither Jehan nor the officers were in sight on the various platforms. How could he have missed them? He raced up the long flight of stairs into the terminal, and saw Detective Dick Auletta standing by the entrance to the lower level, peering over a folded newspaper. When he spied Egan, Auletta lowered his eyes without recognition, obviously awaiting some signal. But Egan, breathing hard, went straight to him.

"Dick, have you seen Frog One?"

Auletta looked quickly up at the other's flushed face and shook his head. "What's happened?"

"I lost him," Egan groaned, rapidly surveying the ramps leading from 42nd Street down into the terminal. "I can't figure it, but I did . . . Let's check some of the other guys."

They hurried about Grand Central, seeking out other officers now posted by various exits, but no one had seen either Jehan or Detectives Meehan and Cahill. Egan felt clumsy and powerless. He and Auletta slumped against the marble counter outside a shuttered New York Central ticket window in the cavernous main terminal.

"What are you gonna do?" Auletta asked.

"Christ, I don't know. If we've blown him, I guess that's the ball game. I better call in. Maybe somebody else has got a lead."

"Why don't we check out the Roosevelt first?" Auletta asked. "That seemed to be their favourite meeting place."

"Yeah, that's a thought," Egan acknowledged, without much genuine enthusiasm. He and Auletta trudged up the stairway to Vanderbilt Avenue and walked two blocks north to the hotel. It was scarcely more than an hour since Egan had happened upon Jehan at the Edison, but the afternoon seemed endless.

After circling the block-square Roosevelt together, the two separated and searched the lobby and lower-level arcades inside. It was fruitless.

They met outside the hotel's Rough Rider Room on the 45th Street side, and Egan decided to call base from the lounge. After a few minutes, Egan rejoined Auletta at the bar, and they ordered two Pepsis. Egan appeared thoughtful.

"So?" Auletta probed.

Egan swallowed a mouthful of cola, set the glass down deliberately, leaned one elbow on the polished wood bar and turned to his companion. "So," he said softly, "Mr Frog One is back in his room at the Edison Hotel."

On the way crosstown to the Edison in Auletta's car, Egan related what he had been told. When he had boarded the shuttle at Times Square and pushed to the head of the car, consciously avoiding looking at Jehan, the Frenchman had left his seat and seconds before the train departed nimbly slipped through the closing doors. Fortunately, Meehan and Cahill had detected this sudden move and managed to scramble to the platform themselves just as the doors closed. Of course, they had had no chance to alert Egan, who continued on to Grand Central rapt in his plans for maintaining surveillance when he got there. Meanwhile, the perplexed officers had followed Jehan up to the street and back to his hotel, where he took an elevator and returned to his room on the ninth floor.

After the return of Jehan, there was considerable agitation among the dozen or so narcotics officers posted in and around the Edison as to how their subject had succeeded in breezing out of the hotel. The next hour was an uneasy jumble of fierce speculation and recrimination, with the New York police and Federal agents generally taking sides against one another.

Shortly, the men staked out in the lobby received word from the French-speaking agent in the room next to Jehan's that Frog One had just had a telephone call from Frog Two. The listening device, which was not attached to the telephone, could pick up only Jehan's end of the conversation. But he had referred to his caller as "*mon petit* François" – surely the missing Barbier – and had said in French: "You were right, I think. It is best to leave it where it is . . ."

This set off a new round of heated speculation downstairs. "What did he mean by 'you are right'?" "It means we burned the tail good, stupid." "*Who* burned it? *I* wasn't sitting on the lobby!" And, as they snapped at each other thus in anger and frustration, Jean Jehan put on his black coat and hat, picked up his cane, and calmly went out for another stroll . . .

Auletta dropped Egan at the corner of 47th and Broadway and drove off. Sapped of enthusiasm, Eddie was struggling to revive his spirits as he again approached the main entrance of the Edison. Suddenly, Jean Jehan came out of the revolving door and walked past him.

Egan took two full steps before stopping short. He whirled, startled to see, as he had earlier, the same tall, dark ethereal figure striding up the street towards Broadway. Jesus, Mary and Joseph – is this a dream? Am I going nuts? Shaking his head, he looked towards the hotel entrance and saw Detectives Meehan and Cahill emerging cautiously behind the Frenchman. Spotting Egan, one nodded in the direction of Jehan up the block. Egan acknowledged with a curt nod of his own and turned after Frog One, with the others trailing.

Jehan again went down the subway stairs at 43rd Street. Egan, half a block behind, couldn't shake the eerie feeling that he was somehow reliving a portion of his life. But Jehan proceeded this time not to the shuttle but to the BMT main line, descending another flight of stairs to the downtown platform. Egan and the others followed separately. Jehan stood on the Local side, apart from a handful of other passengers scattered along the platform. Egan guessed that a train must have just gone through and, because of curtailed Saturday service, he estimated that he would have several minutes to report the situation to base.

The two other detectives drifted apart to opposite ends of

the platform, while Egan looked for a telephone. The only booth he could use without losing sight of Jehan was within a dozen feet of the man. Egan swallowed and with outward brazenness walked in front of Frog One and settled in the booth.

"Send all your available cars to the west side," he told base. "Find out where each BMT local station is and spot a man up at every street exit all the way downtown. If we don't show up with the Frog at one stop, have the guys rotate, keeping a couple of stations ahead. We'll stay with this guy. Got that? Hold it. A train's coming in. Let's see what he does this time. I might hang up fast . . ."

The noisy grey-green subway train squealed to a stop. The doors rattled open, and the passengers got off and those on the platform stepped aboard; all except Jehan who stood quietly, hands clasped gently around the grip of his black walking stick in front of him. When the doors closed again and the train left the station, Jehan and one overcoated man at each end of the platform were the only people visible. Egan said into the telephone: "He didn't get on. Stay with me. I don't want to be wandering around the station."

Another train arrived and departed without Jehan, and now Egan, still in the telephone booth, began to grow restive. "I don't like this," he reported. "He's waiting for something, or somebody . . . Christ, maybe he wants to use this telephone." Egan swung open the folding glass door and raised his voice into the receiver. "I've worked in plenty of joints, bartender, waiter, even a bouncer. All I'm asking is a chance to show you what I can do. Can I come see you today? I'm telling you, I want this job bad." He prayed that his urgent tone had carried over the constant rumble of the subway and that his expression reflected the concern of a man struggling for livelihood.

Several more people had walked onto the platform, one a middle-aged woman in a Kelly green coat with a yellow kerchief around her head who stopped just outside Egan's telephone booth. Jehan came over to her, not six feet from where the detective sat. The elegant Frenchman doffed his homburg and spoke to the woman. He must have been asking directions, Egan thought, for the woman nodded, and with a curt bow Jehan turned to wait for another train. Egan gave the woman in the green coat a hard look, before deciding that she was no more than a passerby.

Another Local clattered into the station, and Frog One seemed to edge towards it. "Here we go, I think," Egan muttered into the telephone mouthpiece. Jehan stepped aboard the train. "See ya," Egan said, jamming the phone into its cradle. He left the booth and hurried to the same car as Jehan. Meehan and Cahill boarded the train at either end.

Jehan sat in the forward corner of the car, gazing blankly up at the advertising placards opposite. There were only five or six other passengers besides Egan. The detective took a seat midway along the car, across the aisle from the Frog, averting his face but keeping the dark figure firmly in the corner of an eye. As the train pulled out of the Times Square station, glancing to his right Egan could see Meehan in the car immediately behind, weaving into position; presumably Cahill was doing the same in the car ahead.

The train pulled into the next stop, 33rd Street. Jehan arose casually and stood studying the subway map next to the door. Egan smiled grimly to himself: he's beautiful; the doors will open, and he'll wait till the last second, and wham! then he'll jump off the train – and I guess I'm supposed to just sit here like a dummy. He hoped the other officers were ready to move.

The doors opened. A man got on, passing Jehan, who had not moved. Action hung suspended for a long second. Then, with a hiss the doors began to come together. Jehan shoved his cane against the rubber edging; all the doors reopened. Jehan quickly stepped out. Egan leaped across the car and out another exit just as the doors were closing again. Egan was grinning.

But not for long. Where was Jehan? He was nowhere in sight. Meehan and Cahill had made it to the platform, and now they were approaching Egan. The train started to move out of the station. The three were alone. And then a familiar figure appeared in a window of the car he had supposedly just left. Frog One, bent slightly towards them, was smiling at the police officers and daintily waving a gloved hand. In a moment, the train had rattled into the black subway tunnel, Jean Jehan with it. There was no way all the exits on the long subway line could be covered this soon.

Egan walked back to his car. It was quarter past twelve. Rays of pale sun were trying to force through the layers of moody grey above. Seventh Street was quiet; there were few pedestrians on the quiet block. Egan sat in the right front seat of the Corvair, chin resting on his left forearm on the back of the seat, looking behind at No. 245 and the small blue Oldsmobile at the curb. The fingers of his right hand played with the holster snap of the .38 Police Special at his hip.

A number of vehicles came through the block from Third Avenue in the next twenty-five minutes, but at twelve-forty Egan sensed something different about one car now crawling past the Fuca house. It held Detective Dick Auletta and Agent Artie Fluhr. Egan grinned, leaned across to the driver's side, and playfully flattened his nose against the window, goggling at them like a clown. Auletta noticed him as they came up alongside and smiled broadly. Fluhr stopped the car next to the Corvair, but Egan motioned them to keep going farther up the street. He got out and walked along the sidewalk after them, glancing back towards No. 245 every few strides.

Fluhr had nosed in near the corner. As Egan climbed in the back and flopped down with a grunt, Auletta greeted him: "Well, has the little man had a trying day?"

"Don't ask," Egan wheezed. "What a mess, huh? You know about my radio crapping out? Christ!"

"Your worries are over," Fluhr smiled. "We brought you another portable unit."

"Beautiful!" Egan twisted around to gaze a long second out the rear window. Turning back to the others, he said: "I wouldn't say our problems are necessarily over, though." And he filled them in on his observations and suspicions.

"So what's the play?" Auletta asked. "Do we go for the collar now?"

"I been thinking about that," said Egan. "And I think I'd

rather wait until Patsy comes out again. I want to see if he still has that suitcase with him. If he does, we'll have to split up and you guys tail him. If he comes out clean, we hit. I'd sure like to have some guys around in any case. You never know what can go wrong."

"Hold it!" Fluhr warned, eyes focused back on 7th Street. "Patsy and Barbara, they're coming out." The three officers, hunched low, watching carefully as the couple got in either side of the Olds. Patsy did not have the blue valise with him.

"Boy, you guys got here just in time!" Egan exclaimed. "Look, Artie, we'll let them pass by here, then you two go get them. I'll run back to the house. I've got to get the warrants out of my car first. Give me that radio, in case we have to talk."

Fluhr handed over the flat, grey rectangular walkie-talkie. They all ducked down out of sight as Patsy's blue compact approached and rolled by to the corner.

Egan waited until the Olds turned right on Fourth Avenue before he clambered out and broke into a sprint back to his own car. Behind him, Fluhr's tyres screeched as he and Auletta swept around the corner after the Fucas. The detective fumbled with his keys, opened the glove compartment and began to sort through the wrinkled sheaf of documents stuffed inside. He snorted impatiently and crammed the entire pile inside his jacket. Radiophone under one arm and his .38 in hand, Egan marched across the street to No. 245.

Joseph Fuca answered Egan's ring. He was a short, scowling old man with untidy grey-white hair and a day's growth of beard, wearing a soiled white shirt with the sleeves rolled to the elbows. "Yeah?" he glowered suspiciously at the burly redhead at the door.

With his free hand, Egan flipped open his shield case. "Police officer. I have a warrant to search this house. You are Joseph Fuca?"

"Policeman? Whatta you wanta? I no—" Fuca's mouth hung open and he blanched as he noticed the revolver in Egan's other fist.

"Just take it nice and easy and we'll get along fine," Egan said evenly, shouldering through the doorway into a small foyer. "Now, you're Joe Fuca, right?" The man was still staring at the gun. "Who else is here?" the detective inquired. Fuca only shook his head dumbly. "Okay." Egan shoved the .38 back into its holster under his leather jacket. "That better?"

He looked the little man over again. His shapeless grey trousers were splotched with old paint, and there also seemed to be traces of a white dust of some kind. His scuffed brown shoes were covered with a powder also. "Okay, old man," he commanded, "let's go inside."

"I no got nut-ting you want," Fuca protested. "Whatta you come—?"

"Fluhr here," a tinny voice echoed out of Egan's armpit. Fuca jumped, startled.

Grinning, the detective brought the transmitter to his mouth. "You got them?"

"We got them."

"Any trouble?"

"Negative."

"Bring them back, kay."

"Ten-four."

Pushing Fuca before him, Egan made his way into the front parlour. The furniture was old-fashioned, mostly stuffed and much of it threadbare; faded white doilies masked arms and headrests and the floor was covered with worn green linoleum. The place looked reasonably tidy, but somehow there was a fetid atmosphere of uncleanliness. Egan could smell the unmistakable, slightly stale aroma of Italian spices.

"Where's your wife?" he asked.

"She's out."

"Too bad. We're going to have visitors – your boy Patsy and his wife."

"Whatta you mean, they justa left." Now the old man glared at Egan. "Why you maka this business? I gotta nutting here!"

"You got somethin' here all right," Egan snapped. "And in

a few minutes we're gonna find it – and mister, you're going to have real trouble."

The doorbell rang. "Stay here!" the detective ordered. He went to the door. Standing outside were Detective Jim Hurley and Agent Jack Ripa. "Hey, gang!" Egan welcomed them. "Come on in. We're about to have a party."

"We heard on the radio," Hurley said. "Any other guys show yet?"

"Not yet."

"Well, there's more coming. You think this is the drop?"

"I think so," Egan said, "but we'll soon find out. Start looking around." As he stood aside in the doorway to let the two officers in, another car drew up outside. It was Fluhr and Auletta with their captives. "Well," Egan exclaimed, "here's our prize package!"

A very sullen Patsy crossed the sidewalk ahead of Barbara and Auletta, then Fluhr followed behind them. The man whom Egan and his partners had been shadowing for months, whose every move had been watched and studied and analyzed and often worried about, somehow appeared slighter to the detective now, less menacing. Patsy's eyes were downcast yet wary. He moved like a trapped animal which fears the finish is near but which still may make one last clawing attempt at freedom should an opening present itself.

Egan propelled Patsy into the parlour, trailed by Barbara, chewing gum, wearing her gaudy blonde wig. Then as Auletta and Fluhr entered, two more cars double-parked on 7th Street and four more detectives joined them. They began to examine the house.

Egan confronted Patsy head-on: "Okay, you can make it easy all around if you tell us right off where the stuff is."

"What stuff?" Patsy snarled. "What the hell is going on here? You better have—!"

Egan brandished his fistful of official documents. "We got warrants for you and practically every place you been the past three months. You, your wife, your house, your two cars, your store, the Travatos, their car, your brother Tony and his house and his car, this joint, your father and mother—" he paused, pleased to note that Patsy had visibly paled, his eyes blinking in obvious surprise – "even your French friends back in New York!"

Patsy was unable to speak for a moment. He shook his head, and looked up. "What French friends? I don't know no French – except Denise Darcel . . ."

"Yeah? Well, then you don't care that they have all been arrested – right after you left them today."

"I don't even know what you're talking about." He was going to try to brazen it through. "What do you want from me?"

"You got a load of junk stashed in this house," accused Egan, aware that he himself was partly bluffing, for he could not be sure that Patsy had not really disposed of the heroin elsewhere and the suitcase he had brought into his parents' house was not clean.

"What's junk?" Patsy asked with the eyes of an altar boy.

Egan, fists on hips, legs planted apart, studied the shorter man with undisguised contempt, his gaze deliberately picking Patsy apart from his face down to his feet. The shoes bore a film of whitish powder, like his father's. The detective glanced over at the elder Fuca's shoes again, then, looking up at Patsy, he snapped to the old man: "Okay, Pop, which way to the cellar?" The minute flicker he saw in Patsy's eyes might have been one of apprehension.

Joe Fuca was clearly reluctant, but he showed them to a door in the narrow corridor connecting the parlour with the rear of the apartment. "Open it," commanded Egan. It was dark below. "Lights!"

Fuca flipped a switch just inside the door. Egan looked down. At the foot of the stairs, lying open on the cement floor, was a blue suitcase. He looked around at the old man and then to the son, a smile beginning to show on his mouth. "If we have to, we'll rip this place apart until we find what we're looking for." Patsy's face was expressionless. His father just glared. "No? Okay. Keep them up here," he told Auletta and the other officers, as he disappeared down the wooden steps.

For a basement, the area below was about as neat as the parlour upstairs. It was a narrow rectangle, extending from the street side of the house to the rear. There was the outside door at the front end and two boarded-up windows. Two other small windows high in the rear wall opened on a back-yard. At that end, the basement was separated by wood-plank partitions into three compartments, like large bins, apparently for storage use. In one corner, by a yellowed washtub, were an electric washing machine and a dryer, in another corner a blackened boiler and water heater. Overhead were the usual grimy pipes and asbestos-covered hot-water ducts. The floor was chipped in spots, but it was swept very clean – a little unusual for even a tidy basement, Egan thought.

He knelt by the open valise. It was empty, but in the corners he noticed filmy traces of a white powdery substance. He explored it with his forefinger, then placed the tip of his finger on his tongue. The taste was acidly bitter. One test of heroin.

Grinning, Egan looked up the stairs to Patsy, standing on the top step, Dick Auletta at his shoulder. "Right *here* there's enough shit to put you away. With your record, you oughta get ten years. But I'll tell you what: for *you*, I'm gonna go for triple that! Put the cuffs on him, Dick."

As he looked up from his crouched position, Egan's attention was caught by a cluster of large dark stains in the faded plaster ceiling over the stairs. He rose and stood on the bottom step and felt gingerly at one of the spots. It was damp, as though recently replastered. There were four such spots, of varying sizes, one more than a foot across. Then, behind the stairs and almost directly below them, for the first time he noticed that all four jets of an ancient gas stove were burning – as though to speed the drying of fresh plaster.

"Well, well!" Egan grinned up again at Patsy, whose expression now was sagging. The detective went over to one of the storage bins in the rear and found an empty wooden crate, and he brought it back to the stove and climbed up onto it. Carefully, he probed one of the wet spots with his fingers, pushing up into the mushy plaster. Now, having tugged his sleeve back from the wrist, he shoved his hand all the way through. His fingers closed around a smooth, lumpy package. It was a plastic-wrapped bag, about the size and shape of a long bag of rice, but filled with white powder. It weighed about a pound – half a kilo of heroin!

"Dick," he called up to Auletta. "You got a field tester?"

"Artie's got plenty."

"Tell him to come down. I think we struck gold!"

Fluhr clattered down the stairs. He whistled when he saw the bundle in Egan's hand. "Look at *that*!"

"Let's give it the treatment."

Fluhr produced a small tin, like a pillbox, and extracted a tiny glass vial containing a clear liquid. He snapped off the top and handed it to Egan. The vial contained a few drops of sulphuric acid and formaldehyde, called a Marquis reagent after the chemist who had developed the test for opium derivatives. Contact with any opium derivative would cause the liquid to turn a purplish colour, the depth of shade depending upon the strength, or "purity", of the narcotic sample. Egan dipped his fingers into the package just taken from the ceiling. He rubbed some of the white powder into the test tube. Almost instantly, the mixture became a deep purple.

"Good Christ!" the Federal agent gasped. "Have you ever seen such a reaction?"

"Never," Egan murmured in awe. "This has got to be the purest stuff anybody's ever seen around here!"

A sullen Patsy Fuca and his wife Barbara, concealing her nervousness by furiously chomping her gum and snapping profane remarks at the officers, were led by Agent Bill Bailey and Detective Dick Auletta to Bailey's car and driven back to 67th Street for a search of their house.

Eddie Egan skipped exuberantly up the rickety steps from the basement to the kitchen, where old Joe Fuca was being interrogated by Detectives Jim Hurley and Jimmy Gildea. Fuca was sitting at the kitchen table steadily working a bottle of whiskey, as the detectives tried to make him tell all he knew about the contents of the blue suitcase. Egan tossed two plastic bags each containing half a kilo of heroin on the table in front of Fuca. "Nothing in the house, huh, Joe?"

Fuca stared at the bags and cried: "Thatsa dynamite. Pasquale tell me that is *dynamite*."

With a disdainful snort, Egan turned to the telephone on the kitchen wall and dialled the number of the police temporary headquarters in the office of the garage back in Manhattan. Sergeant Jack Fleming answered.

"I'm at Fuca's on 7th Street in Brooklyn. I've got a kilo and the shit's still comin' out of the ceiling. Call Chief Carey and ask him to call me here." Egan read off the Fuca number and told Fleming to have Carey ring twice and hang up, then once and hang up.

Egan went back to the basement. He dug into the ceiling, removing one bag of heroin after another. Then, to his surprise, his searching fingers felt cold metal. He pulled out a sub-machine gun.

"Hey, Joe," he shouted up the stairs, "you got a blueprint for this joint? There won't be any ceilings and walls left when we get through down here."

The telephone in the kitchen rang twice, was silent, rang once, was silent again, then began to ring again. Egan stamped up the steps, hugging the half-kilo bags to him. He threw them down on the table and jerked the phone from the hook: "Popeye here."

"What have you got there, Eddie?"

"Six kilos and a machine gun and still counting."

Chief Carey whistled. "Six kilos? Could there be more?"

"Could be *forty*-six. We'll need a lot of men over here with axes and crowbars."

"I'll be there myself," Carey answered.

"Yes, sir." Egan hung up and turned to Fuca and his two inquisitors. "The big man himself is coming over. Better sober Joe up." Egan's beefy hand stabbed across the table, snatching the bottle of whiskey.

Fuca screamed in rage: "Giva my drink!" Fuca's eyes blazed as he shambled to his feet. "You lousy, dirty bastid cop! Bust up my house!" The old man made a clumsy lunge at Egan, trying to strike his face. Egan, with a short, sharp jab to the jaw, sent him sprawling back across the table. Fuca stumbled to the floor and lay still, spittle spewing from his mouth as he breathed heavily.

12

Donnie Brasco:
Unfinished Business

Joe Pistone and Charles Brandt

As discussed in the Introduction, Joe Pistone, or Donnie Brasco, is the apotheosis of the long-term undercover cop, a man able to hold his nerve for over six years of living a lie and who, had it been up to him, would not have stopped operations when they did but would have gone on at ever greater personal risk to see even more wise guys busted, arguing to his handlers that he was on the verge of being "made".

It's fair to say that the cases brought on Pistone's evidence are the chief reason for the weakening of the Mafia's hold on American society in the 1980s, from its heyday in the 1950s, 1960s and 1970s when it was able to corrupt members of even the federal government.

Police forces tend to favour the use of informants over the insertion of highly valuable detectives working undercover, as discussed, for reasons of authenticity. Pistone, however, satisfied this need perfectly: his background in New Jersey, his Sicilian family, and his fluent Italian combined to ensure that he was considered worthy of trust, even from its most justifiably paranoid members, as one of the Mafia's own. He was even mistrusted by FBI staff, at least in regional offices other than New York, on occasion.

Pistone joined the FBI in 1969, and was selected to go undercover at first because his ability to drive trucks meant he could infiltrate a gang stealing and dealing in heavy plant machinery, one of the most profitable thieving rings ever broken in the US at that time.

In 1976 he joined Jilly Greca's operations within the Colombo crime family, which involved truck hijacking for the most part, and then ingratiated himself with Dominick "Sonny Black" Napolitano (who was to wind up sans head and hands in Mariner's Harbor, Staten Island, in 1986 on account of having made Pistone a protégé), Anthony Mirra and Benjamin "Lefty Guns" Ruggiero, of the Bonanno clan. Mirra was also killed, and Ruggiero was slated to be the victim of a hit, but was arrested by the FBI first on Pistone's evidence.

Brasco's information led to more than a hundred convictions (from over two hundred indictments). Finally, Joe Massino ("Joe Bananas"), head of the Bonanno family, was convicted of ordering the death of Napolitano in 2004.

Watching his back, Pistone still travels under assumed names as he consults with law-enforcement agencies around the world, and lives in disguise.

In the latter months of my deep cover I divided my time between Florida and New York. One evening after dinner in New York with Lefty, he and I decided to go to a card game in a walk-up apartment in Little Italy. As we were heading up the stairs, two young white guys were coming down. When they got a step past us they pulled out guns, put them in our backs and demanded our money. I thanked God that Lefty and I had no guns with us. I would have been afraid Lefty would pull his and start blasting away. This would put me in the position of having to blast away to defend myself from their guns and to satisfy Lefty that I was not a rat. Fortunately, we were not about to whack two drug addicts in a stairway. Yet.

Lefty said, "No problem, sport. Just give them your money, Donnie."

Obviously, the robbers had sense enough not to rob the card game, because inside they would have been whacked. They figured it would be safer to get people on their way in with their gambling money. I had about $2,500 in gambling money and Lefty had about $1,500. We turned our money over and they ran out fast.

"So much for the card game," Lefty said. "You got any money in your shoe?"

"Sorry, Left," I said.

"Me neither," he said. "You just saw two dead punks run down the stairs."

Less than two days later Lefty called me to his apartment in Knickerbocker Village on Monroe Street near Little Italy. Lefty's hobby was tropical fish and he had a few aquariums in his apartment. Lefty liked to just look at the fish and watch them swim around. A number of Bonanno wiseguys lived in Knickerbocker Village. They had some kind of in with the management. If they got behind in rent no one bothered them. Lefty had asked me if I wanted an apartment there, but I tactfully had said no. Anyway, Lefty had gotten the names and the hangout of the two robbers. I was relieved that he moved off of wanting them dead, as all he said was, "Go solo. Teach them fucks a lesson both. Get as much of the money you can back."

The robbers hung out in an after-hours storefront on the outskirts of Little Italy. They were both Italian wiseguy-wannabes in their early twenties. They were stupid to think they could get away with it, practically in their own neigh-bourhood, and made more stupid by the drugs they were on.

It was in the middle of the afternoon. I hoped for their sake I would find them because, if I couldn't find them, Lefty might send somebody else who would find them and kill them. Plus, let's face it: I was pissed off. First, they robbed me. Second, they put me in this position of having to cross the line into violence. What I was about to do was another one of those things that was very much unauthor-ized by the Bureau and that could cause me to need a criminal lawyer.

I considered the consequences of telling Lefty they weren't there as I approached. But there they were. The two morons were out in broad daylight standing in front of their hangout. There was a strong grapevine in Little Italy. At that instant I could bank on that grapevine; Lefty would hear every detail of what happened even before I could report it to him.

They were my height; about six feet tall, but at 185 I had thirty pounds on each of them. They were junky skinny. I walked up to one and, boom, I let him have an overhand right. He hit the pavement as if I'd had a roll of dimes in my right fist (no comment). The other one's eyes popped open when he recognized me.

"You stay put," I said. "I'll get to you next. Don't even think about running. You're in no shape to outrun me and it'll only go worse for you."

I looked down at the kid on the ground and realized he was out cold, and so I sprung suddenly and hauled off an overhand right on the other one and he went down. I put the roll of dimes in my pocket and went through their pockets. I got a few hundred, but they had already shot up the lion's share of the money they got from us. Getting the money back was not the point anyway. It was all about the satisfaction to know they didn't get over on you and get away with it.

What I did next I did for each kid's own good. I knew I had to throw them both a good beating or they could still get whacked. You don't put a gun into the back of a made man like Lefty Guns Ruggiero and expect to live. Lefty's son was a drug addict. His son's problems might explain why Lefty only told me to "teach them fucks a lesson both". During my time with Lefty before this incident, Lefty's son pulled a gun and robbed a connected jeweller on Jewellers Row and Lefty had to square that beef with another family that the jeweller belonged to or Lefty's son would have been whacked.

I know this much: the two junky armed robbers didn't get up on their own and walk away from the sidewalk. From the kidney blows they bled piss for weeks. And until the breaks healed they had no use of their fingers for such things as shooting a gun. The whole thing took less than three minutes.

I can't remember if I took any drugs from them. If I did I would have thrown it down the nearest sewer – another unauthorized act.

When I got to Lefty's, he said, "Is it taken care of?"

I said, "It's taken care of."

I gave Lefty the few hundred I recovered and, like a boss, bless his soul, he put it in his pocket without throwing me a dime. Not another word ever was said on the subject.

The Deep End

As an FBI Agent, how deep could I sink into the mud of the underworld of organized crime before I would be too far in to dig myself out? Before I would be off the deep end, out there alone? No undercover had ever been in the position I had been in for as long as I had been in it.

The principal digging tool I had to keep from becoming too deeply involved in criminal activity was what I called the "well-told fiction". I lived a life of deception all the time when I was working undercover, but sometimes I had to develop an elaborate well-thought-out fiction to get myself out of a jam or to allow the operation to continue without compromising it.

While deception had become a way of life in my deep-cover work, from my family upbringing and as a Catholic who still went to Mass when I could sneak away from the crew, and as an FBI agent who reported every few days or so to my FBI handler, distorting the truth was something that went against my grain. It went against my own deep character.

I understood that my deceptions were for a greater good, as if Nazis came to my door and I lied to save the Jews I was hiding in my cellar. To me – and to any student of ethics – that's not lying. But at some point if nearly everything you do is deceptive it can become easier for you to deceive in general. At what point would I be in so deep that I would make a decision to deceive the FBI?

When the fictions start to appear to come true after you tell them, the whole house of deception gets more than a bit eerie. The spookiest for me was when Lefty and I were staying in a hotel in Milwaukee waiting day-after-day for word that the boss of the Milwaukee family, Frank Balistrieri, would agree to meet with us to discuss a joint operation I had promoted.

During the time we were waiting for word from Balistrieri's people, I began to miss my family more intensely than normal and I had a strong desire to dig myself out to see them. I couldn't get away from this proposed meeting with somebody as important as Balistrieri, the boss of an entire family, without an elaborate fiction. I already had a phony girlfriend who I visited in California whenever I wanted to fly home to see my wife. Now I told Lefty that my girlfriend in California had been injured in a car wreck and I had to leave him to be with her. Lefty was so mad when I said I was leaving I thought he was going to explode, or maybe blow me up.

This meeting with Balistrieri was something I had set up with the help of another undercover going by the name of Tony Conte. Our plan was to forge a partnership between the Bonannos and the Balistrieri family in the vending machine monopoly in Milwaukee. It was an expansion of a scheme the Milwaukee family had going already, one in which honest saloon keepers would be required to use only our vending machines or risk problems from the Milwaukee Mafia family. It was one of the biggest breaks of Lefty's career in what he called "the underworld field". This was 1978, a couple years before King's Court in Florida, and it was one of my biggest coups to date at the time. From the Bureau's point of view, the operation we had set up was intended to gather evidence to prove the inner workings of a criminal enterprise consisting of a racketeering alliance between the Bonanno and Balistrieri Mafia families.

While I was telling Lefty that this fictitious girlfriend of mine was in bad shape from her car wreck, he was telling me, "She ain't going to die. What are you worrying about?" Behind my back to Tony Conte, Lefty called me a jerk-off, and wanted to know what was so special about this girlfriend of mine that I never brought her to New York so people could meet her. I withstood Lefty's wrath, called my wife to pick me up at the airport and hopped a plane.

My wife was nearly killed in a car wreck en route to the airport to pick me up. The young woman driving the oncoming car that crossed into my wife's lane and hit her head-on was killed. My fiction instantly had come true. This was the most devastating time of my life. I stayed with my family during the eleven days my wife was in the hospital and for another week after that, which, no matter how you slice it, wasn't long enough. We had barbecues and lived as a family for the first time in a long time. When I was satisfied that things at home were as good as they could be under the circumstances, I returned to Milwaukee.

While we were in Milwaukee working this plan, called Operation Timber, to ensnare the Milwaukee boss in a criminal conspiracy with the Bonanno family, a Milwaukee soldier named Augie Palmisano was blown up in his car. Lefty explained to Tony Conte: "They're blowing guys up because they done something wrong."

To add to his point, Lefty said, "Tony, the responsibility I gave Donnie just now . . . if he fucks up, I'm a dead man." Lefty told us how he would be killed. "If I get sent for, I don't know what I'm getting sent for. They just say to come in. And I'd be getting killed for something I didn't even know."

When the mission in Milwaukee was pretty much accomplished, as far as evidence gathering was concerned for the Bureau, Balistrieri suddenly ended the partnership. Balistrieri refused to return anyone's phone calls. The word that came down was that Balistrieri was mad at Tony Conte for doing "something wrong", something very wrong. According to word from on high, Tony Conte had been seen flirting with Balistrieri's girlfriend. You don't ever disrespect a boss in any way and expect to live another day; you especially don't disrespect him regarding his wife or his girlfriend. As Lefty put it, "That's worse than being a rat or a pimp." On top of that, the sudden dissolving of the partnership without explanation by Balistrieri cost our Bonanno bosses a lot of money, and not just in lost profits.

"Maybe he's a snitch," Lefty said to me behind Tony Conte's back. And worse, "I'm in jeopardy over here and you brought him in." And still worse, "Conte could get whacked at any time over this."

It was now time to get Tony Conte out of the picture

without Lefty and those above him dwelling for long on whether Conte was an informant or an undercover agent or just a bad soldier in need of the ultimate punishment to square things with Balistrieri. Not to mention that, since I brought Tony Conte into our Bonanno crew and introduced him to Lefty and eventually to Lefty's capo and the family underboss for this limited undercover purpose, I had my own safety to consider. Initially we had Tony Conte fake a heart attack to buy us some time. He actually reported to an emergency room complaining of chest pains. But that was only a temporary fix to get him out of immediate harm's way.

Next, we devised an elaborate fiction to extricate Tony Conte permanently without blowing up the rest of my Donnie Brasco operation that we still had in play, or blowing us up. That was big for Conte and me, that part about staying alive. This elaborate fiction also converged eerily with reality.

The elaborate fiction was that Tony Conte had a big score coming up. We told Lefty and our capo at the time, Mike Sabella, that Tony was going to participate in a major art theft that was planned to take place in Chicago and had $250,000 coming to him as his share of the take. We chose art rather than, say, jewellery, because art thieves are in a world unto themselves. It is such a specialized field that an art heist is something Mafia mobsters would not be able to look into and check out with a few well-placed phone calls to bosses in Chicago. Why we chose Chicago, I still don't know.

I told Lefty and our capo, Mike Sabella, that Tony Conte was going to share his Chicago art heist score with us, the way a good crewmember should. All money flows upstream in the Mafia as if that's the way nature had planned money to flow. And the bosses upstream can never get enough. At least half of the $250,000 would go upstream. Such a fact instantly pushes all other thoughts into the back of wiseguys' minds, including thoughts of retribution against Conte.

We concluded this operation in Milwaukee over a year before Carmine Galante got whacked in 1979. After Galante got hit, Mike Sabella got demoted from capo to soldier and

Sonny Black got upped to capo, and Lefty and I went with Sonny Black. Mike Sabella was happy to be demoted at that time because the alternative was to get whacked. At this time, however, Mike Sabella was a big wheel with a lot of power and commanded the extravagant respect these people go for. Big money is a big sign of respect. Waving this kind of big money under Mike Sabella's and Lefty's noses made them forget that they were mad at Tony Conte for doing "something wrong", and for ruining their Milwaukee plans by disrespecting Balistrieri in the girlfriend department.

Now that Tony Conte had an art-theft score to whack up, all of a sudden the word floated down from upstream that it was the inner game of petty Mafia politics – not Tony Conte's flirting with the wrong restaurant hostess – that had queered the deal with Balistrieri. The bosses upstream took Tony Conte off one hook so they could keep him on another hook, one that would put money in their pockets.

No sooner had we devised this Chicago art heist elaborate fiction and told Lefty and Mike Sabella, then out of the blue a real-life art heist worth $3,000,000 was carried out in Chicago. All the big news outlets around the world reported the heist and the enormous value of the art that was stolen. Lefty and Mike Sabella licked their chops. Another fiction of mine instantly had come true. More than spooky. Nothing for nothing, but from the time I went undercover to this very day, everything about everything just seemed to fall into place like it was all meant to happen. Art theft? Chicago? Not Boston, not Los Angeles, not Paris, France – but Chicago? And more than enough value to justify a $250,000 share to Tony Conte? The coincidence was enormous, and enormously helpful.

The rest of the fictitious plot I reported to Lefty, who reported to Mike Sabella, was that Tony Conte had to meet with his confederates to get his share of the three million. The plot twist in our fiction was that the undercover agent they believed was Tony Conte, was simply not going to return from that meeting with his accomplices.

But Lefty was one step ahead of our plot devices. Lefty

gave me a firm order, saying, "I'm holding you responsible. You fly back to Chicago with him. And then you don't leave his side. You go with him to pick up the money, and then you come back in here with him and that money."

I was already responsible for Tony Conte and now I was responsible for this money. People like Augie Palmisano in Milwaukee had been killed for a lot less trouble than I had already caused and was about to cause. When I called Lefty and told him my brand new plot twist – that Tony Conte had gone to the meeting but couldn't take me with him because his pals had told him to come alone, and that Tony Conte had not returned to our hotel room – Lefty said many things. None of them was good.

I'd never experienced Lefty so mad. Among the outpouring of words from Lefty that became embedded in my mind and stuck with me were:

"There ain't a punk in the street that hangs out with a wiseguy could get away with what you two guys done. Forget about it. Youse won't last five minutes in the city of New York.

"I'm so fucking mad. I don't even want to get mad at you right now. I'm fifty-two and I'm willing to spend the rest of my life in jail over this… .

"I'm blowing my top here. You weren't supposed to leave his side. That's why you're there.

"You put me in fucking mean positions with these guys." These guys were Mike Sabella and the other Bonanno bosses all the way to the top. Just as Lefty held me responsible, under penalty of death, Mike Sabella held Lefty responsible, with the same penalty looming.

"Could this fucking guy be a fucking agent, Donnie?"

At that last statement, I thought, why would Lefty's mind go straight to the notion that I might have specific knowledge or insight about something like whether Tony Conte was an agent? If Conte was an agent, shouldn't I be as ignorant of it as Lefty?

And the bar-none scariest words any undercover agent can ever hear about his phony stories while he's telling them was, "Something's fishy".

When enough time had passed to make it obvious to Lefty and Mike Sabella that, whatever the truth might be, Tony Conte was not going to return to the hotel with the money, Lefty called me in Chicago.

"Get on a plane late tonight and come back to New York."

"Why late tonight?" I asked, even though it could only add to my jeopardy by questioning an order. "Why can't I come in now during the day?"

"Because that's the way it is," Lefty said flatly. "You're being sent for and you come in. You come in late at night. You get a cab at JFK and you come directly to Lynn's Bar on 71st. Don't go nowhere else. Don't be seen by anybody. Don't tell anybody you're coming. Straight from JFK to Lynn's. Be there alone at midnight."

Lynn's? A small place that would be empty at midnight. Not too many people would even be on the street at 71st and 2nd at midnight. I couldn't ask Lefty why we weren't meeting in Little Italy where we normally met, a neighbourhood with 24-hour-a-day pedestrian traffic. Midnight. Alone. Straight from JFK. Don't be seen by anybody. Don't tell anybody I'm coming.

This was not the way Lefty had ever talked to me. But I knew Lefty had to do whatever he had to do for putting Mike Sabella into this bad position. And that included whacking me. As Lefty once said, "A little violence never hurt anybody."

"Something's fishy".

Something's fishy on both sides of this equation, I thought. I remembered what Lefty had said to Tony Conte and to me, "If I get sent for, I don't know what I'm getting sent for. They just say to come in. And I'd be getting killed for something I didn't even know."

I'm a lousy gambler. I never win at gambling. But I would be gambling with my life if I went to this meeting.

I never told anyone about this conversation with Lefty, or the ensuing sit-down, until now. I decided to keep the meeting a secret, go to it and take my chances. If I told my FBI handlers that Lefty had ordered me to a sit-down at midnight in an abandoned bar, they never would have let me go. They would know that if they planted backup agents for protection inside an empty Lynn's at that hour, the backup would have been spotted and made. And having backup outside Lynn's would have done me no good. Therefore, having me go to the meeting would have been unacceptable. Having me skip the meeting and return to New York on my own time would have been sure grounds for being whacked – also unacceptable. For all intents and purposes, if I told my handlers about being sent for and the sit-down that would soon follow, the Donnie Brasco operation would have been over.

I decided not to tell the FBI. I was finally in so deep that I was lying to the FBI by omission. Because of my job, I lied by omission regularly in my personal life to those I was closest to, especially my wife. There was so much about what I did that I could not tell her. But she knew it and she didn't expect me to level with her about the things I was doing or the danger I might be in. The FBI, however, expected me to tell them everything. I was finally in the mud at the deep end.

Would this lie by omission to the FBI cause the web of lies I had been telling Lefty and the rest of the wiseguys to come true instantly – like my wife's car wreck and Tony Conte's Chicago art heist? Would I become just another dead rat, a Mafia associate who had done something wrong and paid the price he knew he would pay if he ever fucked up as badly as I had? Would I be dying from the lie I had been living? Was I lying to myself that I could handle this gamble, that it was worth the risk? On that point, I don't think so. And not just because the gamble paid off.

When I teach agents who are about to go deep, I tell them that their most important asset is their mental toughness. People don't realize the power of mental toughness. A lot of people out there don't understand how much you can accomplish just with mental toughness and focus. I saw a lot of it growing up in my Sicilian and Italian neighbourhood in Paterson, New Jersey. It was prized and I had it. That doesn't mean I didn't appreciate the danger of meeting with Lefty at that time in that place, but I was focused and I refused to let go. As I look back, I know I couldn't let go. I didn't have it in me.

I knew that Lefty would go when sent for, and later, when I got to know Sonny Black, I knew that Sonny Black would go when sent for. If I didn't go when sent for, Donnie Brasco was history. If I didn't show up for the midnight meeting, the whole operation would be prematurely over and I would have had to pull myself out of it. Because if I didn't show up when sent for, I would surely be whacked. That's one of the principal grounds for a death sentence – disobedience. And especially failing to come when called. It's actually a part of the Mafia oath when an associate is made; you always come when called. Period.

Lefty knew when he spoke to me on the phone that I had to be thinking that this could be it for me. He's the one who taught me that when they send for you it could be to whack you for something that you didn't even know about. But if I showed up and everything was okay, I would go way up in Lefty's estimation as a stand-up guy who comes in when called for even when it could be the end for him.

Mental toughness includes preparing well in advance to handle whatever could be thrown at you, rehearsing it in your mind like a boxer before a fight. You roll the imaginary camera in your mind and study the film of your opponent's last fight. If you're prepared that way in advance, you don't get confused or panicky by having to make decisions on the spot.

First, I decided I'm not going into any back room. Not that that matters so much, because many hits occur the instant you walk through a door from the outside. Two times .22 with a silencer, behind the ear. I could get it walking in the joint before I even closed the door behind me. I could get it stepping out of the cab. I had to keep my eyes open from the moment the cab pulled up.

Second, I decided I'm going on instinct. If something doesn't feel right when I open the bar door, I'm closing it and turning right around. I pictured myself doing just that.

Mental toughness, at least for me, includes faith. Not a day went by as Donnie Brasco that I didn't subconsciously ask a Higher Power to look over me for the day.

The threat of death was a very real threat to me when I finally opened the front door and took that first step inside. I tried to look as relaxed and normal as possible. I could see Lefty sitting with two wiseguys I knew, but hardly. Otherwise, the place was empty of customers. Not a good sign.

The two wiseguys stood up and moved away from Lefty's table when I stepped in. My first thought was, *what are they doing here?* Did Lefty want these two to get a good look at me to be sure they recognized me if they were supposed to whack me later? Still, on pure hunch, it didn't feel like a set-up, like anything would happen inside Lynn's, but you never know about hunches. And like I said, I'm a lousy gambler, unlucky at playing hunches.

Nothing for nothing, I thought as I walked to Lefty's table, I'm here. I sat to Lefty's side, not across from him. That way if he pulled out a gun, I had a chance at him. And I'd be facing the bar and the two wiseguys.

The two wiseguys sat at the end of the bar closest to the door. I saw that they were boxing me out. They were sitting between the door and me, should I have any inclination to make a broken field run out of the place.

Lefty scowled at me with complete contempt. His eyes were dead and his voice commanding. "Don't say nothing to me right now. You just sit there and take what you got coming."

If this is it, I thought, I'm not going down easy. Lefty's hands stayed on the table. The two wiseguys stayed on their bar stools. We sat in silence. I couldn't break the silence because Lefty told me to say nothing, to just sit there and take what I got coming.

"You know you fucked up," Lefty said. "But I don't know you know how bad you fucked up. Donnie, sometimes I don't know you know nothing. I know you know what happens when somebody fucks up one-tenth as much as you fucked up in this here. When you got it coming, Donnie, for doing something wrong, you got it coming. I don't give a fuck who you are."

"I'm sorry, Left, I'm really sorry. This cost me, too, Left.

Some of that was my money. Plus he took my clothes, my belongings, my plane ticket. I'll make this up to you. I mean it. I'll get us all right on this. I've got some ideas for some scores."

As the apology mixed with the sound of cash, Lefty looked over at the other two wiseguys and they got up, said good-night to us, and left. Were they there to make me understand how serious I had fucked up? Did Lefty send them away to let me know he accepted my half-assed apology? Or would they be waiting for me somewhere?

"I didn't even get a Christmas bonus due to the fact of out there and how it made me look," Lefty said.

After a lot more of this kind of tongue-lashing and poor-mouthing from Lefty, it turns out, Lefty told me, he wanted to meet me way uptown at Lynn's at that late hour because he wanted to prepare me for a meeting I was to have in the morning with Mike Sabella and he didn't want word to get back to Mike that he was doing that. Lefty's act of preparing me for my meeting with Sabella also told me that Sabella had no intention of whacking me at that meeting, as long as I followed Lefty's instructions for handling the meeting.

It looked as if my gamble had paid off. My decision not to tell my handlers that I had been sent for had not backfired on me.

Lefty's advice to me for my conduct at my meeting the next morning with Mike Sabella is advice I pass on to those undercover agents I mentor. Lefty said, "Don't offer nothing. Only answer the questions. Don't show him you're afraid. Look him steady in the eye. Don't show any fear. Don't admit you were wrong, even though we know. This Conte piece of shit was our mark and you shoulda never left him go outside by himself. You shoulda kept a better eye on him so he didn't go chasing after the hostess at the Snug Restaurant, which was Balistrieri's girlfriend. Some looker that girl, but you don't even think like that. Mike will confront you on these parts. But don't you admit none of that. How you fucked this up royally you admit to me some other time, but not to Mike. Look him in the eye. Be respectful. Like I said, Donnie, if I didn't love you how much I love you you'd be fucking dead. Mike don't love you like I do."

Lefty's advice paid off. I got off with a warning. I never again saw the two wiseguys who had been at the bar. The Donnie Brasco deep-cover operation was still in business. And it's a good thing it was. Because the precise things that happened as a result of my continued undercover work ultimately, many years later, were to bring down the entire Bonanno family hierarchy.

Another potentially disastrous incident happened a few years after my gamble at Lynn's paid off. It's another matter I have never before disclosed publicly.

While there are some things I had to do that I will take to my grave and never tell a soul, this is more about something I *decided* to do rather than something I did. In the past I revealed that if there was a situation in which I had to decide between trying to save a wiseguy and risking my own life to do it, or not, I would not jump in and stop the hit on a wiseguy. But I *would* risk my life to stop a hit on a private citizen. What I didn't reveal is what I would do if I found myself in a position of having to put two behind the ear of a wiseguy or risk my own life by not doing it.

My mindset was that the wiseguy would go. I knew the FBI would not stand behind me on something like that. Well, let me call it what it is – murder in the first degree. On top of that there would also be a state charge of first-degree murder in the state in which I murdered the wiseguy, and the federal Department of Justice wouldn't have jurisdiction over the state murder. But to me, I'd rather take my chances with the judicial system than with the Mafia. I'd rather be alive fighting a murder charge.

When you get an order from your boss to kill somebody, you don't hesitate, you don't negotiate, and you certainly don't say, "No thank you, I'll just stay here and play cards."

In an undercover operation you always have to know with whom you are dealing, and I did. If you hesitate when you are given a contract, you will be killed, most likely right on the very spot of your hesitation. A wiseguy who says no to a contract is a dead wiseguy.

Even if you are out on a hit with your crew you are not above danger. If you do not do your part and pull your trigger, too, the other guns could be turned on you then or later. And you could find yourself on the same blood-soaked ground as the intended victim. If the contract happens to be yours, you'd better be the first one to pull the trigger, not the one who fires into an already dead body. That's something a snitch might do.

It goes without saying that, to begin with, you don't want to be in such a position. Even if you don't pull a trigger, but you go out on a hit, you are guilty of murder in the first degree under the theory of accomplice liability known as felony murder. The accomplice, the lookout, the wheelman, is as guilty of first-degree murder in the eyes of the law as the triggerman.

In the late spring of 1981 I was given the contract to find and kill Bruno Indelicato – a made man. He was a cokehead and the son of the murdered Bonanno capo Sonny Red Indelicato. Sonny Red was one of the three capos (along with Dominick "Big Trin" Trinchera and "Phil Lucky" Giaccone) who had been sent for to attend a meeting on 5 May 1981, and when they arrived they were whacked. This downsizing in the Bonanno family occurred a few days before I got the contract to find and kill Bruno.

Bruno, also a capo, was supposed to have attended the meeting, but failed to appear and escaped getting whacked in the massacre with his father. Now they had to find Bruno and kill him before he could retaliate against those responsible for his father's murder.

The May 5th upheaval caused Sonny Black Napolitano, who I had been with for two years by then, to be moved up a rung as acting street boss for the jailed boss Rusty Rastelli. Lefty and I were with Sonny Black's crew and that meant we were moving on up with Sonny Black. Sonny Black was now as big as you could get without being the actual boss.

As acting street boss, Sonny Black was the boss who gave

me the Bruno Indelicato contract. Sonny told me to go to Miami, find Bruno Indelicato, and kill him.

"I think he went to Miami because he's got a $3,000-a-day coke habit and he's got connections with the Colombians down there," Sonny told me. "I want you to find him. When you find him, hit him. Be careful because when he's coked up, he's crazy. He's not a tough guy with his hands, but if he has a gun, you know. . . . He might be down there with his uncle J.B. If you come across them both, just kill them both and leave them there in the street. I want the body found. He's like 140, 150 pounds. Smaller than you. Thin-faced kid. Italian-looking, dark. Always complaining about his bald head. In his late twenties. Bantamweight, petite-looking. He's a dangerous little kid. He's a wild man when he's coked up. . . . Leave him right there in the street."

Sonny gave me a .25 automatic for the job.

I saw Lefty a few minutes later and he already knew I had been given the hit. Lefty told me the Bruno hit would help me get promoted to a made member of the Mafia because it would give me a big hit under my belt. Lefty told me that Sonny had wanted me on the three capos hit, but that Big Joey Massino vetoed it. The prudent Big Joey didn't think he knew me well enough to include me in something that big. Years later Big Joey would point to this with pride.

This ordered hit on Bruno was one matter I clearly and quickly told my handlers. I called Jules the first chance I got, which was 3:30 in the morning. Now that Jules knew, both the FBI and the Mafia would be out there looking for Bruno. That made me figure that my chances of finding Bruno first were almost non-existent. If the FBI found him they would arrest him to get him off the street so I wouldn't have to kill him. If other wiseguys stumbled on him in their ordinary course of activities they wouldn't wait for me to get there to kill him. Whatever wiseguy found him first would kill him first. If I somehow did find him first, I'd have called my handlers in the FBI to snatch him off the street. Unless other wiseguys happened to be along when I found him. Then I'd probably have to kill him or be killed with him.

Because Sonny Black sent me to Miami figuring Bruno would want to be near a supply of coke to feed his huge habit, I danced around all the usual coke haunts in Miami, getting seen everywhere. I was making sure Sonny Black would hear back in New York that I was taking my assignment seriously.

It did occur to me that Bruno Indelicato might get wind that I was the one that had the contract and try to get a shot at me first, or have one of his men who I wouldn't know or even recognize to get off first. But I kept a watchful eye and told myself that the last thing Bruno Indelicato needed to do was go out of his way to try to shoot a shooter. He needed to lay low and keep on the move. Of course, where does it say that a cokehead like Bruno always does what logic dictates?

Nevertheless, in my gut I felt that if Bruno was going to try to whack anybody it was going to be Sonny Black. Sonny Black could never really rest easy until Bruno was gone, and that's why the new acting street boss had given me the assignment in the first place.

A side assignment Sonny gave me while I was looking for Bruno was to drop in on two made men operating for the Bonannos in Hallandale, Florida, not far from Miami. Joe Puma and Steve Maruca were two soldiers who had been under one of the three murdered capos, Phil Lucky, and owed allegiance to the three capos who were massacred. My job was to reassure Puma and Maruca that they were not going to be whacked and to tell them that they now owed their allegiance to Sonny Black.

In a strange way, this assignment was more significant under the Mafia code than the assignment to kill Bruno. Anyone – made, connected, or just some nut – could be given a contract to hit someone. But to have a sit-down of any magnitude with a made man, you had to be at least made. Here I was, a connected man only, not a made man, going to Florida to a sit-down in order to reassure two made men that they wouldn't be hit if they did the right thing. In the sit-down I would be expected to evaluate them both for the slightest attitude or sign of disloyalty or even disappointment that their friends, the three capos, had been whacked. And they would know that I, a mere associate, was sizing them up.

Puma had been so scared after the hits that he hurried to New York to pledge his allegiance to the new power. Maruca made it clear that the three capos' deaths were a part of Mafia life. "Things like this happen. You can't question," he said.

After I was down in Florida awhile Sonny Black called me to fly back to New York. I figured or hoped that my contract to kill Bruno had expired and we would get back to whatever daily scheming presented itself to us in the Motion Lounge in Brooklyn and King's Court in Tampa. Among other things, I was hoping to hear more talk and get more evidence against those who participated in the hit on the three capos.

Which brings me to the other bad incident nobody knows a thing about. One night we were sitting around in the Motion Lounge playing cards and chatting away. Lefty, Jimmy Legs, Nicky Santora, Sonny, and I – all just doing our usual ritual when the phone rang. It was a pay phone on the wall. Sonny Black answered it and I could tell from his look and the tone of his voice when he grunted that he was getting excited.

Sonny hung up the phone and said, "Bruno's in a house in Staten Island."

Lefty got up from the card table and said, "Let's go."

Let's go, I thought. Jimmy Legs and Nicky Santora got up, too. I got up. My getting up, under the law of conspiracy to murder, was an overt act. Immediately upon committing that overt act, I was guilty of conspiracy to murder Bruno.

Lefty's maroon Caddy was parked right outside the front door of the Motion Lounge. Sonny Black, as capo, would not be going, and everybody knew that. Sonny Black gave Lefty the address and directions. Meanwhile I'm thinking, *there is no way out*. Everybody's heavy, including me. We've all been loaded up since the three capos got whacked, in case that multiple hit set off a full-scale Mafia war. I still had my .25 automatic from Miami in my pocket. The others had .38's to .45's. Lefty had a shotgun in the trunk.

If I hesitated in front of my capo, my own soldier, and my

crewmates, I would not have left the Motion Lounge alive. I was on a fast-moving train. I could go to the bathroom, but there were no cell phones in those days. I positively couldn't go outside to use a pay phone at a time like this. There was no way I could contact anyone. I was alone. The statement "Let's go" from Lefty was all it took and everybody knew what to do. This wasn't the first time these guys had done something like this. It never even entered my mind to bolt and run away. They'd get in Lefty's car, catch up to me in a block and I'd be the victim of a drive-by shooting. And then they'd go kill Bruno.

As an FBI agent you're trained to question information you get. Who told you Bruno was there? How reliable is the source? How stale or fresh is the information? Was Bruno seen in the house? What's the layout of the house? All those things went through my mind, but it didn't make any difference. As a Mafia soldier you get to ask no questions. There are no questions in Mafia business. You're trained to go on the word that's given to you. There could have been something else in that call. For all I knew Sonny Black had been told there were three of Bruno's men there with Bruno Indelicato, and maybe Sonny Black chose not to tell us.

Almost from the beginning of my deep-cover penetration into the Mafia my mental toughness mindset had prepared me for this moment. The people I had been assigned to infiltrate engaged in murder the way a cabbie goes through a yellow light. I had to be mentally prepared for the near occasion of murder. I had long ago made my decision of what to do when this predictable occasion arose. If Bruno's there, he's gone. If I have to put a bullet in his head, I will, and I'll deal with the federal government and the Staten Island DA later. There's no doubt they would both charge me for murder. The Bureau would brand me a rogue agent and hang me out to hang. My wife, my daughters, my parents, would all be crushed right along with me, but my decision when it had been made was firmly made.

Meanwhile, we could be walking into a death trap. If not a death trap, then at least a bloody situation. We just killed

Bruno's old man. He knows we're out to kill him. He's a coke-head. He's not going to come easily. There will probably be a shoot-out. Any of his men that are there with him to guard him will be killed, too. I could be facing multiple murder charges. Or worse yet, I got that old dreaded feeling that I would die as a gangster.

We were half out the door and on the street when the phone rang again. Sonny Black ran over and got it, said, "Hold it," and waved us back in while he took the call. We shut the door. When he hung up, Sonny Black said, "It's bad information."

"That's too bad, Sonny," I said.

In my mind, all these years I've been calling that the "miracle of the second phone call". The Higher Power I looked up to each day for protection was looking out for me.

13

Denis Tanner and the Bonnie Doon Bodies

John Harrison

The following sad story concerns an allegedly corrupt cop in small-town South Australia. The beautiful wilderness around Bonnie Doon, about a two-hour drive from Melbourne, has taken on an eerie quality in the light of three interlinked cases, and their unsatisfactory conclusions. Firstly, a suicide that is highly likely to have been a murder; secondly, the body of a transsexual sex worker dumped unceremoniously down an old mineshaft near the same rural property, and thirdly, an unrelated undercover police operation into an amphetamine-dealing ring corrupted by the leaking of information to the suspects under surveillance, possibly by the cop under suspicion for these two killings.

The story is straight out of an episode of crime drama *CSI*, and yet, unlike a neatly scripted plot designed to reach its "reveal" within fifty minutes, it seems not to end with a bang but to continue with guttering claim and counter-claim, until either there will be a further, crucial breakthrough in one case that will shed light on the others, or time will pass and the moving hand, having writ, as it were, will simply move on. In the meantime, two deaths remain unexplained, and either an innocent man is ostracized under the shadow of aspersion, or a guilty man walks free. There's something universal about these unexplained events – reality is not as neat as drama, and life is full of ambiguities. If we find this state of affairs emotionally unsatisfactory, we have to find a way of living with it.

Dramas also leave us with an impression of corruption as something that concerns vast, shadowy conspiracies in the corridors of power, pseudo-Masonic networks or New World Orders. In reality, where corruption occurs, the rotten-apple syndrome is usually, and more prosaically, at work.

Robin Bowles's books *Blind Justice* and *No Justice*, on which the following essay draws, represent the most in-depth look at the following cases. However it should be noted that since their publication, doubt has been cast on the sweeping conclusion of the second inquest into the death of Jennifer Tanner, in 1996 – which attributed responsibility to brother-in-law Denis Tanner – if less so on its conclusion (against the suicide finding of the first inquest), that her death was not self-inflicted. Denis Tanner maintains that evidence that was not presented to the second coroner reinforces the suicide theory.

Two separate investigations have studied events in considerable detail, one by the Victoria Police Kale task force, and one by the federal Office of Police Integrity, and Tanner himself along with an ally, Ron Irwin, has brought further legal action against the Victoria Police over the findings of the former, alleging the fabrication of evidence against him. Detective Inspector Paul Newman and Senior Sergeant Martin Allison face the sack if the disciplinary charges against them are proved, and the Kale task force has already been obliged to settle a sum of $400,000 Aus with another officer, Gerry McHugh, whom it erroneously implicated and bugged. Meanwhile, so many possible courses of events have yet to be dismissed as potential explanations.

It could indeed be the case that Dennis Tanner is linked by coincidence to two women who died without his involvement, after all, and that only the second death, that of sex worker Adele Bailey, was murder. The second inquest into Jenny Tanner's end (prompted by the discovery of Ms Bailey's remains nearby) does indeed seem to have reached a sweeping conclusion in identifying a putative killer, well beyond a finding as to cause of death. In the intervening years, police have maintained that they have insufficient evidence to bring a successful prosecution against Tanner, leaving him in an anguished half-world of being accused but not convicted.

Meanwhile, as reported by Australia's *Herald Sun*, new evidence was passed to the Office of Police Integrity in the summer of 2010 that suggests another officer altogether may have been responsible for Adele Bailey's death, after having enjoyed a sexual encounter with her, unaware that she was a transsexual, and that other officers assisted in the disposal of her corpse. It is, however, alleged that this officer has been known to Denis Tanner since before these events. Whether it could be that justice will reach an explosive conclusion in Bailey's case after all, or we're witnessing another iteration of claim and counter-claim, as police fall out among themselves, remains to be seen.

Why is it that whenever a murder case emerges which involves a cross-gender victim, the story always seems to come across as so much more sordid and enticing? Are we that far desensitized to crime that only the addition of an exotic angle will pique our interest, or does it fascinate us because it indicates the work of a killer who has decidedly kinky proclivities along with a violent nature? When you throw an enigmatic, notorious policeman into this lethal mix, the cocktail becomes that much more exotic, dangerous and irresistible.

The Denis Tanner story is one of the most unusual and intriguing in modern Australian crime; one made even more mystifying by its eventual, unresolved outcome. In an age when police corruption and cover-ups are treated by many people as an ugly but inevitable part of the crime-fighting system, the name Denis Tanner still manages to invoke feelings of curiosity in many, and of sheer terror in a select few.

One of four brothers, Denis Tanner joined the Victorian Police Force on 22 October 1973, graduating from the Academy (22nd out of the 24 in his class) on 15 March 1974. A solid man with an intimidating demeanour, Tanner began active service at Russell Street, then spent time at South

Melbourne and Shepparton, before finally being stationed at St Kilda. At the time (and even today, although to a lesser extent), St Kilda was one of the major hubs for Australia's drug and prostitution rackets, a beachfront suburb dominated by the infamous Fitzroy Street, whose string of skid-row pubs, grimy adult bookshops and neon-lit pinball parlours and fish and chip shops made it Melbourne's own miniature version of Los Angeles's infamous Sunset Strip (unfortunately, it has now become a haven for yuppies, with pretentious coffee houses and overpriced department stores).

Although Tanner was apparently counselled by officers in the 1970s for not following proper procedures, on 4 May 1978 he received a commendation, alongside three other officers, for his dedication to duty and courage, and for the valour which he displayed in the apprehension of a violent criminal.

On 14 May 1978 Denis Tanner arrested Adele Bailey, a New Zealand born transsexual working the streets of St Kilda, on charges of loitering for prostitution and homosexual purposes. A heavy drug user with rumoured connections to the underworld, Bailey had arrived in Australia in the early 1970s, working the streets while trying to save up the $2,000 needed for her sex change operation, which she had done on the cheap in Europe (where you didn't have to undergo a battery of psychological tests or live as a woman for a certain amount of time). It was after her return to Australia that Bailey began to migrate to the St Kilda area, becoming a well-known figure to many of the local cops who patrolled the streets.

When Bailey failed to turn up to her court appearance on 15 September 1978, and when Tanner issued a warrant for her arrest a month later, she had simply vanished from the face of the earth. Her flatmate had arrived home to find the front door ajar and Adele nowhere to be seen.

While Adele Bailey's family and friends undertook a frustrating and fruitless search for answers, Denis Tanner continued his impressive climb up the police ladder, being transferred to the CIB in 1979, and promoted to the rank of senior detective, working in the Major Crime squad.

In 1981 Denis's brother Laurie married Jennifer Blake, with Denis signing the marriage certificate. Although he could never have foreseen it at the time, the marriage would be the seed that would lead to Denis Tanner's eventual downfall and disgrace as a police officer.

Three years after the wedding, on 14 November 1984, Jennifer Tanner's body was discovered in the living room of their farmhouse in the Victorian country town of Bonnie Doon, slumped over her husband's bolt-action .22-calibre rifle. She had been shot twice in the head, as well as through both hands (which usually indicates the victim had been in a defensive position). Her infant son was discovered unharmed in the bedroom, sleeping peacefully.

The two country police officers who were called to the scene were confronted with the sight of Jennifer Tanner's body slumped on the couch, rifle propped between her knees, the barrel pointed into her profusely bleeding head (Laurie Tanner claimed that when he found his wife's body he didn't notice the bullet holes through both hands).

The death of Jennifer Tanner was extremely suspect from the outset. The police at the scene decided to call in Alexandra-based Ian Welsh; however, the Detective Sergeant, known as "Columbo" to the locals, decided against visiting the crime scene to personally investigate, even after he was informed of the discovery of a second bullet cartridge lying near the body. Incredibly, Welsh also decided that fingerprinting, photographs and forensic tests were not necessary (Welsh would deny ever having received the initial telephone call at the 1997 inquest into Jennifer's death).

While suicide was to be the initial consensus in the death of Jennifer Tanner, Bill Kerr, the older of the two constables who had been first on the scene (Don Frazer being his partner), harboured a number of serious doubts, which he kept to himself for a number of years. Kerr – well aware that Jennifer was the sister-in-law of Denis Tanner – wondered about the cup of coffee and plate of biscuits that were sitting next to Jennifer's body, and why she would leave her baby alone in another room. The position of the body also troubled him, along with the bloodstains on the couch. It almost seemed as if the body had been lying down at some point, before being propped up in a seated position.

There was also no suicide note and, as the two officers made the trip to break the news to Jennifer Tanner's parents, Kerr noted a police radio message, which revealed that Denis Tanner was not at his Footscray apartment when Melbourne police arrived to see him.

Amazingly, the morning after Jennifer's death, another of Denis Tanner's brothers, Bruce Frederick, was allowed to enter the farmhouse and clean up the site of the apparent suicide, potentially erasing evidence at a possible crime scene. The initial inquest into Jennifer Tanner's death was held in late 1995 and, although some fingers and whispers of suspicions were clearly directed at Denis Tanner (he was represented by well-known attorney Joe Gullaci),[1] the police's handling of the death was considered so botched that the laying of any murder charges was considered impossible, with an open finding being the verdict of the inquest.

Controversy continued to dog Denis Tanner throughout the latter half of the 1980s. In March 1988, he was believed to be responsible for selling information to big-time drug dealers William Hackett and Terrance Moon, who were the focus of a major undercover investigation into an amphetamines distribution ring (which police had dubbed Operation Mint). It is claimed that Tanner received vital information regarding the operation from a drug squad officer who worked at the same building, then used a former policeman to pass the details on to Hackett and Moon. (In October 1989, the detective suspected of leaking news to Tanner resigned six weeks after being questioned on the matter by Chief Inspector Tony Warren.)

Denis Tanner transferred to the country town of Benalla in December 1988, holding the rank of detective sergeant (his wife, also in the police force, resigned from her position at the Altona station in order to be with him). It wasn't long after the move that Tanner was being counselled by his superiors at Benalla, for using inappropriate language.

The following February, Tanner seriously hurt his knee during a vicious struggle with a criminal in the Benalla cells. Two months later, he requested forty days leave to recover from stress and anxiety, no doubt brought on by the growing widespread allegations that he was suspected of serious corruption.

Upon Tanner's return to duty in June 1989, he was interviewed by investigators in relation to Operation Mint, and was later informed by Police Commissioner Neil Comrie that Command intended to demote him to the Police Reserve, which eventuated in January of 1990, after Deputy Commissioner Brendan Crimmins wrote a letter to Denis Tanner in regard to Operation Mint, in which he clearly branded Tanner a crook. Tanner immediately appealed the transfer.

Tanner's appeal to the Police Services Board was heard by former Police Commander Eric Sutton, former policeman Fred Leslie and Country Court Judge Walsh. The appeal – in which eleven serving and former police, ranked from constable to chief inspector, told the hearing that Tanner was a valuable and trusted member of the CIB – was successful, and his transfer to the Police Reserves was overturned. The Services Board believed that there were clear indications of corruption in Operation Mint, but Tanner's link to any of them could not be proved.

THE FARM GIVES UP ITS SECRETS

On 20 July 1995, Mick Bladen and his friend Dave Worsley, Melbourne residents who frequently journeyed to Bonnie Doon for campouts and mountain-climbing treks, were returning from a day's exploring when they came upon the old, and long disused, Jack o' Clubs mineshaft, situated on a property not far from the farmhouse where Jennifer Tanner died. Named after the unknown original owner of the mine – because of his skill at playing blackjack – the mine yielded fine, rich concentrations of gold in the late 1800s, but had been long since tapped out and abandoned, a large cherry tree growing by the entrance its only companion.

On a whim, Bladen and Worsley decided to venture down the mineshaft, descending via a rope tied to the cherry tree. What they found down there was not what they had expected. Reaching the first level ten metres down, Worsley shone his torch down on to the next level of the shaft and, with a sudden wave of fear surging through him, solved a seventeen-year-old mystery. Adele Bailey had been found.

The partially clothed skeleton was wearing lingerie, high-heeled boots and jewellery. Although the remains were too old to establish a definite cause of death, a number of Bailey's bones were broken, and several police officers privately revealed to author Robin Bowles that Adele had probably been either kicked to death or "copped the chicken" (a police slang term for almost choking someone to death, then letting them go from a height).

Tanner's clear link to Bailey,[2] combined with Andrew Rule's[3] article in the Sunday 9 June 1996 edition of the *Sunday Age* (which probed the inconsistencies surrounding Jennifer Tanner's supposed suicide), led to the original inquest into Jennifer's death being quashed, and the re-opening of a new inquiry, which was designated Operation Kale.

Less than two months after the mineshaft discovery, the old Tanner homestead – which had been sold shortly after Jennifer's death to an absentee owner – mysteriously burnt to the ground. The fire began outside and engulfed the building before firefighters could arrive. Any DNA or forensic evidence which may have been recovered was gone for good.

The new inquest into the murder of Jennifer Tanner began in October 1997. In his opening address, Jeremy Rapke made public for the first time the name of Sergeant Helen Golding. It was revealed that Golding, godmother to Denis Tanner's children, and formerly his wife's best friend, had received a series of death threats. When Golding herself appeared in the courtroom a week later, she looked stressed out and visibly nervous, and a weapon check had been conducted on everyone who entered the court.

Golding revealed to the court that she had contacted the Jennifer Tanner task force in October 1996, after reading the

Sunday Age piece. Since giving a statement about Denis Tanner to detectives, she had not been able to sleep properly, and had been too scared to even walk her dog or ride her horse alone. She had also received a number of disturbing, and none too subtle, messages through the mail. She was sent a dagger (covered in fake blood), leaflets from funeral homes, a sympathy card with "you're dead" written on it, a .22 calibre bullet, and a wreath with the message "Time Runs Out", which was left on her front doorstep. She also received a letter containing her current work roster, with the words "I miss you" inscribed on it.

Bill Kerr, the constable who kept his suspicions to himself when first called to the scene on the night of Jennifer Tanner's death, was also called to the stand. Kerr told the court that he had believed Jennifer Tanner was murdered ever since the autopsy two days after her death showed that she had two bullets in her skull, as well as bullet wounds in each hand. Kerr also recalled his claims that he had called detective Ian Welsh to inform him of irregularities at the scene, only to be told by Welsh to continue to treat the investigation as a suicide, and not to gather evidence as if it were a crime scene. Kerr also said he had become frustrated by his superiors, who repeatedly denied his requests for forensic tests on the rifle, and for a list of questions to be put to Denis Tanner. He also expressed his curiosity when he heard the radio report revealing that Tanner had not been at home when police called in shortly after the discovery of Jennifer's body.

(Denis Tanner's wife Lynn claimed that her husband did not return home until early morning on the night Jennifer died. After initially claiming that he had been at the horse races at the time of the death, Tanner changed his story months later, telling homicide detective Albert Fry that he had been providing security at a bingo night in the inner Melbourne suburb of Albert Park. Tanner was never officially questioned over his change of alibi, despite the fact that the race meeting which he originally claimed to be at had not even taken place on the same night as Jennifer Tanner's death.)

Don Frazer, the constable who accompanied Kerr to the Tanner home, told the coroner he regretted the way things were handled on the night Jennifer Tanner was shot (he had progressed to the position of sergeant by the time he faced the inquiry).

Superintendent Peter Fleming – who would later join the anti-corruption unit – assisted the coroner in the 1985 autopsy of Jennifer Tanner. Fleming testified that he felt the investigation of Jennifer's death was inadequate at every level, adding that he had been concerned that nothing was being done to rectify it. He recalled a heated meeting with homicide squad officers where Albert Fry seemed adamant that the death was a suicide, and was supported by his superiors, who refused to investigate the matter.

Bruce Frederick Tanner, who appeared to be tense and borderline aggressive throughout his time on the stand, explained his own curious behaviour in the immediate after-math of Jennifer's death. His version of events were that his mother had telephoned him at around 6 a.m. with the bad news. Setting off to Mansfield to comfort his parents (as well as brother Laurie), Bruce Tanner decided to stop off at the farmhouse where the shooting had occurred, where he went in and cleaned up the grisly aftermath. When asked why he did this, rather than head straight to his grieving family, Bruce explained that a policeman had claimed that his mother would be expected to clean up the scene, and he was not prepared to let her suffer through that. Unfortunately, he was unable to recollect the name of the police officer who had given him this information.

Leaving the court with his family after his day on the stand, Bruce Tanner was walking to his car when his brother Denis swung his briefcase into the groin of a *Herald-Sun* photographer. As he drove away, Bruce Tanner flung the door to his car open, knocking the same photographer to the ground.

Among the other statements given during the hearing was that of the doctor who performed the initial autopsy on Jennifer Tanner's body, who admitted that he tried at the time to make the two head wounds, as well as the two wounds on the hands, fit the police's dogged opinion that the death was a suicide.

Coroner Graeme Johnstone delivered his finding into the 1984 death of Jennifer Tanner on 10 December 1998, stating that she had been killed by her brother-in-law, Detective Sergeant Denis Tanner. The courtroom sat galvanised as Johnstone told them that Denis shot her at least three times with her husband's bolt-action .22 rifle.

Despite the finding – along with the public outrage and damning media coverage which followed it – charges were not laid against Denis Tanner. It seemed obvious that much of the evidence considered by Johnstone would be inadmissible in a criminal trial, and with no eyewitnesses and any forensic evidence long since destroyed, there would be insufficient substantiation to put Tanner before a jury.

Still, the findings had highlighted the gross ineptitude of the initial handling of Jennifer Tanner's death, and put the heat of the spotlight clearly on Denis Tanner. For the media and news-hungry public, it was also an enthralling curtain-raiser to the forthcoming inquest into the death of Adele Bailey, which finally got under way in early 1999.

At the Bailey inquest, one of the most damning statements was that of a former insurance clerk, Mrs Janine Fletcher, who claimed that Mark O'Loughlin, a former client, policeman and friend of Denis Tanner, had boasted of the parties which had taken place at his holiday home at Bonnie Doon, where prostitutes and strippers were taken along. Fletcher also overheard O'Loughlin talking about how the police would regularly let the transsexual prostitutes get roughed up by the men in their holding cells.

Fletcher further identified Denis Tanner as having the same eyes as a policeman who had pulled her over in her car and threatened her after she had questioned her employer over a suspicious insurance claim lodged by O'Loughlin. Fletcher said she processed three insurance claims for Mark O'Loughlin with insurance broker Complete Financial Services in the early 1980s. One of the claims was for cash and a large amount of alcohol stolen from O'Loughlin's Bonnie Doon holiday house.

The claim which forced Mrs Fletcher to raise her suspicions was for the theft of jewellery from O'Loughlin's car. When she noticed a similar lot of jewellery being advertised for sale in *The Trading Post*, Fletcher called the number listed in the ad, only to find it being answered by the South Melbourne police station where O'Loughlin was based. Fletcher's boss, Denis Jones, told her to back off when she pointed out the advertisement to him (Jones kept a number of police officers on his books as clients).

A week after raising the issue with her boss, Mrs Fletcher was pulled up by a plain-clothes policeman, whom she later identified as Denis Tanner. Fletcher told the court that Tanner told her in no uncertain terms to keep her nose out of other people's business, and to leave his friends alone. Fletcher, whose confrontation with Tanner left her rattled and scared, later received a number of threatening telephone calls. She eventually decided to contact police after reading the 1996 article on the Tanner case in the *Sunday Age*.

Unlike the Jennifer Tanner inquest, the Adele Bailey hearing was relatively short. Because of the age of the crime, and the lack of any usable, concrete evidence, Coroner Jacinta Heffey was left with no choice but to make an open finding.

Not long after the Bailey hearing – on 28 July 1999 – Denis Tanner resigned from the police force. He escaped having any murder charges laid against him after senior prosecutors informed the Victorian Director of Public Prosecutions that there was no reasonable prospect of obtaining a conviction. He was last known to be working as a cab driver.

On 13 March 2002, John Silvester reported in *The Age* that Chief Commissioner Christine Nixon had called in the federal police to investigate a claim of perjury against Victorian police officers on the murder task force that investigated Denis Tanner over the murder of Jennifer Tanner and the death of Adele Bailey.

The federal police were particularly interested in the task force's decision to place listening devices in the house of a serving policeman, Senior Detective Gerry McHugh. It is alleged that Senior Detective McHugh may have been at a party with Denis Tanner at Bonnie Doon, where Adele Bailey either overdosed and died, or was killed, in 1978. The Supreme Court granted a warrant to install listening devices in McHugh's Mildura home. McHugh, a policeman with more than twenty-five years' experience, later found the devices. Subsequent investigations found that McHugh was not at the Bonnie Doon party and was not involved with Adele Bailey's disappearance.

A FATAL LINK?

Was there a connection between Jennifer Tanner and Adele Bailey, a link which would bind these two very different personalities together in the cold, black void of death? Nothing points to the pair ever having met in life – the most popular explanation would seem to be that Jennifer Tanner had the misfortune to stumble upon the secret of what lay in that abandoned mineshaft out the back of her property, and either threatened to talk or was silenced before she ever had the chance to do so.

Another popular theory bandied about suggested that the murders of Jennifer Tanner and Adele Bailey were completely unrelated (save for the likelihood that they were committed by the same person), that Jennifer was killed because she was unhappy with her marriage and planning to divorce her husband, and someone was not prepared to see part of the family assets handed over to her (Laurie Tanner had already been through one very costly divorce with his first wife, Sally).

Of course, this is all now just a matter of speculation and, although we have many of the individual pieces, it seems highly unlikely that we will ever view the complete picture. When one drives through the outskirts of Bonnie Doon – about two hours out of Melbourne – it is easy to be convinced of a strange eeriness, and feeling of foreboding, that hangs in the air. It is not so much a feeling of current danger, more the echo of an evil, one that's all too human, that once pervaded the farmlands. It provides a grim reminder that horror can indeed lurk within serenity and beauty, and the evils of crime and corruption can spread its wings far beyond the claustrophobic, dirty confines of the metropolis.

And somewhere out there, another killer has gotten away with murder.

NOTES

1. A short but tough man with a gravelly voice and the required penchant for courtroom drama, Joe Gullaci's reputation helped him win both high-profile policemen and organized crime figures as clients. At his first trial in 1973, he represented a transsexual prostitute, Vicky Liddy, who had attacked a customer with a broken bottle after he refused to pay up. Although Liddy was found guilty, Gullaci was able to win her a greatly reduced sentence, and he quickly graduated from representing prostitutes and low-rent drug dealers to defending some of the country's biggest criminal cases, including that of Raymond Patrick Bennet, the mastermind behind the 1976 Great Bookie Robbery (where six gunmen robbed millions of dollars from bookmakers at the Victorian Club). When Bennet was shot outside a courtroom in 1979, by a hit man disguised as a lawyer, Gullaci pushed Bennet's wife Gail out of the line of fire, then later took her to hospital to visit her fatally injured husband. Joe Gullaci was appointed a County Court judge in June 2002.

2. Throughout the early 1980s, most police department watch house books – large, cumbersome leather-bound volumes – were destroyed to make way for shelf space as computerized systems slowly took over. For historical purposes, a select few of the old volumes were kept for display in the Police Museum. Ironically, some of the books kept were the St Kilda police station volumes from October 1976 to January 1979, which contained complete records of Adele Bailey's arrests during that time. The records showed that Bailey had been arrested by Tanner, which in itself was not uncommon as it would have been part of Tanner's job tasks at the time, but it did provide Operation Kale investigators with clear proof that Bailey and Tanner were known to each other.

3. A senior reporter for *The Age* – specializing in stories on crime and corruption – Andrew Rule was one of the most prominent journalists attached to the Denis Tanner investigation. His 1996 *Sunday Age* piece on the inconsistencies of the initial Jennifer Tanner death enquiry helped pave the way for the new inquest, and many of the people who decided to testify at the subsequent inquests into both Jennifer Tanner and Adele Bailey claim they decided to come forward after reading Rule's article. (While researching the piece, two heavy roof tiles were thrown through the window of Rule's car as it was parked outside his home.) A recipient of the 1996 Australian Journalist of the Year award, Rule has also written on the Port Arthur Massacre, and has penned (with John Silvester) the popular series of *Underbelly* books, published by Sly Ink, which chronicle true Australian crime cases. Rule also narrated a 1996 television documentary on the Denis Tanner case.

14

The Onion Field

Joseph Wambaugh

A somewhat controversial figure on account of his role in the 1986 J. C. Smith murder trial in Pennsylvania (which is still confusing, if unintentional in its consequences for that case), Wambaugh was nevertheless, at the height of his powers, a fresh new voice in crime fiction. His first novel, *The New Centurions*, published in 1971, was a bestseller thanks to its realistic portrayal of the uniform beat cops of the LAPD, and prefigured the wave of realistic cop TV dramas, from *Hill Street Blues* to *The Wire*, as well as the character-driven, journalistic prose and wisecracking, black-humoured police officers of David Simon's books and scripts.

Upon first publication, Wambaugh had been an LA cop for ten years or so, and he continued to work as an LAPD detective for a time while a successful author: "I would have guys in handcuffs asking me for autographs." His position in the force inevitably became untenable, and, though it kept faith with the idea of the cop as a frontline worker for the preservation of civilization, his first novel on leaving the LAPD, *The Choirboys*, featured flawed, jaded cops, wrecked and morally compromised by a lifetime's police work. It was a further departure from the unalloyed, trilby-wearing hero cops of comic books, *Elliot Ness* or *Dragnet*.

The Onion Field, Wambaugh's first non-fiction book, written in 1973 while he was still a serving officer, is a taut and tragic tale in the manner of Capote's *In Cold Blood*. It features the story of two plain-clothes LAPD officers who were abducted from their unmarked car in 1963. The following extract narrates what happened next – events that kick off a labyrinthine series of events that culminated in two men facing the death penalty, and one man – the surviving cop – feeling like a failure for the rest of his foreshortened life. In that way, it's a study of the kind of masculine outlook in which an individual won't allow himself to see himself as a helpless victim, however accurate that may be, and hence let himself off the hook over the things he did not do, however impossible to accomplish they may have been.

"A typical Hollywood Saturday night," said Jimmy Smith, the tension festering in his guts, as he looked at rows of cars jammed up for blocks. "And everybody's too law-abidin' or too scared of cops or too fuckin' lackadaisical to even toot their horns or swear at the guy in front."

Jimmy thought of the Spanish automatic in his belt and what if the miserable thing went off by itself and shot his dick off? And yeah, that was somethin' else to worry about. What if I killed myself with my own goddamn gun by squirmin' around the wrong way in the seat? Bang! Off goes the cock and there I am, sprawled there dyin' in the street. Bleedin' to death! And he considered putting the gun in the glove compartment to get it out of his belt.

"Goddamnit," Greg said. "I'm getting out of this traffic. We'll head back toward downtown until we spot a liquor store to knock off."

"But I thought you wanted to take off this market out here in Hollywood?"

"Too goddamn much traffic, Jim. We made the wrong turn off the freeway. We'll find something on the way downtown."

As Ian Campbell drove the Plymouth into the alley near Gower Avenue on his ninth night with Karl, 9 March 1963, he spotted some mauve-coloured flowers in a window box, and rolling up his window against the night chill said, "The sweet peas and azaleas are starting to bloom. That must mean spring is here. I keep warning mine of the Ides of March."

Karl Hettinger grinned in the dark at his big-shouldered improbable partner who talked quaintly of flowers and bagpipes. Then Karl realized he had never heard a set of pipes firsthand.

"I'd like to hear you play those bagpipes sometime, Ian," he said as the little maroon Ford passed by the alley westbound on Carlos.

Gregory Powell was heading north on Gower when he decided to circle the block to the west. He turned on Carlos Avenue, saw the short street called Vista Del Mar straight ahead, and mistakenly thought Carlos Avenue dead-ended there.

"Hearing me play the pipes can definitely be arranged," Ian chuckled. "No one else wants to listen to me. My wife and kids and friends run away screaming when they just see me blow up the bag. I wait for unsuspecting people like you to ask me."

Ian slowed in the alley, flashing his two-cell light towards some shadows in an apartment house doorway, but it was just two bony cats slinking through the alleys, prowling hungrily.

The little maroon Ford made a turn and was coming back their way.

It was now 10:00 p.m. and the unmarked Plymouth police car known as Six-Z-Four was emerging from the alley onto Carlos when the coupé crossed their headlight beam and they saw the two gaunt young men with their leather jackets and snap-brim leather caps in their little car with Nevada plates.

They would have aroused the suspicion of almost any policeman in Hollywood that night. It was patently obvious that they were not ordinary out-of-town tourists cruising the boulevard. The caps were rare enough, but with matching leather jackets, they were almost absurdly suspicious, even contrived. It was as though they'd just driven off the Columbia Pictures lot farther south on Gower, two extras from a Depression-era gangster film, caricatures, Katzenjammer Kids.

But still, Ian and Karl had to look for something more tangible, something to tell the court for probable cause in case they came up with an arrest. They could not, or would not, depend upon their own ability to articulate a well-grounded suspicion, nor the court's ability to understand the several intangibles which go into the decision to stop and frisk and interrogate. So they looked for and immediately found something else: the tried and true "rear plate illumination".

Even if the Ford's licence plate lights had not been out, it is doubtful that Ian Campbell and Karl Hettinger would have let this car go its way. The little Ford looked "too good", which in police jargon means it looked too bad, too suspicious, a "good shake". It had to be stopped and a reason found to search.

The little Ford had but to turn left on Vista Del Mar and it could have proceeded south to Hollywood Boulevard and never have been stopped by Six-Z-Four that night, but Greg decided on a U-turn, and on their ninth night together, the partners made their last wrong turn on Los Angeles streets.

"Fuckin' dead ends," Jimmy grumbled when they turned around. "We always seem to be runnin' into dead ends."

"We should check these two," said Ian as the little Ford stopped for the red light at Gower.

"All right. When do you wanna take them?"

"Right now," said Ian, who pulled up behind the coupé, turned on his red light, and tooted the horn.

Gregory Powell glanced into the rear-view mirror, tightened his grip on the steering wheel, and said: "Cops!"

As the coupé turned the corner into Gower and stopped, Karl saw the heads move a bit closer.

"Let's be careful," said Karl.

Jimmy *felt* the red light before seeing it, felt the heat from the red light searing the back of his neck, and he was whispering, "I knew it. I *knew* it," even as he unzipped the brown leather jacket Greg had bought him, removed the .32 automatic Greg had bought him, and gingerly dropped it on the floor, kicking it across the car with his new thirty-five-dollar shoes. Greg's eyes were glued to the mirror and the kick was subtle but sharp enough so that the gun ended up very close to Greg's left foot where Jimmy wanted it. It was far enough from Jimmy so that he could swear that Greg had just picked him up hitchhiking and that he knew nothing of the two guns in Greg's possession. Weren't they in Greg's name? And in case that story didn't work he was sure he could come up with others.

"Just take it easy, it may just be a ticket. Just sit tight," Greg said, looking at Jimmy for an instant, and Jimmy tried to answer, wanted to say something sarcastic, but found himself unable to speak.

He could not take it easy, was in fact frantic, wanting as much distance as possible between himself and Gregory Powell when the cops found the gun on the floor at Greg's feet, and the one in Greg's belt. Who knows, this maniac might just try shooting his way out! Jimmy wouldn't put that past him, and he just wanted to show the cops he was only riding along with this guy, a hitchhiker, that's all.

I got nothin' to hide, and I just gotta be cool, gotta be cool, he told himself. But he was all the way to the right, as far as he could sit in the little coupé, and still felt too close to Greg, felt at that moment like they were Siamese twins. And then he leaped out of the car and looked into the eyes of Karl Hettinger, who was flashing his light, advancing slowly on the sidewalk.

Jimmy came forward, fear bursting all over him, and Karl reached inside his sport coat, placed his right hand on the gun butt in the cross-draw holster, and said what he knew was obvious enough despite the unmarked car: "Police."

Jimmy Smith froze at the sound of the word and threw his hands in the air.

Karl's pulse bucked. He glanced inside the car at Greg and quickly back at Jimmy standing stock still on the sidewalk, hands high in the air, though Karl had neither drawn his gun nor told Jimmy to raise his hands, and Karl knew for certain. Any policeman would have known. Something. There was something. Narcotics perhaps. They looked like hypes, but Ian was on the street side of the car and couldn't see Jimmy's panic signals.

Jesus, what if he sees the gun? thought Jimmy. What if Greg starts shootin'? Christ, I gotta get away from this maniac!

Karl's eyes were not close set, nor did the irises bleed into the pupil, but Jimmy was to forever remember Karl's eyes as being close set and glittering behind his plastic-rimmed glasses. Jimmy bore it as long as he could, about five seconds. Then he said, "What's the trouble, officer?"

"Police officers," said Ian to Greg, coming up on the driver's side, not bothering to show a badge, because it went without saying that these two would certainly know they were police. He wanted one hand free since the other held the flashlight.

"Oh, Lord, I know what I'm getting a ticket for this time," said Greg, with only a faint hope that he could bluff the cop, knowing that plain-clothes police don't write traffic tickets. Knowing that when you get stopped by them it's usually a frisk and questioning. He knew it the first instant he looked up at the big policeman, seeing his dark sport shirt buttoned at the throat, and his old grey flannel slacks, and his well-worn sports jacket, knowing they were on something other than normal uniform patrol or traffic details. He *knew* there would be no traffic ticket.

"Would you mind taking your licence out of your wallet?" asked Ian.

"Sure."

"How long have you been in town?" asked Ian, glancing at the licence.

"We just got in today."

"Would you mind stepping out of the car?" asked Ian, handing back the licence.

Greg placed the driver's licence in the left front pocket of his leather jacket and lifted and loosened his gun.

"What's this all about?"

"It's just routine."

"Okay. Okay." Greg smiled, shaking his head and sighing, seeing Ian open the door and step back, seeing that Ian held only a flashlight in his hand. Greg turned to his right to back out, then wheeled to his feet.

Ian was looking at the Colt in Greg's hand and stepping backwards slowly, unbelieving. Then Greg was behind him, holding him at the back by a handful of jacket, dizzily remembering the things he had learned in the prison yards about police disarming movements. So he clutched the big policeman by the jacket, and if he felt him turn he could push away and step back, and . . .

Karl had been watching Jimmy, who was licking his lips, cotton-mouthed, stone still in the flashlight's glare, asking, "What's the trouble, officer?" And then Karl saw Ian coming around the car, with the suspect walking behind *not* in front, and that was wrong, all wrong. And then Greg peeked from behind Ian's back and said, "Take his piece," to Jimmy Smith and fluids jetted through Karl's body and he jerked the six-inch service revolver from the cross-draw holster and pointed it towards the man who was almost completely hidden behind Karl's much larger partner.

"He's got a gun on me," said Ian. "Give him your gun."

And then no one spoke and Karl pointed the gun towards the voice, but the voice had no body. It was like a dream. He was pointing his gun towards Ian, towards a glimpse of black cap and a patch of forehead showing around Ian's arm, and there was no sound but the car sounds, tyres, cars humming past on Gower, and headlights bathing them in the beams every few seconds. But no cars stopped or even noticed and Karl found himself now pointing the gun at Jimmy Smith, who was like a statue, and then Karl aimed towards the voice again. It was so incredible! It couldn't happen like this. Back and forth went Karl's gun and he was crouched slightly as on the seven-yard line at the police combat range. But this wasn't the combat range. There was no sound except from passing cars.

Ian spoke again: "He's got a gun in my back. Give him your gun."

Then Karl looked at Ian, hesitated, and let the gun butt slide until he was holding it only with the thumb and index finger, the custom wooden grips smooth and slippery between his cold wet fingers. Then he held it up and Jimmy, dark eyes shining, walked towards him and took Karl's Colt revolver.

Jimmy Smith held the gun clumsily in both hands at chest level and raised it towards the street light on Gower and squinted with astigmatized vision, like a primitive seeing a gun for the first time. And it *did* seem to him like the first time. This was a cop's gun! It was all so unreal to him.

For another moment then they were inert. All four of them. Four brains fully accelerated, four bodies becalmed. Staggered. Inertia for a long moment. Four young men bathed in the purple glow of the street light. Detachment on the faces. Total bewilderment. Two policemen facing that which all policemen firmly believe can never happen to them. Two small-time robbers, fathoms deep, holding the Man at bay. Four minds racing. Tumbling incoherent thoughts.

Perhaps the first one to move was Karl Hettinger. Hands upraised, he began moving the big five-cell flashlight, ever so subtly, in a tiny circle, the beam flashing into the street, striking the windshields of the cars which passed unconcerned every few seconds. Then Ian noticed, and hands upraised, did the same with his little two-cell. Then Greg saw what they were doing and said, "Put those goddamn hands down."

Jimmy Smith stopped holding the gun to the light, stopped staring at it in wonder, and began trying to fit a Colt service revolver with a six-inch barrel into a four-inch pocket. He turned, staring from one to the other until he heard Greg's command, then he shoved the gun into his belt. Perhaps without a command he would have remained there forever.

"Get over there," Greg said, nodding towards the coupé, and hearing the voice, Jimmy wanted to obey. Then he realized Greg was talking to the cops, so he waited for his own orders.

Then it came. His chance. His final opportunity to order fate. Greg said, "Jim, go back to the police car and park it closer to the kerb so we won't draw any more heat. And turn out the lights."

Jimmy nodded vacantly and Greg said to the policemen, "Get in the car."

"Where do you want me?" asked Ian, standing at the right side of the little maroon coupé.

"Behind the wheel," said Greg, who was thinking, watching, examining both men, sizing them up. At first it was merely Ian's physical presence which guided Greg. He was a big man. Put the big man behind the wheel where he can be watched more closely. The little man in the back.

"Where do you want me?" asked Karl.

"In the back."

Karl struggled with the seat trying to pull it forward, not realizing it was a one-piece backrest and would not move.

"It's stuck," said Karl.

"Goddamnit, get in that car and I mean right now. Climb over the seat!"

Then Karl was inside behind the seat, sitting on the floor of the coupé, knees up to his chin. In the cramped space behind the only seat, on the metal floor of the car, flashlight in hand, pulse banging in his ears so that it was actually hard to hear for a moment.

Jimmy Smith was wrestling with the gears of the police car and with the emergency brake, but most of all with his courage.

"Won't move," he mumbled aloud to himself. "Got it in drive and it won't move!"

He fought with the Plymouth, stepping on the accelerator and killing the engine each time he was caught by the emergency brake. Jimmy Smith didn't know that emergency brakes on late model cars were no longer controlled by clumsy levers hanging down. He desperately yanked on the emergency foot brake but didn't know to tug the little chrome lever under the dash. He had been away too long.

"If I'd only knew about late model cars," he was to say later. "I coulda drove off in that police car. I coulda cut him loose right there. But I couldn't get that fuckin' brake off."

"Hurry up," Greg yelled, and Jimmy gave up, got out of the car, looked towards Hollywood Boulevard, looked towards escape and made his last choice. He walked towards the Ford hopelessly.

"I couldn't get the brake off," Jimmy said to Greg who was seated in the passenger side of the coupé, Colt pointed at Ian's belly, hammer cocked.

"Leave the goddamn thing. Leave it," Greg said, sliding slowly close to Ian to make room for Jimmy in the front.

At that moment a carload of teenagers drove by, talking loudly and laughing. One glanced at Jimmy for a moment and Jimmy became aware of the big revolver under his leather jacket and then the teenagers drove on. Jimmy got in the coupé.

"Did you check the police car for our licence number?" asked Greg. "They probably wrote it down when they stopped us."

"Yes," Jimmy lied, wanting to get away, to get away now, to have one more chance to cut Greg loose. If he just had one more chance.

"Where's the other gun?" Greg asked Jimmy, drilling Ian with his eyes, keeping the Colt at his belly, watching Ian's hands on the steering wheel. Already the little car was starting to reek from the smell of fear and sweat from the four of them.

"Where's the other gun?" Greg repeated.

"What other gun?" Jimmy asked, thinking of the automatic, hoping Greg would not notice that Jimmy had kicked it under Greg's side of the seat. And then Jimmy added further confusion to the moment by adding, "You mean the .45 automatic?"

And then Greg, not knowing that Jimmy was referring to the Spanish Star .32 automatic, felt panic, suddenly thinking there was still another cop's gun unaccounted for.

"Was this guy carrying a .45?"

"I dunno," said Jimmy, totally bewildered now, not knowing how many guns there were, or where they were.

"Well look around the floor for the goddamn .45 then," said Greg frantically.

"Gimme that flashlight," Jimmy said to Karl, and with the

bright five-cell light he found the .32 automatic on the floor just under the edge of the seat where he'd kicked it. Now he had two guns in his lap: his own automatic, and Karl's Colt service revolver.

"This is all the guns there is," said Jimmy.

"Okay, all the guns are accounted for," Greg said in exasperation. "Now let's get outta here." And to Ian, "Do you know how to get on the freeway to Bakersfield? I want Highway 99."

"Yes," Ian answered. "We can go up the street here on Gower and get on the Hollywood Freeway."

"Well get going," said Greg. "Don't break any laws and don't go fast, because if you get us stopped you're both dead."

Jimmy switched his glance from Karl in the back to his partner Gregory Powell, and rode most of the trip in an uncomfortable twisted position where he could occasionally look at Karl.

Greg's voice had lost its rasp and was coming back normal and confident. "Son of a bitch, we couldn't be any hotter," said Greg, and Jimmy thought he detected a bit of elation in his voice. "I've already killed two people. I didn't wanna get in this business, but now that I'm in it, I gotta go all the way."

Oh Jesus, Jimmy thought. Greg was breathing regularly now and saying crazy things, and sounding like some punk Jimmy would expect to see in an old movie and, oh, Jesus.

"Why did you guys stop us?" Greg asked.

"Because you had no lights on your licence plate," Ian said as he drove onto the ramp of the Hollywood Freeway.

Greg's gun hit Ian's ribs. "Just a minute. Where're you taking us?"

"This is the way to the Hollywood Freeway. I'm going the right way," said Ian steadily.

"It's the right way," said Karl, peering up over the window ledge from his place on the metal floor, looking over the space back there – finding a hubcap, rags, a bumper jack and handle, cans – nothing that could be of much help against two men and four guns in a cramped and tiny car, with one man holding a cocked revolver in the driver's belly.

"We're going on the freeway to the Sepulveda off-ramp. And that'll take us to the Ridge Route," Ian explained.

"Jimmy," said Greg, "your job is to look to the rear and cover that guy. And also to look for a tail."

"Okay," Jimmy mumbled, thinking: Thanks for telling them my name, you dumb . . .

"How often you guys check in on the radio?" asked Greg.

"About every hour," Ian said.

"I figure that gives us a fifteen-minute head start," said Greg, who would occasionally glance back at Karl. He and Jimmy were sitting twisted to the left, towards the two policemen. Greg said to Karl, "Don't try anything funny back there, because I got it in your partner's ribs."

"I won't," said Karl. "We've both got families. We just want to go home to our families." And he pulled the corduroy sport jacket up around his chin because he was suddenly very cold.

"Just keep that in mind," Greg said, and now Jimmy sensed that Greg was totally relaxed.

Jimmy hated him more than he ever had because he himself was breathing so hard he was hyperventilating, and his heart was hammering in his throat. From this time on, Jimmy could never think of his friend as Greg. It would be Powell from this moment, whenever he thought of him, whenever he would dream about him.

Ian said quietly, "Don't get excited, but there's a radio car up ahead." And everyone in the car went tense as Ian kept up the steady speed in the slower lane, approaching the police car which was stopped in front of them.

"It looks like a roadblock, Jimmy," said Greg, voice razor thin. "Get ready!"

"It looks like they're writing a ticket," said Ian. "That's all. I'm just going to drive by at an even speed."

"Okay," Greg whispered. "Remember. Remember. If we get stopped . . ."

"Yes," Ian said, and they passed the police car at the Sepulveda off-ramp and then they were on Sepulveda Boulevard making good time in the night-time traffic, catching most lights green, and each man was beginning to think about what all this meant, and to make and reject his own plans.

"Can I give you some advice?" asked Ian after several minutes during which time no one had spoken. The wind rushing through the window chilled them all because they were still sweating freely, but the car was filled with the smell of fear on all of them, so the window remained partly open.

"Go ahead," Greg said.

"You should take off those caps. Nobody around here wears them and we're liable to get stopped."

Greg immediately took off his cap, but Jimmy ignored the advice. Fuck it, he thought. I ain't showin' them my hair. And I ain't takin' no free advice from a cop. At night, in this dark little car, if I just keep my mouth shut or talk like a white man when I have to, they ain't even gonna know my race. And if Powell don't run off with his fat mouth and tell them all he knows about me, well shit, I might get out of this yet, I just might.

And after a few more blocks of driving, Greg reached down on the floor with his free hand and picked up the Schenley's and began drinking.

"If you drink in a moving car the Highway Patrol might stop us," Ian said, and Greg put the bottle down sourly.

Karl peered over the ledge seeing they were passing Van Owen. Already his legs were cramped up, and he longed to stretch out.

Jimmy stopped thinking and listened to the tyres hum and the wind rush, and occasionally he blinked when an oncoming driver failed to dim his lights. Then Greg said, "Do you guys have any money?"

"I've got ten dollars," Ian said, characteristically knowing exactly how much money he had.

"I've got eight or nine," said Karl.

"If you take our money it'll get you clear to San Francisco," said Ian, with a faint hope that the gunmen might be tempted by the few dollars. Might drop them off now. Might run for it up the highway in the little Ford. Or might feel that the policemen believed they would run to San Francisco, and then head in the other direction. Might do anything, but might just release them. That hope faded quickly as Greg snorted and said, "You know better than that."

They were quiet for a few more miles, and Karl tried to see his watch in the darkness, but could not. His stomach was twisted and he was sweating so badly the watch was sliding down his wrist. But Karl was not idle. He was looking at them, listening to the voices, staring hard whenever one turned. He would have to describe the faces later, and the car, and the voices. He tried to get a better look at the guns, but could not, except occasionally when the darker man pointed one at him over the top of the seat, his eyes like berries. The sight blade looked to Karl like his own gun.

Karl watched the blond one chew his lower lip with a craggy overbite. Then Greg said: "Here's the plan. We're gonna take you guys up on the Ridge Route, drive you out on a side road, drop you off, and make sure you have a long walk back to the highway."

Now Karl felt the tension subside a bit. It was partly what Gregory Powell said, and partly the friendly tone of his voice. The voice had softened now with the barest trace of hometown middle America in it. "With just a little bit of cornpone twang," as Jimmy Smith was to put it.

So a more relaxed Karl said, "You know, those guns are paid for out of our own pockets. Would you do us a favour and after you drop us off, unload them and heave them into the brush so we can get them after you leave?"

"We don't make that much money," Ian added.

"Sure." Greg smiled. "I think we can do that." And now, even Jimmy's breath was coming at regular intervals.

They were driving through Sepulveda Pass, out of the heavy traffic. The infrequent street lights made it utterly impossible to see what time it was, so Karl gave up. Once in a while he would glance up at Ian, whose hands did not change position on the wheel. Ian looked calm except that there was a trickle running down the right side of his neck disappearing under the collar.

Greg said, "There's a lake up here."

"It's a reservoir off to the left," Karl said.

"You're damn right there is," snapped Greg, turning, mouth like an iron bar, as though Karl had challenged him. Karl felt himself go tight again. The abrupt change in tone, for no reason, puzzled and upset him.

They could see the reservoir shimmer in the moonlight and then they were near the Mint Canyon turnoff. After that, Sepulveda turned into the Ridge Route.

"Give me your money," Greg said, and Karl removed his wallet carefully, seeing Ian do the same. Karl opened his with both hands and held it up for Greg to see and took out his nine dollars.

"We have a hideout a few hours from here where we'll be safe," Greg said. And this was more than Jimmy Smith could bear. For the very first time he rebuked Gregory Powell.

"Shut up. Don't tell these guys anything." And the moment he said it he stiffened, but Greg didn't seem to notice what he'd said.

The tyres hummed on the highway, and Karl looked up and could gauge by the frequency of the stars how far they were getting from the smoggy skies of Los Angeles.

"Where does that road go?" Greg asked suddenly.

Karl raised up and said, "That's the Mint Canyon turnoff. It eventually swings right back into Highway 99 here."

"I know it does. I was just checking," Greg said sharply.

Then they were four or five miles up the Ridge Route and Karl looked out and felt an overwhelming sadness mingle with the fear and he said to no one in particular, "I was fishing out here two days ago. With my wife. She's pregnant with our first."

"Shut up!" Jimmy Smith said. "Shut your mouth!"

"That's all right," Greg said soothingly. "Let him talk." And then Greg leaned over to Jimmy and whispered, "Let them talk. Don't make them nervous."

Jimmy Smith was thinking: Fuck you and fuck the lake and I don't give a fuck if it's covered with fuckin' fishes. And you and your knocked-up ol' lady, I don't give a fuck about any of it.

Now as he watched Greg's head turn on its swivel from time to time, he became even more angry, hating *everything* about Powell, especially that rooster neck. Then Jimmy became aware that Karl was speaking to him.

"Can I change positions if I keep my hands in sight? My legs're going to sleep."

"Stay where you are. I'm cramped too," said Jimmy, sticking the gun muzzle an inch or so over the seat once again.

Greg leaned over and whispered something to Jimmy. Then Greg said aloud, "We changed our plan. We're gonna hold you guys until we stop a family car. We need hostages. We're gonna stop a family car and when we get one we'll let you guys go, but let me give you a piece of advice. I know you guys got a job to do, but if you turn us in before we can get away we'll kill every member of the family. Understand?"

"Yes," Karl said, realizing at once the absurdity of it, and feeling once again in danger.

Jimmy Smith was to tell later what had been whispered. "He said to me, 'Jimmy, I told you it was only a matter of time before it would come to this. It's either them or us. Remember the Lindberg Law?' And I got an awful cold feelin' all of a sudden. '*Them or us. Them or us.*' I couldn't get it outta my mind, what he said. But I didn't know for sure what he meant. I never knew of no Lindbergh Law exactly. I mean, I felt like it meant death. And I wondered about the way he said, 'I told you it was only a matter of time.' He *never* told me. He musta told somebody else, because he never told me. And he said, '*Remember* the Lindbergh Law.' Just like we talked about it before. I never heard of no such thing. Like, he was talking to me about things I never talked to him about. I started getting a bad bad feelin' then."

Karl worried over the whispered conversation and he wished the car muffler wasn't noisy, and that he wasn't down on the metal floor just over the differential of the car with the sounds banging around him, reverberating. He hoped that Ian could hear something. He hated the whispered conversations. But the blond man talked reassuringly. He talked so much he interrupted Karl's thoughts. When Karl was getting very edgy and feeling desperate, the blond one would say something to reassure. It was the other gunman Karl wondered more about, the dark one. What was he thinking? He seemed more volatile. Would he be a threat at the end of their journey? And now the dark one turned and looked at Karl again. He didn't talk enough for Karl to know for sure, but he seemed to be a Mexican. If only he'd talk more, Karl thought.

Then Greg turned and in a quiet voice said to Jimmy: "We oughtta pull a stick-up to get some money. Do you think you can handle these guys? If you think so, I'll go into the next likely place and take it off." Then he raised a bottle of Schenley's and took a deep swallow.

"Are you crazy?" Jimmy whispered, caution be damned. And Jimmy was to say later, "Powell's head turned on his long neck like a bird and I knew I shouldn't a said that word. Jesus, not then. The gun in my hand, the automatic, was pointed right towards him. I tried to make it up by humorin' him. I said real casual, 'Well, maybe I oughtta pull a job, Greg. You watch the cops and I'll go in someplace in Gorman here and pull a job.' And I held my breath hopin' he'd see how fuckin' insane it was and he took a little drink and said, 'No.' He shook his head and said, 'No.' And that was the end of that. Jesus."

Now Karl suspected that Ian was sharing his bad vibrations. The blond one was erratic and the dark one had just said something about pulling a robbery.

Ian said casually, "How're you fixed for gas?" and looked hopefully towards the gas station at Gorman. But the blond one looked at the panel and said, "We got plenty," and smiled. Then Jimmy Smith took a long desperate pull from the bottle, turning nervously as he drank, to keep an eye on Karl.

Now they were past Gorman, almost on that part of the highway known as the Grapevine. They were at the top near old Fort Tejon, with a view of the great, bleak, lonely San Joaquin Valley. The car started the long descent.

But while they were closest to the clouds, Ian Campbell looked up, ducking his head because the roof was low. He looked up and Karl pushed his glasses higher on his nose and followed Ian's eyes. Up. Up. But there was nothing. Only the black sky. Vast in this immense valley. Stars flickering close and familiar, as they do at the top of the Tehachapi Range.

Now Karl felt this was where he belonged. Out here. Where he'd always wanted to be. In cultivated land where things grow. Where the air is so pure and brisk it hurts. And now perhaps, out here in the farmlands, near the earth, he was somehow safe. Perhaps this nightmare was a city dream. He looked at his partner, who was switching his gaze from the road every few seconds as though he had never seen a great sparkling sky before.

The abandoned felony car was not discovered until eleven o'clock. By midnight, several police supervisors were belatedly panic-stricken and plans were formulated to search the area. At fifteen minutes past midnight a command post was established at Carlos and Gower. All residences, apartments, buildings in the area were being systematically checked. Many were carefully searched for any sign of the missing officers. Motorcycle units were called in for traffic diversion. Press relations were established, and all nightwatch units were held over to assist in the search. No resident of that Hollywood neighbourhood slept until later that night when the search was abruptly called off.

During the descent down the mountain, the blond gunman turned all the way around to look at Karl. Or rather his head did. The torso seemed to remain motionless as the head twisted on the axis. The face was so thin and taut it was skull-like, but the voice was pleasant and it lulled, and he said: "Here's your money back, I won't be needing it."

And now Karl could have wept for joy because he was at last certain they were safe. The gunman was giving back the money. He'd never do that if . . . And then his thought was interrupted by the dark one, who again pointed the gun at him and stared for a second or two. So Karl put the money in his sock and waited.

Then Greg said, "You should have that gun on half cock, Jimmy," and he reached towards Jimmy's automatic and Karl heard the sound of the slide working, and then the blond one said, "It's on full cock. Ease down the hammer to a safe position." And he said. "There. Now it's ready to go. You don't have to keep pointing over the seat. If anything happens, just fire through the seat. You'll stop him quick enough."

Then Ian's gun in Greg's belt began poking him in the lower abdomen so he pulled it out and put it on the seat between himself and Jimmy.

With the automatic cocked and ready, Jimmy opened the glove compartment and put Karl's gun inside.

Then Greg said to Ian, "What kind of a shot are you?"

"I'm not very good," Ian said.

"Yeah? How're you classified on the police force? Sharpshooter? What?"

"Just a marksman. Not very good."

"You been in the army?"

"Marines," said Ian.

"See any combat?"

"I was in Korea during the war."

And now the wind was blowing the little car and it seemed to be an effort to keep it in the number two lane and talk to Greg at the same time.

"Well I'm an expert shot," said Greg. "In my business you gotta be good. I killed one man with a gun and another with my hands. And Jimmy here can tell you about how I shoot."

You fuckin' fool, thought Jimmy Smith. You fuckin' *fool*.

But Ian did not respond. He continued wrestling the car through the wind which was whistling around them now, making it difficult for Karl to hear every word. Ian's silence seemed to anger Greg, who said, "Pull in at the next rest stop. I'm gonna give you a chance to see if you can beat me on the draw. I'll give you back your gun and we'll have a little contest."

Oh, please, Jimmy thought. Oh, please, man, don't say nothin' wrong, don't do nothin' wrong. And he looked down the steep grade to his right and wondered, what if something happened now at seventy miles per hour. If something . . .

But Ian did not reply, and Greg nodded and smiled towards Jimmy who sighed sharply and took another drink.

Jimmy was to say, "That big cop talked intelligent all the way, not like some dummies you meet on the police force, and now I respected him because he was sayin' and doin' just the right things for the fuckin' crazy man. And I jumped in and said, 'You're right, man, right not to fight him. Cause my partner here is some shot. Like, I seen him make a tin can jump like a country girl at her first dance.'"

Jimmy smiled at Greg, who returned the grin and seemed satisfied.

Karl saw Greg's head move towards Jimmy again, and he strained forward, but heard only the muffler's roar. Jimmy Smith was to say later, "Powell told me, he said, 'Jimmy, remember, if you have to shoot a policeman, save one bullet for you.' He said that, and my asshole slammed shut again."

When they reached the valley floor, Jimmy Smith for the first time believed they were going to make it. *Had* made it. They were less than an hour from the motel and the station wagon – a *cold* car. They had kidnapped two cops and were walking away from it. It was hard to control his exultation. "I know where there's a dirt road," he said to Greg. "I used to work around the Bakersfield area." And they were at the Maricopa turnoff, where they had been earlier in the day with the shorted-out tail lights.

"Turn off here," Greg said, and Ian did, and the road curved west over the highway.

"Do you want me to go straight?" asked Ian, now headed west.

"Yeah, if you turn it'll take us back to 99."

And Jimmy was straining his eyes for a place, anyplace. A dirt road. Just a place. And then there were some dusty tyre tracks out of the fields to the south. The tyre tracks meant a road, and suddenly Greg said, "Pull over and turn around."

Ian eased the little Ford to the side and made a U-turn on the lonely quiet highway and Karl's heart began pounding with new vigour, as did Ian's, as did Jimmy Smith's and Gregory Powell's, as each approached his destiny. Then Ian made a right turn on the dirt road heading south towards Wheeler Ridge, south on the long dusty dirt road.

Karl strained upward, tried to see, but as far as he could see was black loneliness and quiet. The smell of sweat and whiskey was suddenly unendurable. Then Greg said: "That's the farmhouse you're going to hike back to. To make your call."

But it wasn't that far. It wasn't that far! Were they going to handcuff them? It wasn't that far to be logical!

They had driven ninety miles. They had four-tenths of a mile to go down the dirt road, down towards the ridge.

"I see it," Karl said. "I see the farmhouse." That sight, that farmhouse in the middle of these lonely fields with its little lights, gave him hope. Somehow here, next to the earth, with *his* kind of people, on *his* kind of land, somehow he would be safe.

"We gotta tie these guys up," said Jimmy.

"No, if we tie them up they'll be here all night long and freeze to death," said Greg.

"Well, we oughtta tie them up just a little bit, you know, so they'll work themselves loose."

"No," Greg said vacantly. "We'll just let them go."

And Jimmy was to confess at a later time, "Jesus. It dawned on me then. It really hit me!"

And then they came to a dirt road which crossed the one they'd been driving on.

"Do we turn here?" asked Jimmy Smith, and his voice was shaking and he rubbed his mouth with nicotine-smudged fingers, face numb, head feeling oppressively heavy.

"No, just keep going," said Greg.

"It looks too soft. We'll get stuck," Karl said, feeling that he could not bear it. Not another moment. Wondering if his legs would hold him when he stood. They were cramped, and weak from the fear.

Then they came to another dirt road which crossed this one and Ian again slowed to a crawl. There was a large ditch in front of them in which a huge, recently installed gas line was lying, waiting to be buried.

"This is the spot," Greg said. "Turn left and then turn around."

While Ian made a careful U-turn in the soft dirt, Greg said, "You get this car stuck and you're both dead."

"Don't chatter the wheels," Karl said to his partner. "You might get the rear wheels stuck." But Ian managed the turn and was now driving back towards the ditch, the little car pointing the way they had come.

"Stop the car," Greg said. "Turn off the lights. This is where we're going to let you go."

Jimmy Smith turned and looked at Karl Hettinger, who was sitting knees up, hands hanging limply over his knees.

"I just started lookin' at him then. I don't know why. He seemed to have big hands, the way they was hangin' over his knees, and I noticed that, and I noticed the other officer was a pretty big man because I couldn't see around him out the side window on the driver's side. And I don't know, I just noticed little things about them ever since I got the bad feeling. Ever since Greg said he didn't wanna tie them up. And now I was breathin' funny again. Couldn't get enough air, seemed like. And I could hear wind screechin' through. Screamin' like. I hated that goddamn wind. And I just saw the big ditch there where they was fixin' to bury that big silver pipe. All the dirt was piled up beside it and I thought, I hope he don't drive off into that ditch. And then for the first time I started feelin' cold. Cold!"

Then the car was stopped. The lights were turned off. Greg wanted the lights off.

"Get out, Jim," Greg said.

Then a hand picked up Ian Campbell's Smith and Wesson which was on the seat between them.

Jimmy alighted and walked around the back of the car. Then Greg backed across the seat, still covering them with his Colt.

"Get out," Greg said to Ian, and now Greg was standing beside the door on the passenger side. Ian got out and faced towards the rear, towards Jimmy Smith, and Ian put his hands in the air.

"Get out," Greg said to Karl.

"Do you want me to climb over the seat?"

"What've you got in your hands?" Greg said unexpectedly.

"Nothing. See, I'm going to keep my hands in sight," said Karl, crawling over the little seat in the darkness, using only his elbows.

"You're doing it just right," said Greg.

Then Karl was standing beside the driver's door of the little coupé on Ian's left. He put his hands in the air and the two policemen faced Jimmy Smith, who stood several feet from the rear fender of the car, pointing his automatic at them, more in front of Ian than in front of Karl. It was just past midnight.

The silence rang in their ears during those seconds. There was no sound. No crickets. Only the wind howling.

But there was something. And then Ian recognized it. It was onion. They were between two sections of onions just beginning to sprout now in the month of March, already pungent. And it may have been the onion or the wind or something else, but Ian Campbell wiped his eyes quickly and then raised his hands high again. It may have been the landscape, so endlessly flat, so desolate at night, the earth so dusty beneath the crust, that the wind was blowing powdery choking dust balls all around them. The eye craved mountains, the heart shrank from the vast solitude, but the soaring ranges were far to the east and north, as far as the horizon. It looked to Karl like pictures of the moon, grey and desolate. Under a black sky like this, and except for the wind, the moon would be exactly like this, terrible in the darkness.

Now it seemed bitterly cold to Ian Campbell as he stood to the right of Karl Hettinger, and once, with their hands upraised, their fingers touched for an instant. Though Karl's fingers were icy, the touch of a hand of a friend helped calm Ian, and until they were safe at last, it would be better to think of other things, or anything, perhaps of the pipes, as he'd done all his life in troubled moments, as he'd done in Korea or in frightening moments as a policeman.

Though it was not the clearest of nights – now sporadically cloudy as puffy spectres scudded past the moon – still one could *feel* the stars all around. It was on such nights many years ago that Ian loved to march by the tarpits. Perhaps Ian deliberately thought of the pibroch, of playing "MacCrimmon Will Never Return" and vowed that when this was over, when he was home again, he *would* master the great pibroch.

The silence was broken by the sound of Gregory Powell's footsteps, scraping on the crust of earth as he rounded the back of the car in the darkness. Karl could not see his face in the moonlight, just the hair, short and dark blond, and the triangle of the face. Now he and Ian were looking at Gregory Powell, at the long neck and the shadowy face and the gun in his hand, the hand in deep shadows, and Gregory Powell walked over to Jimmy Smith and leaned close and appeared to whisper, but no man except these two would ever learn the words he whispered, and then Gregory Powell moved to his right so that he was in front of Karl Hettinger. Jimmy Smith moved slightly to his right, just as he did on the desert that day in Henderson, Nevada, and he stood almost behind Gregory Powell. Jimmy held a gun in his right hand, the hand with L-O-V-E tattooed across the fingers. And though Gregory Powell was more directly in front of Karl Hettinger, he continued to look at Ian Campbell, at the *big* man, his gun pointed towards the policeman's feet.

Despite the cold wind, sweat poured down Ian's ribs and chest and burned his eyes, so he closed them, and perhaps it made it easier to imagine the pipes, to hear them wailing far back in the funnel of the wind. Perhaps it calmed him.

Jimmy Smith said later, "The big cop seemed relaxed, you know?"

Gregory Powell said to Ian Campbell, "We told you we were going to let you guys go, but have you ever heard of the Little Lindbergh Law?"

Ian said, "Yes."

And Gregory Powell raised his arm and shot him in the mouth.

For a few white-hot seconds the three watched him being

lifted up by the blinding fireball and slammed down on his back, eyes open, watching the stars, moaning quietly, a long plaintive moan, and he was not dead nor even beginning to die during those seconds – only shocked, and half conscious. Perhaps his heart thundered in his ears almost drowning out the skirl of bagpipes. Perhaps he was confused because instead of tar he smelled onions at the last. He probably never saw the shadow in the leather jacket looming over him, and never really felt the four bullets flaming down into his chest.

Jimmy Smith was to say later: "I can only remember his arm and hand. His *hand*! Each time a bullet hit him, his hand would jerk and jump up. Like he was grabbin' for you. Like he was grabbin' for your leg in the dark there! I'll never forget that arm."

Jimmy Smith shouted in horror, "He's still *movin'*!"

But if Ian Campbell did not hear the voice, nor the staccato explosions, nor feel the four bullets bursting his heart, perhaps he believed that the bagpipes screamed and screamed.

15

Godfather of Night: My Life in America's Hidden Greek Mafia

Kevin Pappas

Fear the Greeks when they come bearing gifts – especially if those gifts are expensive jewellery, bags of coke, or super-fast, expensive Porsches. Pappas tells the story of the American Greek Mafia, less well known than their Italian cousins but no less lethal, a fixture of the 1970s and 1980s cocaine scene in Florida and Georgia. Miami was a well-known hedonists' hotbed, popularized by *Miami Vice*, but Pappas was able to operate smoothly out of Atlanta, couri-ering for others and then rising to the top of his own empire thanks to having forged direct links with major Colombian suppliers. Rubbing broad shoulders with African-American gangs dealing crack and redneck bikers trading crystal methamphetamine, it seems as if the arrangement not to poach each other's product lines ensured that matters stayed quiet (by drug-trade standards) and business, running smoothly, boomed.

Pappas did some very bad things! But he's insightful as to his motivations – raised in a quieter area of Florida by upstanding, Jehovah's Witness parents, he endured an ambiv-alent relationship with the man he thought was his father. However, when Pappas was seventeen, the elder man fell ill and died, revealing in the process that young Kevin had in fact been sired by the head of the local Greek Mafia . . . As much as any seventeen-year-old who has found the reason for his sense of unease and dislocation in life might do, he sought his father's acceptance, and that of his brothers and sisters, but thought the best of his mother all the while. When it was not forthcoming, he grew a business to rival his real father's, at least while it lasted, moving big, fat Greek bags of coke to high-end dealers, and keeping himself well away from the fiddly business of street deals and end users.

However, his care was insufficient to avoid detection, ultimately – drug dealers at every level face the dilemma that they're sales people after all, and have to pitch to someone at some point. Discretion and professionalism can ensure they have as long a crack at the business as possible. But the writing is, in the end, on the cell wall – if you can't do the time, don't do the crime, as they say.

In the following extract, Pappas first experiences the unwelcome involvement of the FBI . . .

What made my business in the beginning was my Rolodex. I knew everyone in Atlanta, beginning with the Falcons. I got to know the players and the staff so well that even the Falcons' coach walked me into the locker room one day. It was like being introduced around by the Pope.

My first real sales were to football players. There were a few guys who grew up in Griffin, Georgia, who would come into the Gold Mine and buy diamond stud earrings or custom necklaces. I started hanging out and partying with them. Pretty soon I was going to bashes at mansions and meeting the Atlanta Hawks. Through them I met musicians: Atlanta was just beginning to be a powerhouse in the industry. I moved into a penthouse apartment next to this R&B star who had a string of big hits during the eighties, and soon I was hanging at his place, too. My circle of customers and friends just kept getting wider and wider.

Maybe my Tarpon Springs days paid off in Atlanta. I knew how to be the outsider who made friends in a community he didn't belong to. I was the white guy at every black party, just like those years when I was trying to fit in with the Greeks. I could dance, I could talk shit with the best of them, and I was a comedian. Plus I had powder for sale. You just couldn't have a party in Atlanta without me.

During the Falcons games, I would hang out with the wives and girlfriends in their section, talking them up. The only difference between me and a regular fan was that I had a .38 strapped to my ankle in a leather holster. I had started wearing it after I started dealing. I had guns everywhere: my glove compartment, under my seat, a shotgun behind the counter at the Gold Mine.

One time I was hanging with the Falcon families at a game when cops started running down the aisles towards our seats. They had their guns drawn and they came right to my row. Someone had seen my holster and called 911. Luckily, it was empty – I'd left my gun at home.

But the incident didn't help my PR. The Falcons' coach found out who I really was and banned his players from contact with Kevin Pappas. He said I was a bad influence. Never mind that his guys were coming to *me*.

I felt it was safe because I knew who they were; I knew their families, their girlfriends, their wives. They weren't informants for the government. They had enough money to pay for the merchandise and they had enough smarts not to fuck up their contracts and their business because they were professionals. So I kept telling myself this wasn't real drug trafficking.

I was spending money like water. The jewellery business was doing well, but I was living over my head. I needed another source of income. So I started letting people know that if they needed a ki or a half a ki, I was the guy.

Word got out fast. We'd get calls from the rich people in Buckhead. We had politicians. We had cops. We had street people. We had a lot of weightlifters, a lot of bodybuilders, a whole bunch of strippers. We had corporate America. We even delivered to some of the best office buildings in Midtown Atlanta – lawyers needing their morning refresher or mortgage brokers celebrating a big sale. Car dealers, for some reason, were big clients of ours. There was one guy who owned a string of exotic car dealerships. He was good for half a ki a week. And that was just for him, his buddies, and his clients. In the eighties, coke was what a good cigar is now – the capper at the end of a deal.

And just like the Vegas casinos, drug dealers have whales. High rollers. And you had to service them like they were special. Anytime of the night they called, you got out there and took them the dope. Big sales meant lower risk. You had to take care of your premium clients.

The junkies were different. They got no respect. They were barely hanging on to life anyway. We had a way of testing the purity of the stuff when we wanted to confirm it; we'd take it to a street guy and give him a hit. People laugh when I tell them, but there's actually nothing better than taking it to a junkie. Sometimes they would come close to OD'ing and then we knew it was pure, 97 or 98 per cent. And the funny thing was that was the shit that the junkies wanted. They didn't resent us for almost killing them, not at all. They'd be like, "Hey, can I get some more of that?"

It was like a medical trial for addicts. We had people lining up to be test subjects.

We also had test kits. We cut a triangle in the ki and we put the kit in and if it turned a royal blue it was 98 per cent pure. Later, when we were buying directly from the Colombians and the Ochoa clan, everything we got from Colombia was guaranteed at 96 to 98 per cent. Everything. It came with a money-back guarantee. If the purity was anything less, they'd make it up to you on the next load.

Tyrone had a friend he introduced me to during this time. He was a good ole boy with a mullet haircut, looked like Billy Ray Cyrus with a really bad complexion. Pure country. He always wore jeans and a T-shirt and big belt buckle. Everyone called him Lee.

Lee didn't draw much attention to himself, but he was always around. I thought he was just a local boy who was living large. He was a car wholesaler, which meant he was always driving around Atlanta looking for new merchandise and had plenty of time to hang out at the Gold Mine. And he had a wicked bad coke habit.

I never thought much about Lee. He was an okay kind of guy. A casual acquaintance. I should have been paying more attention.

The scene wasn't like it is today. This was before crack, before Miami became the murder capital of America because the Colombians were killing everything that moved. Before the war on drugs. It was socially acceptable to bust out a bullet casing – that was the carrier of choice for the club crowd – and tap out a few lines of coke.

I didn't feel like a criminal. I knew what I was doing was against the law, but being a cocaine dealer was different. It had cachet. It was cool to be a coke dealer. Everyone wanted to be my friend. I'd walk into a club and there would be an "Oh, wow, look who's here" look in people's eyes. They knew the party was on.

At this point, I was doing odd jobs. Whatever you needed me to do in the drug trade, I was available. I was still learning my way and so I couldn't pick and choose my assignments. A lot of the times I was asked to go down to Miami and take a package up to Atlanta. Sounds simple, but it wasn't.

Using the highways during the eighties was dangerous. There were so many profile checks being done on A1A coming out of Miami that you had to basically be in disguise just to have a hope of getting through. The guys they had working those checkpoints were phenomenal. If you were driving a Chevy Malibu looking like a surfer, but you had a Rolex on your wrist, they'd pull you over. So you had to make sure that you profiled your own guys before they went out onto the road. You couldn't put Kevin Pappas in a Malibu. You'd have to put him in a Porsche – with my jewellery, my tan, and all that, I just looked like a Porsche guy.

The roadblocks could make your hair turn grey while you waited to go through them. They had these big ladders with high-powered lights that would shine down on the car, and they had two dogs. We got to know the set-up so well that we even knew the dogs' names: Champ and Bear. I'll never forget: they even had the Highway Patrol vests on with their names on them. Champ and Bear held my life in their hands and you would actually have to spend hours thinking how to outsmart them if you wanted to survive. Forget the cops – you had to think like a drug-sniffing dog to beat the game.

You'd see the red tail lights ahead of you and then the lights thirty feet up in the air, and you'd say to yourself, "Oh my God, is the stuff packaged right?" You'd have five or ten ki's in the trunk, and there'd be forty cars ahead of you, so you'd have time to go over every step of the wrapping and storing of the dope to see if there was a shot at getting caught. Some idiots would see the roadblock ahead and they'd pull a U-turn to get away from it. But of course the GHP has chase cars waiting for you to do that, and they'll get you before you've gone two miles.

So you just don't turn around. Not when you're loaded. You bite the bullet. I remember coming up to Champ and Bear with ten ki's in my trunk in a black Porsche 944 and my heart was practically coming through my chest. The handler brought the dogs up and they walked around and sniffed, walked and sniffed. I was sitting there, trying to act bored, flashing my diamond bracelet, trying to seem like some hotshot lawyer who has a hot date waiting up the coast. I tried to look annoyed but I was terrified.

There were no hits. I sailed through. But if you don't think a drug trafficker earns his money, you try sitting on a baking-hot piece of asphalt with enough dope to put you away for the rest of your life sitting six feet behind your ass.

A lot of these runs were for a guy named Billy Solomon. Tyrone introduced me to him, and he was like Tyrone on an international level – a step up. Billy was Bahamian, and back then the Bahamas was the trans-shipment point between Colombia and the United States. Billy was heavy into the heroin business, the cocaine business, and money laundering. He was a big dude – 6ft 2in, 285 pounds, with a goatee, black as the ace of spades.

So when Billy gave me the job of delivering five kilos to his contact in DC, I said yes right off.

I called Jose and he agreed to come along with me on this other job. We took along two other hard-asses who did runs with us. We drove the shit up 95, hoping we wouldn't get spotted. Everything went fine, and we breathed a sigh of relief when we finally pulled into DC. But then we realized we had another problem: We didn't know where the fuck we were going.

The directions were off, because pretty soon we were wandering the city craning our heads out of the car window looking for street names. It doesn't take long in DC before you end up in the wrong part of town. We started on Pennsylvania Avenue and passed the White House – with five ki's in the trunk and guns all over the car. I'd never seen the White House before, and I just couldn't believe I was seeing it on a drug run.

"Jose, this cannot be happening."

"Yeah, it's happening," he said. "Where the fuck is this house? I'm going to kill Billy when we get back."

We drove around and finally pulled up to what we thought was the house. But we were in shorts and T-shirts and it's like forty degrees out. We looked like hicks on steroids. And we quickly became a target.

We were sitting in the car talking about what to do next when we saw four or five black guys, neighbourhood guys, walking towards us, all dressed in Timberlands and down jackets and jeans. They didn't look like they were coming to offer us directions. One of them pulled up his jacket and I saw a flash of silver.

"Get the fuck out of here!" I yelled.

Jose hit the gas and we nearly ran over one of the guys as we peeled off. I could see his face as we went by. He wasn't scared. He was angry. We were fat targets who were getting away.

We finally found our way to the entrance to US 95 by sheer luck. The whole ride back, I was thinking, *There has to be a better way.* I needed to figure this game out or I was going to die a very stupid death.

★   ★   ★

I liked to put forward the image of invulnerability. If you don't care about living, you can appear to be indestructible. You'll take any job, no matter how dangerous. But a year after the DC job, I had a load on my back hauling ass through Alligator Alley coming out of Miami. I was in a truck with 150 kilos packed in a red convertible Chevy, kind of a surfer ride. And all of a sudden, I just felt exposed. I looked at my situation from a profiler's point of view.

I pulled over. I called the guy I had just done the pickup from and said, "I can't do it. I'm a dead giveaway." Truth was, my nerves were shot. I was done. I knew that part of my business was finished. So when you start thinking about the repercussions, it's time for you to get up, get out, or change up.

At the time, I felt it was a strike against me that I couldn't go through with the drop. But now I see that I was just getting smarter. There's no profit in risking your ass as a mule. I wanted to be the guy making the deals.

There were three types of merchandise. You had a yellow-based petroleum cut, which was what we called the wash cocaine, the bottom of the barrel, the sludge. It was popular for some reason with our black customers. They liked it because they were remelting it and stepping on it and because it's got a real strong flavour to it. It's pasty, it's sticky – a nasty cut in my opinion, but some people loved it.

The second wash is acetone. It smells like nail-polish remover. That cut is what you called a high-level norm. It was the industry standard. It melted very quickly, so it was good for freebasing. And it held up well when you stepped on it, so the traffickers could make money on acetone wash and they loved that.

Then you take a pure cocaine that's 98 per cent and it has ether-based wash. That ether base is so potent that it can break blood vessels and make your nose bleed. So if you're snorting cocaine and you're leaning down to do a line, that ether-based shit was so strong that often your nose would be squirting blood.

You could take this tablet and you could hold it up and

thumb your finger on it, and it would actually flake and cascade down. If you know anything about cocaine, that's good. It was like the finest caviar; the quality was amazing. Cesar Uribe cut the coke for the Ochoa clan and his nickname was the Mad Cook. He knew how to take the coca leaves, process them into a paste, wash that, and purify it in such a way that the stuff was like candy. It was really a connoisseur's cocaine. We took a lot of pride in that. Later when I hooked up with the Ochoas, people knew that we had good merchandise and they would pay five grand more for it because that'd mean that they could take it to the streets and put more weight on top of it.

The price of the product depended on how much you were buying. You'd sell ki's and half ki's at one price and you'd sell small weight at another price. Then you'd gram it down and eight-ball it and quarter-ounce it down to another price.

This is how the maths worked: each kilo had two tablets, or bricks; each one was 500 grams per. At that time, kilos went for $18,500. You'd take that kilo and you put another half a ki on it – cutting it with baby laxative or whatever. Now you've got 1,500 grams. You break that into eight-balls at three grams per. By the time you're done you can piece out that ki and make $100,000 on it.

But when you break a ki down into 1,000 grams and try to sell those one at a time, that's a thousand chances to go to jail. You make a better profit but you increase your vulnerability. I'd rather flip ten ki's and make ten grand a ki than have four ki's and break it down and make a million. Because I'd rather be more secure.

South Florida was glorified because of *Miami Vice*, but everyone understood that Miami was hot as a pistol. If you lived the high life in Miami, your life was very short.

There were rabid gun-shooting crazy jackasses on every block. And while Atlanta was controlled by American-born gangsters, black and white, Miami was filled with cultures you might think you understood but you didn't: Jamaicans, Haitians, Cubans and Colombians.

The murders there were terrible for business. Life

expectancy for a drug trafficker was low. Rule of thumb was you wouldn't last more than five to seven years. Not only does the violence make the local news every night, but you get the feds interested. Once it becomes a headline, prosecutors and the DEA and the ATF want to come to your town and make their reps.

And another thing people don't realize is that all that killing messes with your personnel. The turnover of people within the hierarchy of the trafficking gangs was so rapid you didn't really know who to trust and who not to trust. You'd go down there and make a deal with X and come back two months later and X had been found dead in a mail sack by the side of the road. So who do you deal with? You open yourself up to danger every time you make a new connection. You couldn't really put your stake in the ground in Miami because the players there were so big and so ruthless. For me, it was a fun place to go and visit but not a place to do business.

Atlanta, on the other hand, was the hidden jewel. Big city, glamorous, southern women, a sun town. And you didn't take your life in your hands stepping outside your door. It was still a major cocaine hub, but it didn't make the headlines. I got into the cocaine game at the exact right time, and in the right place, too.

Cocaine was innocent back then.

Lee, the redneck junkie, started showing up at the Gold Mine at all hours. Tyrone brought him around and I tolerated him. He was snorting up more coke than I thought was humanly possible, but back then I didn't know that many junkies. Lee was a stone addict.

He was also a narc.

His cover was that he was so fucked up. No one thought he was an undercover guy because he was a pill-popping, drug-smoking maniac. Narcs have this thing of saying that they do drugs to protect their cover, but Lee was way beyond that. He was hooked, no question. And we all would see it. And that was a kind of badge of authenticity. If you're that strung out on the stuff, there's no way you're a pig.

Later Lee got busted for being a dirty cop and having a drug problem. But we just thought he was a redneck who liked to party.

So one Christmas Eve, I had an event at the Gold Mine. I had about twenty guys who came in – the champagne was flowing, everyone was dressed to the nines, and at the end of the night, the tradition was that each man would buy his girl-friend or wife a nice piece of jewellery.

By one or two in the morning, there were only a few people left – Tyrone and a few of his guys. And Lee, of course. You couldn't pry him out of my store with a crowbar if there was blow around.

So Lee asked one of the guys, "Hey, let me get a bump."

I was sitting behind the counter, and one of the guys gave me a baggie and I handed it to Lee. He put lines down on the glass counter and snorted it. No big deal. It was just Lee being Lee.

A week later, I was working with my mother behind the counter. All of a sudden, cars squealed up into our little gravel parking lot and guys started pouring out. The Georgia Bureau of Investigation and the Sheriff's Department and a couple of other agencies busted down my door and stormed in with guns drawn, screaming, "Freeze, stand against the wall!" And I was like, "What the fuck?" They told me they were charging me with the intent to distribute cocaine. One gram. Fucking Lee.

The detectives took me in the back room. My jewellery store had a hair salon adjacent to it, and they had a storeroom with a table and chairs. We sat down.

"Listen," this one good ole boy detective told me. "We really don't give a shit about you. We know you got caught up with this thug Tyrone. We've been after him for a long time. He thinks he's slicker than butter. Tell us where the merchan-dise is coming from and you walk. Or better yet, why don't we work a deal and we'll set him up?"

They actually said that to me. I couldn't believe that. These guys were below amateur.

"Listen," I told him. "It's been an hour since you arrested

me and it's already all over the street. Tyrone Meeks knows everything that happens in this little redneck town."

They told me they had a plan to get him. There's only one thing worse than getting busted. It's getting busted by cops who have no idea what you are facing. Tyrone had Douglas, and Douglas would come see my mother with an electric drill if he had to.

"I got my mom and my family, that's all I got. And I know they'll hurt them."

"Son, you can forget about all that. We'll protect you."

That's all I needed to hear. There was no way these guys would put my mother and her family on twenty-four-hour protection. The case just wasn't that big.

I told them to call my lawyer.

There was a prosecutor in Atlanta who was on a witch-hunt for Tyrone. I had fallen into the trap; they barely knew who I was. I refused to rat. And the judge and the prosecutor were so angry that I wouldn't flip they ended up giving me ten fucking years. For one gram.

When I heard "ten years" in the courtroom, I wanted to throw up. I turned around and looked at my mom, but before I could say anything they handcuffed me and they took me out of there. They took me to GDCC, Georgia Diagnostic Classification Center, where the state's death row is housed. That's the highest-level penitentiary in the state of Georgia and that's where they put me because I had so much time.

I was nineteen years old.

I didn't have the ability to feel remorse; I was too busy being eaten up with aggravation. I was already aggravated that my mom moved my ass from Florida to Georgia. I was already dealing with this whole idea of "Am I a Pappas or am I a Cunningham?" I wasn't getting anybody's acceptance. And now I was sitting there thinking ten years of my life was gone. Ten years in an eight-by-ten cell, twenty-three hours a day.

And all I could think about was my brother Louie, free and safe. I couldn't get the idea out of my head that he was much better off with me out of the picture. That he'd be thrilled my sorry ass had ended up in jail. The desire for revenge was all I could feel.

In the prison system in Georgia, you're not allowed to have any outside contact for the first eight weeks. You're allowed no visitation, no letters, no communication of any sort for eight fucking weeks. It fucked up my world.

I was scared and confused. I spent four months at GDCC, working as an orderly and making friends with the guards. It was all I could do to keep sane. I'm naturally hyperactive and there's nothing worse for that than being locked in a cell. I was climbing the walls inside of a week.

After four months, they transferred me to a chain-gang work camp in the north Georgia mountains. I was cleaning the side of the road, swinging what we called a yo-yo, otherwise referred to as a bush axe, with a corrections officer behind me with a pump shotgun.

I wrote to Lukie (*his natural father*) asking him to use his connections. He sent me money to help hire a lawyer, but that was it. Money always seemed to be Lukie's way of showing me where I stood: *You're worth a few grand, but not my name or my acceptance.* It was always a bittersweet thing for me: I would have much rather had a note where he said that he cared about what happened to me. But it was always cash and no message.

Thank God for Alexis. She was my girlfriend at the time, the *Penthouse* centrefold model. Alexis was 5ft 3ins, 101 pounds, blond hair, and emerald green eyes, with an ass that would stop a clock. She was a good ole country girl from Conyers, Georgia. And she loved me to death.

In jail, you are judged by the quality of the women who show up to see you. You don't want some broken-down old lady coming in and embarrassing you. Alexis would show up and everyone would know that she was a centrefold, and they would crowd in to see her and be like, "Oh my God". She'd walk in wearing this cute little skirt and the officers would do anything she asked them. And when Alexis came in, she came with cash because she was a stripper. So she'd put a couple hundred bucks on the books for me every week so I could get extra food from the commissary.

The *Penthouse* model with a heart of gold. God bless her. What folks don't realize is that when you are put in the slammer they seize all your money, close all your accounts, they take all your clothing, jewellery, cars, and any other assets. And the streets close their doors on you. Any money that's owed to you is simply written off. Alexis helped me save my image when I was really down and out.

On one of those visits, she said to me, "Kev, I can't go through this anymore. When you get out, let's get our shit together."

"I will," I told her. And I had every intention of doing that.

The Colombians stepped into the picture when I went to jail. They knew of me through my Lebanese suppliers, half the Colombians are of Lebanese descent and they all knew one another in Atlanta. When they saw that I wouldn't roll over on Tyrone, they made some payoffs and greased some palms to rush my case through the Pardons and Parole Board.

I had no idea what was happening. But after the Colombians worked their magic, all I knew was that I would be on parole for eight more years, but fuck it, I was free.

16

Fallen Angel: The Unlikely Rise of Walter Stadnick in the Canadian Hell's Angels

Jerry Langton

In North America, Hell's Angels, beneath the stereotype of wild guys who like to throw rambunctious, dirty parties, remain a force to be reckoned with in organized crime. It's said of outlaw bikers, as it used to be said of the Mafia, that they only kill each other. This wasn't exclusively true of Canada's Biker Wars, a struggle for drug-trafficking turf that took place between 1994 and 2001. But kill each other they certainly did in abundance. Some one hundred and sixty bikers died as the Hell's Angels duked it out with the rival Rock Machine MC.

With the spoils at stake, it's almost no wonder. Wolodumyr (Walter) Stadnick of Hamilton, Ontario and his colleague Donald Stockford administrated a system of laundering drug profits from which, the RCMP estimate, the Angels earned $111,503,361.00 Can (around £72 million) between March 1999 and December 2000 alone. One wonders if the prospects and hangarounds who'll follow – or anticipate – any order in the hope of becoming fully patched chapter members would be quite so ardent for some desperate glory if they thought of the mind-blowing amounts someone was creaming off the top of their collective endeavours. Probably, and they'd want to make it themselves.

Stadnick and Stockford were convicted in June 2004 of conspiracy to commit murder, gangsterism and drug trafficking. However, Stadnick also beat three charges of attempted murder and thirteen of first-degree murder. The pair eventually lost an appeal in August 2009 on the conspiracy charges, but with sentences of twenty years apiece and time served taken into account, are eligible to apply for parole from early 2011.

Stadnick was responsible for forging links with other chapters to extend the Quebecois drugs trade out across the prairies, and the pair were heavily involved in HA activities in British Columbia, Manitoba and Ontario. But there was no evidence that either ever pulled a trigger or ordered a specific hit on any of those who opposed their expansionist plans. Angels, it seems, simply know what has to be done. (And if they're wrong, well, everyone will get over it.) Metaphorically, the pair were something like central African leaders, mineral-rich, suited and booted in the corridors of power, perhaps even talking democracy, while their rag-tag forces intimidate potential rival clans with sexual abuse and the taking of child soldiers. How responsible is the general for his soldiers in the field? How far will it play to argue an excess of zeal on the part of his followers?

The case against them, conducted in English, relied heavily on two informants, Stephane Sirois and Stephane Godasse "Old Shoe" Gagne, neither of whom would you be likely to find at a Quaker meeting. As Mr Justice Jerry Zigman of the Quebec Superior Court put it: "Gagne testified that in 1997, he was a cold-blooded killer but did not necessarily enjoy what he was doing. Nonetheless, it was his job. He stated that he did what he did in order to climb the ranks of the organization and that he had a desire to get into the Hell's Angels. The court does not believe that Stephane Gagne deserves a medal for his past ruthless and vicious behaviour but the court is of the opinion that he is telling the truth in his sworn testimony."

The RCMP also had another long-term informant, Dany Kane, a contract killer, and files stolen from a police computer were found in Stockford's house. These featured the photos of other outlaw-biker leaders. Zigman again – "The reason why Stockford had the binder of photos at his residence was because he was a participant in the conspiracy to murder them . . . He certainly did not have the pictures at his residence so that he could admire the faces of his enemies." And so the conspiracy charges stuck.

Stadnick was, in fact, a smooth operator, ruthless when necessary, but aware of the value of consensus, too. At 5ft 4ins he is diminutive, especially for a biker. Nothing seems to mark him as someone with remarkable management skills, able to unite a bunch of feral, far-flung and dissolute bikers into a well-oiled business empire, a McDonald's of drugs with biker wings instead of golden arches. His favoured tactic was to muscle in to new markets simply by undercutting the existing dealers in those towns – the classic introductory offer that becomes exclusive once the competition disappears.

One Canadian journalist has called him the Henry Kissinger of the Hell's Angels. Stadnick served as national president of the Hell's Angels for six years. However, his masterstroke was to create a new chapter – with a difference – that went live towards the end of 1994. The Nomads were an über motorcycle club, a mobile inner circle featuring the most loyal and battle-hardened bikers, a kind of praetorian guard. This enabled Stadnick to confuse law enforcement with "puppet" clubs that could be set up and dissolved as required, removing him further from potential apprehension and ensuring his direct links with violent crimes were tenuous. The Nomads were, of course, to be the sole supplier of drugs to these puppet clubs.

In a culture where many meet a violent death at the end of a gun, it's ironic that the most harm Stadnick ever suffered was inflicted by a priest. In September 1984, Stadnick's chopper was hit by the man of the cloth as he raced to see the Pope speak at Montreal's Olympic stadium. In a parody of divine judgement, its petrol tank exploded, leaving Stadnick with third-degree burns to his upper body, nose and hands.

The recent spate of arrests had weakened the Alliance and convinced the Hell's Angels they were on the ropes.

With the war winding down, the Hell's Angels became increasingly focused on their enemies in the authorities and within their own organization. An edict even came down from the Nomads that Hell's Angels and their associates stop wearing their colours in public and reduce the size and number of parties. After the police found the bomb in the Hydro van on 23 August, Boucher became convinced there was a snitch in the Hell's Angels.

The cops knew exactly where the van was and what to look for; it didn't seem possible for them to know what was going on without a tip. Worse yet, an SQ officer flippantly let it slip that they had a mole in the Hell's Angels' inner circle. Cops try to intimidate suspects with claims like that all the time, but this time Boucher thought there was more to it, especially after other officers got angry at the one who told him. Although he'd been loyal to him in prison, Stéphane "Godasse" Gagné was Boucher's prime suspect. It was his bomb the police mysteriously found and Boucher figured that Gagné could have chickened out of his first job, especially with the Desrosiers incident fresh in everyone's memory.

His fears were unfounded. Gagné was proving his worth with the Rockers. While serving under the watch of Boucher's right-hand man, Tousignant, and Paul "Fonfon" Fontaine, Gagné distinguished himself as a drug salesman and frequently lobbied to prove his worth to the club in other ways. Before they'd let him join a "football team" (what the Montreal Hell's Angels called their killing squads), they told him he had to wait. But Gagné was too ambitious and impatient for that. Christian Bellemare was an old friend of his and had been selling his drugs since the days before Gagné got involved with the Hell's Angels. Their long-standing friendship had allowed Bellemare a certain amount of leeway as far as debts were concerned, but when he'd run up a $12,000 tab at the same time Gagné needed to prove a point, he was in big trouble.

In the spring of 1997, Gagné and another would-be Rocker, Steve Boies, invited Bellemare up to a party in the Laurentians. After they got good and drunk at a chalet bar,

Gagné suggested they go outside for a joint. When they were out of sight of the chalet windows, Gagné pulled out a gun. Realizing he was the intended victim, Bellemare took off and started climbing over one of the snowbanks that surrounded the parking lot. Just as he was getting over the top, Gagné shot him and Bellemare tumbled over backwards onto the pavement. They were surprised to see he wasn't dead, so Gagné grabbed the barely conscious man by the shirt, pointed the gun at his forehead and pulled the trigger. It jammed. Exasperated, he put his hands around Bellemare's throat and started squeezing. When Gagné was satisfied the man was dead, he left the body where it was, and he and Boies kicked enough snow over it so it wouldn't be discovered until they were back in Montreal. The plan probably would have worked if they had killed Bellemare, but they hadn't. Strangled merely into unconsciousness, the victim dug himself out of the snow and made it back into the bar where a waitress called 911. Although Gagné had not managed to kill anybody, he'd made his point. He was certainly willing to become a murderer.

Boucher was becoming obsessed with the idea that he had a rat in his midst. Since he couldn't find out who was telling the cops about what the Hell's Angels were doing, his plan was to make the cops too scared to do anything about it. Under his new plan, the Hell's Angels would murder police officers, prosecutors, judges and others who tried to put members behind bars, thereby inciting enough fear in the authorities to leave the Hell's Angels alone and to ensure that, even if a biker was arrested, he'd never be convicted. Of course, the plan also had a personal side. Like many organized crime leaders, Boucher had very little love for authority figures and he wouldn't have minded seeing a few of them dead. So to kick off the operation, Boucher targeted the people he hated most, the ones he considered stupid and beneath his contempt, the ones who had treated him the worst over the years: prison guards. And, although Boucher didn't realize it, with Kane behind bars, there would be nobody to warn the RCMP.

True to the Nomads' philosophy, Boucher pushed the job down to his underlings, Tousignant and Fontaine. Although both men had a great desire to please their boss, neither wanted to take on such a hazardous job. According to Vincent, the man who claimed to be friends with both Boucher and Stadnick at the time, the belief among Montrealers at the time was that when a biker killed another biker, the police and prosecutors considered it a natural part of the business they were in. When a biker killed a civilian, it was sad but fairly routine. But if a biker were to kill an authority figure, he would be in real trouble. But Boucher wanted a prison guard dead, so it had to happen. This was the kind of job that normally would have fallen to Kane, but he was in jail awaiting trial on the MacFarlane murder, so Tousignant and Fontaine turned to another eager young thug, Stéphane "Godasse" Gagné.

They could hardly have picked a better candidate. Gagné was obsessed with becoming a Hell's Angel, and he had a personal grudge against prison guards. Not only had they thrown him into the heart of Rock Machine territory in Bordeaux, but a group of seven guards had beaten him severely in Sorel. He jumped at the chance to take one down. As with many East Enders, when Gagné thought of jail or prison, he thought of the nearby facility in Rivière-des-Prairies, a sort of holding pen for maximum-security prisoners on their way to court. After he cased the prison several times under the cover of darkness, Gagné found a section of the chain-link fence he could crawl under. From there, he found a spot in the trees where he could watch the parking lot. After a few nights, he fixed on a target.

Of all the cars that arrived and left – mostly rusted old minivans or cheerless economy cars – one stood out. Five nights a week, a man in a suit, who left earlier than all the others at shift change, strode into a brilliantly white spotless Buick Park Avenue that was always parked in the closest spot to the door. Clearly, he was someone important. Not wanting to take any chances, Gagné followed him out of the parking lot one night. Gagné knew that unless he got his victim on the highway, he'd never be able to get away from the crime scene. He was disappointed when he tailed the man in the big white Buick. Instead of turning off on the Autoroute Métropolitaine into the suburbs, the Buick kept driving down Boulevard Henri-Bourassa into the city. Disappointed, Gagné was mentally running through his list of potential victims when he got an urgent page to report to Boucher's office.

When he arrived at Rue Bennett, Tousignant was waiting outside. He took Gagné to a bar and told him that Boucher was getting impatient for results and that they would be working together from now on. The plan was simple. Gagné and Tousignant would follow a prison guard onto the Autoroute Métropolitaine on a motorcycle, kill him just before the bridge to Laval, cross over, dump the bike in a mall parking lot and drive away in a stolen car. When it came time to do the job on 26 June, Tousignant picked the most un-Harley bike he could find, a wildly low-slung silver Suzuki Katana racer. The two men sped to Rivière-des-Prairies and waited in the darkness until shift change. When the first guard left in an old Jeep Cherokee, they followed him until he passed the Autoroute turnoff. Tousignant then stopped the Suzuki, turned it around and twisted his right wrist until they were back at the prison.

Just as they arrived, they saw a short, heavyset guard get into a white Plymouth Voyageur and drive out of the parking lot. Tousignant followed. When the minivan turned onto the Autoroute Métropolitaine, the bikers knew they'd found their quarry. Diane Lavigne, the daughter of a veteran prison guard and one of the first women ever to serve as a guard in Quebec, was driving in the slow lane. She only took the Autoroute Métropolitaine about a mile before she turned off on the Chemin-des-40 Arpents to her house in St-Eustache. Tousignant brought the Suzuki even with the minivan. Gagné pulled out his revolver and fired into the open window three times. He hit her twice, the second one passed through her arm and her left lung before coming to a stop in her back-bone. She was dead before the Voyageur came to a stop on the shoulder. Tousignant then sped into Laval, where they dumped the bike, burned their clothes and fled in a stolen Voyageur. Danielle Leclair was another Rivièredes-Prairies guard; she was driving on Autoroute Métropolitaine about a quarter mile behind Lavigne. She saw the Suzuki, even swerved to avoid it at one point, and heard some cracking noises. When she recognized Lavigne's minivan by the side of the road, she considered stopping, but didn't.

When news of the murder hit the media the next day, Gagné, Tousignant, Fontaine, Boucher and others celebrated. They were surprised to find out the victim was a woman and, after some ribbing, Boucher put his arm around Gagné and told him not to feel bad. He didn't. After receiving his Rockers prospective membership, Gagné interpreted their gratitude as an indication that he was one more murder away from his full patch. But it would have to wait. About a week later, a young drug dealer was driving around the East End in a stolen car when he spotted Gagné wearing his Rockers patch (Fontaine and Tousignant earned prospective Nomads memberships). Eager to make his own Rock Machine prospective patch, the driver plowed his car into Gagné's Harley and fled. Gagné suffered injuries bad enough to keep him out of commission until late August. When he emerged, he resumed his duties as a drug dealer and started planning for another hit. Fontaine advised against hitting another prison guard. Without any information from Kane, Lavigne's murder was being treated as an isolated incident. Although the hit was professionally done, some elements – like the Japanese bike – put the police off the scent. Another, similar killing might make it obvious who the real killers were. But Fontaine was missing the point. Boucher's master plan was to destabilize the Quebec government and make them fear the Hell's Angels. Following a model set down by the cocaine barons of Colombia, Boucher wanted to terrorize the police and judiciary into submission. Making it obvious was a key element to success. The next victim would be another prison guard.

On 3 September, Gagné and Fontaine were hiding in the trees at Rivière-des-Prairies when they selected a victim. They followed Richard Auclair and Gagné suggested they kill him at a stoplight just before he turned onto the Autoroute. Fontaine, who had appeared nervous to his partner from the start, begged off, saying he didn't think the escape route was safe. Gagné disagreed, but respected his decision. On the ride home, Fontaine revealed that he was having a problem with killing a guard. "Killing a Rock Machine – that doesn't bother me; they're our enemies," he said, pointing out that he had no grudge against the guards. "They mean nothing to me." He also wanted to make sure that Gagné knew that if they were caught they were guaranteed twenty-five-year sentences. Fontaine's arguments didn't have much effect on his partner, though. Gagné had already murdered one guard and was desperate for his full patch.

They were back in the woods again on 8 September. When Boucher found out that it was Fontaine who had hesitated, he wanted to know why. Fontaine said he didn't like the risk of taking motorcycles, so Boucher got him a little Mazda 323 hatchback and a Dodge Caravan minivan. Not only was Fontaine back on the job, but Boucher suggested he be the triggerman, although Gagné would carry a gun for backup.

That morning, twelve buses left from Rivière-des-Prairies to pick up prisoners and, when one turned towards where the getaway Caravan was parked, the bikers followed it in the Mazda. As government vehicles must, the bus stopped when it came to a railway crossing. Robert Corriveau, the relief driver, was in the front passenger seat when he saw a fat man dressed in black in front of the bus. He appeared to have a gun. Before he could say anything, Fontaine climbed onto the hood of the bus and emptied his .357 Magnum in the direction of Pierre Rondeau, the driver. Through a shower of tiny glass cubes, three bullets entered his body. One bounced around inside, shredding most of his internal organs. Stunned, Corriveau watched as Fontaine slid off the hood and ran away, but he didn't see Gagné until he heard the click. Gagné's 9 mm, aimed at Corriveau's head, had jammed. Corriveau hid under the dashboard. Gagné slid off the hood and calmly walked around to the right-hand side of the bus. Through the window in the door he could see Corriveau huddled in a ball and he shot every bullet he had before leaving. Somehow, every one of them missed Corriveau; but one hit Rondeau, whose heart was still faintly beating.

Prison guards and employees in Quebec were in a state of panic in the fall of 1997. Two of their peers had been professionally murdered and police had no real supects and no hard evidence. But the guards themselves were ready to make their own less formal investigation. Working day in and day out with many people who'd enjoy seeing them dead, the guards could make educated guesses as to which groups and individuals would be able to carry out such an elaborate plan. Many of them remembered the list of their names and home addresses found in a prisoner's cell in Archambault prison back in 1992. Even if the police didn't realize it, or didn't say it out loud, the prison guards knew who was killing them – the Hell's Angels.

That fall, anxious guards noticed people taking pictures of their houses and cars. Some reported being followed as they drove to and from work and even on their jobs. Their panic turned to terror on 14 October, when a prison guard's house was burglarized. While his most saleable items – TV, VCR, computer – were left untouched, the thieves did take something far more frightening – two complete guard uniforms, two extra shirts and a pair of handcuffs. Fed up with a lack of help from police, the prison guards took the investigation into their own hands. A combination of their own recollections and a brief, sometimes brutal, questioning of every man on his way into Bordeaux prison soon led them to the accurate conclusion that Stéphane "Godasse" Gagné had at least something to do with the murders. It made sense – he was a vicious thug out to prove a point and he had experienced some really bad times with guards. Among the other names bandied about were André "Toots" Tousignant and Paul "Fonfon" Fontaine, who were also involved. As prisoners were released from Bordeaux and other institutions, they took what they'd learned from the guards' unsubtle investigation directly to the Hell's Angels.

Serge "Pasha" Boutin was a successful drug dealer for the

Pelletier brothers. He ran their operations in Montreal's gay village. When the war broke out, he sided with the Hell's Angels and assumed the same role as a member of the Rockers. Just before Halloween, one of his street-level dealers – fresh out of Bordeaux – told him what the guards were saying. The next time he saw them, Boutin called Gagné and Fontaine into his office. He told them that the guards were spreading rumours that they were the killers. When neither said anything, Boutin waited until they left and called Boucher. Boucher then called Gagné and set up a meeting on the busy corner of Rue Ontario and Avenue de Lorimer. He told Gagné that the prison guards knew he was the murderer, and that they knew this because he was such a bastard to them behind bars. Gagné struggled to maintain his composure. He left the meeting wondering if he would be eliminated as a threat to Hell's Angels' security.

A few days later, Mom Boucher arranged to meet Gagné on the sidewalk in front of his Rue Bennett headquarters. When he got there, Gagné started gushing about all the security precautions he had taken and that if the guards suspected him it was because he had fought with them in Sorel. Boucher calmed him down and told him it was time to hit another "screw". Gagné didn't understand; the police were everywhere and everybody knew the Hell's Angels were behind the prison guard murders. Boucher laughed. "Not to worry, we'll do the police, we'll do judges and prosecutors too," he told Gagné. "But that's not for you, dear Godasse, you've already done your job." Then he gave Gagné a different assignment. He was to tail members of Montreal's Italian Mafia in an inconspicuous grey Chrysler and videotape them using a camera concealed in a box of tissues. Nobody ever told him, but Gagné was sure Boucher was planning a war against the Mafia.

Although the prison guards and public were outraged by what they perceived as a lack of action regarding the guard assassinations, the Montreal police were quietly and effectively chipping away at the biker infrastructure. Under the codename Project HARM (Hell's Angels, Rock Machine), police were buying drugs in bars undercover, then arresting the vendors and closing the establishments. It was running smoothly until the night of 4 December, when four plain-clothes cops were sent to bring down an escort agency in Rosemount that was known to have biker connections. When a frantic call for backup came in, the only available officer was André Bouchard, commander of the Montreal police. When he arrived he saw four cops, guns drawn, surrounded by fifteen bikers and their women. The cops were screaming at the bikers, telling them to get on the floor. But the bikers were clearly unafraid of the officers and one even threatened them, saying, "You think you can shoot us all?"

Bouchard, a veteran of the days when officers beat up bikers on sight, made the difference. Arriving in his full dress uniform, complete with gold braid and gongs, he approached the biggest biker, sized him up, holstered his gun and then punched him in the jaw. The biker went down in a heap and the others got on the floor.

The police had stumbled upon treasure. In the back of the escort agency, they found a map of Montreal annotated with every Hell's Angels-associated bar, complete with their contacts and whose responsibility it was to get them drugs. Armed with that information, Bouchard sent out every available officer that night. Before sunrise, the Montreal police arrested 28 Hell's Angels associates, confiscated $2.5 million in drugs, 18 cars and 67 illegal weapons. But like a diamond amongst gold dust, they also found Steve Boies. There seemed to be little special about him, a regular street-level dealer, but when the police found almost four kilos of cocaine stashed in his house in Berthierville and a pager that linked him to a bombing attempt on a Rock Machine clubhouse, it was enough to put him away for a long, long time and he knew it. Boies then pulled out his get-out-of-jail-free card and started talking. He had some important friends and they had done some bad things.

Boucher, Gagné and Tousignant didn't know about the arrests. They were at Boucher's South Shore farmhouse going over the final details of an ambitious plan. The 20th anniversary of the Hell's Angels in Canada was approaching and a celebration was scheduled for the following night. Boucher surmised that if the Rock Machine had any fight left in them, they'd almost certainly have to strike then. As part of a comprehensive overall security plan, he had rented two helicopters with the plan of putting Tousignant in one and Gagné in the other. They would circle the Sorel clubhouse and shoot any invaders from above. After much of the meeting was over, Gagné received a call on his cell phone and excused himself. Taking Tousignant's car, he sped down Route 132 until he came across a phone booth (Hell's Angels never discuss anything of importance over cell phones) in Verchères. He called Benoît Cliche, his lawyer, back. It was bad news. Boies had been caught and had turned informant. Gagné sped home to St-Hubert, grabbed his wife, packed a few bags and got back on the road. He hadn't gotten very far on his way east when his wife convinced him to find a place to stay for the night. When he spotted a motel just outside St-Hyacinthe at 11 p.m., he stopped. As soon as he opened the door, he saw the lights and heard the sirens. The SQ had been tailing him since he'd left Montreal.

Back at the SQ offices in Montreal, Gagné sat in an interrogation room across the table from a faintly familiar face. His interrogator was Sgt Robert Pigeon, the same officer who had made the arrest that sent him to Bordeaux in 1994. Pigeon told Gagné he knew about the attempted murder of Christian Bellemare. Gagné told him he wasn't going to talk and asked to call his lawyer. According to Gagné's later testimony, he tried three times between 3.00 and 3.30 a.m., but Cliche did not answer. Gagné returned to his seat and declared again that he had nothing to say. Pigeon knew Gagné and was pretty sure he lacked the intellect or ambition to mount two very intricate and successful attacks on the prison guards, especially when he recalled how poorly he'd pulled off the attempt on Bellemare's life. His theory was that if Gagné was actually just the triggerman (as Boies had assumed), he was the SQ's only chance at catching the architect of the assassinations. That man, Pigeon correctly surmised, was Boucher. Gagné called his lawyer again at 6.24 a.m.; there was still no answer. When he returned, he looked at his questioner and asked, "If I talk, how many years will I get?"

It says a lot about either Pigeon's persuasiveness or Gagné's character that he folded. In truth, Boies had told the police little of value. The only mention of Gagné that wasn't pure speculation was a reference to his asking Boies to clean his garage and get rid of some clothes. But Gagné didn't know that. After consulting with his wife, he made the deal. Another fact Gagné did not know until Pigeon told him was that he was liable for the murder of Pierre Rondeau, the second prison guard. Although he had never actually intended to shoot Rondeau, one of the bullets he'd shot at Robert Corriveau had hit him. Forensic experts determined that the bullet entered Rondeau's body before he died, making Gagné at least partially responsible for his murder. In Canada, the murder of two officials guarantees a mandatory twenty-five-year sentence with no hope of parole. If the charge implicating him in Rondeau's murder was dropped, Gagné would face a twenty-five-year sentence with a chance at parole after fifteen years for the murder of Diane Lavigne. The police also offered $400 a month in cash and to drop any charges against his wife. Before talking to his lawyer, Gagné spilled his guts.

17

Homicide: A Year on the Killing Streets

David Simon

Before TV series *The Wire*, many people's only association with the city of Baltimore, Maryland were the funky, funny films of John Waters. After viewing the tensely scripted, compelling drama, that image changed to a city with the suburbs of Washington, DC or Oakland, California – a ruthless drug-dealing and murder capital. (For which it shares with Oakland the excuse of being a port.)

Homicide is one of a trinity of books on the subject, along with Simon's follow-up, *The Corner* (itself the basis for a miniseries), and fellow series-writer Rafael Alvarez's *The Wire: Truth be Told*. Simon's tone is that of a love-it-or-hate-it muscularity that at times seems to carry scant regard for the victims of crime or the foot soldiers caught between the threats of long-term imprisonment or certain death. It's a holiday in other people's misery, an unmarked-cruiser ride through Baltimore's ripped backside. But in that it accurately reflects the mindset of the hard-bitten plain-clothes detectives assigned to Baltimore's homicide unit. It captures how they shut off their minds because the best option on anyone's terms is to get the job done.

The following extract details how, nevertheless, murder cases do not always come from bandanna-wearing gang-bangers straight out of central casting, and how premeditated, purely manipulative evil can come in altogether smaller and less threatening packages, who notch up a chillingly high body count nevertheless . . .

Friday, July 22.
    "Aw Christ, another Bible."

Gary Childs picks the open book up off a bureau and tosses it onto a chair with a dozen others. The bookmark holds the place even as pages flutter in the cool breeze of an air conditioner. Lamentations 2:21:

> *Young and old lie together*
> *In the dust of the streets;*
> *My young men and maidens*
> *Have fallen by the sword.*
> *You have slain them in the day of your anger;*
> *You have slaughtered them without pity.*

One thing about Miss Geraldine, she took her Good Book seriously, a fact confirmed not only by the Bible collection, but also by the framed 8-by-11 photographs of her in her Sunday finest, preaching the good news at storefront churches. If salvation is ours through faith rather than works, then perhaps Geraldine Parrish can find some contentment in the wagon ride downtown. But if works do count for anything in the next world, then Miss Geraldine will be arriving there with a few things charged to her account.

Childs and Scott Keller pull up the bed and begin riffling the stack of papers stuffed beneath it. Grocery notes, telephone numbers, social service forms and six or seven more life insurance policies.

"Damn," says Keller, genuinely impressed. "Here's a whole bunch more. How many does that make now?"

Childs shrugs. "Twenty? Twenty-five? Who the hell knows?"

The search warrant for 1902 Kennedy gives them the right to seek a variety of evidentiary items, but in this instance, no one is gutting a room in the hope of finding a gun or knife or bullets or bloody clothes. On this rare occasion, they are looking for the paper trail. And they are finding it.

"I got more of them in here," says Childs, dumping the contents of a paper grocery bag onto the upended mattress. "Four more."

"This," says Keller, "is one murderous bitch."

An Eastern District patrolman who has been downstairs for an hour, watching Geraldine Parrish and five others in the first-floor living room, knocks softly on the bedroom door.

"Sergeant Childs . . ."

"Yo."

"The woman down there, she's sayin' she feels faint . . . You know, she's sayin' that she's got some kind of heart condition."

Childs looks at Keller, then back at the uniform. "Heart condition, huh?" he says, contemptuous. "She's having a heart attack? I'll be down in a minute and you can really watch her fall out of her chair."

"Okay," says the patrolman. "I just thought I'd tell you."

Childs sorts through the jetsam from the grocery bag, then wanders downstairs to the front room. The occupants of the rowhouse are clustered together on a sofa and two chairs, staring up at him, waiting for answers. The sergeant stares back at the plump, sad-faced woman with the Loretta Lynn wig and red cotton dress, a genuinely comic vision under the circumstances.

"Geraldine?"

"Yes I am."

"I know who you are," says Childs. "Do you want to know why we're here?"

"I don't know why you're here," she says, patting her chest lightly. "I can't sit like this. I need my medicine . . ."

"You don't have any idea why we're here?"

Geraldine Parrish shakes her head and pats her chest again, leaning back in her chair.

"Geraldine, this is a search-and-seizure raid. You're now charged with three counts of first-degree murder and three attempted murders . . ."

The other occupants of the room stare as deep gurgling noises begin to rise in Geraldine Parrish's throat. She falls to the carpet, clutching her chest and gasping for air.

Childs looks down, moderately amused, then turns calmly

to the Eastern uniform. "I guess you might want to call for that medic now," he says, "just to be on the safe side."

The sergeant returns upstairs, where he and Keller continue dumping every document, every insurance policy, every photo album, every slip of paper into a green garbage bag – the better to sort through it all in the relative luxury of the homicide office. Meanwhile, the paramedics arrive and depart within minutes, having judged Geraldine Parrish healthy in body if not in mind. And across town, at the Division Street rowhouse of Geraldine Parrish's mother, Donald Waltemeyer is executing a second warrant, digging out another thirty insurance policies and related documents.

It is the case to end all cases, the investigation that raises the act of murder to the level of theatrical farce. This case file has so many odd, unlikely characters and so many odd, unlikely crimes that it almost seems tailored for musical comedy.

But for Donald Waltemeyer, in particular, the Geraldine Parrish case is anything but comedic. It is, in effect, a last lesson in his own personal voyage from patrolman to detective. Behind Worden and Eddie Brown, the forty-one-year-old Waltemeyer is Terry McLarney's most experienced man, having come to homicide in 1986 from the Southern District plainclothes unit, where he was a fixture of large if not legendary proportion. And though the last two years have taught Waltemeyer everything he needs to know about handling the usual run of homicide calls, this case is entirely different. Eventually, Keller and Childs and the other detectives assigned to the case will return to the rotation and it will be Waltemeyer's lot to serve as primary investigator in the prosecution of Geraldine Parrish – a probe that will consume half a year in the search for victims, suspects and explanations.

In a unit where speed is a precious commodity, it's the rare case that teaches a detective patience, providing him with those last few lessons that come only from the most prolonged and complex avenues of investigation. Such a case can transform a cop, allowing him to see his role as something more than that of an ambulance chaser whose task is to clean up one shooting after another in the shortest time possible. And after a month or two, or three, this sort of sprawling case file can also drive a cop to the brink of insanity – which for Waltemeyer isn't all that long a journey in the first place.

Just yesterday, in fact, he was gnawing on Dave Brown's leg about one case or another when Brown felt compelled to whip out Rule 1, Section 1, from the department's Code of Conduct and read verbatim, to wit:

"'All members of the department shall be quiet, civil and orderly at all times and shall refrain from coarse, profane or insolent language,' And," added Brown, glaring at his partner, "I emphasize the word 'civil'."

"Hey, Brown," said Waltemeyer, making an obscene gesture. "Emphasize this."

It isn't that Dave Brown doesn't respect his partner, because he does. And it isn't that they can't work together, because when they have to, they do. It's just that Waltemeyer is constantly trying to explain police work to Brown, an exercise in condescension that Brown will accept only when it comes from Donald Worden, no one else. But even on his best days, Waltemeyer is quite possibly the most volatile detective in homicide, with a hair-trigger temper that never ceases to amaze the rest of McLarney's squad.

Once, soon after Waltemeyer had come downtown, McLarney himself happened to be busy talking to one of several witnesses from a murder. He called Waltemeyer over and asked him to handle one of the interviews, but as he began explaining the details of the case, he quickly realized that it was simply easier for him to talk to the witness himself. Never mind, McLarney explained, I'll do it myself.

But later, at several points during the interview, McLarney looked up to see Waltemeyer's face staring at him from the hallway. Three minutes after the end of the interview, Waltemeyer was in the office, pointing a finger in McLarney's face and raving wildly.

"Goddammit, I know my job, and if you don't think I can handle it, to hell with you," he told McLarney, who could only watch with detached awe. "If you don't trust me, then send me back to the goddamn district."

As Waltemeyer stormed away, McLarney looked around the office at his other detectives, who were, of course, biting the sleeves of their sport coats to keep from laughing aloud.

That was Waltemeyer. He was the hardest worker in McLarney's squad, a consistently aggressive and intelligent investigator, and two days out of every five he was a confirmed mental case. A Southwest Baltimore boy and the product of a large German family, Donald Waltemeyer was a source of endless delight to McLarney, who would often distract himself on a slow shift by goading his new detective into a tirade against Dave Brown. If Brown could then be made to respond, the result was usually better than television.

Heavyset, with a ruddy face and a mop of thick, coal black hair, Waltemeyer suffered his most embarrassing moment in homicide one morning at roll call: a sergeant read an announcement that Waltemeyer had been named the hands-down winner in a look-alike contest for his portrayal of Shemp, the forgotten Stooge. In Waltemeyer's considered judgement, the author of that little item would survive only as long as he remained anonymous.

Neither temper nor appearance had prevented Waltemeyer from becoming a first-class street police in the Southern District, and he still liked to think of himself as the same down-in-the-trenches patrolman he had always been. Long after his transfer to homicide, he made a point of staying close to his old bunkies in the district, often disappearing at night with one of the Cavaliers to visit the Southern's holes or shift-change parties. It was as if there was something a little disreputable about his having gone downtown to CID, something for which a real cop ought to apologize. The vague embarrassment Waltemeyer so obviously felt at having become a detective was his most distinctive trait.

Once last summer, he made a point of taking Rick James out to lunch at Lexington Marker, where the two bought tuna sandwiches from a carryout vendor. So far, so good. But then, instead of taking the meal back to headquarters, the older detective drove to Union Square, parking the Cavalier in his old patrol post.

"Now," said Waltemeyer, pushing the driver's seat back and spreading a napkin over his trousers. "We're going to eat like real police."

In McLarney's opinion, Waltemeyer's unswerving adherence to the patrolman's ethic was his only real weakness. Homicide is a world unto itself, and the things that work out in the district don't always work downtown. Waltemeyer's written reports, for example, were no better than district quality when he first came to homicide – a typical problem for men who spent more time on the street than at the typewriter. But in homicide the reports genuinely mattered, and what fascinated McLarney was that after mentioning the value of coherent paperwork to Waltemeyer, the detective set out on a successful, systematic campaign to improve his writing ability. That was when McLarney first realized that Waltemeyer was going to be one hell of a detective.

Now, neither McLarney nor anyone else could teach Waltemeyer much that was new about working murders. Only the cases themselves could add to his education, and only a case such as Geraldine Parrish could qualify him for the advanced degree.

The case actually began back in March, though at the time, no one in the homicide unit recognized it for what it was. In the beginning, it appeared to be nothing more than a routine extortion case: a complaint from a twenty-eight-year-old heroin addict who claimed that her uncle wanted $5,000 to keep her from being murdered by a contract killer. Why anyone would want to kill a brain-dead like Dollie Brown was unclear; the girl was a fragile little wraith with no known enemies, tracks on every appendage and very little in the way of money. Nonetheless, someone had tried to kill her, not once, but twice.

The first attempt was almost a year ago, when she was shot in the head during an ambush in which her thirty-seven-year-old boyfriend had been slain. That, too, had originally been Waltemeyer's case, and though it was still an open file, Waltemeyer believed that the boyfriend had been the intended victim and that the shootings had been drug-related. Then, after being released from University Hospital's shock-trauma unit back in March, Dollie Brown had the misfortune to be standing on Division Street when an unknown assailant cut her throat and ran away. Again, the girl survived, but this time there could be no doubt of the intended victim.

In any other environment, two such assaults in a six-month period may have led an investigator to believe that a campaign to end Dollie Brown's life was indeed under way. But this is West Baltimore, a place where two such incidents – absent any other evidence – can be safely regarded as coincidence and nothing more. The more likely explanation, Waltemeyer reasoned, was that Dollie's uncle was simply trying to capitalize on her fears and cheat her out of the $5,000 cheque she had received after the shooting from the state's crime victims compensation board, a government agency that provides financial assistance to those seriously harmed by violent crime. Her uncle knew about that money and told his niece that in return for the cash, he would intervene by killing the man who had been trying to kill her.

Working with a special undercover unit of the Maryland State Police, Waltemeyer had Dollie and her sister, Thelma, wired up with Nagra recorders and sent under police surveillance into a meeting with her uncle. When the man again demanded the money to prevent the impending murder, the extortion attempt was captured on tape. A week or so later, Waltemeyer made an arrest and closed the file.

Only in July did the Dollie Brown case become truly bizarre, for only then did a murder defendant with the singularly appropriate name of Rodney Vice begin talking to prosecutors, trying to cut a deal for himself. And when Rodney Vice opened his mouth, the plot didn't just thicken, it positively congealed.

Vice had been implicated as a go-between in the contract slaying of Henry Barnes, a middle-aged West Baltimore man who had been killed by a shotgun blast as he warmed up his car on a cool morning in October. The victim's wife had paid Vice a total of $5,400 for his services in procuring a gunman to kill her husband, thereby allowing her to collect on a series of life insurance policies. Vice had given a Polaroid photograph of Barnes and a shotgun to a tightly wound sociopath by the name of Edwin "Conrad" Gordon. Told that the intended victim usually warmed his car in front of his rowhouse every morning, Gordon was able to get close enough to use the shotgun at point-blank range. Henry Barnes left this world never knowing what hit him.

All would have gone according to plan had Bernadette Barnes been able to keep her silence. Instead, she admitted to a co-worker at the city social services building that she had arranged her husband's death, telling the woman, "I told you I was serious." Alarmed, the co-worker called the police department, and after several months of investigation by the detectives on Stanton's shift, Bernadette Barnes, Rodney Vice and Edwin Gordon were all in the Baltimore City Jail, tied together in a single prosecution report. Only then did Rodney Vice and his lawyer begin shopping some cooperation around, searching for a ten-years-or-less deal.

At an 11 July proffer session with lawyers and detectives at the Mitchell courthouse, Vice was asked how he had known that Edwin Gordon was a man capable of carrying out a contract murder. Nonplussed, Vice assured the detectives and prosecutors that Gordon had been in that line of work for some time. In fact, he had been killing people for an East Baltimore woman by the name of Geraldine for several years now.

How many people?

Three or four that Vice knew about. Not to mention that one girl – a niece of Geraldine's – who wouldn't die no matter how many times Gordon tried to kill her.

How many times did he try?

Three, said Vice. After the most recent occasion, when he had shot the girl in the head three times to little effect, Gordon was particularly disheartened, telling Vice, "It don't matter what I do, the bitch won't die."

Checking back with Dollie Brown that same day, Waltemeyer and Crutchfield confirmed that Geraldine Parrish was indeed her aunt and that the young woman had indeed been assaulted a third time. She had been walking with Aunt Geraldine back in May, when the older woman told her to wait on a Hollins Street stoop while she went to get something. Seconds later, a man ran up and shot her repeatedly in the head. Again, she was treated and released from University Hospital; incredibly, she mentioned nothing to the investigating officers about the previous attempts on her life. McAllister handled the Hollins Street shooting, and knowing little of Waltemeyer's extortion case two months earlier, he wrote nothing more than a brief twenty-four-hour report.

As Vice spoke, a new tale was being added to the lore and legend of the BPD homicide unit, that of the Unsinkable Dollie Brown, the hapless, helpless niece of Miss Geraldine Parrish, alias the Black Widow.

Rodney Vice had a lot more to say about Miss Geraldine, too. After all, Vice told the gathering, it didn't exactly stop with Dollie Brown and the $12,000 in insurance policies that Aunt Geraldine had obtained in her niece's name. There were other policies, other murders. There was that man back in 1985, Geraldine's brother-in-law, who had been shot on Gold Street. Edwin Gordon had taken that contract as well. And then there was the old boarder who lived at Geraldine's house on Kennedy Street, the elderly woman whom Gordon had to shoot twice before he finally killed her off. It was Miss Geraldine herself who sent the old woman out to a Chinese carryout on North Avenue, then signalled Gordon, who walked calmly up to the target and fired one shot to the back at point-blank range, then issued a coup de grâce to the head after the victim fell to the sidewalk.

Veteran detectives left the courthouse with their heads spinning. Three murders, three attempted murders – and that was just what Vice happened to know about. On their return to the homicide office, open murder files dating back as many as three years were suddenly being yanked from the oblivion of the filing cabinets.

Incredibly, everything in those files conformed exactly to Rodney Vice's account. The November 1985 murder of Frank Lee Ross, the common-law husband of Geraldine's sister, had been handled by Gary Dunnigan, who at that time could find no motive for the slaying. Likewise, Marvin Sydnor had worked the fatal shooting of Helen Wright, sixty-five, who had been boarding with Geraldine on Kennedy Street; lacking any solid information about the murder, he had presumed that the old lady had been killed in a robbery attempt gone awry. Not that Sydnor hadn't found a few loose ends in a routine interview with Geraldine Parrish; he even tried to polygraph the landlady, but he gave up when she produced a cardiologist's note saying that her health could not stand the stress of a lie detector test. True to Vice's account, the old woman had been shot in the head several weeks before being murdered but had survived the first assault – a redundancy that had also been written off as inner-city coincidence.

The sheer amount of new information made clear the need for a special detail, and Waltemeyer – because he had handled the original March extortion complaint as well as the initial shooting of Dollie Brown – soon found himself reassigned to Gary Childs's squad on Stanton's shift. He was joined by Mike Crutchfield, the primary detective on the Bernadette Barnes case, and later by Corey Belt, the bulldog from the Western District who had done so well on the Cassidy investigation. At Stanton's request, Belt had been returned to homicide from the Western ops unit specifically for the investigation of Geraldine Parrish.

They began with detailed interviews of Dollie Brown and other relatives of Miss Geraldine's, and what they heard became more incredible with each telling. Everyone in the family seemed to know what Geraldine had been doing, yet everyone seemed to have regarded her campaign to trade human lives for insurance benefits as an inevitable, routine bit of family business. No one ever bothered to call the police – Dollie, for one, had said nothing about her aunt during the extortion probe – but worse than that, many family members had signed insurance policies for which Geraldine was the beneficiary. Nieces, nephews, sisters, brothers-in-law, tenants, friends and neighbours – the detectives began learning of

hundreds of thousands of dollars in double-indemnity policies. Yet when people were being shot, no one who knew
anything about it had bothered to voice so much as mild
apprehension.

They feared her. At least they said they feared her – and
not just because they knew of the sociopaths that Geraldine
Parrish employed for her insurance killings. They feared her
because they believed that she had a special power, that she
knew voodoo and hexes and all kinds of Carolina backwoods
garbage. She could bend a man to her will, make one marry
her or make one kill for her. She told them that stuff and,
after a time, when people began dying, they actually took to
believing it.

But Aunt Geraldine's power wasn't at all obvious to anyone
outside the family circle. She was a semi-literate lay preacher
with a grey Cadillac and a white stone rowhouse with fake
panelling and dropped tile ceilings. She was heavyset, and
ugly, too – a thoroughly unattractive woman whose penchant
for wigs and fire-engine-red lipstick suggested a $20
Pennsylvania Avenue prostitute. Geraldine was a hard fifty-
five years old when the city homicide unit finally kicked in
her front door and that of her mother's house on Division
Street.

The search of both addresses takes hours, as Childs, Keller
and Waltemeyer find policy binders and other papers strewn
throughout the two rowhouses. Long before the search at
Kennedy Avenue is complete, Geraldine departs in the back
of an Eastern District wagon, arriving at the homicide office
well before the investigators. She sits stoically in the large
interrogation room as Childs and Waltemeyer arrive and
spend another hour or so in the coffee room scanning the
insurance policies, photo albums and documents seized in
the two houses.

The two detectives immediately notice a proliferation of
marriage licences. As far as they can tell, the woman is
married to five men simultaneously, two of whom were living
with her on Kennedy Avenue and were taken downtown as
witnesses following the raid. The two men sit together like

bookends on the fishbowl sofa, each believing the other to be nothing more than a tenant at the East Baltimore home. Each is confident of his own place in the household. Each has signed a life insurance policy naming Geraldine Parrish or her mother as the beneficiary.

Johnnie Davis, the older of the two husbands, tells detectives that he met Miss Geraldine in New York and had, over his own objection, been intimidated into marriage and brought to Baltimore to live in the basement of the Kennedy Avenue rowhouse. Without fail, Miss Geraldine confiscated his disability cheques at the beginning of every month, then returned a few dollars so that he could buy food. The other husband, a man by the name of Milton Baines, was in fact Miss Geraldine's nephew and had rightly objected on grounds of incest when his aunt insisted on marriage during a trip back home to Carolina.

"So why did you marry her?" Childs asks him.

"I had to," he explains. "She put a voodoo curse on me and I had to do what she said."

"How did she do that?"

Baines recalls that his aunt had cooked him a meal using her own menstrual discharge and watched as he ate. Afterwards, she told him what she had done and explained that she now had power over him.

Childs and Waltemeyer exchange glances.

Baines rambles on, explaining that when he continued to express concern about marrying his mother's sister, Miss Geraldine took him to an old man in a neighbouring town who spoke briefly with the bride-to-be, then assured Baines that he was not, in fact, related to Geraldine.

"Who was the old man?" Childs asked.

"I don't know."

"Then why did you believe him?"

"I don't know."

It was not to be believed – a murder case with cosmic insanity as the only common frame of reference. When the detectives tell Milton Baines that the old man living in the basement is also Geraldine's husband, he is stupefied. When they explain to him that both he and his rival were living in that house like hogs waiting for the slaughter, corralled by a madwoman who would eventually trade them in for a few thousand dollars of insurance benefits, the man's mouth drops in abject wonder.

"Look at him," says Childs from the other side of the office. "He was the next victim. You can almost see the H-file number stencilled on his forehead."

Waltemeyer guesses by the marriage licences and other documents that husband number three is probably in Plainfield, New Jersey, though whether he is dead or alive isn't immediately clear. Husband number four is doing a five-year bit at Hagerstown on a gun charge. Husband number five is somebody by the name of the Reverend Rayfield Gilliard, whom Geraldine married this past January. The good reverend's whereabouts are uncertain until Childs goes to the blue looseleaf binder that lists unattended deaths for the year. Sure enough, the seventy-nine-year-old Gilliard's marriage to Miss Geraldine had lasted little more than a month; his sudden departure had been attributed by the medical examiner's office to natural causes, though no autopsy had been performed.

There are also the photo albums, in which Miss Geraldine had saved not only the Reverend Gilliard's death certificate but also that of her thirteen-year-old niece, Geraldine Cannon, who, according to an accompanying newspaper clipping, had been in her aunt Geraldine's care when she succumbed to an overdose of Freon in 1975 – an overdose ruled accidental, though pathologists attributed it to a possible injection of Ban deodorant. On the following page of the album, the detectives find a $2,000 insurance policy in the child's name.

In the same album, they locate more recent pictures of Geraldine with an infant girl and soon learn that she had purchased that child from a niece. The baby would be found later that week at a relative's house and would be taken into custody by the Department of Social Services after the detectives match that infant to at least three life insurance policies totaling $60,000 in double-indemnity benefits.

The list of potential victims has no end. An insurance policy is found for a man who had been beaten and left to die in a wooded section of Northeast Baltimore; however, he survived the attack and was later located in a rehabilitative hospital. Another policy is found for Geraldine's younger sister, who died of unexplained causes several years back. And from one page of another album, Childs pulls out a death certificate, dated October 1986, for a man named Albert Robinson. The manner of death is listed as homicide.

Childs takes the document and walks to another blue binder that contains a chronological list of Baltimore homicides. He opens the binder to the 1986 cases and scans the column of victims:

Robinson, Albert B/M/48

10/6/86, shot, NED, 4J-16884

Nearly two years later, the case is still open, with Rick James as the primary detective. Childs takes the death certificate back into the main office, where James is at his desk, absently poking at a chef's salad.

"This mean anything to you?" Childs says.

James scans the death certificate. "Where'd you get this?"

"Out of the Black Widow's photo album."

"Are you shittin' me?"

"Uh-uh."

"Hot damn," says James, jumping up to grip the sergeant's hand. "Gary Childs done solved my murder."

"Yeah, well, someone had to."

A smokehound *(ageing drug addict)* from Plainfield, New Jersey, Albert Robinson had been found dead by the B&O railbed at the foot of Clifton Park, shot once in the head. The man's blood-alcohol level at the time of death was 4.0, four times the legal standard in drunk driving cases. Working on that murder, James never did figure out why an alcoholic from north Jersey was dead in East Baltimore. Perhaps, he had reasoned, the man was a hobo who had hitched a southbound freight only to be shot to death for some unknown reason as the train meandered through Baltimore.

"How does she connect with Albert?" asks James, suddenly fascinated.

"I don't know," says Childs, "but we know she used to live up in Plainfield . . ."

"No shit."

". . . and I got a feeling that somewhere in that pile of papers we're gonna find an insurance policy on your man."

"Oooooo, you makin' me feel all warm an' happy inside," says James, laughing. "Keep talkin' that nice talk."

Inside the large interrogation room, Geraldine Parrish adjusts her wig and applies another coat of makeup, using a small mirror. None of this has made her any less conscious of her appearance, such as it is. Nor has she lost her appetite; when detectives bring her a tuna sub from Crazy John's, she puts away the entire thing, chewing slowly, pinkies raised as she holds the ends of the sandwich to her mouth.

Twenty minutes later, she demands to use the ladies' room and Eddie Brown walks her as far as the door, shaking his head and smiling when his prisoner asks if he would be coming inside.

"You go on ahead," he tells her.

She is in there for a good five minutes, and when she steps back into the hallway, it's with a fresh coat of lipstick. "I need my medicines," she says.

"Well, which medicines do you need?" asks Brown. "You had about two dozen different ones in your purse."

"I need all of them."

Visions of an interrogation room overdose dance through Eddie Brown's head. "Well, you ain't getting all of them," he says, walking her back down the hallway. "I'll let you pick three pills."

"I got rights," she says bitterly. "Constitutional rights to my medicines."

Brown smiles, shaking his head.

"Who you laughing at? What you need to get is some religion . . . stand there laughing at people."

"You gonna give me religion, huh?"

Geraldine saunters back into the interrogation room,

followed by Childs and Waltemeyer. In the end, four detectives will take a crack at this woman, laying the insurance policies on the long table and explaining over and over that it doesn't matter whether she actually pulled the trigger.

"If you caused someone to be shot, then you're guilty of murder, Geraldine," says Waltemeyer.

"Can I have my medicines?"

"Geraldine, listen to me. You're charged with three murders already, and before this is over you're probably going to be charged with some others. Now's the time to tell us what happened . . ."

Geraldine Parrish stares up at the ceiling, then begins babbling incoherently.

"Geraldine . . ."

"I don't know what you're talkin' 'bout, Mistah Poh-leeces," she says suddenly. "I didn't shoot no one."

Later, when the detectives have given up on the notion of a coherent statement, Geraldine sits alone in the interrogation room, waiting for the paperwork to catch up with her before she is transferred to the City Jail. She is leaning forward, her head resting on the table, when Jay Landsman walks by the one-way window and glances inside.

"Is that her?" says Landsman, who has just come on the four-to-twelve shift.

"Yeah," says Eddie Brown. "That's her."

Landsman's face creases into an evil grin as he slams an open palm hard against the metal door. Geraldine jumps in her seat.

"Whhhhooooaaaaaaaaaaa," wails Landsman in his best approximation of a ghost. "Whhhhooooaa, mmuuurrder . . . MMMUUURRDER . . ."

"Aw Christ, Jay. Now you fuckin' did it."

Sure enough, Geraldine Parrish dives under the table on all fours and begins bleating like a crazed goat. Delighted with himself, Landsman keeps at it until Geraldine is prone on the floor, bellowing at the metal table legs.

"Whhhhhooooaaaaa," moans Landsman.

"Aaaaaaaaahhhhhh," screams Geraldine.

"Whhhhooooaaaaaa."

Geraldine stays down on the floor, whimpering loudly, as Landsman strolls back into the main office like a conquering hero.

"So," he says, smiling wickedly, "I guess we're probably looking at an insanity defence."

Probably so, although everyone watching Geraldine Parrish's performance is now utterly convinced of her sanity. This writhing-on-the-floor nonsense is a calculated and naive version of the real thing, an altogether embarrassing performance, particularly when everything else about her suggests a woman vying for a special advantage, a manipulator measuring every angle. Her relatives have already told detectives how she would boast about being untouchable, about being able to kill with impunity because four doctors would testify to her insanity if need be. The musings of a sociopath? Perhaps. The mind of a child? Probably so. But a mind genuinely unhinged?

A week ago, before the search warrants were even typed, someone showed Waltemeyer an FBI psychological profile of the classic black widow serial killer. Prepared by the behavioural sciences unit at the Quantico Academy, the profile suggested that the woman would be thirty years or older, would not necessarily be attractive, yet at the same time would make great efforts to exaggerate her sexual prowess and manipulate her physical appearance. The woman would probably be a hypochondriac and would more likely than not enjoy portraying herself as a victim. She would expect special treatment, then pout if it was not forthcoming. She would greatly overestimate her ability to sway other people, men in particular. Measured against the profile, Geraldine Parrish seemed to be the product of Central Casting.

After the interrogation, Roger Nolan and Terry McLarney are both escorting Geraldine Parrish to the City Jail, following her down the sixth-floor hallway, with Nolan walking directly behind the woman.

"Just before the elevators, she stops suddenly and bends over," Nolan later tells the other detectives, "as if she's trying to make me run into her fat ass. I tell you, that's what she's really about . . . In her mind, she really believes that if I get a good feel of her ass, I'm gonna fall in love with her and shoot Terry McLarney with his own gun and ride off into the sunset in an unmarked Chevrolet."

Nolan's psychoanalysis may be sufficient to the occasion, but for Waltemeyer, the long journey into the mind and soul of Geraldine Parrish is just beginning. And while every other detective in the room is content to believe that they already know everything there is to know about this woman, it is now up to Waltemeyer to determine just how many people she killed, how she killed them and how many of those cases can be successfully prosecuted in court.

For Waltemeyer, it will be an investigation unlike any other, a career case that only a seasoned detective could contemplate. Bank statements, insurance records, grand jury proceedings, exhumations – these are things that no patrolman ever worries about. A street cop rarely takes the work beyond a single shift; one night's calls have nothing to do with those of the next. And even in homicide, a detective never has to worry the cases beyond the point of arrest. But in this investigation, the arrest is just the beginning of a long, laboured effort.

Two weeks from now, Donald Waltemeyer, Corey Belt and Marc Cohen, an assistant state's attorney, will be in Plainfield, New Jersey, interviewing the friends and relatives of Albert Robinson, finding one of Geraldine's surviving husbands and delivering subpoenas for bank and insurance records. Much of the evidence involves an interstate paper trail, the kind of detail work that usually inspires a street cop to nothing more than tedium. But the three men will return to Baltimore with the explanation for the migration of Albert Robinson to East Baltimore and his subsequent murder.

Brought once again to the interrogation room from her jail cell, Miss Geraldine will once again confront a detective who lays the insurance policies in front of her and once again explains the truth about criminal culpability.

"You not makin' any sense," Geraldine will tell Waltemeyer. "I didn't shoot no one."

"Fine with me, Geraldine," the detective says. "It doesn't matter to me whether you tell the truth or not. We just brought you here to charge you with another murder. Albert Robinson."

"Who's he?"

"He's the man from New Jersey you had killed for ten thousand dollars of insurance money."

"I didn't murder no one."

"Okay, Geraldine. Fine."

Once again, Geraldine Parrish leaves the homicide unit in handcuffs and, once again, Waltemeyer goes back to working the case, expanding it further, searching this time for answers in the death of the Reverend Gilliard. It is a deliberate, often tedious process, this prolonged investigation of a woman who has already been arrested and charged with four murders. More than a string of fresh street shootings, it demands a professional investigator. A detective.

Months into the Parrish investigation, McLarney will walk by Waltemeyer's desk and overhear a lecture that the detective is delivering with calm sincerity. The beneficiary of Waltemeyer's new-found wisdom will be Corey Belt, the prodigy from the districts whose detail to homicide was extended for the Parrish investigation. At that moment, Belt wants very much to respond to a lying, recalcitrant witness in the Western District way.

"Back in the Western," Belt tells Waltemeyer, "we'd just throw the asshole against a wall and put some sense into him."

"No, listen to me. This isn't patrol. That kind of stuff doesn't work up here."

"That stuff always works."

"No, I'm telling you. Up here you got to be patient. You got to use your head."

And McLarney will stand there, listen a little longer, and then move on, delighted and amused at the notion of Donald Waltemeyer telling another man to shake off the lessons of the street. If there was nothing else to her credit, the Black Widow had at least taken a patrolman and turned him into a detective.

Donald Waltemeyer's career case went to trial in 1989, as prosecutors brought Geraldine Parrish into Judge Bothe's court for the murder of Albert Robinson, the alcoholic from Plainfield, New Jersey, found dead by the railbed in Clifton Park in 1986. Geraldine knew Albert Robinson from her storefront church in Plainfield, and years earlier she had convinced him to sign a life insurance policy that named her as the beneficiary. Of the four murders with which she was charged, the slaying of Robinson proved to have the most corroborative evidence. A trio of prosecutors told jurors an incredible, at times almost comical, tale in which Geraldine and a handful of other conspirators drove to New Jersey and lured Robinson into a car with promises of alcohol. Hours later, they shot him and left him for dead in a copse near Atlantic City. Robinson survived with only superficial wounds, but he was so drunk that he remembered nothing of the incident. A few months later, the gang returned to New Jersey, lured the drunk into the car once again, and this time drove him to Baltimore, where a teenage friend of one of Geraldine's nieces finished the job on the B&O railbed, leaving Rick James with a stone whodunit.

Geraldine disappointed no one at the trial. At one point, she threw a conniption in the jury's presence, flailing in her chair and spitting foam from the corners of her mouth. A bored Elsbeth Bothe ordered her to behave, ending the demonstration. Later, on the witness stand, Geraldine claimed she was duped by men who made her turn over the insurance policies and identify the prospective victims for them.

She wasn't convincing, and in this instance a jury had little problem agreeing on a verdict. Geraldine Parrish was sentenced to life in prison, after which she pleaded guilty to the remaining three murders and received concurrent life sentences. No one was more relieved to see the case end than

Donald Waltemeyer, who returned to the rotation full time immediately after the trial.

Waltemeyer's partner, Dave Brown, no longer lives in a state of perpetual torment. For the last two years, Donald Worden has granted the younger detective a certain grudging acceptance, if not respect. It is true, however, that in the summer of 1989 the Big Man began charging Brown twenty-five cents apiece for his phone messages.

As for Terry McLarney himself, he continues to cling to the brotherhood. In 1989, he ignored a persistent cough until he could barely stand, then spent months recuperating from a bacterial infection around his heart. He was not expected to return to homicide, which is to say he was back in four months, looking leaner and healthier than he had in years.

18

One Child at a Time: Inside the Fight to Rescue Children from Online Predators

Julian Sher

The following extract goes behind the scenes of new police units established to investigate cross-border Internet crimes. Recent law-enforcement approaches to paedophilia and the solicitation of underage sex represent one way in which undercover police work is changing: in the future, some highly effective police officers who assume false identities – in contrast to the regrettably necessary risks run by brass-necked operatives such as Joe Pistone – may in fact remain desk-bound. From the point of view of top-brass police decision-takers, this is a good thing – if risk can be avoided, it should be.

The involvement of Interpol, the international law-enforcement support and data dissemination service, in the pursuit and capture of Canadian paedophile Christopher Neil in Thailand in 2008 – a gift to Britain's tabloids, who dubbed him "Swirly Face" owing to the software he had used to disguise himself in abusive images he posted online – represented an effective future direction in policing. German, Thai and Cambodian police worked together to identify their suspect, with the Germans providing technical support. The inter-jurisdictional nature of the Internet has made this kind of policing essential.

The Internet provides new opportunities for data theft and online fraud, and in that context too, the targeted surveillance of IP addresses looks set to grow. The following extract goes beyond the lurid news stories, examining three cases in which predators have been brought to book using a "mixed economy" of online and traditional, offline undercover techniques. Together, these represent the future of undercover policing.

> —*Are you a police officer, or do you work for any law enforcement agency?*
> —*No, I'm in the ninth grade.*
> —*Good, thank you ... lots of cops online pretending to be girls.*
> —*They don't let ninth graders in the CIA!!!!*
> —ONLINE CHAT BETWEEN A FORTY-FOUR-YEAR-OLD MAN
> AND AN UNDERCOVER FBI AGENT

A fifty-seven-year-old man from Liverpool, England, sends money to a twelve-year-old girl for bus fare so she can travel two hundred miles to see him on Valentine's Day. An employee in his fifties at a Michelin tyre factory in Nova Scotia, Canada, pretends to be a seventeen-year-old lesbian in order to seduce a teenage girl from Toronto. A forty-four-year-old weapons designer for the US Department of the Navy can't wait to meet his thirteen-year-old date at a mall in Maryland.

Three men. Three countries. All three assumed false personae on the Web – pretending to be much younger than they were. What they never suspected was that the joke was on them: the "girls" at the other end of their steamy email courtship were undercover cops, often male police officers, at that. Sometimes the police take over the identity of a real child who has been ensnared by an older man; other times the agents have built entirely fictitious online characters to lure the predators.

In the shadowy world of Internet intrigue, the predator and the police play what seems to be a dangerous game of cat and mouse. Except that it's not a game, and the fates of real children are at stake. In the US, the police call these types of predators "travelers"; in the UK, the offence is called "enticing"; in Canada, it goes by the name "luring". But it amounts to the same thing: grown men prowling the Web looking for lonely children, the underage victims. According to a study published in the *Journal of Adolescent Health*, 76 per cent of the victims of online abuse met the offenders in a chat room; another 10 per cent hooked up via email.

To catch these men, police have to get inside the minds of the predators, figure out how they think, what turns them on and what risks tipping them off.

These are not men who sit at home content to trade illicit pictures of children or even to take pictures of their own children being abused; instead, they actively seek out complete strangers to assault. These online lurkers are the Web's equivalent of the proverbial "dirty old men" in the park, turning the Internet into their playground. To stop them, police have had to come up with equally devious undercover techniques that sometimes push the envelope – going too far, their critics say, into the morally dubious and legally tricky terrain of entrapment.

"Are you a cheerleader?" the man asked the thirteen-year-old girl in the online AOL chat room called "I love older men". It was one of many anonymous meeting places on the Web filled with lonely children in America. They come to play, to pretend – and sometimes to meet up with men who are deadly serious about their intent.

"Must be hot if you're a cheerleader," George Paul Chambers wrote. The girl dutifully sent him her photo, and over the next four months he courted her until she agreed to meet him at a bakery shop in a mall. Chambers must have thought it was his lucky day when he made that date at the mall, but he had the misfortune of crossing paths with one of the FBI's keenest undercover operatives: Emily Vacher, the investigator who worked closely with the Toronto police and helped the FBI dig up the forensic filth on Burt Thomas

Stevenson's computer in North Carolina after Jessica's rescue. Vacher has a fervour for her job made all the more intense by the long road she took to get there.

"I'm a Jewish kid from outside Manhattan," she says with a laugh. "I didn't know any police officers, much less any FBI agents."

She got a bachelor's degree at an upstate New York college, then enrolled in pre-med studies at Cornell. She did volunteer work as a paramedic, but at the last moment switched from medicine to get a Master's in counselling and education. She ended up working with children with disabilities – until she decided she wanted to be a lawyer.

"At twenty-four, I had four degrees, and my mother said that I had to go work," Vacher jokes. Her first job at a law firm allowed her to concentrate again on children, through education law. When she asked a colleague who had been an FBI agent what it was like to be part of the famed bureau, "he just lit up. The way he talked about it – I wanted to feel like that at work."

The next day she went down to talk to the FBI and within a few weeks found herself at the training centre in Quantico, Virginia. There she heard about the FBI's Innocent Images programme, and her mind – finally – was made up. "I knew I wanted to do something where I either got to work with or help kids," she says. In the spring of 2001, she was lucky enough to get her first posting in Baltimore, not far from the Calverton headquarters. In the months following the 9/11 attacks, like almost everyone else at the FBI, she was consumed by anti-terrorist work. In December 2001, she finally began training to become the FBI's latest undercover Internet agent.

The FBI had to make sure that its agents talked and looked like teenagers. Early on, the bureau brought in a couple of real teenage girls – one was the daughter of an agent – to school the adult agents in the lifestyle and lingo of the wired generation. Online predators often ask for pictures from the children they are in contact with, but FBI agents – and other police officers from around the country who began to emulate the bureau's undercover work – could hardly use pictures of real children. So they called on the image specialists at NCMEC, who usually spent their time employing the latest photomanipulation software to "age" children who had been missing for many years. For the adult undercover agents, it was the reverse: NCMEC's experts were tasked with mastering the art of "age regression".

"It snowballed," says Steve Loftin, one of MCMEC's image specialists, who was getting a half-dozen requests a week from agencies across the country.

Sometimes Loftin uses an officer's childhood photos and only has to alter the clothing or hairstyle to match the right decade. Other times he asks them to have a picture taken of themselves in a childlike setting – on a swing or clutching a teddy bear – and wearing age-appropriate clothing. Then Loftin goes to work, changing bone density, altering muscle definition, smoothing out skin and adding some baby fat.

A few hours' work, and decades have been wiped out.

Changing appearances was the easy part for Emily Vacher. She decided she didn't need any technical wizardry. She dug up a snapshot of herself at thirteen in a summer camp performance of *Grease* – decked out in a white T-shirt and a brown leather jacket. She might have looked thirteen in the photograph, but how could Vacher, at the time thirty-two, think and sound like a teenager? "I don't have children, I haven't been thirteen in a while, and when I was thirteen the world was a different place," she said.

To pick up teen habits, Vacher spent a lot of time on the phone with a thirteen-year-old niece, listening to her voice, expressions and grammar (or lack thereof). When she visited her niece's home, she checked out the latest posters on her bedroom wall; Vacher became a regular reader of *Teen People* and *Teen Vogue*, an avid MTV fan and an aficionado of boy bands. Her homework paid off. One adult correspondent, who happened to have a real teenage daughter enthralled with heartthrobs like the Backstreet Boys and *NSYNC, once asked her if she favoured lead singer Lance or Justin. Vacher, immersed in teen culture, could easily come up with the convincing answer of a connoisseur.

For her first undercover role, Emily Vacher took the name EmmaMDGurl – the MD standing for Maryland. With as many as ten or twelve men pursuing her online at a time, Vacher had a notebook in front of her when she went online to keep her stories straight and make sure she was telling the right lies to the right people. "These predators use the same system," she says. In one raid, she discovered that a man had a bulletin board filled with index cards for all the girls he had been pursuing – their names, their ages, siblings, bra sizes and even whether thcy had pubic hair. "So they would check on us just as much as we would check on them," the FBI agent says. "It's important as an investigator to be consistent."

To maintain that consistency, she modelled as much of her online persona as possible after herself. EmmaMDGurl had an eight-year-old sister, just as Emily Vacher did when she was thirteen; both the online fictitious girl and the real-life FBI agent enjoyed playing lacrosse. Other parts of her story were concocted to help her undercover work: for example, she pretended that she split her time between the homes of her divorced parents so that she could explain away long absences from her computer, claiming she didn't have Internet access at her father's house.

Vacher liked to joke that catching online predators was not rocket science – until the day she caught a rocket scientist.

George Paul Chambers, a forty-four-year-old father of two young daughters, worked at the Naval Surface Warfare Center in Indian Head, Maryland, developing weapons and building systems to disarm explosives and landmines. "His brilliance is outstanding," his defence lawyer later said.

When Vacher signed on to the AOL chat room called "I love older men" just after 4 p.m. on 1 February 2002, she had been an FBI agent for less than a year and assigned to the Innocent Images project for only three months. Suddenly she found herself immersed in the murky universe of cyber-stalking, where adult males shed a few years and most of their inhibitions as they go hunting for vulnerable girls online.

To avoid any suggestion of entrapment, the FBI's under-cover cops are trained not to initiate contact, not to be forward, not to make any suggestions for meetings but only to respond. So Vacher was as passive as could be. "I went into that room and I didn't say a word," she says. "I was just sitting there and he contacted me."

"Do you like older guys?" came the query from laxfan314, the AOL screen name that Chambers used (short for "lacrosse fan").

Over the next four months, the navy weapons designer doggedly pursued what he thought was a precious cheer-leader. He didn't waste time. On that first day, he sent EmmaMDGurl a picture of his penis. He eventually sent a picture of his face as well, albeit one that showed him ten years younger. Vacher sent him the photograph of herself at thirteen. They would talk several times a week. She had to put in long hours because she could only go online in the afternoon after "school" was out; she came in on the week-end to work from the FBI's secure computers (which could not be traced) because she could not sign on undercover from home. Chambers often asked if her parents or any adults were home as they chatted online. He pushed to talk to her on the phone, but she refused. He soon wrote about getting together to meet his young cheerleader in person.

Chambers must have had some fears as well. On 24 March, he asked EmmaMDGurl if she worked for the FBI.

"Since when does the FBI hire teenagers?" she replied.

Later that same day, he again asked if she worked for any law enforcement agency.

"Uummmmm no," she replied.

Two months later, on 21 May, Chambers raised his worries one more time. "Are you a police officer or do you work for any law enforcement agency?" he asked.

"No, I'm in the ninth grade."

"Good, thank you . . . lots of cops online pretending to be girls."

"They don't let ninth graders in the CIA!!!!"

The FBI agent playing a ninth grader was busy doing her

homework on her online chat partner, running background checks to ascertain his real identity. A subpoena to AOL revealed basic information about Chambers; the picture he sent Vacher matched a driver's licence photograph of George Paul Chambers that the FBI obtained.

All that was left was the face-to-face meeting. Vacher had repeatedly delayed and cancelled, in part to give Chambers every opportunity to bail out. He kept insisting, until finally the date was set for Saturday, 6 June. There was no mystery about what would transpire once the navy scientist met the thirteen-year-old schoolgirl.

"He wanted to have sex with me," says Vacher. "When I had mentioned the issue of condoms during our chat, he specifically told me that he was not going to bring condoms because he wanted to get me pregnant."

As hard as it is to fathom, Chambers had good reason to believe a girl in a chat room would want such a meeting; as Vacher and other investigators would discover, plenty of real girls find themselves ensnared in Internet-initiated relationships with older men.

EmmaMDGurl suggested they meet at a bakery on the second floor of the Howard County mall in Columbia, Maryland, where her "mother" could drop her off. Chambers got into his car that day and drove the fifty miles from the Naval Surface Warfare Center in Indian Head, never spotting the FBI cars that were following him.

When he got to the rendezvous site, Chambers stood about twenty-five feet from the bakery, waiting for his teenage date, who never showed. Instead, FBI agents moved in to arrest him.

"I can't believe I came out here today," he said, according to later testimony by one of the agents. "My life is over."

In his car, the FBI found a computer Zip disk containing child pornography; more pictures turned up on his home computer. Back at the FBI office, Emily Vacher walked into the interrogation room where Chambers was seated. "He was one of my first cases, so I was still a little nervous," says Vacher. "As a new agent, you don't want to make mistakes.

But I was also excited: what I'd just done was potentially save a real child from harm."

For all his brilliance, the navy scientist still had no idea that the young field agent sitting across the table from him was the thirteen-year-old cheerleader he had been plotting to assault. Chambers declined to speak without his lawyer present, so Vacher sent him off to jail. The next morning, she picked him up and took him to his first appearance in front of the judge. Only later, through court papers and as the trial unfolded, did Chambers discover who EmmaMDGurl really was.

It was surprising that Chambers opted for a trial. In these kinds of cases, the defendant often goes for a guilty plea and a lesser sentence, because the details of his attempted online seduction of a child are so explicit – and downright embarrassing – that few want a jury or the public to hear them.

"It was my first trial as an agent, and I had obviously put a lot of time into the case. I was the undercover, I was there at the arrest, I did all the investigations," says Vacher. "I was scared to death."

Given the amount of evidence against him – naturally, Vacher had saved every scrap of conversation, every image he had sent – Chambers had only one viable defence strategy, a tactic almost all Internet predators use because it offers their sole chance with jurors: it was all a fantasy.

"It's a way of stepping out of your real life; you could be somebody else for a while," Chambers testified, insisting that he went to the mall out of curiosity, with no plans of sex. His attorney told the jurors that his client was "a nice guy with a crazy twist. But he's not a sexy guy," the lawyer said. "On the Internet, though, he can be Don Juan."

The real culprit, he argued, was the FBI and its special agent Vacher, who tried to lure and entrap Chambers. At one point in his cross-examination, the defence attorney asked Vacher if she thought her picture as a thirteen-year-old was "sexy". The judge berated him for "inappropriate" questions. Vacher took it all in stride. After all, she had been an attorney herself. Still, she was upset by the defence's insinuation that she took pleasure from her online encounters. "He was trying to make it seem like I got any kind of amusement out of this, like I enjoyed the sexual chat with his client. And I'm thinking, Ugh. The last man on earth. This behaviour is revolting.

"You just hope that a jury of twelve people will listen to our side, listen to their side and decide who is telling the truth."

But they couldn't decide.

After eleven hours of deliberation over two days, the jurors failed to reach a unanimous verdict. Most were certain he was guilty, but there were at least three holdouts, including the jury forewoman. "People do misrepresent themselves [on the Internet], and it's not a gross misrepresentation for him to engage in something like that and not know," she said. With a hung jury, the prosecution could have dropped the case or opted for a plea bargain, but they chose instead to go after Chambers again.

Vacher wanted to be sure she won the next time. When Chambers's second trial began, in March 2004, she was ready to attack the weapons designer for what he had said under oath the first time. "I got a transcript for the entire trial, and I went through it with a fine-tooth comb," explains Vacher.

The navy scientist had testified that child pornography was "repulsive" to him. Vacher pored through the logs of thousands of chats on Chambers's computer. "I found conversations that he was having not only with other children but also with other paedophiles, looking at images of children being sexually abused."

Chambers also insisted he had never had sex with anyone he met online because after all, that was just his fantasy world. From his computer logs. Vacher tracked down a young woman – legally an adult, at eighteen – whom Chambers had met in an AOL chat room, but ended up with in a hotel room. Finding the woman was one thing, persuading her to testify quite another. "She was completely scared, and you could feel empathy for her," says Vacher, "but I told her that her testimony was important to make sure that somebody who had a sexual interest in children was not on the street."

The woman had lost a lot of weight since she had met Chambers, so he did not recognize her at first when she showed up at trial. When she walked to the stand, however, it sunk in; he stood up and ran out of the courtroom. Running from the evidence was not as easy. In his summation, the prosecutor attacked head-on Chambers's claims that his online actions had all been make-believe.

"The question in this case is, Where does the fantasy end and the reality begin?" said the prosecutor. "If you fantasize about going to Ocean City, Maryland, it's a fantasy. When you get in your car and drive there, it's reality."

The reality began for George Paul Chambers when the jurors came back, united this time, with a guilty verdict. Reality sank in deeper in June 2004, when the judge sentenced him to six years in prison.

Chambers's only comment was, "Obviously, I think six years in prison is ridiculous."

Vacher, for her part, just wanted to move on. "There are no winners here. Not only did he commit the crimes, but he has a wife and children, so the damage is done. Besides, I had other had guys to catch."

Oddly enough, Chambers was not the last military man Vacher had a hand in arresting. Six months after the first Chambers trial, the Maryland police asked the FBI for assistance in an undercover sting they were running. Wayne David Sharer was a decorated navy commander and pilot who used his computer at the Pentagon to solicit sex on the Internet from what he thought was a twelve-year-old girl. Like Chambers, he travelled to meet her – in his case, to another mall in Columbia, where he was arrested. He got three years in prison.

Vacher caught flak for her undercover work. As one of the rare luring cases to go to trial, the Chambers case garnered a lot of media attention, including some sniping from commentators such as Joe Bob Briggs, whose shoot-from-the-hip columns were syndicated by United Press International. He took Vacher to task because she "flat-out lied" to Chambers when he asked if she was a cop (as if an undercover cop buying drugs from a dealer would flash his badge before making the buy). His main beef was that "there's no victim" in this crime; instead of going after "hard-core child molesters", the FBI was chasing "some lonely guy ... [who] is crossing imaginary lines with the equivalent of a blow-up party doll."

Such arguments infuriate Vacher, who points out that, far from entrapping people, she always gives them an escape hatch. "I never raised the issue of having sex, never raised the issue of meeting in real life, never," she says. "I don't sit in a chat room and say I'm thirteen and I want to have sex with an adult. They don't have to hit on me. If you're not interested in having sex with a child, then don't write to me."

And far from fantasies about a "blow-up party doll", the online predators are after real flesh-and-blood targets. Indeed, at times Vacher is required to take over the identity of an actual child who has fallen into a risky Internet trap.

In one such case, a Virginia girl had begun an intense online relationship with an older man from Colorado. Her parents, when they discovered what was going on, alerted the police, and the file landed on Vacher's computer.

"He wasn't hiding his intentions: he was looking for a teen sex toy," says Vacher. He mailed her cash for a bus ticket, confident that his teen target would travel by bus from Virginia to Colorado. FBI agents arrested him as he waited for the bus to arrive, expecting a teenage girl to step out and greet him.

"What would have happened to her?" Vacher asks. "If anyone wants to make the argument that what I do is wrong or pushing the bounds of the law, look at that child. If it's not me at the end of the computer, it's going to be a real child they're going to assault."

Between 1996 and 2004, the number of Innocent Images cases opened increased by over 2,000 percent – from 113 to 2,645 – and an equally impressive 1,195 per cent increase in convictions or pleas. "Like shooting fish in a barrel," says Arnold Bell, the unit chief of the Innocent Images project since 2002. Bell did six years in the army, followed by years of police work on homicide cases and Los Angeles gang wars. This was just another battlefront for him, albeit ever shifting and evolving.

At headquarters in Calverton, Bell has more than twenty people at work on various undercover stings. By 2005, the task force boasted that it had generated more than three thousand leads in the United States and two thousand abroad. Every agent who does similar work in the field – and there are more than forty of them in twenty-eight FBI bureaus scattered across the country – goes through an intensive undercover boot camp. The FBI has also hosted investigators from a dozen countries at its Calverton training centre – including a steady stream of Canadians.

Paul Gillespie of the Toronto police was one of the first to make sure his squad took advantage of the FBI's expertise. In late November 2002, a team of investigators from the Child Exploitation Section of the city's Sex Crimes Unit went down to Calverton, including a young detective named Paul Krawcyzk, who had just joined the squad five months earlier. "It was amazing," he recalls. "They seemed so ahead of their time. It was a real eye-opener."

The four-day course – including sessions with Emily Vacher – had an immediate impact. Within a week of returning to Toronto, Krawcyzk got his first undercover assignment. A woman had contacted the police with concerns that her fifteen-year-old younger sister, Rebecca,* was getting too close to a stranger she had met in an MSN chat group called "Girls4Girls". Rebecca had a learning disability, and her mental age was closer to ten. Her new friend called herself Karla Conrod; she claimed to be a seventeen-year-old student at Clayton Park High School, outside of Halifax. Her online profile sounded wholesome and cheery:

Nickname:	Goldilocks1121
Name:	Karla
Age:	17
Gender:	Female

Favourite Things: Read mystery novels
Favourite Quote: Only 2 things in life are free, fresh air
                   and happiness

Karla sent Rebecca two photographs of herself: they showed
a young blonde. In one shot, she had pulled down her bra to
expose a breast but kept on her underpants and shoes; in the
second photo, she was lying on a blanket, nude, with her legs
spread. Rebecca and her Nova Scotian friend talked about
the possibility that Rebecca could visit over Christmas.
Rebecca had supplied her real name, her home address and
phone number, the address of her school and a photograph
of herself.

Krawcyzk had doubts that Karla was who she claimed to
be. But he also knew that even if he could prove that Karla –
whoever she or he was – was trying to lure Rebecca for the
purposes of sex, he could not make an arrest because the age
of consent in Canada was fourteen. But the Toronto cop
figured that anyone who was trying to lure a teen into sex was
also likely a trader of child porn online. He could at least try
to nab the suspect for that.

With the permission of a reluctant Rebecca – who was
still convinced that her online friend was genuine – and
her mother, Krawcyzk took over the girl's account and
immediately changed the password to make sure he alone
had access to it. He discovered that Karla had sent sixty-
one messages to Rebecca in the previous eight days.
Krawcyzk was certain that Karla was an older man. Now
he had to convince the suspect that he was fifteen-year-old
Rebecca. It was not easy. Rebecca had not kept any copies
of her outgoing emails; thankfully, in many of Karla's
replies the original message was included, so the Toronto
cop could get a sense of how Rebecca talked. "Basically,
no grammar, no upper cases, just one big run-on para-
graph," Krawcyzk says.

He pulled it off, and Karla kept the chat coming. By early
December, Karla felt comfortable enough to send her young
friend some child pornography. In one email with the subject

header "u and me with her" she attached a JPEG file showing a young girl lifting up her skirt and exposing her genitals. The message read:

> Rebecca, I wish u and me can please her.
> What do u think? Love Karla

Krawcyzk had enough to lay a charge for the possession and distribution of child pornography. Now he just had to find out who Karla really was. He ran an IP trace and found that most of the communication came from the large Michelin tyre plant in Pictou, Nova Scotia. Krawcyzk passed the file on to the RCMP; they did more digging and were able to trace the messages to a single desk computer. It belonged to Ronald Stuart Laing, a supervisor at the company who had worked there for twenty-three years. Married, with no children, the fifty-six-year-old apparently was so new to computers that he did not even own one at home and learned all of his skills at work.

When police arrested him, they found eighty more images on his office computer. He pleaded not guilty, but on the morning of his court appearance he switched his plea. In theory, he faced a maximum penalty of five years for possession and ten years for distribution, but he needn't have worried. The judge called the images shocking, but he accepted a joint recommendation from the prosecution and the defence that Laing serve just one year under house arrest. The Toronto cops were going to find that, no matter how hard they worked to gather evidence, many judges were reluctant to sentence the defendants to any real jail time.

Still, Krawcyzk and his fellow team members kept ferreting out predators in the months and years that followed. Detective John Menard never ceases to be amazed at how desperate the online predators are. In one case run by the Toronto team, he recalls, an officer working undercover as a thirteen-year-old girl had no fewer than fifteen males clamouring for sex with her within twenty seconds of going online.

In another investigation, the Toronto team snagged the

pastor of an evangelical church. Kenneth Synes spent four months trying to groom what he thought was a twelve-year-old girl. "The chat became more sexually explicit, to the point that he was prepared to drive across the city and meet in a public place," says Detective Constable Scott Purches, who did the undercover work. US authorities eventually contacted the Toronto cops with evidence that the pastor had tried looking for victims south of the border as well, with no apparent success.

Synes, discharged from his church, pleaded guilty and got a year in jail for his sins.

In the United Kingdom, undercover Internet work is taken so seriously that police officers have to get special accreditation before they can become keyboard criminal catchers. About ninety-five "covert Internet investigators" have been trained at a national course run by the Association of Chiefs of Police Officers.

At New Scotland Yard, one of those qualified undercover agents is Jim Pearce, a chain-smoking detective constable who shares his cramped quarters with five other investigators from the High-Tech Crime Unit at the Yard's headquarters, near St James's Square. The modern banks of computer hard drives, image scanners and hacker software seem out of place in the old-fashioned office filled with battered desks, with its fading paint and scuffed floors. Pearce has a bone-weariness etched on his face and a darkness in his eyes that only a veteran cop who has seen it all can carry off with grace. His Liverpudlian-accented speech, like his detective work, is slow and methodical. He walked the beat in London's Battersea district for seven years as a uniformed bobby, then put in eight more years in the Clubs and Vice squad, patroling the seamier side of London. Now he patrols the underbelly of the Web, and is finding that the technology has changed but not the crime.

His first undercover case began when the local Cambridgeshire police were contacted by a panicked mother on Christmas Eve 2004. She had discovered that her twelve-year-old daughter, Alison,* had been flirting online with an older man who said he was eighteen. The family had reason to be nervous. The Cambridgeshire county, after all, had been the site of the notorious murders in the town of Soham just two years earlier, when the entire country was gripped by the disappearance of two ten-year-old girls; they were later found dead, after having been lured into the home of a school caretaker. Alison had gone to the same school as the two victims.

Alison's older brother had discovered her online communications with the man, dating back to the previous July. They had met on a children's site known as Pogo.com, which allowed users to chat while they played games; the man and his young target soon migrated to more intimate talk through instant messaging. When police came to the family home that Christmas, they found a heart-shaped piece of paper inscribed with what appeared to be the man's initials in the girl's room, along with a Christmas card and several letters, all proclaiming his love for her. The stranger had convinced Alison to let him use one of her friend's addresses for the packages and gifts he sent to her.

In one letter, he gave Alison his address on Longreach Road in Liverpool. A discreet police check there turned up a fifty-seven-year-old resident named Oliver Jordan. The man did have an estranged teenage son who lived with his mother. The police were fairly confident that the predator was the father and not the teen, but they could not be certain. Worse still, there was not enough evidence yet to lay a charge: the man's courtship of the girl had been inappropriate but, to date, not explicitly sexual. And while he had spoken to Alison about meeting, he had not yet made any specific arrangements.

They decided to call in Scotland Yard to ask Jim Pearce to take over the girl's online identity. Pearce was keen, but realized he faced numerous challenges. By this time, it was already 18 January, and there had been an unexplained gap of two weeks of silence from Alison. Moreover, Jordan had an intimate knowledge of his prey, having corresponded with her since July; Pearce, on the other hand, knew little about teenage girls, much less about this particular child from Cambridgeshire.

"Basically, you've got this lonely twelve-year-old who's probably got her first ever boyfriend, even though he's a virtual one," says Pearce. "It's her little secret."

With the family's permission, the police made a mirror-image copy of her hard drive. Pearce wanted not just her chat logs but all her directories – to get a sense of what she was doing in school, what her musical tastes were (a boy band named Busted seemed high on her list) and how she organized her life and her thoughts. He also had to learn how she spoke, or at least typed. He noticed, for example, that she always signed on with Jordan – who used the screen name james00231 – by saying, "Hi James, Wot u up 2?"

Pearce wrote out pages of notes, including lists of Alison's frequently-used abbreviations, such as BF for "boyfriend," G2G for "got to go" and OIC for "oh I see". Four days later, Pearce was ready to flip the switch and go online as Alison. By now, it was Saturday, 22 January 2005. Jordan had not heard from Alison since 3 January when he had sent her a New Year's card. Pearce sent a simple instant message: "Hi James, please talk to me."

All he got back was an automated response from Jordan: "I'm away from my computer."

On Sunday night, Pearce typed in another short missive as Alison, saying she would be home after school the next day.

The response he got back on Monday was cold and harsh: "Look, I don't know who you are, so please don't send me any more stupid IMs [instant messages]," Jordan wrote. "I'm sick of your little games. If you persist you'll leave me no alternative but to inform AOL about you invading my privacy."

"This is blowing up the first day," a worried Pearce told his police mates. The police knew Alison had told Jordan that her brother was on to them and had reported something to her mother; they hoped Jordan was just worried about that and did not suspect that the authorities were involved. Still, it was obvious that their suspect was on edge. "What can we do to try to get him back on our side?" they asked themselves.

Pearce went back into the logs and found a conversation in which Alison asked Jordan about a girl named Sally he had met at a pool. Taking a chance, Pearce wrote a new message: "Look, if you don't want me as your girlfriend because of the girl at the pool, please tell me. I love you."

"Why have you not been talking to me online or by letter?" Jordan shot back. "Answer me: why not?"

Pearce, as Alison, played the soft touch: "Doing school stuff. I just wanna know, do you still love me?" He added an explanation for her erratic behaviour, telling Jordan that Jimmy, Alison's brother, had "said something to Mum, that's why I'm not being allowed online".

"I missed you, Alison," Jordan replied, apparently consoled. "Yes, I still love you."

Pearce continued to run the sting for almost two weeks. By early February it was time to pull in the line. The police had confirmed beyond a doubt Oliver Jordan's real identity. They got hold of the photos he had supplied for a passport application. His handwriting on the application was the same as that on the note he had written on the New Year's card to Alison. Now that they had proof that they were speaking to a fifty-seven-year-old man, the police had to see if he would follow through on his promise to meet a twelve-year-old.

"I want you here, I don't care how I do it, I just want you here with me," Jordan wrote.

"I want to be with you, but how?" Pearce asked.

Jordan came up with a scheme. Alison had her half-term school break starting the next Monday, 14 February – Valentine's Day. Through her friend, he would send her £30 in cash and a bus schedule for her trip to Liverpool from Cambridgeshire.

"Don't tell your mum about this," he cautioned. "Delete my details off your computer. Let me know what coach you're getting and I'll come meet you."

Pearce played the innocent: "I'm only twelve. How am I going to get on the coach?"

"Look, just tell them that you're being met at the other end; it won't be a problem," Jordan assured her. Then he detailed what he had planned for their first face-to-face meeting: "Do you still go to bed naked? I'll undress you slowly until you're naked and kiss you all over."

Now at last the police had everything they needed to lay a grooming charge: Jordan had sent his victim travel money and made clear his sexual intentions. All that remained was to spring the final trap.

Jordan had told Alison that he was having problems with his computer and that she should send confirmation of her trip by mail, since he would not be online. The police figured he was being cautious, trying to ensure that there was no electronic trace of his rendezvous with the girl. Scotland Yard got a hand-writing specialist to pen a Valentine card in Alison's style, telling Jordan she would be on the afternoon bus to Liverpool. Pearce had hoped to arrest Jordan as he waited with his Valentine flowers for his young date to arrive at the bus terminal. But they made one mistake: the card was delayed in the mail.

As the Liverpool police ran their surveillance on Jordan's home, they noticed he had gone out to buy new bedding; he had also visited the bus station to get information on the schedules. But by late afternoon on Valentine's Day he had not left his house. They made the decision to move in for the arrest all the same.

The late card arrived the next day, but by then Jordan was already in custody – and in deep trouble. He had the misfortune of trying to seduce Alison just after a new law came into force making "grooming" a crime even if the person never touched or even saw the victim. Jordan faced a maximum of fourteen years, but a guilty plea served him well: he got three years in jail, a permanent spot on the Sex Offenders Registry and a lifetime ban on working with children.

Pearce never spoke to the real Alison either before or after the case; that was standard dispassionate police procedure. But he did find out from her family that they had told her what the police had done to save her.

*   *   *

Barely four months after the arrest of Jordan, Pearce and his colleagues at the Yard found themselves in an even more bizarre online chase, trying to track a predator claiming to be a female nurse in her late thirties.

She said her name was Holly Chadwick. Like "Karla" from Nova Scotia, Holly too claimed to be a lesbian. Her photo in her Hotmail profile and in an online dating club known as Hi5.com showed a plain-looking woman in her thirties; she said she was a nurse who had been hurt by a man in a previous relationship, which seemed to make her sympathetic in the minds of impressionable teens. "These young girls feel they have a trusting older woman as a friend," Pearce explains. Holly persuaded vulnerable girls she met online to perform sex games for her with their webcams.

Pearce had the suspect's Hotmail address, though he had his doubts that Holly was, indeed, female. In her Hotmail profile, Holly cited Oscar Wilde's famous line, "We're all in the gutter, but some of us are looking at stars." By coincidence, Pearce had seen that quotation inscribed on the statue of the well-known playwright near the Charing Cross Tube station when he used to work at the local police station close by. There was also a hospital nearby, so another Scotland Yard detective spent hours going through their employee photos to see if a female nurse matched Holly Chadwick's online photo.

No luck. The only way to catch Holly was through what Pearce called "good old-fashioned police work". He went undercover, assuming the role of a fictional twenty-two-year-old lesbian named Samantha, who had a fifteen-year-old sister. He set up an account in the same chat rooms where Holly hung out, and the two of them easily struck up a friendship. Holly explained that she went online at an Internet café because she did not have a Net connection at home. Scotland Yard ran an IP trace on Holly's chats and determined that the suspect was frequenting a large Internet café near Trafalgar Square – not far from Oscar Wilde's statue.

They were closing in, but not there yet. Every computer in the café would have the same IP address, and there were five hundred machines spread over four floors. The police had to come up with a better way to narrow down the target. Pearce could by now predict when Holly would come online and for how long. A fellow detective, Sean Robbie, and another officer went to the café, posing as employees, while Pearce kept chatting with Holly. The two cops went around with clipboards, asking customers if they needed any help – and looking over shoulders to see what people were doing online. Within minutes, Robbie spotted the person chatting with Pearce (they could even see the photo Pearce was using in his fake profile as Samantha on the suspect's computer); as police had suspected, Holly was a he, not a she. With the camera in his mobile phone, Robbie snapped a picture of the man.

When the suspect left the café, the police followed him home. That gave them an address and quickly his full name – and his criminal record. Alan Pemberton was on the Sex Offenders Registry. Before the days of widespread Internet use, he used to phone young children, pretending to be a doctor, and persuade them to perform "medical exams" on their private parts. Pemberton's photo in police files matched the grainy shot Robbie had taken inside the café.

All that remained was the final sting. Holly arranged to meet Samantha at Victoria Station; she even asked Samantha to bring her fifteen-year-old younger sister to make it a three-some. As Pemberton was typing out the arrangements for the rendezvous on the computer in the café, the police were discreetly standing not far away, this time with a video camera filming his keyboard crimes. They moved in to make the arrest; with Pemberton in custody, one of the officers typed the last message that would ever come from Holly Chadwick, the nurse who liked quoting Oscar Wilde.

Back at the Yard, Pearce smiled as he saw the words appear on his computer screen: "All secure."

Pemberton was convicted of sending child abuse images to Pearce and – more seriously – of inciting someone to rape a child. "It was very satisfying," says Pearce. "Paying him back for deceiving others."

Deceptions within deceptions. A male child abuser pretending to be a female nurse chatting with a twenty-two-year-old lesbian who was in fact a middle-aged male Scotland Yard detective. Pearce closed the file, but he could not help wondering how many other predators were out there, pretending to befriend a lonely child.

*Real names not used.

19

The Terrorist Hunters

Andy Hayman and Margaret Gilmore

Andy Hayman's *The Terrorist Hunters* gives an insight into the confusing and at times tragic years at the start of twenty-first century, when millennial euphoria gave way to a guarded fear of terrorist attack in the wake of 9/11, from Britain's top anti-terror cop of the time.

Andy Hayman CBE, QPM, now retired to journalism, looks set to remain a controversial figure for some owing to his role in the initial investigation of British tabloid the *News of the World*'s celebrity telephone-hacking activities. No friend of satirical magazine *Private Eye*, he has been a subject of the smears and counter-smears over conduct that seem to be the currency of the internecine career politics that take place at the top of the force in Britain, where influence over the appointment of top cops by politicians remains the norm. (A constitutional Hobson's choice it may be. But, given the knee-jerk views expressed by elective police chiefs in the USA, long may it continue.)

Nevertheless, Hayman's "horse's mouth" account of five confusing years in which the UK re-learned how do deal with a terrorist threat not seen since the PIRA ceasefire of 1994 is required reading for students of anti-terrorist operations as they are conducted in the field. From the assassination of dissident Russian journalist Alexander Litvinenko in 2006, through an impolitic dawn raid on an innocent household in east London's Muslim community, to the tragic shooting at Stockwell underground station of hapless Brazilian electrician Jean-Charles de Menezes (who had the misfortune to live in the same block of flats as a "live" terror suspect), Hayman's account does not shy from the fact that, in the real world, undercover and uniform anti-terror policing is very far from an exact science.

Free from the backside-covering tone that creeps into some career police biographies, Hayman's account nonetheless describes a world in which Britain's cops and the security service, whatever their failures, scrabbled sincerely to protect the public in the face of an unknown threat – one that could be as small in outcome as the fart from an inexpertly made fertilizer bomb, or as unimaginably large as 9/11.

There is little to tell between a terrorist and a sympathizer, and who'd want to live in, or defend, a society in which radical chic and the free exchange of ideas were not welcome? A terrorist is not a terrorist until they begin to commit acts of terror – this is both a tenet of a free society and a necessary standard for prosecution. The dilemma this poses for policing and preventing terror while preserving the freedoms that terrorists seek to destroy is at the forefront of Hayman's mind, and those of his colleagues, in the following extract. Hayman's support, at the time, of the proposals of Britain's Labour government for ninety-day detention without charge, for example, would appear based on the operational dilemmas he experienced, rather than on an authoritarian instinct in itself.

Anti-terror policing is on the one hand a matter of undercover, softly-softly skills, and on the other, when overt policing is called for, an often massive and swift response, given the potential proximity of fissile material and other tools of terror. In earlier chapters of his book, Andy Hayman describes the dawn raid in Forest Gate in 2006. Based, as their belief was, on faulty intelligence, the Met thought that two residents of a particular property were possessed of enough explosive materials that, despite their proximity to West Ham United's Upton Park ground, they planned to blow a lot more than bubbles.

In the event, a family was terrorized into thinking they were the target of a violent robbery and one of the two innocent young men who sought to defend it received a flesh wound in the arm. Explaining the rationale behind this policing own-goal, Hayman discusses the possible presence of detonable explosives as the reason why "this would have to be a size-twelve boot kicking the door in." As throughout, he explains, with commendable frankness the messy, necessary, all-too-human inexactitude of anti-terror and covert policing in real, "live" operations, times when over-reaction can seem preferable to under-reaction. Sometimes, he seems to say, people have to do what's justified, to leave the rest of us free to discuss right and wrong…

There is nothing like long-term surveillance to bring results.

We had our suspicions about a group of people who would meet in a street in east London and needed to establish whether or not they were a terrorist cell. Our surveillance operated a covert camera to get excellent shots of the group meeting. The slightest loss of nerve, even a blink of an eyelid towards the group, would not only have exposed the surveillance team but might also have blown the entire operation.

From then on, for months we put the suspects under surveillance and followed them. We logged everything they bought; we filmed and listened to them and used all sorts of other intrusive techniques to get a wide view of what they were up to. MI5 and Counter-Terrorism Command had been granted permission to do this through warrants from senior police officers and from government. And this was why.

MI5 had been watching young Muslims who had been travelling to obscure parts of Pakistan and Afghanistan for years. They had studied those who were associates of people belonging to terrorist cells that had already been uncovered: in 2004 a group had been planning a conventional fertilizer bomb on a club or shopping centre. Some who knew them had no links whatsoever with terrorism – but others did.

The intelligence agencies also investigated young British Muslims who had gone to obscure parts of the

Pakistan–Afghanistan border at the same time as the 7 and 21 July bombers, or who'd been in the region at times when intelligence suggests groups of the Al-Qaeda leadership had gathered to recruit and train young militants.

Against this background the agencies became concerned about one particular group who had been to Pakistan.

Friends and acquaintances of these men noticed they were particularly angry at the continuing deaths of innocent Muslims in Iraq and Afghanistan, and signs in them of behavioural change. We put them under surveillance.

One of the men visited Pakistan, and on his return journey investigators opened his baggage, took a look and resealed it. We found evidence in his case that could be used to detonate and make bombs. Now we were really worried. With MI5, we set up one of the UK's largest ever surveillance operations.

One of the men we were watching appeared to take on the role of quartermaster, buying items like clamps, drills, syringes, glue and latex gloves – things he couldn't possibly need in quantity in everyday life and which could potentially be used to make explosives. Our undercover officers saw him throw away empty hydrogen-peroxide bottles.

We were on the trail as the cell bought a flat in cash. Was this to be the bomb factory? We upped the ante – eaves-dropping on the property. Now we listened to all their plans. We watched them make and test peroxide explosives. We filmed their methodology, constantly assessing whether public safety was at risk if we continued the surveillance. We watched them construct devices. Our scientists tried to copy what they were doing, and concluded that if a detonator was attached, the devices were viable as bombs.

MI5 overheard them discussing numbers – were they referring to the number of targets the group planned to attack? Another time we heard them make numerous calls to chemicals companies.

They applied for new passports and junked their old ones to hide visits to Pakistan – which they clearly knew fitted the profile of the modern terrorist.

By now we were convinced they were planning an attack

– but we wanted to let the operation run so that we could collect as much evidence as possible to prosecute them rather than simply disrupting their plans.

At this point John McDowall, deputy head of Counter-Terrorist Command and the senior investigating officer in charge of this particular operation, rushed rather breathlessly into my office. Peter Clarke, his boss, was not around and he had something important enough to tell me in person.

He told me the surveillance information suggested the men were planning an attack bigger than the attacks in the USA on 11 September 2001, right here in the UK. Imagine the effect if they succeeded – the horrendous loss of life.

Then I took a mental step back. We were on top of this. I felt confident that we would not allow the plot to come to fruition. The only caveat I had was that we didn't know if other terrorist cells were running parallel to this one: what if this was the second and the first was close to fulfilling its plans? It was an unnerving thought, but we had no evidence to suggest this was part of a wider conspiracy. I knew that at John's level there was communication daily, sometimes hourly with MI5. We spoke and decided to let it run. Once again we pushed the surveillance button, upping it to an even higher level to ensure nothing was missed. At this point the police were chairing the Gold command meetings because we had moved on from pure intelligence-gathering and were now, with our surveillance tapes, gathering firm evidence we hoped to put before a court once we had arrested and prosecuted the cell – as we wanted to.

We had another flat in London under surveillance too. To our incredulity we heard several of the suspects record what appeared to be suicide videos full of anti-Western rhetoric. We knew from past experience this didn't mean the attack was imminent – but it might be close. We still felt we had the tactical advantage: we were keeping tabs on the men but there was more to be done in gathering evidence which might stand up in court.

The stakes were high. We couldn't tell where the planned detonation would occur. An error on anyone's part now might mean at best loss of evidence but at worst catastrophic loss of life.

We had briefed our counterparts in America on the alleged plot. At the highest level they were looking for reassurance that this was not going to slip through our fingers. I was briefing the home secretary on progress, he was briefing the prime minister, Tony Blair, and *he* was briefing the US President, George Bush.

The operation had been going on for weeks. We knew where the men were, and where they lived. We knew everything about their lifestyles, their movements, their acquaintances, friends and families. We had them bugged and they were followed 24/7. We had contingency plans in place if we suddenly needed to arrest them. None of my senior team had had a holiday for a year, so some weeks earlier we had decided to take a leaf out of Eliza Manningham-Buller's book. Immediately after the 7 July attacks she'd sent staff home in anticipation of the long haul – she wanted some rested and ready for when others became exhausted. I knew we would be working ridiculous hours once we moved in to make arrests so we fixed our summer breaks. John went away first, followed by Peter, and on Peter's return I left for La Manga in Spain with my wife, family and some friends. I knew it was unlikely that I'd get the full two weeks. Peter and I had half speculated that, given the pace of the operation, by the time I left we were probably seven or eight days away from the arrests.

I went equipped with a secure satellite phone, having arranged with Peter that I would speak to him every evening at 8 p.m. A couple of days into the holiday, things were on a stable footing. I was about to order dinner and decided to make the agreed 8 p.m. call just ahead of that. Peter reiterated that I probably had another three or four days before I would need to come back ahead of the arrest phase. We hung up. I sat down to my paella. Less than an hour later, the cork hardly out of the wine bottle, he was back on the phone. Things had changed.

The Americans it appeared felt it was getting dangerous

and that we should bring the operation to a close. We didn't want to do that. We believed we could gain more evidence and thus a better chance of securing convictions if we let things run a little longer. Our US counterparts were especially worried about a man we suspected – but couldn't prove – could be pulling the strings in Pakistan and might even be a vital link between the men we were following in the UK and Al-Qaeda. The Pakistani authorities arrested him.

It happened as I settled down to my dinner in Spain. We were caught unawares and colleagues in the UK were forced to take action into which we would normally have put considerable time and planning. We had no choice but to move in on the cell. If, as we suspected, the man was linked, his detention might scare them and push them into accelerating their planned attack: we had to get to the men in the UK before they found out he was in custody. We couldn't risk letting this run on now, Peter said, and I agreed. We'd gathered evidence we felt incriminated them. We strongly felt that an attack was imminent – and just as we could close our side of the operation early, so could they.

I felt frustrated that I wasn't in the UK. I hadn't really wanted to leave for my holiday but had known it was the right thing to do. All I wanted now was to get back to be part of the team. I had a very small window in which I could return before things went crazy: once news of the suspected plot was published I knew international security measures would be tightened.

My plan B was to fly home in a UK military aircraft but that would be expensive. Instead my backroom team pulled out the stops. At 9 p.m. they were set the task of getting me to the UK, and within half an hour they had booked me on to a scheduled flight leaving Alicante at midnight. I should be home before the public knew anything about the plot.

I rushed back to the apartment and packed a few essentials – I was not calm as I was anxious to get a cab and make the hour-long journey to the airport in good time for the flight. I ran outside and flagged down a passing cab. In it, I gathered my thoughts, systematically checking what I would do when I arrived in the UK. Then I did the usual travel check: money, passport. To my horror I discovered that in my panic to get packed I had taken my six-year-old daughter's passport rather than my own. Time was tight but I had to make the half-hour round trip back to the apartment. I felt sick – and incredibly silly. Fortunately I caught the plane – just.

Meanwhile the home secretary, John Reid, had been pulled out of a football match: he had been watching Chelsea play at Stamford Bridge in west London. Peter briefed him on the plans to begin the arrests.

I landed at Gatwick Airport and was met by Sussex Police Special Branch, who drove me to my waiting car and driver. I changed from my polo shirt and shorts into a suit, and on a blue-light run we raced through the night to New Scotland Yard, Peter and the team.

I was stunned by the progress they had already made. The task was to spontaneously locate and arrest more than a dozen people – an incredibly tall order because we didn't have the luxury of choosing when to do it: early morning, while they were still asleep would have been normal. I think the police service often operates at its best in these types of circumstances: contrast this operation with the one in Forest Gate, where we had spent hours poring over risk assessments and health and safety guidelines and still got it wrong. This time there was no fuss, no drama and no time for studying health and safety rules, just fast, old-fashioned police work.

At 5 a.m. Peter Clarke and I drove across Parliament Square to a COBRA meeting chaired by the home secretary. On the way Peter told me that when John Reid heard we were going to pull the surveillance operation, he had said he felt it was near on impossible for us to achieve the arrests. Now, some eight hours later, I took a back seat, immensely proud as Peter, in his understated manner, informed the meeting that nearly everyone of the suspected key players was already under arrest.

In a way this was not the end but the beginning of the investigation. We believed we'd stopped an appalling plot, but we also knew that this could cause chaos for the public. We were in familiar territory: we increased security causing immense public inconvenience but, because the men might face trial, the law prevented us publishing much detail about what they were accused of.

As is often the case at times like this, as the arrests were made, the threat assessment for the UK was once again raised to Critical, implying an attack might be imminent. Intelligence assessed that unknown cells, either in the UK or abroad, might try to undermine the arrests by carrying out an attack.

The Critical signal sent a warning to private and public organizations, to ports and airports, power stations and so on that they should adopt their most stringent security precautions. At Scotland Yard we implemented the Rainbow List to protect the public. We also went to great lengths to keep mainstream Muslim communities in the loop. Those we arrested were Muslim, but held extreme views and espoused violence in a way that the majority of Muslims abhorred.

It crossed my mind, as that long night turned into day, what crazy times these were. The police and security agencies had dealt with the fatal terrorist attacks of 7 July 2005, the fatal shooting by police of Jean-Charles de Menezes, the failed bombs of 21 July 2005, and now this. Anyone of those events would have challenged the command resilience of the Met.

I drew back significantly from private briefings to the press: I felt that it would be totally irresponsible to give any hint as to why these extra security measures had been introduced and relied on the trust and confidence the media, I believed, now placed in me. I kept what I told them fairly general, and asked for their cooperation, assuring them that when the time was right I would give them a blow-by-blow account. Other Whitehall departments took a different view: someone was clearly briefing the details – probably because, as I had felt after the 7 July attacks, they wanted speculation kept to the minimum. Without crossing the line of inappropriate disclosures, they were giving as much information as possible so that the reporting was responsible and not scaremongering.

The arrests meant we had to instigate thorough searches of homes, offices and all the other places used by the suspects.

Also, we had to start analysing their phone and computer records. As soon as the arrests started we made arrangements for lawyers specializing in terrorism to camp alongside our officers in Scotland Yard. We were downloading evidential material in real time – that is logging, filing and prioritizing everything that we found on computers seized during the searches, everything that the suspects said in interviews, everything we discovered about who they'd called or emailed. The lawyers had a wall chart with each defendant's name on it: when key elements of evidence were relevant they would be written up under an individual's name. They wanted to be absolutely clear when they felt a defendant could be charged and there was a viable chance of a successful prosecution.

The moment from arrest to charging is always a race against time – and never more so than in this case. We were up against it. The scale of the evidence we were bringing in was vast. Almost everything belonging to, or that had crossed the paths of, the suspects had to be analysed and logged. By law, we are expected to have the key elements of our case and the main evidence gathered by the time the suspect is charged; clearly we can't always do this and often continue investigating after that. If anything played into the debate of extending the length of time we could hold a suspect between arrest and charge, this did. In the past month the limit had been raised from fourteen to twenty-eight days but we had supported the government's moves for a longer period of detention. The home secretary was acutely aware of the importance of this case to that debate and keen to discover if it would show the need for powers to hold suspects longer before they must be charged. It was another example of how politics and policing were becoming closely intertwined.

The political argument was the last thing on our minds: we had a job with a time limit and had to make the most of what we'd got. I also had to deal with the internal police politics. One of the scenes we had identified shortly before the arrests was a house close to a large recreation area where people walked dogs. We'd seen the group going there and lying face down to communicate, and suspected the place was being used not just for meetings but for something more sinister. We had no proof but thought they might have a hide there.

That search was a logistical nightmare. We decided that, come what may, we would search the entire area of heath thoroughly. It was huge, hilly, with a mix of dense woodland and open spaces with many foot-and bridle-paths – a popular spot with people and with deer, badgers and other wild animals. Some areas back on to residential areas and others are popular meeting places for lovers. We were digging up every single piece of turf, combing under every bush and through all the undergrowth. Nothing would be left untouched. If we had ended the surveillance operation weeks earlier we would not have found that house and we certainly would not have searched that common ground.

For the surveillance officers who'd followed the suspects day and night for many months before, the arrests of the suspects were the pay-off they were looking for: it would now be the job of lawyers to use what they had found to see if they had enough to prosecute the men.

* * *

Our surveillance officers are brave, but other men and women working for us have, arguably, an even tougher job. I cannot emphasize strongly enough the steely nerve of our undercover officers, or agents, as they're known in MI5. These people nurture and befriend a criminal or terrorist, leading a double life, so that eventually they can be exposed and brought to justice.

Take the South Mimms case. Our tactics were conventional. We needed to track a suspect. Intelligence suggested he was trying to purchase firepower, including a ground-to-air missile-launcher. Several years previously we had discovered what we believed were early plans to use such weapons around the perimeter fence at Heathrow Airport. It looked to us as if someone had flattened the ground in preparation to bring them in. All airports now have dedicated patrols that randomly check places on the perimeters from which planes could be shot down.

In the frenetic days after the July bombings in 2005 we heard that one Kazi Rahman was looking to buy arms. He had links with terrorists but until then it had been thought that he wasn't personally involved. An undercover MI5 officer, using the name Salim, befriended him, and offered to introduce him to an arms dealer. That dealer was an undercover police officer known as Mohamed. For months the three were wheeling and dealing as Rahman upped the stakes, ordering more and offering more cash. His wish list included a Man Portable Air Defence System (MANPADS), a shoulder-launched surface-to-air missile.

Undercover officers are chameleons, a breed unto themselves. I'm amazed at how close they get to their quarry. On one particular operation I recall an undercover officer being asked by a major criminal if he'd be his best man – how the hell can a police officer infiltrating a criminal gang get *that* close to the top man? It must be an innate skill, not one you can acquire on a Home Office training course. The undercover officers used in drugs work are impressive, but for a different reason. Because we're asking them to infiltrate drugs-users and dealers, they have to be young, which means they're less experienced and therefore more open to the dangers of undercover work.

The annual V concert at Chelmsford is held over two days and the pop fans camp overnight. When I was in charge, we ran a massive undercover drugs operation. Officers were looking for dealers and therefore posing as buyers; they averaged less than five years' service but they operated as if they had fifty years under their belts. Any undercover officer has to be tough and cool to infiltrate and become a trusted friend within the criminal and terrorist underworld. The job is to gather intelligence and turn that into evidence, which they give anonymously in court. Little can beat an undercover cop describing to a court and jury the inside story of criminal activity.

As 2005 wore on we reached the point in the arms-dealing case where we had to force a sting: the cover would have to be blown for the simple reason that our "arms dealer" could not produce the arms. We decided on South Mimms as a rendezvous, a common meeting point for criminals and cops. It's at the junction of the M25 and the A1 heading north. The service station there is busy day and night.

With any sting, the operation must not overstep the mark. The agents can't encourage or entice the criminal or they'll be accused in court of setting them up. The actions and words of the criminal or terrorist must be spontaneous. Our MI5 agent and the undercover police officer were wired up. Plain-clothes officers, some of whom were armed, provided backup nearby, watching and waiting, ready to move in.

It was like a movie set: at the centre there was a van, ostensibly with the missile-launcher and other guns inside, while the rest of the car park was overrun with undercover cops, some in cars and vans with cameras, others on motorbikes in case the target ran. Round the corner the Silver commander was in radio contact with Gold at base. Finally the terrorist appeared, weaving through families, coach parties and other travellers, and walked up to the van. As he did, his undercover "associates" turned on him and the backup cops moved in.

Rahman was jailed for possessing guns, silencers and ammunition for the purposes of terrorism. Had he got his missile and carried out his threat to shoot down a plane, hundreds of innocent people would have died. His trial judge said that what he had been trying to buy was "dreadful and dangerous". He added: "I have no doubt what was intended was the deaths of large numbers of citizens." This type of sting often concludes with a guilty plea in the courts – a sign of the overwhelming strength of the evidence.

Plots like these were not thwarted solely by undercover work. The work of the human spies was complemented by state-of-the-art bugs, microphones, and the amazing Internet technology that underlies nearly every modern-day investigation. Take the mobile phone. Even as a police officer I'd smile at what I and others are prepared to say when we're using one – "I can't talk about this or that", then going on to do so, sometimes making the most indiscreet revelations on the train or in the office. We just forget ourselves. Mind you, so does the criminal.

When a terrorist or other criminal uses a mobile, though, they're telling us much more than the content of their conversation. We can pinpoint the area from where they made the call and work out who they called. We used this technique to track one of the 21/7 bombers to Rome. We can check all telephone records, mobile and fixed-line, to build a retrospective picture of a terrorist's activities. Which brings us back to the argument for extending the time we can hold suspects before we have to charge them: the longer we have, the more closely we can examine bank accounts and Internet, computer and mobile usage before the suspect has to be charged or released.

In the early days the authorities were cautious about revealing eavesdropping and bugging methods in court. They were worried that if the criminal learnt how they had been bugged the tactical edge for the investigation would be lost. I totally support that view. However, I was delighted when Sir Ken McDonald, the director of Public Prosecutions, and Eliza Manningham-Buller, at MI5, agreed that some surveillance evidence could be made public because the greater need was to achieve convictions. The constraints they placed on what could be released were pragmatic and did not disclose anything above what the average member of the public would expect from spies. After all, many a celebrity has been bugged by tabloid newspapers in scandal scams so people know that pinhole cameras can be concealed in tiepins, that most furniture can be used to conceal listening devices and that mobile-phone conversations and text messages can be monitored. Despite that knowledge, though, criminals need the mobile phone and can't resist speaking to each other in public places where they can be overheard.

Even with my limited experience of doing surveillance work I have sat in a bar just feet away from a house burglar talking to his criminal handler, describing the loot he had stolen the night before and was trying to sell on. This enabled us to follow those two individuals for the next couple of days and catch them red-handed.

In my role as the UK police lead for countering terrorism at New Scotland Yard, I advised the government on the benefits of keeping telephone, email and Internet data for at least twelve months. I cited cases where such details had been critical in bringing terrorists to justice. After the 7 July attacks, the then home secretary Charles Clarke sent me to Berlin to do the groundwork on introducing new European Union rules to this effect. I had no idea, of course, that several years later the powers that were introduced as a result would also be used to target fly-tippers, tax- and housing-benefit dodgers and trading-standards swindlers. They were certainly not intended for that. This is where I believe civil-liberties campaigners have a very good point. I am all for using these things to catch those who threaten our society but I don't approve of "mission creep", which means they're used for other, lesser, things.

The mobile phone was the key to almost everything in one recent case. It was exploited by the terrorists and by us. The attack happened on 29 June 2007. There was no intelligence to go on so we had to identify those responsible quickly as they were terrorists on the run. We and MI5 pulled together all our capabilities.

It was a Friday night in the West End of London. Thousands of people were out and about, enjoying a night on the town. The area was full of noisy revellers, young people queuing to get into popular nightclubs, couples enjoying late-night meals as the theatres and cinemas ended their evening performances, celebrities and the super-rich at their favourite haunts. Central London was buzzing, as it is every Friday night. And, also as every Friday night, the emergency services were out in force too, police and ambulance staff dealing with the inevitable incidents, accidents and crimes that come with large gatherings of people.

In the middle of all this a sinister and potentially devastating terrorist plot was unfolding, carried out by doctors – the very people you and I would expect to be helping society, rather than planning mass murder. They drove up to one of the most popular and well-known clubs in Haymarket in which five hundred plus people were dancing and drinking the night away. They left one car outside Tiger, Tiger, the other by the nearby late-night bus stop. The vehicles were Mercedes saloons, innocuous enough in central London at that time of night – they might have been minicabs, or have belonged to members of the public.

They were packed with a lethal cocktail of gas canisters, petrol and nails. If set alight, they would create massive fireballs and explosions that would send the steel nails flying through the air at terrible speed. There can only have been one aim: to cause maximum injury to many innocent people. The terrorists also left a mobile phone rigged to the bombs in each car: the plan was that when they rang the first mobile from another phone it would trigger the explosion – a ploy often used by the IRA. As people ran away from it they might be caught in the second detonation – a cowardly, outrageous act by people who should have been curing, not killing people.

The terrorists, thank goodness, had been careless and the mobile detonators failed to work. We know from their phone records that the bombers repeatedly called the mobiles in the cars to no avail. A passing ambulance crew detected vapours and reported the first car. By the time we realized there was another, through CCTV and eyewitness reports, it had been removed because it was illegally parked and taken to an underground car park.

This meant that there were two mobile phones – one in each car – with details that quickly identified the bombers and the new phones they were using – they recorded the numbers of the phones that had been dialling in as the bombers tried to detonate the devices. Instead of leaving a bomb wreck the culprits left vital clues for us. They fled north, with us in hot pursuit.

We now finally traced the details of who they were, using the phone and car details. To our shock one was an NHS doctor who, American intelligence sources suggested, used to belong to an Al-Qaeda-inspired cell in Iraq before coming to the UK. MI5 had fleetingly come across him before, mixing with people of extremist views, though not with anyone known to be involved in terrorism. This was another case that would push us to realize many more on the fringes of extremist activity should be followed up.

By 5 a.m, we had found their bomb factory in Scotland. But they were not there. By lunchtime on the Saturday we had reliable intelligence they were in Scotland though, near Glasgow. But it was like looking for a needle in a haystack. We didn't know the car, we didn't know where they were heading. As we followed them from London, we knew we were still about half an hour behind them.

I was sitting in my office, taking calls, ensuring resources were available, keeping forces whose areas we were travelling through up to date. We didn't know if the men were suicidal but we had to get to them before they attacked again. In the background the television was showing Saturday-afternoon sport: it was around three o'clock, and to this day I remember the feeling of helplessness as the Sky newsflash came through and we saw the story unfold before our eyes. The second I saw it, before I'd had word from anyone else, I knew we were too late. Once again, the terrorists had got through on my watch. The manhunt was over: the bombers had driven their fuel-packed jeep up on to the pavement and straight into the doors of the passenger terminal at Glasgow Airport.

Initially we didn't know if there were injuries or deaths, though we soon saw the heroism of the public, which, it transpired, would save the day. The driver was seriously injured and would later die, but his passenger was wrestled to the ground by passers-by, then arrested.

So, I was in my office. Peter Clarke and John McDowall were still upstairs in theirs. Once we knew it had been a suicide attack and that the bombers had survived, there were two imperatives. First I had to deal with the fact that we were operating in a different judicial territory: I needed to be sure we recognized and observed Scottish law; second, I was detached from the crime scene and, with my national responsibilities for terrorism, I had to exert some control over that. There would probably be disagreement between ourselves and the Scottish authorities as to who would be in charge. I was confident the chief constable of the Strathclyde Police,

Sir Willie Ray, would have no qualms whatsoever in handing me jurisdiction over the terrorist investigation, but I was less confident that the Scottish Lord Advocate would allow it. Yet again the vulnerability of UK policing to political structures was exposed.

I thought that a disproportionate amount of effort was directed towards convincing the Scottish Lord Advocate that it was right to hand the case to London. Although this amounted to a couple of days, this was time which could have been better directed towards the investigation. In the future a signed protocol may reduce similar handover hours. I think Peter Clarke swung it. I sent him immediately to Scotland in a military helicopter to take charge on the ground. His influence and negotiating skills secured the agreements we needed, though not before some amazing playground antics from some of the politicians. I remember one particular video-conference call conducted in COBRA where we and government ministers in London were communicating with Scottish ministers. The Scots were determined they were equipped not only to deal with the investigation but also to try any suspects in their courts. No one was prepared to give way.

We had been so lucky in not having had mass casualties at Glasgow Airport: the attack had taken place on the first day of the Scottish summer holiday and there were four thousand people at the airport. If the vehicle had got through the doors there would have been massive loss of life – yet here we were having an ugly debate over who had primacy, heels dug in. And there was nothing to say there wouldn't be more attacks, perhaps as retaliation. Intelligence analysts had raised the threat level from Severe to Critical for the next few days.

The police took a different view from the politicians: officers from both forces were cooperating brilliantly on the ground, sharing offices and getting on with the job. Both the Met and Strathclyde Police knew it was sensible to give the lead to London where we could make connections with other cells and cases and draw on our considerable experience in hunting terrorists. It took a couple of days but, eventually, logic prevailed and the case came to us.

I know I keep banging on about the frustration of politics but this example, along with many others I have mentioned [in original book], is surely starting to make a strong case for detaching politics from policing. At times I think some politicians can't help themselves. The lure of getting in the spotlight or having hissy fits over who is most important simply gets in the way. And, quite frankly, it's despicable.

The Haymarket-Glasgow case highlights the importance and the difficulties of using legal powers as a tool in fighting terrorism. The day after the Glasgow attack I realized just what an ass the law had become. I was summoned by the new prime minister, Gordon Brown, to Downing Street. He'd only been in power a few days.

"Is the whole of the country pulling together to prevent further attacks?" he asked me. It was a terrible moment. I'd had a good rapport with Tony Blair but I hadn't yet built a relationship with the new incumbent at Number 10. I looked him in the eye, fingers crossed behind my back, and reassured him we were on top of the job.

I was taking a punt. If it went wrong I would have to return and tell him the powers his government had given us to fight terrorism had been baulked at by some chief constables who weren't using them and who, in my view, were making our job of tracking terrorists harder.

Let me explain. Section 44 of the Terrorism Act, 2000, gives police and the home secretary powers to define any area in the country, over any period of time, when we can stop and search any vehicle or person, and seize articles of a kind which could be used for terrorism – even if there are no grounds for suspicion.

Our intelligence told us that terrorists did not stay at home: they travelled to terrorist camps to train, or to potential targets, or to meet other members of their particular cell. The 7 July bombers had gone to training camps in Wales, for example. And yet we had the crazy situation where some chief constables chose to invoke Section 44 and some did not. Take Cumbria: we knew terrorists were travelling there to train and bond but its chief constable didn't use Section

44. Neither did Bedfordshire Police, even though we knew Luton was a hot bed of extremism. Terrorists were able to travel across counties knowing that in some places the chances of being stopped and searched or questioned were nil. In the wake of the Haymarket and Glasgow bombs, we were trying to create a hostile environment in case other terrorists were planning to attack. Part of our wider tactic was to make it more difficult for them to move around, especially if they were carrying bombs.

So, on that Sunday morning, as the world woke up to the developments in Glasgow, I had called an emergency meeting of the Association of Chief Police Officers (ACPO) Advisory Group. Senior officers from across the country were gathering in London and I was banking on persuading everyone to invoke the powers of Section 44 – hence my little white lie to the prime minister that they were already working together to do all they could to hunt down those behind the latest attacks.

I drove from Downing Street to the Yard. The streets were quiet, just a handful of tourists around, armed police patrolling the bastions of power around Whitehall, street cleaners and me. The journey took about a minute in the car. Inside, New Scotland Yard was buzzing.

There were about fifty senior officers in the room when I walked in. I was immensely grateful to the then deputy commissioner, Sir Paul Stephenson, for attending the meeting to support the operation. His presence meant that the discussion had real significance.

I explained to the meeting why I wanted them to invoke Section 44 nationwide. I explained it would be initially for the month of July and that the Home Office approved the plan. Many chief constables gave me a hard time. They did not want it to be used in their area because they believed it might upset sensitive communities and create too much controversy. I thought this was political correctness gone bonkers – and wondered if, in some cases, they just didn't want the hassle they'd get from civil-liberties groups. We were fighting terrorists hell-bent on murdering innocent civilians anywhere in the UK – as Glasgow had proved – and the government had given us powers to make it more difficult for them to move around, yet those on our own side didn't want to use them. Sir Paul piled in with strong support, and by the end I thought we had convinced most. Some had to get further clearance in their areas but in the main, throughout July 2007, Section 44 was in place over huge tranches of the country. That morning I was able to return to the prime minister and say with more certainty, and relief, that our colleagues in other forces were on board.

Isn't this a fascinating way of working? It's rather twee and typically British, yet it has the potential for disaster. The contrast with the Serious and Organized Crime Agency (SOCA) is telling. Its director general simply circulates in the UK a tactic he feels appropriate. Yet in terrorism, which is at least equally serious, no one can do that.

Other legal powers have proved invaluable in hunting terrorists. In the early days after the 11 September attacks in the USA, we were concerned that key suspects were allowed to operate freely because we hadn't strong enough evidence to bring them to court. We were given powers to detain them without trial, as long as a judge who specialized in terrorism was convinced of the need for us to do so in a secret hearing involving, among others, MI5. When this was challenged in the courts it was deemed unlawful and we were given the power to put these suspects under control orders instead. Only a handful of suspects are held in this way – we far prefer to bring them to trial. But I believe that the power to do this has enabled us at the very least to disrupt and thus prevent some plots.

Although I advised government on what we needed, I was still detached, of course, from the process of law-making that was the job of lawyers and politicians. It was assumed, correctly in the main, that we'd take what weapons we could – and if that meant stronger legal powers to fight terrorism, that was all to the good.

I was now getting my head around a much newer threat: the increasing power of the Internet. Over the years the use of fingerprints and DNA to achieve convictions has been overwhelming. When a terrorist leaves his physical fingerprints at the scene of crime it's clearly incriminating and puts the onus on him or her to explain why they're there – a fantastic tactical edge for the police. Now, there are modern equivalents too: the cyberspace fingerprint and the financial fingerprint. We've shifted significant resources away from conventional detectives to financial investigators and computer hackers. You'll have seen how, when we arrest terrorist suspects, detectives remove literally tons of computers, hard drives, documents including bank statements, credit cards, phone sim cards, mobile phones, etc. Each of these items can reveal the equivalent of a fingerprint for the investigator. A mobile sim card contains all phone and text-messaging traffic – we've often found new leads and suspects thorough sim-card analysis. It doesn't tell us what was said, but it provides us with a point of contact to interrogate.

Computer hard drives do the same: they'll show email traffic and Internet usage – not what was written but patterns of contact. When we want to establish what was said or written we have to bug or eavesdrop and that means obtaining a warrant from the home secretary.

As for financial analysis, every time someone uses a credit card or hole-in-the-wall cash dispenser, writes a cheque or transfers money, they reveal lots of information that helps the investigator build a picture of them. Sixty pounds withdrawn from a cashpoint will give a location, a specific time at which the suspect was there – which makes getting hold of the relevant CCTV footage from local cameras much easier and, bingo, we have an up-to-date photograph. If he's on the run and has shaved or dyed his hair, we'll know. We've often trapped fugitives by following their cash withdrawals.

Petrol stops also give us masses of information – a time and place, CCTV pictures of the car they're driving and others they're travelling with. Automatic Number Plate Recognition (ANPR) also has a role to play here.

As we exploit the new technologies, though, so do the terrorists. In October 2005 the arrest of two terrorists planning an attack in Bosnia led us to a man with whom they were in Internet contact in London. Younes Tsouli was king of the Internet terrorists and he was helping the pair prepare their attack from his modest room in Shepherd's Bush. He conspired through cyberspace, under the name of "Terrorist 001", with people he never met face to face, promising he would eventually meet them "in a better place" – i.e. in heaven. He would browse the Internet searching for home videos made by US troops in Iraq, then pass them on to terrorists who would study them for details about the inside of US bases there so that their attacks could be more lethal. Al-Qaeda leaders in Iraq used him to build websites and he became the main distributor of their evil videos.

It was only after his arrest and our IT experts had unravelled the secrets on his computer that we realized just how significant he was. Information on his computer led to terrorist arrests all over the world, including the UK. Tsouli and his two co-conspirators were jailed in 2007 for incitement to commit murder through the Internet. He's now serving sixteen years in Belmarsh high-security prison in south-east London.

The cyberspace plot presented a new challenge to us all. Imagine men who had never met but who had a common desire to commit mass murder of innocent victims for the purpose of terrorism. They have minimal knowledge and expertise on how to mount attacks. They have little idea of how to organize themselves and belong to no real terrorist association, yet all those prerequisites are achieved over time through the Internet. It's like paedophile-grooming: the paedophile looks to befriend and influence a potential victim. The cyber-terrorist does the same. In this particular case the men involved had never met physically: their contact was through email.

Their case showed just how far Al-Qaeda's propaganda has spread via the Internet.

Our surveillance society means we are all watched and monitored as never before. Some may not like it – civil libertarians from all persuasions continue to argue it's gone too far. I believe it's a necessary part of life, a vital weapon in our armoury if we are successfully to hunt and prosecute terrorists.